# Classroom
# Management
# Strategies

# Classroom Management Strategies

## Gaining and Maintaining Students' Cooperation

James S. Cangelosi

*Utah State University*

Longman

New York & London

Classroom Management Strategies: Gaining and Maintaining
Students' Cooperation

Longman Inc., 95 Church Street, White Plains, N.Y. 10601

Associated companies:
Longman Group Ltd., London
Longman Cheshire Pty., Melbourne
Longman Paul Pty., Auckland
Copp Clark Pitman, Toronto
Pitman Publishing Inc., New York


Executive editor: Raymond T. O'Connell
Production editor: Elsa van Bergen
Text design: Lynn Luchetti
Cover design: Charlene Felker
Illustrations: Marie DeJohn
Production supervisor: Judith Stern


**Library of Congress Cataloging-in-Publication Data**

Cangelosi, James S.
  Classroom management strategies.

  Bibliography: P.
  Includes index.
  1. Classroom management.   2. Teacher-student
relationships.   3. Rewards and punishments in
education.   I. Title.
LB3013.C3259   1988     371.1'02     87-3662
**ISBN 0-582-28638-7 (pbk.)**


Compositor: TC Systems
Printer: The Alpine Press, Inc.

87 88 89 90 9 8 7 6 5 4 3 2 1

To Amy

# Contents

# Preface

The most commonly expressed complaint of students, teachers, parents, and school administrators alike regarding schools involves a lack of pupil discipline, poor classroom management and control, and disruptive student behavior. A tenth grader remonstrates, "School is a joke! I don't learn anything because the teachers are so busy trying to keep order that they don't take time to teach." One sixth grade teacher's comment is indicative of the feelings of thousands of her colleagues that teach at every level: "I became a teacher because I love knowledge and I wanted to help children. But these pupils don't want my help! They won't sit still long enough to learn anything—except how to drive me out of the profession!" Another teacher's lamentations are all too common: "I used to look forward to each school day. Now, I start days hoping I can survive until school is out without being driven crazy, overly embarrassed, or physically harmed." One parent expressed his dilemma: "My taxes go to support public education, but I had to find a private school for my child where teachers controlled students with good old-fashioned discipline." A recent high school graduate suggested that "Teachers should exert more control. I just played around in school . . . rarely paid attention or did homework. Now I'm paying for my fooling around. I wish my teachers had made me work and learn." A school principal stated emphatically. "The number one thing that I look for when hiring a new teacher is the ability to maintain discipline and order. What good does it do a teacher to know all the subject matter and pedagogy in the world if he can't keep the kids in line?"

Teachers can blame student inattentiveness, lack of effort, disruptive behaviors, and general lack of cooperation on their students' own flaws or on the lack of support provided by society, families, and school administrators. But thousands of teachers do overcome seemingly impossible circumstances and elicit their students' cooperation in the face of unfavorable student attitudes and school conditions. These teachers run efficient classrooms where student cooperation is the rule rather than the exception. Students of these teachers are achieving and learning to be successful. How can a teacher obtain her or his students' attention, effort, and cooperation? That is the question addressed by *Classroom Management Strategies: Gaining and Maintaining Students' Cooperation.* This text's suggestions for helping teachers to effectively obtain and maintain students on-task and engaged in lessons are an outgrowth of extensive school teaching experiences and of the findings of numerous studies that dealt with student motivation, behavior management, student engagement, and classroom organization.

Principles and techniques for obtaining and maintaining students' cooperation will not be understood and applied by teachers unless those teachers are exposed to a wide variety of examples demonstrating the principles and techniques in everyday, realistic classroom situations. Thus, this book does not simply make suggestions, it explains them and brings them to life via 425 scenarios drawn from a wide variety of teaching situations from prekindergarten to college. Each scenario (used to demonstrate an idea, successful technique, or unsuccessful technique) is drawn from an actual experience. Many of them (resulting from interviews with teachers) "get into a teacher's mind" and follow that teacher's thought processes as he or she formulates a solution to a discipline problem.

*Classroom Management Strategies: Gaining and Maintaining Students' Cooperation* is presented in four parts:

Part One (chapters 1 and 2) deals with some basic ideas which need to be understood before one is in a position to apply the practical suggestions presented in the remainder of the text.

Part Two (chapters 3 through 6) demonstrates ways for teachers to communicate with students, organize their classrooms, and design and conduct lessons so that students choose to be cooperative and involved. These chapters suggest measures for preventing discipline problems and inattentiveness from ever occurring.

Part Three (chapters 7 through 10) presents teacher-initiated solutions to problems of disruptive student behaviors, lack of student engagement in lessons, and poor student cooperation.

Part Four (chapter 11) raises a word of caution about trying out these ideas and methods for the first time.

This book combines ideas from learning theory, behavior modification principles, recent works on student engagement, counseling psychology, and commonsense principles discovered by highly successful classroom teachers. It is designed for use as a textbook for college level courses that are concerned with helping preservice and inservice teachers to effectively manage student behaviors and solve classroom discipline problems.

I am indebted to the hundreds of classroom teachers and students whose ideas and examples influenced the writing of this book. I am particularly appreciative of the assistance provided by my very dear friends Ruth Struyk who provided invaluable help with research and copyreading, April Diffie who contributed her ideas and marvelous talent to the artwork, Izar Martinez and Charlie Duke for their administrative support, Ray O'Connell and Elsa van Bergen for their highly professional work as editors and Barb Rice for her copyreading and counsel.

# part one

# What Causes Students to Cooperate?

# What Causes Students to Be Uncooperative?

# 1

# Thinking About Your Role as a Teacher

The purpose of this chapter is to introduce you to a model for organizing your thoughts about teaching. An understanding of this model and the terminology associated with it will help you grasp the ideas presented in Chapter 2 and learn to apply the techniques and suggestions that are presented in chapters 3 through 10 of this textbook. More specifically, Chapter 1 is designed to help you:

1. examine your personal commitment to gaining and maintaining students' cooperation so that: (a) you enjoy satisfying teaching experiences; (b) your students are provided with optimal learning opportunities
2. analyze what you do as a teacher along the lines of the six steps of "the Teaching Process Model."
3. know the meaning of the following terms: allocated time, transition time, student engagement, on-task behavior, off-task behavior, and disruptive behavior.

## THE DIFFERENCE BETWEEN A MISERABLE AND A PLEASANT TEACHING EXPERIENCE

Some teachers seem to be constantly struggling to get students' attention, gain some semblance of order, confront disruptions, and maintain enough energy to get through their planned lessons. Other teachers have given up the struggle, having decided that today's students are so unmotivated and uncaring that it is futile to attempt anything more than surviving the school day. Then there are those teachers who orchestrate smoothly operating classrooms where students cooperatively and efficiently go about the business of learning with minimal disruptions.

Why does it seem so easy for some teachers to conduct productive lessons while other teachers' struggles do nothing more than wear them down? Teaching is hardly ever easy, but it is enjoyable for some because they implement proven classroom management ideas and principles for gaining students' cooperation. Why should you learn to apply these ideas and principles? Two reasons come to mind: (1) The satisfaction and enjoyment that your teaching experiences provide you are dependent on how well you develop efficient methods for leading students to cooperate with you; (2) You are responsible for providing your students with a learning environment that is conducive to achievement and free from disruptions, distractions, and threats to their safety and well-being.

Before examining this book's suggestions for gaining students' cooperation and for confronting discipline problems, your attention is briefly directed to an examination of your role as a teacher.

## THE TEACHING PROCESS MODEL

### Ms. Martinez's Learning Unit

Ms. Martinez is an English teacher at Carver Street Middle School. She is very concerned about her students' inability to communicate effectively in writing. In her opinion, they need to think about the different ways readers interpret what they write and they need to edit their own writing so that it conveys what is intended. For one of her classes of 32 students, Ms. Martinez develops a creative writing unit to help her students achieve this goal. She designs, prepares, and implements a number of learning activities over a 10-day period. For example, one day she divides the 32 students into five groups of six or seven each. Within each group, one student reads a paragraph he or she had written for homework. The other students then discuss the meaning of the paragraph as if the writer were not present. The writer, who is not allowed to enter into the discussion, listens and takes notes on how the classmates interpreted the paragraph. The writer is to later modify the paragraph in light of the discussion. This activity continues until all students have had a chance to read their paragraphs and hear them discussed.

Near the end of the 10-day unit, Ms. Martinez uses a posttest to help her evaluate just how aware of readers' interpretations her students have become and how effectively the students learned to edit what they wrote.

### An Analysis of What Ms. Martinez Did

The idea for Ms. Martinez's unit grew out of her belief that her students needed to improve their writing and editing abilities. Deciding to do something about that need, she *determined a learning goal*. To help her students achieve that goal, she *designed learning activities* and then completed the preparations (e.g., rearranging her classroom to accommodate five small groups working independently) for the learning activities. The term *learning activity* refers to what a teacher plans for students to experience to help them achieve a learning goal. When Ms. Martinez's students were writing paragraphs, reading them to their small groups, listening to others read, discussing what was read, taking notes, and rewriting paragraphs, those students were *engaged in learning activities* and Ms. Martinez was *conducting learning activities*. Finally, Ms. Martinez evaluated how successfully her students achieved the unit's goal.

## A General Model for Any Learning Unit

You, like Ms. Martinez, teach learning units by effecting the six steps of what is referred to throughout this textbook as the *Teaching Process Model:*

### Illustration 1.1. The Teaching Process Model

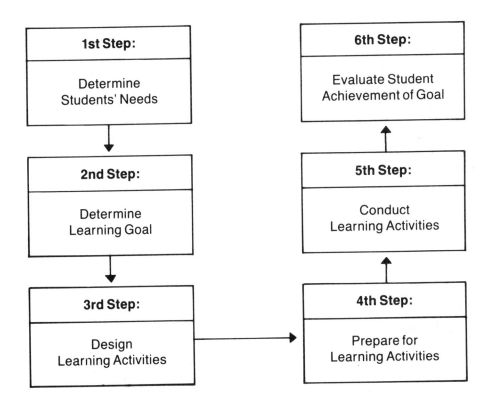

**1st)** Determine needs of students
**2nd)** Determine learning goal
**3rd)** Determine appropriate learning activities
**4th)** Prepare for the learning activities
**5th)** Conduct the learning activities
**6th)** Determine how well students have achieved the learning goal

The Teaching Process Model will serve two functions in this textbook: (1) It will help us relate suggestions and techniques about how to gain students' cooperation to specific aspects of teaching; (2) It will be used to organize our thoughts on how to teach students to supplant uncooperative behavior with cooperative behaviors.

## ALLOCATED TIME AND TRANSITION TIME

The third step of the Teaching Process Model requires you to determine and plan your students' learning activities. Suppose that the learning activities that you plan for one school day calls for one group of students to: (1) read a passage from a book; (2) discuss what they read; (3) listen to you give a brief lecture; (3) respond individually in writing to questions appearing on a worksheet; (4) read another passage and write a brief essay for homework. The time periods of that day that, according to your plan, you *intend* for your students to be engaged in these learning activities are referred to as *allocated times*. Obviously, allocated time cannot take up an entire school day. On the day you conduct the four learning activities, time must be devoted to, among other things: (1) getting your students assembled and attentive; (2) assigning the reading and directing them to begin; (3) calling students' attention away from the reading and preparing them to attend to your lecture; (4) upon completion of the lecture, getting the worksheets distributed and directing them to answer the questions; (5) calling a halt to the worksheet activity and assigning the homework. Time periods, like the five just enumerated, that exist *between* times allocated for learning activities are referred to as *transition times*.

## STUDENT COOPERATION, ENGAGEMENT,
## AND ON/OFF-TASK BEHAVIORS

Throughout the book problems, procedures, techniques, and a variety of classroom situations are illustrated in scenarios, such as the examples which follow.

Mr. Issac directs the 28 first graders whom he teaches to remove their paints from their supply boxes and to complete a previously assigned art project. Buster takes his paints and begins working on the project. Elysia picks up a bottle of yellow paint and throws it across the room, splattering several students.

Ms. Saunders, a high school history teacher, is in the midst of conducting a class discussion on the reasons why the U.S. Congress rescinded prohibition in 1933. Lia listens intently to the discussion and occasionally expresses her thoughts on the causes. Amy quietly sits at her desk daydreaming about riding horses.

Coach Murphy directs 18 of his football players to take two laps around the field. Hewitt begins running while Ricky hides behind the blocking dummies until the others have completed the exercise.

Buster's, Lia's, and Hewitt's behaviors, as described in the three examples, are cooperative. Because they were acting as their teachers had planned, their behavior is referred to as being *on-task*. The time Buster spent working on his art project was time Buster spent *engaged* in the particular learning activity that Mr. Issac had planned for him. Lia appeared to be spending the time that Ms. Saunders had allocated for discussing why the U.S. Congress rescinded prohibition by becoming involved in that discussion. Thus, Lia, like Hewitt in the third example, was engaged in a learning activity. In general, students who are cooperating with a teacher and doing what the teacher planned for them to do are displaying on-task behavior. If on-task behavior occurs during a period of allocated time, the on-task behavior is also referred to as *student engagement in a learning activity*. On-task behavior can occur either during allocated time or transition time. Engagement can occur only during allocated time.

In the first of the three examples just given, Elysia's behavior was very uncooperative. She was *off-task* because she was not attempting to follow Mr. Issac's directions and she failed to become engaged in the planned learning activity. Amy's behavior, in the second example, was not as disruptive as was Elysia's, but Amy was still off-task as she was insufficiently engaged in the discussion (i.e., neither listening nor contributing) during the time Ms. Saunders had allocated for the discussion. Similarly, Ricky was off-task and not engaged in Coach Murphy's planned learning activity.

## DISRUPTIVE BEHAVIORS

When Elysia flung her paint across Mr. Issac's room she was not only displaying off-task behavior, but her behavior also probably prevented or discouraged other students from being on-task and engaged in the learning activity. Amy's off-task behavior (i.e., quiet daydreaming) probably did not disturb any of the other students nor interfere with the chances of others being on-task. The off-task behavior that Elysia exhibited is referred to as *disruptive;* Amy's off-task behavior was not disruptive. Off-task behaviors such as students talking to one another during times allocated for them to be listening to a presentation, interrupting a speaker, being generally discourteous, clowning, and acting out violently are usually thought of as disruptive. Off-task behaviors such as students allowing their minds to wander from the topic at hand, daydreaming, being quietly inattentive because of the effects of drugs, failing to complete homework assignments, skipping class, and cheating on tests are usually thought of as non-disruptive. In general, a student's behavior is disruptive when it encourages or causes other students to be off-task.

Disruptive behaviors are the sources of most teachers' greatest fears (Abernathy, Manera, & Wright, 1985). Teachers who are considered by their supervisors to have poor classroom control and discipline problems are teachers whose students display unusually high levels of disruptive behaviors. Teachers really have little choice; they must deal one way or another with student disruptions. However, off-task behaviors that are not disruptive, especially disengagement during learning activities, should also be a prime concern of teachers. The really effective, concerned teachers conscientiously work at identifying off-task behaviors, even those that are not disruptive, and they work with deliberation to keep students on-task and engaged in learning activities (Cangelosi, 1986).

## FACING THE PROBLEM OF KEEPING STUDENTS ENGAGED

The problem of maintaining discipline in schools continues to be, as it has been for at least the past 17 years, the number one concern of students, teachers, parents, and school administrators (Gallup, 1986). For typical classrooms, some research studies suggest that students are engaged in learning activities for no more than half of the time that is allocated for those learning activities (Jones, 1979). Other studies place this figure nearer 75 percent (Goodlad, 1984). The time allocated to learning activities averages only about 40 percent of the total time students spend at school. Thus, the average amount of time students spend actively engaged in learning activities ranges (depending on which study you believe) between 20 percent and 30 percent of the time they are at school (Latham, 1984).

Why is it that in the average classroom students spend what appears to be an inordinate share of their time either off-task or in transition between learning activities? Should not students be engaged in learning activities for a larger portion of the school day?

When the proportion of allocated time that students spend engaged in learning activities is increased, students' achievement of learning goals increases (Fisher et al., 1980). While some reports suggest that both the school year and the school day should be lengthened to accommodate more allocated time (National Commission on Excellence in Education, 1983), others clearly display that through effective planning and organization teachers can increase allocated time, without lengthening either the school day or year, by minimizing transition time (Latham, 1984). Furthermore, by applying some rather elementary classroom management and discipline techniques, teachers can lead students to be engaged in learning activities for more than 90 percent of allocated time (Evertson, Emmer, Clements, Sanford, & Worsham, 1984; Fisher et al., 1980; Jones, 1979).

What goals you establish for your students to achieve; how you plan, prepare for, and conduct learning activities; how you evaluate your students' achievement; how you organize and manage the classroom setting; and the manner in which you communicate with students and their parents will be major influences on how much of your students' time is spent cooperatively engaged in learning activities. Of course other factors, many of which are out of your control, will also influence how well your students cooperate. Unsympathetic school administrators, uncaring parents, lack of needed supplies and facilities, unmotivated students, students with emotional disabilities, students with learning gaps, students with learning disabilities, overcrowded classes, and more work than is possible in 24-hour days are major culprits. But dwelling on causes outside of your control will not be a productive means for you to begin increasing students' time on-task and engaged in learning activities. Rather, address this question: "What can I, as the teacher in charge of students, do?" If you are willing to do what you can to get and keep your students' cooperation, then you are ready to work your way through the remainder of this text.

## Self-Assessment for Chapter 1

Exercises to reinforce what you learned from this chapter are contained in this section; answers or responses to the items of an exercise are provided in the next section, "Reviewing Your Self-Assessment."

I. Examine the following scenario and then on a separate sheet of paper respond to the items that follow in light of your examination:

Because Ms. Kobayashi believes that most of her 33 home economics students do not adequately practice comparison shopping, she decides to conduct a learning unit designed to better enable students to assess the cost-benefit value of products that are sold in stores. During one of the unit's learning activities, which involves students cutting ads out of newspapers, Corine and Gordon toss balled-up newspaper scraps at one another. Ms. Kobayashi decides to put a stop to their activity by speaking to them privately and directing them to clean up the area during the time when the rest of the class is field-testing the fruit salad that was made during another learning activity. Both Corine and Gordon cooperatively clean up and do not disturb the class during subsequent lessons of the unit. Therefore, Ms. Kobayashi concludes that they will be less likely to clown around in future class sessions. At the end of the unit, a test is given and Ms. Kobayashi decides that 11 of the 13 students who scored significantly higher than the test average are quite proficient at assessing the cost-benefit value of products.

A. Within the context of the example Ms. Kobayashi completed a teaching cycle dealing with (1) assessing cost-benefit values, and (2) another in which she dealt with a discipline problem. Using the following outline, list what she did for each of the six steps of the Teaching Process Model.

1. *For the cost-benefit unit:* Ms. Kobayashi implemented the first step of the model when she decided what?
   She implemented the second step when she decided what?
   What did she decide when she implemented the third step?
   What are some of the things she might have done while implementing the fourth step?
   What are some of the things she probably did in carrying out the fifth step?
   What did she decide when implementing the sixth step?

2. *For dealing with the discipline problem:* What decision might Ms. Kobayashi have made in carrying out the first step of the model?
   She implemented the second step when she decided what?
   What did she decide when she implemented the third step?
   What are some of the things she might have done while implementing the fourth step?
   What are some of the things she probably did in carrying out the fifth step?
   What did she decide when implementing the sixth step?

B. A number of instances of allocated time occurred in the example. What was one?

C. A number of instances of transition time were implied by the example. What was one?

II. Following are some brief descriptions of student behaviors. Label each according to an appropriate combination of the following: (1) on-task; (2) off-task; (3) engaged; (4) disruptive.

A. Ms. Romano directs her first graders to complete seven math problems from a worksheet. Several students begin doodling and drawing pictures after briefly trying to work one or two of the problems.

B. Mr. Finegan tells his third graders that it is time for them to put away the materials with which they have been working at learning centers and to get to their reading groups for the next lesson. Dale puts away the center materials and immediately goes to his reading group area and waits. Adonis places some of the colored rods from the learning center on Mary's head. Mary yells at Adonis, and the two begin arguing.

C. Charlene, Marion, and Rufus are eleventh graders engaging in a lively conversation as they wait for Mr. Bench to enter the classroom and begin chemistry class. Mr. Bench arrives, asks for silence, and asks Marion to demonstrate an experiment that had been tried for homework. Marion begins the demonstration. Except for Charlene and Rufus, who continue to socialize, class members watch and listen to the demonstration.

III. Make a list of some of the factors that lead students in many classrooms to spend an undesirably low proportion of school time engaged in learning activities. Circle those factors on your list that you, as a teacher, can control.

*Reviewing Your Self-Assessment* ─────────────────────────

Because the questions raised by the items in the exercise in which you just engaged are somewhat open-ended, an exact answer key cannot be provided. You should, however, evaluate your responses in light of the sample answers and comments appearing in this section.

Regarding item I–A, the scenario suggests that Ms. Kobayashi followed the Teaching Process Model in planning and conducting her unit on comparison shopping and that while she conducted that unit, she also followed the Teaching Process Model to teach Corine and Gordon to be on-task. The application of the Teaching Process Model to discipline goals, as it is applied to academic learning goals, may be a strange idea to many. However, as is suggested in Chapter 7 of this text, if you treat student displays of off-task behavior as indications that students need to learn something, you are more likely to deal effectively with discipline problems when they arise.

With respect to the cost-benefit unit, Ms. Kobayashi implemented the first step of the model when she decided that most of her students needed to be able to practice comparison shopping. The second step was implemented when she set the goal of learning how to assess cost-benefit values. The principal difference between the first and second steps is that a teacher who only determines that students have a particular need has not yet decided to do something about that need. As a teacher, you identify many needs that your students have that never lead to learning goals. You cannot, nor do you have the right or responsibility to, take care of all of your students' needs. The student needs that fall within your responsibilities and with which you are reasonably capable of dealing lead to learning goals. Ms. Kobayashi could have decided that other needs would take priority over learning comparison shopping and she could have chosen not to move to step two of the Teaching Process Model. In this example, however, she decided to act upon recognition of that particular need.

She implemented the third step by planning to have students cut out newspaper ads and carry on other activities that are not given in the example. What she did to carry out the fourth step (i.e., preparing for learning activities) is not explained; try to imagine what she might have done. For example, she may have collected particular editions of newspapers with some especially helpful advertisements, distributed the papers and scissors, and grouped the students in a way that would benefit the smooth operation of the lesson. For the fifth step, she explained to them what to do with the ads and supervised the cutting-out activities. In the sixth step, she decided, probably among other things, that 11 of the 13 high-scoring students were quite proficient at assessing the cost-benefit value of products.

With respect to the way she dealt with the discipline problem, it appears that Ms. Kobayashi decided, in the first step of the model, that Corine and Gordon's disruptive behavior should cease. There are times when a teacher may identify a need, such as that some off-task behavior should cease, and wisely choose not to deal with that need. Dealing with the unwanted behavior may, for example, itself create more disruption. But Ms. Kobayashi chose to deal with Corine and Gordon's disruption and, therefore, went on to the second step of the model by deciding to get them to stop tossing paper balls. The third step was implemented by deciding to speak to them privately and directing them to the clean-up task. You really have to use your imagination to fill in a fourth step. Possibly, she saw to it that the rest of the class was able to remain busy while she directed Corine and Gordon to a private spot for the conversation. The fifth step was, of course, speaking to them and directing them to clean up. Her evaluation that they had been adequately discouraged from repeating such behavior provided the sixth step.

Regarding items I–B and I–C, there are many examples you could have given. The time Ms. Kobayashi planned to spend with students cutting out ads was an example of allocated time. Time spent directing the students from their newspaper-cutting activities and into their fruit salad-tasting activities was an example of transition time.

Regarding item II, those of Ms. Romano's students who doodled during time allocated for working math problems displayed off-task behavior. Doodling is usually not disruptive. The Mr. Finegan example involved transitional time rather than allocated time, so there was no opportunity for students to be engaged in learning activities as was the case in the Ms. Romano example. Dale's behavior appeared to be on-task, while Adonis' and Mary's seemed both off-task and disruptive. During the transitional time before Mr. Bench asked Marion to demonstrate the experiment, Charlene's, Marion's, and Rufus' talking did not seem inappropriate.

However, when Marion began the demonstration, Charlene and Rufus' conversation became off-task and may have been disruptive, depending on whether or not others were distracted. Marion and those students who paid attention were displaying on-task, engaged behaviors during the demonstration.

Regarding item III, any list of factors that I make will not be any more meaningful than the one you gave. Carefully examine your list and compare it with ones provided by others who are also interested in the topic of classroom management and discipline. Think of ways that your actions can combat or at least mitigate the effects of the factors on students' levels of cooperation and engagement in learning activities.

## Supplemental Readings

Some of the topics you read about in each chapter are also referred to in the list of readings which, as is the case here, follow Self-Assessment exercises. You may find some of them helpful.

Abernathy, S., Manera, E., & Wright, R. (1985). What stresses student teachers most? *The Clearing House, 58,* 361–362.

Cangelosi, J. S. (1982). *Measurement and evaluation: An inductive approach for teachers* (pp. 9–21). Dubuque, IA: Brown.

Cangelosi, J. S. (1986). *Cooperation in the classroom: Students and teachers together* (pp. 9–12). Washington, DC: National Education Association.

Denham, C., & Lieberman, A. (Eds.). (1980). *Time to learn* (pp. 7–72). Washington, DC: U.S. Department of Education and the National Institute of Education.

Gallup, A. M. (1986). The 18th Annual Gallup Poll of the public's attitudes toward the public schools. *Phi Delta Kappan, 68,* 43–59.

McGarity, J. R., & Butts, D. P. (1984). The relationship among teacher classroom management behavior, student engagement, and student achievement of middle and high school science students of varying aptitude. *Journal of Research in Science Teaching, 21,* 55–61.

Parker, W. C., & Gehrke, N. J. (1986). Learning activities and teacher decisionmaking: Some grounded hypotheses. *American Educational Research Journal, 23,* 227–242.

# 2

## Thinking About Teaching Students to Cooperate

Chapter 2 is designed to help you:

1. realize that on-task behaviors and engagement in learning activities are learned responses that you should plan to teach your students.
2. be aware of the basic contributions of each of the following schools of thought: the Kounin, the Jones, the Ginott, the Glasser, the Dreikurs, the Canter, and the behaviorist approaches.
3. know the meaning of the following terms and be able to comprehend communications that use them: positive reinforcer, destructive positive reinforcer, naturally occurring punishment, contrived punishment, destructive punishment, negative reinforcement, isolated behavior, and behavior pattern.

### STUDENTS LEARN TO COOPERATE

Here are some examples of student behaviors that are commonly observed in school settings:

After being told by their second grade teacher to work out the computations on a worksheet, Jaylene begins computing while Fred, another student, begins doodling and drawing pictures of robots on the worksheet.

Instead of doing the push-ups that his physical education teacher assigned for homework, Woodrow watches television and eats snacks.

During history class, Janet listens to her teacher's lecture on the European Industrial Revolution while two of her classmates, Sophie and John, chat about their plans for going out that night.

Jaylene and Janet were on-task and engaged in learning activities; Fred, Woodrow, Sophie, and John were off-task. Which group, the on-task one or the off-task one, displayed behaviors that were more natural for people? Think about the contrasting behaviors of the two second graders, Jaylene and Fred. Would a seven- or eight-year-old, when handed a pencil and a sheet of paper containing numerals, be more inclined to begin manipulating the numerals or to begin doodling and drawing? Is it surprising that Woodrow would prefer watching television and eating snacks to doing push-ups? Isn't it normal for two adolescents, such as Sophie and John, to be more interested in talking to each other than in listening to a lecture on the European Industrial Revolution?

Sitting at a desk, thinking about academic topics, completing writing exercises, trying to memorize steps in a process, doing calisthenics, and discussing mitosis are simply not the kinds of things people are inclined to do in the absence of either the imposition of a special structure (e.g., a school) or extraordinary motivation. You should keep in mind that students *learn* to be on-task and engaged in the learning activities you plan for them. On-task behaviors are typically less natural than off-task behaviors and, consequently, you can expect your students to be on-task only if you have *taught* them to choose on-task behaviors over off-task behaviors.

The question, of course, is, "How do you teach students to choose to be on-task?" Over many years this question has been addressed by enough reports, journal articles, books, and papers to fill a library. From these works, a number of schools of thought on the general topic of student discipline and classroom management have emerged. Sometimes mistakenly thought of as being in opposition (e.g., the Ginott approach versus the Behaviorist approach), these theories actually complement one another when the best ideas and insights from each are taken into consideration. Each of the next seven sections of this chapter presents some of the basic ideas associated with a major school of thought on how students can be taught to be on-task.

## THE KOUNIN APPROACH: WITHITNESS AND ORGANIZATION

### Kounin's Research

Beginning in the 1950s and continuing into the 1970s, Jacob Kounin conducted studies examining the influence of certain teacher behaviors on the tendencies of students to be on-task (Kounin, 1977). These studies involved classrooms from kindergarten through college.

## Withitness

One of the major implications from these studies involves the impact of a teacher's *withitness* on the behaviors students exhibit in classrooms. Kounin coined the term "withitness" to refer to a teacher's awareness of what is going on in the classroom. The proverbial teacher with "eyes in the back of his or her head" has withitness. Teachers who are fully aware of practically everything going on in their classrooms are likely to have their students on-task. Kounin emphasized the importance of students knowing whether or not their teacher is with it. He found that students tend to judge their teacher as having withitness if:

1. When discipline problems occur, the teacher consistently takes action to suppress the misbehavior of exactly those students who instigated the problem. (This displays that the teacher knows what is happening. If on the other hand, it appears to the students that the teacher is likely to blame the wrong person, they conclude that the teacher is not with it.)
2. When two discipline problems arise concurrently, the teacher typically deals with the more serious one first.
3. The teacher decisively handles instances of off-task behaviors before the behaviors either get out of hand or are modeled by others. (For example, if third grader Bernie begins creating a tower out of the colored rods that he is supposed to be using to validate answers to multiplication problems, a with-it teacher will take action to get Bernie back on-task before the tower tumbles over or other students begin building their own.)

## The Impact of Teachers' Responses to Misbehaviors

Kounin also studied how a teacher's handling of one student's misbehavior affects the behaviors of other students. He found that when a teacher responds to the misbehavior of one student so that other students understand exactly what about the behavior is unacceptable, the other students are less likely to exhibit that misbehavior in the future. This effect was stronger for elementary level students than for older ones. It was also discovered that when a teacher's response to a student's misbehavior includes anger, threats, physical handling, or indications that the teacher is stressed, other students become anxious and nervous, but the chances that they will exhibit the misbehavior themselves in the future are *not* reduced.

## Concurrently Dealing with a Number of Events

According to Kounin, it is very important for teachers to be able to manage a classroom so that they can deal with a number of events concurrently.

Compare how two teachers handled instances of off-task behaviors in their classrooms as described in the following two examples:

> Ms. Farnsworth is explaining certain aspects of human digestive systems to her class of 31 tenth graders when she notices Ekpe and Ross whispering to one another. She stops her explanation and announces: "Please pay attention you two! It's very important for you to understand this. . . . Now where were we? . . . Oh, yes! As I was saying . . ."

> Ms. Gordin is explaining certain aspects of human digestive systems to her class of 31 tenth graders when she notices Rich and Jonathan whispering to one another. She continues with her explanations to the class as she moves nearer to Rich and Jonathan. They continue their whispering. Without the least interruption to her lecture, she moves between Rich and Jonathan and gently touches Rich on the shoulder. The two stop and appear to begin attending to the lesson. She continues to observe all of the students, including Rich and Jonathan as the explanation progresses.

How would you prefer to have handled the students' whispering—as Ms. Farnsworth did, or as Ms. Gordin did? Ms. Gordin simultaneously handled two events: her explanation about digestive systems to the whole class and two students' off-task behaviors. Ms. Farnsworth, on the other hand, interrupted her lecture to take time to handle the whispering. Her failure to deal with both situations at the same time caused other students to become disengaged from the learning activity.

## Smoothness of Transitions

According to Kounin's studies, student engagement and on-task behaviors are dependent on how smoothly teachers move from one learning activity to another and how efficiently transition time is used. Examine the following three examples:

> Mr. Condie is grading papers at a desk while his fifth grade students individually work on a writing assignment at their places. Suddenly, he announces: "Okay class, you can finish that later, let's take out our history workbooks and start answering the questions beginning at the bottom of page 74. Here we go. Jean, how would you answer number one . . . ?" Some of the students, who were involved with the writing assignment when Mr. Condie suddenly announced the new activity, do not hear what was said. They continue to write although history questions are being read. Others stop writing, but have to inquire from classmates to what page they should turn. There is quite a delay before the majority of the class is engaged in the history lesson.

> Ms. Jesundas announces to her fourth grade class: "I see that everyone

is finished with the calculator drill. Please see that your calculator is off and put away in its box. . . . Very good! Now, we're going to begin working on something you'll really enjoy. I want everyone to get out one sheet of paper and a pencil. . . . Joseph, get those other things off of your desk. . . . Thank you, Joseph. Okay, as I was saying, you should have just one sheet of paper. . . . That's the way to do it, Mark! . . . You should have one sheet of paper, and nothing else, except for a pencil on your desk. . . . Oh! Rachel, your pencil needs sharpening. We'll take care of that in a moment. Now, you're really going to like what we're going to do. Take your paper and. . . ."

With the aid of an overhead projector, Mr. Saville is demonstrating to his accounting class one system for recording certain types of business transactions. While referring to an example involving consolidation of loans, Mr. Saville pauses and asks, "Have we ever explained what 'consolidation of loans' means?" Dorothy: "No, we never did get to that." David: "Yeah! What does that mean?" Mr. Saville: "I thought we had covered that, but I guess not. . . . Open your text to page. . . . Let's see. . . . Here it is! Page 139. . . . Everybody's got it? . . . Good! Now read the part under heading six dash four on consolidating loans." Gwynn: "Mr. Saville, we already read this! This was a homework assignment." Other students express their agreement, while only a few suggest that they hadn't read the section. Mr. Saville: "In that case, put your books away and let's get back to our new recording system. . . . Now, as I was explaining before. . . ."

Mr. Condie failed to get all of his students' attention before attempting to provide them with directions for an upcoming learning activity. The transition between the time allocated for the writing activity and the time allocated for answering history questions was not smooth. With some students continuing to work on the first activity, others changing activities, and still others beginning the new task, the transition time was marked by confusion. While Mr. Condie did not attend to details and attempted to make the transition between two learning activities too rapidly, Ms. Jesundas may have never gotten the second activity underway. She wasted so much of her students' time with minute details, taking care of isolated problems of individuals, and trying to convince her students how enjoyable the activity would be, that her students got bored by what she had planned for them to do before they ever got to do it. Mr. Saville interrupted one lesson to begin another and then returned to the first while the second activity was abandoned. Although such interruptions cannot always be avoided, they do make it difficult for students to remain engaged in a learning activity. At least some of Mr. Saville's students would still have been thinking about who was right regarding the alleged homework assignment when he was expecting their attention to be refocused on his demonstration.

### Group Focus

Kounin emphasized the importance of a teacher using strategies to keep all students in a class focused on a topic. In the following two examples, one teacher seems unconcerned about maintaining the group's focus, while the other consciously tries to direct all students' thinking:

> Mr. Drake is leading a discussion session with his 28 sixth graders on a short story they have just read. Mr. Drake: "Mary, why do you think Joey didn't go back to school?" Mary: "Because he thought his friends would make fun of him." Mr. Drake: "What did the story's author say to make you think that?" Mary: "Well, remember, when . . ."
>
> Ms. Grimes is leading a discussion session with her 28 sixth graders on a short story they have just read. Ms. Grimes: "Think about why Joey didn't go back to school. . . . Okay, we're ready to hear what you think. Why didn't Joey go back to school, Mary?" Mary: "Because he thought his friends would make fun of him." Ms. Grimes: "What in the story do you suppose made Mary believe that, Devon?" Devon: "She probably thinks . . ."

Ms. Grimes did not let the group session become a private conversation between herself and only one or two students. She used strategies designed to keep the entire group focused on the topic at hand.

Kounin also found that teachers could reduce boredom and increase engagement in learning activities by: (1) keeping students apprised as to what they were accomplishing as lessons progressed; (2) injecting challenges for the students to confront at different stages of the lesson; (3) using a variety of approaches from one learning activity to another.

Subsequent chapters of this text, especially chapters 3, 6, 9, and 10, include material that is designed to help you put ideas emanating from Kounin's studies into practice.

## THE JONES APPROACH: BODY LANGUAGE, INCENTIVES, AND EFFICIENT HELP

### Studies of School Time

Utilizing the results of studies that involved hundreds of observations in elementary and secondary school classrooms in a wide variety of settings (e.g., inner city and suburban), Fredric Jones has developed and promoted techniques for managing classrooms and motivating students through the Classroom Management Training Program centered in Santa Cruz, California. Observations indicated that for typical classrooms 50 percent of allocated time is lost because of off-task behaviors (Jones, 1979). While some teachers fear that students will be openly defiant and hostile and that violence will erupt in their schools, Jones found that 99 percent of off-task behaviors take one of several forms: students typically will be either talking out of turn, clowning, daydreaming, or moving about without permission. Antisocial, dangerous behaviors only represent a fraction of the time students spend off-task. Massive timewasting seems to be epidemic in schools.

Many teachers and school administrators who have participated in workshops through the Classroom Management Training Program have found that student engagement time is markedly increased when teachers adhere to Jones' suggestions regarding use of body language, incentive systems for students, and efficient individual help for students. The remainder of this section presents some of those suggestions. Some subsequent chapters of this text (e.g., chapters 3, 4, 6, 7, 8, 9, and 10) provide you with help on developing your own techniques for implementing those suggestions.

## Body Language and Proximity

Through the use of eye contact, facial expressions, gestures, your physical proximity to students, and the way you carry yourself, you can communicate that you are in calm control of the class and mean to be taken seriously. Direct eye contact between two people often makes those people uncomfortable. Consequently, teachers and students are inclined to look away when their eyes meet. However, Jones has found that control over a classroom situation is exerted when a teacher uses her or his eyes to continually monitor the students, often pausing to look directly into the eyes of individual students. By focusing your eyes on individual students and managing to do this regularly for all students, you communicate that each student is personally an important part of what's going on in the classroom. Occasionally winking at, smiling with, or making a positive hand gesture (e.g., thumb up) to a student when you have caught her or his eye helps communicate that you are very aware and interested that she or he is there. How does Jones' suggestion about eye contact relate to Kounin's emphasis on withitness?

As you might expect, students who see the teacher nearby are more likely to be on-task than students who are farther away. You should consider planning learning activities so that you are free to roam among your students rather than being stationary (e.g., at a lecture stand, chalk board, or behind a lab table). Chapter 6 will provide you with practical suggestions for conducting learning activities, even lectures and demonstrations, so that you are able to move among your students and encourage engagement.

Which teacher, in the following two examples, do you think displays the more effective use of body language?

Mr. Tramonte's students are working on individual assignments at their desks as he moves about the room answering questions and providing help. While explaining something to Charlie, Mr. Tramonte realizes that Bonnie and John, two students seated behind him, are off-task and becoming disruptive as they talk with one another. Without turning his body around, Mr. Tramonte looks over his shoulder and yells, "Knock it off! I don't want to hear any more yakking."

Mr. Brown's students are working on individual assignments at their desks as he moves about the room answering questions and providing help. While explaining something to Iris, Mr. Brown realizes that Dustin and Annie, two students seated behind him, are off-task and becoming disruptive as they talk to one another. Mr. Brown softly tells Iris, "Excuse me, I'll be back within 40 seconds." Mr. Brown pivots and faces Dustin and Annie. He calmly walks directly toward them and squats down so his eye level meets theirs. With his shoulders parallel to Dustin's, he looks Dustin in the eyes and softly says, "I would like for you to get to work without talking." He immediately turns directly to Annie, achieves eye contact, and repeats the message. Standing up, he pivots and returns to Iris.

The body language displayed by Mr. Brown was more in line with Jones' suggestions than that displayed by Mr. Tramonte.

## Incentives

Jones' training program encourages teachers to use systems of *real* incentives for students. In the first of the two following examples, Ms. Robertson uses a typical approach to motivating on-task behaviors; in the second, Ms. Samples uses an approach that exemplifies Jones' method:

While directing her fourth graders to answer questions at the end of a reading lesson, Ms. Robertson announces: "I know you can be my best class ever! Let's see how quickly you can get these questions answered correctly! The first three of you that show me all 12 correct answers will get stars on their papers to bring home and show their parents!"

While directing her fourth graders to answer questions at the end of a reading lesson, Ms. Samples announces: "You have exactly 17 minutes to work on these questions. I want you to answer as many of the 12 questions as you can in that time. I will be walking around watching you work. If every one of you works on the questions without stopping for the entire 17 minutes and no one disturbs anyone else, the class can pick out one video from the library and we will watch the first 30 minutes of it right after lunch."

Because Ms. Samples has used this tactic before, the fourth graders know not to complain that it wouldn't be fair for the whole class to miss the video if only one or two children are uncooperative. Such complaints have been non-productive in the past, but peer pressure has served as an effective control. They also don't inquire about how the class will select the video, because they know from experience that Ms. Samples will come up with something. However, Emily does ask: "Ms. Samples, what will we do after lunch if we don't watch the video?" Ms. Samples: "If we don't watch a video, I'll let you help me clean the room for 30 minutes right after lunch."

There were at least two factors to prevent Ms. Robertson's effort from providing her students with *real* incentives: (1) Some students may have wanted to be a member of Ms. Robertson's "best class ever" and have a star on their paper; however, such incentives were probably not strong enough to maintain 17 minutes of continuous work. (2) The vast majority of Ms. Robertson's students realized they have virtually no chance of being one of the first three successful finishers; the competition was no motivation for those who were in greatest need of motivation.

Pre-scheduled opportunities to watch a video, have free time to talk or play, or listen to music (with earphones) may be more appealing than less tangible rewards. Ms. Samples' approach provided incentives to all the students, not only the few who had a chance to be early finishers.

## Providing Individual Help

The following scenario illustrates one other concern raised by Jones' research findings:

> Mr. Dupont-Lee's eleventh graders are individually working at their places on an exercise on factoring algebraic polynomials. About 12 of the 27 students have their hands raised beckoning Mr. Dupont-Lee's help as he moves among them tutoring one and then another. When he gets around to Brenda, she says, "I don't know how to do these." Mr. Dupont-Lee: "What is it you don't know how to do?" Brenda: "I don't understand enough to know what I don't know!" Mr. Dupont-Lee: "Let's look at number three here. Did you look for a factor common to all the terms?" Brenda: "Well, all the terms have three as a factor." Mr. Dupont-Lee: "Then what can you. . . ." In the meantime, other students are waiting and feel they cannot continue with the exercise until Mr. Dupont-Lee helps them. But he doesn't get around to all those requesting help and more and more students become disengaged from the learning activity.

Teachers were observed providing individual help, as did Mr. Dupont-Lee, and then they were asked how much time they thought they averaged with each student helped. The teachers thought they spent between 1 and 2 minutes; actually they averaged about 4 minutes with each student (Jones, 1979). Four uninterrupted minutes is too long to spend with one individual student while others are waiting for help. You can be far more efficient than Mr. Dupont-Lee in the way you provide individual help to your students. Chapter 6 will provide you with some suggestions.

## THE GINOTT APPROACH: COOPERATION THROUGH COMMUNICATION

### Describing Instead of Characterizing

Through publications appearing in the 1960s and early 1970s, Haim Ginott offered solutions to common communication problems that parents experience with their children and teachers experience with their students. Ginott (1965, 1972) emphasized that the messages adults send have a profound effect on the self-concepts children and adolescents form about themselves. What may seem to be only subtle differences in the ways teachers consistently use language can be a major determinant in how students view themselves and how willing they are to cooperate. Here are two contrasting examples to illustrate a major Ginott theme:

> Ms. Robinson is conducting a learning activity in which her sixth graders are describing how reading a particular poem made them feel. "I began to remember back when I was only about seven years old when . . . ," Justin is saying when he is interrupted by Theresa who blurts, "Yeah, because you still are seven! Who wants to hear what a baby like you thinks?" Ms. Robinson: "Theresa! What a rude little girl you are! Why can't you be more thoughtful? Continue, Justin. It is too bad that one discourteous person hurt your feelings! You are definitely not a baby. Please go on."
>
> Ms. Hebert is conducting a learning activity in which her sixth graders are describing how reading a particular poem made them feel. "I began to remember back when I was only about seven years olds when . . . ," George is saying when he is interrupted by Lamona who blurts, "Yeah, because you still are seven! Who wants to hear what a baby like you thinks?" Ms. Hebert turns to Lamona and firmly, but calmly, says, "George has the floor right now. I am angry because you stopped us from hearing what George was saying." Turning to George, Ms. Hebert says, "George, you were saying that the poem had you remembering when you were seven. I would like for you to continue."

Ms. Robinson addressed Theresa's character; she labeled her as "rude." Ms. Hebert, on the other hand, did not bring Lamona's personality into question; she did not hang a label on Lamona. Instead, Ms. Hebert addressed the situation and targeted Lamona's rude behavior rather than Lamona herself. Lamona's rudeness needs to be eliminated, not Lamona herself. Paramount in Ginott's work is this principle: Teachers should verbalize to students descriptions of situations and behaviors and never value judgments about individuals themselves.

Ms. Hebert described a situation when she said, "George has the floor right now." She also described her own feelings by saying, "I am angry because your interruption stopped us from hearing what George was saying." According to Ginott, teachers should recognize, rather than deny their feelings, both their own and those expressed by students. If, as a teacher, you are not angry very often, you are more likely to have students' full attention during those times when you are angry. Ginott suggests that you take advantage of such times to model the way in which you want your students to handle their anger. Ms. Hebert indicated that she was angry, but displayed complete control and never resorted to name calling, insults, or sarcasm. She focused on getting back to the business at hand and getting students re-engaged in the learning activity.

## Avoiding Labels

Teachers are often reminded (e.g., in psychology courses and professional journals) that they should not be sarcastic with students nor identify students with undesirable labels (e.g., "dumb," "rotten," or "poor reader"). Ginott, of course, agreed that this deplorable, but not uncommon practice is detrimental to obtaining students' cooperation and maintaining on-task behaviors. However, Ginott also pointed out the dangers of placing *any kind* of characterizations or labels, even seemingly desirable ones (e.g., "smart," "good," or "fast reader"), on students. Consider the following example:

> Upon returning one of her students' science test papers with a high score, Ms. Johnson remarks, "Whitney, you proved you are quite a scientist. Thank you for being such a good student!" Whitney feels proud and better about himself because of Ms. Johnson's remarks. Jana, who overheard Ms. Johnson's remark to Whitney, thinks, "Since I had a low test score, I must be a bad student who can't do science."
>
> Later, Whitney gets nervous, fearing that he won't score high enough on subsequent science tests to live up to Ms. Johnson's label. When science gets difficult for him, he is tempted either not to try, lest he fail to live up to the label, or to cheat on tests and at least maintain his status in the class.

## The Detrimental Effects of Praise

Sometimes teachers think that by praising students themselves, rather than only their work and their behaviors, they gain more control over those students. The students' self-esteem then becomes dependent on what others (e.g., teachers) think of them. Ginott warned of the dangers of getting students hooked on praise. In the first example of this section, Ms. Robinson suggested that Theresa had hurt Justin's feelings. She assured Justin that he is not a baby. Ms. Hebert, in the contrasting example, avoided suggesting for a moment that Lamona could influence how George felt about himself. She assumed that George was capable of determining for himself whether or not he was a baby.

## Focusing

While you are still thinking about the two examples involving Ms. Robinson and Ms. Hebert, please call your attention to one other difference in the two stories. Ms. Hebert responded to Lamona's disruptive behavior by describing the situation and then directing the students back on-task. Ms. Robinson, on the other hand, raised at least one irrelevant issue when she asked Theresa, "Why can't you be thoughtful?" Unless Ms. Robinson wanted to waste class time listening to Theresa explain why she can't be thoughtful, she didn't really want Theresa to respond to that question. Why, then, did she prevent her class from re-engaging in the learning activity?

The influence of Ginott's work is ubiquitous in this text. Chapter 4, in particular, suggests practical ways for you to apply Ginott's principles to your own teaching situations.

## THE GLASSER APPROACH: RATIONAL CHOICES

### Inexcusable Behavior

In the privacy of their school's conference room, two teachers, Mr. Green and Ms. Mena, have the following conversation:

> Mr. Green: "Thanks for meeting with me. I want to talk to you about Bartell Hopkins. Wasn't he in your class last year?" Ms. Mena: "Yes, and I'm glad you've got him this year instead of me! How's he getting along?" Mr. Green: "Terrible! When I asked him for his homework today, he told me, it was . . . pardon me, I don't mean to be gross, but I'm just quoting . . . ." Ms. Mena (interrupting): "Don't worry, I've heard everything after 14 years in the classroom and most of it I heard from Bartell last year.

What did he say?" Mr. Green: "He told me it was up his ass, and I was welcome to come and get it." Ms. Mena: "Is that all! You should have heard some of the foul things he came out with last year. You know, Bartell is an abused child. Ever since he was a baby, he's had an uncle, his father (some father!), and heavens knows who else take advantage of him in every grotesque way. It's a wonder the poor lad behaves as well as he does." Mr. Green: "I didn't know! No wonder he acts like that. I'm sorry I sent him out of the room today when he mouthed off at me. I'll begin to be more tolerant with him."

It is probably well that Mr. Green now knows some of Bartell's background and, therefore, can better understand his behavior. However, according to William Glasser (1965, 1977, 1978, 1986), understanding why a student exhibits undesirable behaviors is no reason to tolerate such behaviors. Glasser emphasizes that students are rational beings and are quite capable of choosing to cooperate and be on-task. Mr. Green should never waiver in his insistence on high standards of conduct from Bartell in spite of Bartell's unfortunate background. Glasser would remind Mr. Green that he and other teachers may provide Bartell with his only opportunity to learn acceptable behaviors. The idea is for teachers to lead students to focus on their choices of behaviors while in school and to never accept excuses for improper behaviors.

## Meetings and Conferences

Rules for governing classroom conduct and maintaining students on-task should, according to Glasser, be established cooperatively by teachers and students. It is vital for rules to be strictly enforced. Students must be able to predict the consequences, both desirable and undesirable, of their behavior choices.

Classroom meetings and one-to-one conferences between student and teacher are important tools for leading students to rationally choose how they will behave relative to school activities. Glasser recommends that teachers routinely hold three types of classroom meetings: (1) meetings concerned with students' social conduct in school; (2) open-ended meetings for discussing intellectually important subjects raised by the students; (3) meetings concerned with how well students are progressing relative to the curricula. Class meetings, as well as one-to-one conferences, are conducted so that solutions to problems are addressed, while faultfinding and name-calling are out of order.

One-to-one conferences are used to help students identify a particular problem behavior, make a value judgment regarding that behavior, and make a commitment to supplant on-task behavior for the problem behavior. Here is an example:

For two consecutive days during the times that Mr. Dean, a high school industrial arts teacher, allocated for students to work on a project, Elmo either sat and stared into space or slept. Responding to this display of off-task behavior, Mr. Dean met privately with Elmo and had the following conversation:

Mr. Dean: "Thank you for coming. Sit right here." Mr. Dean takes a seat directly in front of Elmo so that he can readily achieve eye contact. Mr. Dean: "Were you in shop class today?" Elmo: "Yeah, you saw me there." Mr. Dean: "How long were you in shop class today?" Elmo: "I was there the whole time; I didn't skip out or nothin'! Somebody else might of slipped out, but I didn't." Mr. Dean: "I don't want to talk about anybody else, just what you did in shop class today. Tell me one thing you remember doing in shop today." Elmo: "I watched you show us how to use that new machine." Mr Dean: "And what did you do after I finished showing you how to use the drill press?" Elmo: "I dunno, I guess I went to sleep." Mr. Dean: "Do you remember what I asked you to do right before you went to sleep?" Elmo: "Work on my project, but I was tired." Mr. Dean: "I'm sorry you were tired, but would it be better for you to sleep in shop or get your project done?" Elmo: "But the project is so boring!" Mr. Dean: "I'm sorry that doing the project bores you. What happens if you don't finish your project by next Monday?" Elmo: "I know, you've told us; we don't pass shop." Mr. Dean: "Not passing shop, is that good or bad for you?" Elmo: "That's bad, that's real bad!" Mr. Dean: "Do you want to pass shop?" Elmo: "Of course!" Mr. Dean: "What will it take for you to pass shop?" Elmo: "Do my project." Mr. Dean: "By when?" Elmo: "Monday." Mr. Dean: "What will you do so that you'll have it done by Monday?" Elmo: "I'll have to work on it this week." Mr. Dean: "When will you have time to work on it?" Elmo: "In class, that's the only time you let us work on it." Mr. Dean: "That's right. And there are only 2 more class days for you to get it done. You don't have any time to waste. What are you going to do in class tomorrow when I assign the class to work on projects?" Elmo: "I'm going to work on my project." Mr. Dean: "What if you're tired?" Elmo: "I'll work on my project anyway." Mr. Dean: "You've made a smart choice. Would you be willing to write me a note telling me that you will work on your project tomorrow? I'll use the note to remind me to leave you at least 45 minutes of class for your project and to remind you of your commitment."

## THE DREIKURS APPROACH: MISTAKEN BELIEFS

### Democratic Classrooms

Rudolf Dreikurs (1968) stressed that teachers should be neither autocratic nor permissive if they expect students to be cooperative in the classroom. Resentment and power struggles are among the unpleasant consequences of autocratic teachers' use of coercion to control students' behaviors. Permissive teachers, who fail to establish and enforce rules for conduct, leave their students confused and lacking in guidance for being on-task. Dreikurs wrote on the advantages of "democratic" classrooms where students: (1) have a voice in the determination of rules; (2) suffer the logical consequences of their own misbehaviors rather than submit to arbitrary punishment administered by teachers; (3) are motivated to be on-task because of the intrinsic benefits derived from being on-task (e.g., achieving a skill by being engaged in a learning activity) rather than because of extrinsic benefits (e.g., avoiding ridicule or reaping praise).

## Mistaken Beliefs About Social Acceptance

Because students desire to be accepted members of a social group and because they are able to control their own behaviors, Dreikurs suggested that student misbehaviors are attributable to mistaken beliefs about what will obtain the recognition they seek. He identified four types of mistaken beliefs that lead to misbehaviors: (1) attention getting; (2) power seeking; (3) revenge seeking; (4) displaying inadequacy.

After failing to gain recognition as a result of on-task behavior, a student may resort to off-task behavior in an attempt to achieve the recognition of a teacher or other students. Dreikurs referred to this as the "attention-getting mechanism." When you recognize one of your students displaying the attention-getting mechanism, you should, according to Dreikurs, see to it that the student is ignored. Attention-seeking students prefer being punished, admonished, or criticized to being ignored. Attention should be afforded the student when he or she is on-task and cooperating.

"Power seeking" refers to the mistaken belief of students that if a teacher doesn't let them do what they want, then the teacher does not approve of them. Power-seeking students attempt to provoke teachers into a struggle of wills. Teachers, who follow Dreikurs' advice, refuse to play such games. Compare how the teachers in the following two examples responded to students' attempts at displaying defiance of authority:

> During the transition time between when Ms. Burnside's fifth graders worked on a spelling exercise and when she planned for them to report on findings of a science experiment that was assigned for homework, Steve stands up on top of a work table in the back of the room and begins to clown. Some of the students laugh at his antics. Steve remains on the table even after Ms. Burnside directs the class to begin the science activity.
>
> Ms. Burnside: "Please get down and take your seat, Steve. It's time for us to share what we learned from the experiments." Steve: "I'm not getting down." Ms. Burnside: "Yes you are!" Steve: "You can't make me!" Ms. Burnside: "Oh yes I can! Who do you think you're talking to, young man?" Steve: "Who do you think I'm talking to?" Ms. Burnside: "Boy!

You have just 5 seconds to get off that table or you'll be mighty sorry! . . . One . . . two . . . three . . . four. . . ." Steve grins as he hops off the table and slowly walks to his seat.

During the transition time between when Mr. Ruiz's fifth graders worked on a spelling exercise and when he planned for them to report on findings of a science experiment that was assigned for homework, Rubin stands up on top of a work table in the back of the room and begins to clown. Some of the students laugh at his antics. Rubin remains on the table even after Mr. Ruiz directs the class to begin the science activity.

Mr. Ruiz: "Rubin, I would appreciate you taking your seat right now." Rubin: "No, I'm staying right here. You can't make me get down!" Mr. Ruiz: "In that case, Rubin, I won't try." Mr. Ruiz directs his attention to those students sitting at their places and says, "Who would like to tell one thing that surprised them about the experiment?" Some students raise their hands and nearly all become engaged in the lesson. Rubin is left standing on the table.

Ms. Burnside allowed Steve to draw her into his power-seeking game. Consequently, valuable class time was lost. Many other students probably never got well engaged in the lesson, once it finally started, because they continued to think about the nasty exchange that had just occurred. Steve's belief that the classroom is a place to have power struggles was confirmed. Ms. Burnside may think she won the battle of wills. However, because she heightened rather than defused the game, as did Mr. Ruiz, she unwittingly challenged Steve to try her again some other time.

Seeking revenge is closely related to power seeking. Power-seeking students are likely to develop resentment toward those to whom they have lost battles of the wills. They feel hurt by others who have displayed power over them. Consequently, they want to hurt others to display their own power and thus achieve status. After failing to achieve satisfaction through seeking attention, power, and revenge, students are likely to become so discouraged that they give up and use displays of inadequacy as an excuse for not trying. Dreikurs found it extremely difficult for teachers to deal effectively with students burdened by the last two of the four mistaken beliefs. He suggested that teachers help students recognize the mistaken beliefs under which they are operating. Examples of teachers confronting students with their mistaken beliefs in response to displays of off-task behaviors are contained in chapters 7, 9, and 10 of this text.

## THE CANTER APPROACH: ASSERTIVE DISCIPLINE

### Six Suggestions

Lee and Marlene Canter researched the traits of teachers whose students displayed high levels of on-task behaviors. Their research led to a formulation of principles and techniques by which teachers take charge of their own classrooms in a forceful, but calm, manner. Thousands of teachers have trained at workshops, read literature (e.g., *Assertive Discipline: A Take Charge Approach for Today's Educator* [Canter & Canter, 1976]), attended lectures, and viewed films forwarding the Canter approach known as "assertive discipline."

The Canter approach urges teachers to: (1) utilize the assertive response style that is associated with assertion training (Salter, 1949; Wolpe & Lazarus, 1966); (2) recognize fallacies in reasons for excusing off-task behaviors; (3) specify exactly what types of behaviors will be required and what types will not be tolerated; (4) develop a plan for encouraging on-task behaviors and discouraging off-task behaviors; (5) persist in following through with the plan; (6) seek and expect support from parents and instructional supervisors.

## The Assertive Response Style

An assertive response style is characterized by openness, directness, spontaneity, and appropriateness. Ms. Wilford displays an assertive response style in the following example:

> "Mrs. Wilford, you know that report you wanted us to turn in Friday?" says Russ, one of Ms. Wilford's history students. Ms. Wilford: "Yes, Russ. What about it?" Russ: "Well . . . could we wait 'til Monday to give it to you?" Other students in the class begin to chime in with comments such as, "Oh! Yes, please, Mrs. Wilford." Russ (smiling): "There's a game Thursday night and I know you want us to support the team!" Marie: "You wouldn't want us to miss the game?" Barkley: "Be nice, just this once."
> Ms. Wilford is tempted to "be nice" and enjoy the applause she knows she'll receive if she gives in. However, she also realizes three things: (1) Delaying the assignment will cause the students to fall behind in their schedule of learning activities; (2) If she doesn't get the reports until Monday she won't be able to read and annotate them over the weekend and consequently, she would be inconvenienced; (3) If they will adjust their own schedules, the students are quite capable of completing the report on time without missing the game.
> Ms. Wilford announces to the class, "I understand that you are worried about making it to this important game and still being able to finish the report on time. You have cause for concern. Because changing the due-date will mess up our schedule and because I need the weekend to go over your papers, the reports are still due on Friday." "That's not fair!" cries Dennis. "Yes, I know it seems that way to you. Now, let's turn our books to page 122. . . ."

A less assertive teacher in Ms. Wilford's situation may have feared jeopardizing his or her relationship with the students by not agreeing with their seemingly reasonable request. In reality, Ms. Wilford's assertive reply is likely to enhance her relationship with the students for two reasons: (1) Students begin to realize that she takes their work very seriously and that her plans for them are well thought out and not changed whimsically; (2) Had she changed her plans and not allowed herself the weekend to go over the reports, the personal inconvenience she suffers might lead to feelings of resentment directed at the students.

The recommended assertive response style is neither hostile nor passive. The teacher in the first of the following three examples displays an assertive response, the second a hostile response, and the third a passive response:

> Lori loudly yells out during an independent work session, "Help! Mr. Clark, I can't do these!" Mr. Clark: "We don't shout out in here. Quietly raise your hand if you want me to help you."

> David loudly yells out during an independent work session, "Help! Miss Lancy, I can't do these!" Ms. Lancy: "You screech like a little girl! If you yell like that again, you're gone, Buster!"

> Tamara loudly yells out during an independent work session, "Help! Ms. Slovaki, I can't do these!" Ms. Slovaki: "Why must you yell at me? I hope you try and raise your hand next time."

## Inexcusable Behaviors

Like Glasser, Canter warned teachers not to let excuses deter them from insisting on appropriate student behavior. Peer pressure, inadequate parenting, learning disabilities, personal stress, and poor health are just some of the factors that make it more difficult for some students to be on-task than it is for other students. However, it is a fallacy that the presence of such factors excuses students from being responsible for their own behaviors.

## Teacher Needs

The needs of students are emphasized throughout educational literature. Canter emphasized the needs of teachers. He discovered that many teachers have difficulty specifying exactly what behaviors they need for students to exhibit and what behaviors they need for students to avoid. Ask yourself the question, "As a teacher, how do I want my students to behave so that my need to have a smoothly functioning classroom is met?" Do your answers specify observable behaviors or are they couched in vague generalities? When asked what they want from students, Canter and Canter (1976) reported the following among replies given by teachers: "I want the kids to act good." "I want them to be good citizens and have positive attitudes."

"I want the children to respect me and each other." "I don't want hassles from the boys who are troublemakers."

Before you, as a teacher, are in a position to formulate plans for encouraging students to behave as you need them to behave (i.e., on-task) and discouraging them from behaving otherwise (i.e., off-task), you need to specify the desirable and undesirable behaviors. Rather than the vague, general words used by teachers in Canter's aforementioned examples, Canter recommended that the list specify conduct regarding such things as following directions, completing assignments, and not leaving the classroom without permission. Even the most clever of your plans for keeping students on-task will not work unless you persist in following through with it.

## Support from Parents and School Administrators

Students' parents and instructional supervisors (e.g., principals and department heads) have a vested interest in the success of classroom operations. Thus, Canter's assertion that teachers should seek and expect support from parents and supervisors seems quite reasonable. In many locations, school-wide systems based on Canter's assertive discipline have been instituted. One such system operating in a junior high school involves the following:

> Just prior to the opening of school each year, parents of students enrolled in Alpine Junior High receive a description of the "assertive discipline" program. Students', parents', teachers', and administrators' responsibilities to the program are explained. Parents are asked to sign and return to the school office a form indicating that they have read the material and are willing to comply with the stipulations of the program. An orientation to the program is provided for the students during the first week of school.
>
> Alpine Junior High's assertive discipline program includes the following features:
>
> 1. Each classroom teacher specifies for students the rules for classroom conduct. During the course of the year, new rules may be decided upon and occasionally an old rule may be deleted. An up-to-date list of rules is always displayed in the classroom.
> 2. The first time each day a student violates a rule during a particular class session, the teacher writes the student's name on a designated area of a chalkboard. The number of the rule that was violated is put next to the name. The teacher does not say anything about the transgression; she or he only writes the name and numeral on the board and continues with the planned activity.
> 3. The second time a student violates a rule (not necessarily the same rule), the number of that rule is added to the name appearing on the

board. Again, the teacher makes no other response to the off-task behavior.

4. Upon the third violation of the rules in the same class period, the student must leave the class and report to a detention room. Again, the teacher does not take class time to talk to the student about the matter. The teacher only indicates that a third violation has occurred and the student is already aware of the consequences.

5. There are no penalties or requirements for students who have no more than one violation during any one class period.

6. Students with two violations are required to meet with the teacher after school to discuss the misbehavior and map out a plan for preventing recurrences.

7. The parents of students with three violations must appear at school to discuss the misbehavior and make plans for preventing recurrences with the student, the teacher, and another school official. The student may not return to the class where the violations occurred until a plan has been worked out with the parents.

## THE BEHAVIORIST APPROACH: CONDITIONING RESPONSES

### Learned Responses

With the initial impetus from the works of Watson (1914), Dunlap (1919), and others who focused attention on learned, rather than instinctive, human behavior, behavioristic psychology has flourished and provided a research-based foundation for today's theories and principles for teaching students to be on-task. Particularly notable are the investigations of B. F. Skinner (1953, 1954) who examined the effects of stimuli on learning when the stimuli occurred *after* a response or act. Such investigations led to the following general conclusion that is fundamental to the behaviorist approach for managing behavior: *Behaviors (i.e., responses) that are followed by rewards (i.e., satisfying or pleasant stimuli) are more likely to be repeated than behaviors that are not. Aversive stimuli or punishment following a behavioral response tends to discourage that response from recurring.*

### Behavior Modification

A student's conduct is thought of as a complex set of responses that have been conditioned by his or her environment. *Behavior modification* refers to the behaviorist approach by which students' environments are manipulated to increase the chances of desired behaviors being rewarded while undesirable behaviors go unrewarded. Students are thus conditioned toward being on-task. Detractors of behavior modification point out:

1. The goal of behavior modification programs is to condition observable behaviors. Consequently, character development is neglected while students learn to "go through the motions" of being well-behaved.

2. Behavior modification programs often depend on providing students with extrinsic rewards that have no natural association with the behaviors they are designed to encourage. Students, for example, may be given trading stamps for doing homework. Consequently, the students come to expect such prizes for simply meeting routine responsibilities.

3. Conditioning students' behaviors is suggestive of treating human beings as if they are robots that lack free will.

Proponents of behavior modification answer the first of these three criticisms by noting that controlling students' behaviors cannot wait for character development. Besides, by practicing desirable behaviors, one learns self-discipline. The second criticism is confronted with the argument that students often need extrinsic rewards to *initially* choose to be on-task. After on-task behaviors become habitual, then the students begin to recognize the intrinsic values and no longer need to be bribed. In the aforementioned example, the students eventually will find satisfaction from what they learn by doing homework. Thus, the intrinsic motivation (e.g., satisfaction gained from learning) replaces the extrinsic motivation (e.g., promise of trading stamps).

The third criticism, dealing with free will, involves questions that are more appropriately addressed in a treatise on philosophy.

The suggestions in this text are provided to you with confidence that they will work because of the wealth of research findings from behavioristic psychology. Before you begin considering the specific methods for gaining students' cooperation that are dealt with in subsequent chapters of this text, there are some concepts with which you should be familiar. They are explained in the remainder of this chapter.

## ISOLATED BEHAVIORS
## AND BEHAVIOR PATTERNS

While Ms. Bernstein is explaining to her sixth grade class what they will be doing in an upcoming learning activity, Harry interrupts, "Aw no! That'll be boring!" This is one of the few instances in which Harry ever interrupts a speaker in class. It is atypical for Harry to interrupt.

While Mr. Diel is explaining to his sixth grade class what they will be doing in an upcoming learning activity, Valerie interrupts Mr. Diel with a comment as she has done on numerous other occasions over the past month.

Dianne virtually always completes the homework that her teacher assigns.

One night Jessica completes her homework assignment. Usually she doesn't bother with doing assignments.

By interrupting Ms. Bernstein, Harry displayed an off-task, disruptive behavior. Because such interruptions are not typical for Harry, that instance of being disruptive and off-task is said to be an *isolated behavior*. Valerie, on the other hand, habitually interrupts Mr. Diel and so Valerie's off-task, disruptive behavior is just one display in a continuing *behavior pattern*. Similarly, Diane is simply displaying what is a regular behavior pattern for her by choosing to be on-task and do homework assignments. In the instance where Jessica did homework, she was deviating from her regular pattern and was, therefore, displaying an isolated behavior.

It is important for you to differentiate between behaviors that are part of a pattern that your students have incorporated into their general conduct and behaviors that are isolated displays and are not habitual. Would you not expect Ms. Bernstein to deal with Harry's isolated instance of interruption differently from the way Mr. Diel should attempt to teach Valerie to break her habit of interrupting others?

## POSITIVE REINFORCERS

Ever since Barry began regularly training with weights in physical education class, he really likes the way he feels. He frequently receives comments from classmates about how good he looks and how strong he is.

During class discussions, Sandra often interrupts speakers with "put-downs." Others in the class usually laugh at her remarks.

Dale has a desire to lose weight. He attends a weight reducing class several times with no resulting loss in weight. Dale ceases attending the class.

A week ago, two-year-old Morris attempted to get his father, who was involved in a telephone conversation at the time, to hold him. "Dad, Dad, hold me," Morris said in a calm voice. His father continued talking on the phone without paying attention to Morris. Morris persisted with his requests becoming louder and sounding more and more distressed. Finally, Morris was lying on the floor, screaming and kicking so that his father could no longer hear himself or the other party on the phone. At that point, Morris' father picked him up. Similar incidents have occurred since then. Now, when Morris wants to be picked up, he just throws himself on the floor and begins screaming and kicking.

Nancy always does the written work assigned in Mr. Washington's class where each paper is returned to her with comments and suggestions. Nancy hardly ever does the written work assigned in Ms. Taylor's class; Ms. Taylor never returns written work.

Sandra, Morris, and Nancy each display a voluntary behavior pattern. Barry is regularly engaged in the learning activities planned for the weight lifting class, Sandra frequently interrupts speakers, Morris routinely throws temper tantrums, and Nancy consistently completes written assignments assigned by Mr. Washington. On the other hand, Dale chooses not to attend weight reduction classes and Nancy chooses not to do written work assigned by Ms. Taylor. Why are some behavior patterns continued, while others are discontinued or never established? Obviously, Barry perceived that his participation in weight training classes were paying off for him. The way he felt and the comments he heard left him with that impression. Because the way he felt and his classmates' comments encouraged him to continue being engaged in weight training, they are referred to as *positive reinforcers* for that particular behavior pattern. Similarly, Sandra's classmates' laughter served as a positive reinforcer to Sandra's habit of interrupting speakers with put-down remarks. Being picked up served to positively reinforce Morris' temper tantrums. Mr. Washington's helpful feedback on written assignments positively reinforced Nancy's behavior pattern of completing assignments.

People will not retain a behavior pattern or establish a new one in the absence of positive reinforcers. Dale no longer chose to attend weight reducing class when he perceived his attendance went unrewarded. Nancy felt that doing Ms. Taylor's assignments was fruitless; thus, without positive reinforcement, she did not elect to do the work.

By definition, a *positive reinforcer* is a stimulus presented after a response that increases the probability of that response being repeated in the future. In the example about Barry, the *response* from the definition is Barry's engagement in weight training sessions; the *stimuli* are the way Barry felt and the compliments he received from classmates.

On-task, as well as off-task, voluntary behavior patterns are established *only* because of the presence of positive reinforcers.


## DESTRUCTIVE POSITIVE REINFORCERS

Ms. Coco announces to her ninth grade class, "Because you have been so cooperative with me today, I will not assign any homework for you to do tonight!"

Students in Ms. Lambert's kindergarten class receive candy for completing assignments on time.

Mr. Breaux asks his third graders, "Who can tell me why the man in the story did not want to leave his house in the morning?" A dozen of the students eagerly raise their hands. Mr. Breaux: "Jackie?" Jackie: "Because he didn't want to go to work." Some of the other students say, "No! Mr. Breaux, Mr. Breaux!" Mr. Breaux: "Okay, Ory, can you help out Jackie?" Ory: "Because he thought his friend would return to see him." Mr. Breaux: "Very good, Ory! That is correct! You are one of my very best readers!" Ory beams happily.

A teacher used positive reinforcement to encourage on-task behaviors in each of the three previous examples. Ms. Coco's fifth graders were rewarded for their cooperation by being exempted from homework assignments. Ms. Coco's tactics probably served to encourage students' cooperation in the future. However, she might have unwittingly taught her students that homework assignments are unimportant and not doing homework is better than doing homework.

In the second example, the motivation of anticipating a piece of candy may encourage Ms. Lambert's students to complete their assignments, but it may also teach them undesirable eating habits.

Mr. Breaux positively reinforced Ory's commendable answer with praise. However, Ginott (1972) warned against getting students hooked on praise. Also, Mr. Breaux may have unwittingly taught Ory to hope others (e.g., Jackie) will be unsuccessful in order to enhance his own opportunity to be the star of the class.

In each of the three scenarios, the positive reinforcer for a targeted behavior (e.g., cooperation, finishing assignments, or comprehending a reading) had an undesirable side effect (e.g., teaching the unimportance of homework, unhealthy eating habits, or undue competitiveness among students). When a positive reinforcer for one behavior has undesirable side effects on other behaviors, it is referred to as a *destructive positive reinforcer*. Selecting positive reinforcers for on-task behaviors that are not destructive is a main concern of chapters 4, 7, 8, 9, and 10 of this text.

## CONTRIVED AND NATURALLY OCCURRING PUNISHMENT

### Two Types of Punishment

By definition, *punishment* is a stimulus presented after a response that decreases the probability of that response being repeated in the future. Because they tend to affect students differently, you should distinguish between two types of punishment: (1) *contrived* and (2) *naturally occurring*. Here are some examples illustrating the difference:

Leonard falls asleep while Mr. Tessier, his tenth grade health teacher, lectures. After the lecture, Mr. Tessier directs Leonard to bring to class the following day a 1,000-word essay entitled "Why I Should Not Sleep in Class."

Bill falls asleep while Mr. Vasse, his tenth grade health teacher, lectures. When Bill awakens, he realizes that he does not know what was explained during the lecture. The next day, Bill's fears are confirmed as he fails the test over the objectives that were covered by the lecture.

Oddly enough, if Leonard happened to find that writing the essay provided him with an opportunity to be comical or to vent some frustration, the assignment might positively reinforce the off-task behavior. Please assume, however, that this was not the case and that writing the essay served as punishment for *getting caught* sleeping in class. Mr. Tessier designed the punishment specifically to get Leonard to regret having slept in class. But having to write an essay is not a natural consequence of sleeping when one should be paying attention in class. Thus, Mr. Tessier used *contrived punishment* in dealing with Leonard's disengagement from the learning activity.

Bill also received punishment, but Bill's punishment was a natural consequence of his sleeping when he should have been paying attention. Hopefully, Bill will make the connection: "If I miss out on Mr. Vasse's lecture, I won't learn what will be on the test." What Bill suffered took the form of *naturally occurring punishment*.

## The Effects of Naturally Occurring Punishment Compared to Those of Contrived Punishment

Here is an example of a teacher utilizing naturally occurring, rather than contrived, punishment:

Ms. Brock's kindergarten class is working in two groups: the "Busy Bees" and the "Chipmunks." The Busy Bees have just finished working on a project in which they used scissors, paste, and cardboard. Ms. Brock tells them, "While I show a short filmstrip to the Chipmunks, I want each of you to put away your scissors and paste and then clean up these scraps from the floor and table. When I return, I will read this story to you." Ms. Brock displays a book. The Busy Bees eagerly anticipate hearing the story.

As Ms. Brock begins showing the filmstrip to the Chipmunks, the Busy Bees start giggling and playing instead of following her directive to clean up. Six minutes later, Ms. Brock returns to the Busy Bees with the storybook in hand. "Oh, my goodness! This floor is still a mess and your scissors and paste are still out," she says. "I am sorry, Busy Bees, but now I will have to help you clean up this mess and I won't have time to read the story to you." As she begins picking up along with the students, Ms. Brock continues, "I know you are disappointed. It is too bad that we still have to clean up and there won't be time left for the story."

If Ms. Brock consistently continues to use this strategy, her students will soon realize the automatic consequences of being off-task. Ms. Brock's words and manner communicated that she did not withhold the promised story *because* the students failed to pick up after themselves. She conveyed that the story was not read *because* the time set aside for the story would simply have to be used for cleaning.

The differences between contrived and naturally occurring punishment may seem so subtle as to be unimportant. But over time, the differences are monumental in terms of effects on students (Dreikurs, Grunwald, & Pepper, 1982). In the following example, Ms. Webb confronts a situation identical to that in Ms. Brock's example; however, Ms. Webb uses contrived punishment:

> . . . As Ms. Webb begins showing the filmstrip to the Chipmunks, the Busy Bees start giggling and playing instead of cleaning up. Six minutes later, Ms. Webb returns to the Busy Bees with the storybook in hand. "Why is this mess still here?" she asks. "Okay, because you didn't cooperate with me and pick up as I told you, I am not going to read this story. Maybe next time you'll know to listen!"

Do you see the subtle differences between Ms. Brock's and Ms. Webb's handling of the situation? Ms. Webb blamed her failure to read the story on the students' failure to follow directions. She turned the incident into something personal. Consistent handling of such situations will lead to an antagonistic rather than cooperative relation between Ms. Webb and her students. In time, students will learn to avoid getting caught while still enjoying some of the benefits of being off-task. When Ms. Webb raises irrelevant questions such as "Why is this mess still here?" they will have ready answers such as "I was picking up, but Otis didn't!" and "I tried to pick up, but Nadine kept bothering me!"

In contrast, Ms. Brock blamed her failure to read the story on the lack of time. Of course, the lack of time was a consequence of the area not being clean. Ms. Brock focused on what must be done. The question of why the area had not been picked up was not raised. Rather than communicate an "I'll get you for this" tone, Ms. Brock shared the students' unhappiness at not having time to read the story.

Frankly, some teachers use contrived instead of naturally occurring punishment because the off-task behaviors do not have undesirable naturally occurring consequences. If, for example, a teacher assigns students to do work that has no evident benefit for them, then the students will not recognize any logical drawbacks for neglecting the work. Faced with such situations, teachers resort to the threat of contrived punishment to coerce students to cooperate.

## Unwittingly Administered Punishment

You should keep in mind that on-task, as well as off-task, behaviors can be discouraged through punishment. Teachers are ordinarily unmindful of such misfortunes when they do occur; here is an example:

> Barlow spends 2 hours figuring out and completing a computation exercise in which he is to find out the products of 28 pairs of three-digit whole numbers. Barlow correctly executes almost all of the steps in the process for all 28 items. However, because he repeats a one-step error pattern in 19 of the items, only 9 of his final answers are correct. Without explanation as to *what* he did wrong nor any indication of what he did right, Barlow's teacher returns his "corrected" work with 19 'X' marks and '32% F' at the top of the paper.

Might Barlow's teacher's response discourage him from making such diligent efforts in the future? How could Barlow's teacher have avoided punishing his diligent efforts and still communicated to him that 19 of the answers were incorrect? Is there something the teacher could have done to see that Barlow's efforts were actually positively reinforced although he had incorrect final answers?

## DESTRUCTIVE PUNISHMENT

A positive reinforcer is destructive if it has undesirable side effects. Punishment can also be destructive if it produces undesirable side effects in addition to discouraging some targeted behavior. Here are two examples; for each identify the behavior being punished and a possible undesirable side effect that the punishment might cause:

> Mr. Norton is in the habit of assigning extra math problems to students who are disruptive in class.

> Ms. Chamberlain catches Quinn, one of her tenth graders, shooting paper clips across the classroom. She sends him to an assistant principal who administers three swats with a wooden paddle to Quinn's buttocks.

Mr. Norton's punishment of extra math problems for disruptive behavior may effectively reduce incidences of disruptive behavior. However, if it teaches students that math is a form of punishment and should be avoided, then Mr. Norton's punishment is destructive. Besides discouraging him from getting caught again shooting paper clips, Quinn may learn from his experience with the assistant principal that it is okay for one human being to strike another. The undesirable effects of corporal punishment are well documented (Hyman & Wise, 1979) and will be addressed in Chapter 7 of this text.

## NEGATIVE REINFORCEMENT

For many, but not nearly all, instances in which a student is off-task, negative reinforcement can be a powerful mechanism for getting that student to choose to be on-task. By definition, *negative reinforcement* is making the removal of punishment contingent upon a specified change in the behavior of the individual being punished. Here is an example:

> Ms. Dirks directs her preschool class to put away the musical instruments they've been playing and to wash up for their midmorning snack. Jay continues to blow his horn. Ms. Dirks goes over to Jay and says, "It's time to put your horn away and wash your hands." Jay slams the horn to the floor and screams, "No, no! I don't want to eat! I wanna play!" Ms. Dirks: "Jay, you don't want to eat. That's fine, but I want you to put away your horn, wash your hands, and sit with the rest of the children while they eat." Jay throws himself on the floor, kicks his feet and yells incoherently. Ms. Dirks remains calm as with gentle firmness she gets Jay to his feet and walks him to the back of the room over to a chair that faces away from the other students. Ms. Dirks: "Jay, you are to sit in this chair until you have decided to get control of yourself, put away your horn, wash your hands, and sit with the rest of us." She leaves him in the chair. It takes about four minutes for Jay to calm himself down when he hops off the chair, puts away his horn, washes his hands, and joins the group.

How does negative reinforcement relate to punishment and to positive reinforcers? Like positive reinforcement and unlike punishment, negative reinforcement focuses on the behavior to be exhibited rather than the one to be inhibited. Ms. Dirks used punishment by having Jay sit in the chair. However, she allowed Jay to choose *when* the punishment would be terminated. The promise of ending the punishment acted similarly to a positive reinforcer in that it encouraged the on-task behavior. Ms. Dirks would have used only punishment if she had told Jay to sit in the chair for five minutes or until she told him he could get up. Instead, she used negative reinforcement because the removal of the punishment was contingent on Jay's decision to cooperate.

Chapters 8, 9, and 10 of this text will expose you to examples of teachers using negative reinforcement to teach students to supplant off-task with on-task behaviors.

## Self-Assessment for Chapter 2

Here are activities covering some of what you learned from Chapter 2 to this point. When you have completed the exercises, please compare your responses with the answers or comments provided in "Reviewing Your Self-Assessment."

I. Chapter 2 contains the statement, "On-task behaviors are typically less natural than off-task behaviors. . . ." What did the author mean by that statement? Explain why you agree or disagree. If the statement is true, what are some of the major implications for the way in which teachers plan their learning activities?

II. Select the one best response for each of the following multiple-choice items:

A. A teacher's withitness, according to Kounin, refers to which one of the following?

1. How well students respect that teacher
2. How enthusiastic that teacher is about the learning activities she or he conducts
3. How aware the teacher is of what is going on in the classroom
4. How well the teacher's students remain on-task and engaged in learning activities

B. According to Jones' studies, which one of the following forms of off-task behavior occurs the least number of times in schools?

1. Fighting among students
2. Talking out of turn
3. Mind-wandering and daydreaming
4. Students attempting to make others laugh

C. Jones suggested that teachers should:

1. avoid direct eye contact with one student at a time, in order to prevent showing favoritism.
2. not use hand gestures as a form of communication, because hand gestures send ambiguous messages.
3. avoid stationing themselves at a distance from students during learning activities.
4. address all questions a student has when providing individual help.

D. Ginott urged teachers to:

1. avoid expressing personal feelings.
2. praise students for being on-task.
3. describe situations for students.
4. tolerate misbehaviors that are a function of students' family backgrounds.

E. Which one of the following remarks made on a student's test paper is most in line with Ginott's suggestions?

      1. "It appears that you should review the area-of-a-triangle formula."

      2. "It appears that you are quite a mathematician."

      3. "You didn't study hard enough."

      4. "Apparently you are the kind of student who diligently prepares for tests."

**F.** Glasser recommended that teachers:

      1. avoid discussing discipline problems with students.

      2. lead students to make value judgments about their own behaviors.

      3. utilize group processes to embarrass students into choosing on-task over off-task behaviors.

      4. tolerate disruptive behaviors whenever the causes are understandable.

**G.** According to Dreikurs, all students have a desire to:

      1. display power.

      2. call attention to themselves.

      3. achieve revenge.

      4. gain recognition.

**H.** According to Dreikurs, which one of the following is most distasteful to the attention-seeking student?

      1. Being punished

      2. Being criticized

      3. Being ignored

      4. Being praised

**I.** The assertive response style that Canter recommends for teachers is characterized by:

      1. concern for students' needs.

      2. honesty.

      3. hostility.

      4. passiveness.

**J.** Canter suggested that with assertive discipline teachers need to:

      1. be independent of a need for help from parents.

      2. depend on help from parents.

      3. hold parents responsible for their children's behaviors.

      4. find out if parental influences are causing students to misbehave.

**K.** Behavior modification programs are based on the belief that:

      1. Human conduct is influenced by positive reinforcers that follow certain acts.

      2. Extrinsic motivation is more important in shaping human behavior than is intrinsic motivation.

      3. Human beings are like pigeons in that their conduct is primarily a function of instincts.

      4. Environmental influences can explain all forms of human behavior.

**L.** It is important for a teacher to identify whether a student's display of off-task behavior is isolated or is part of a behavior pattern because:

    **1.** Behavior patterns are instinctive whereas isolated behaviors are learned.

    **2.** Isolated off-task behaviors should be tolerated whereas habitual off-task behaviors should never be tolerated.

    **3.** Students can control isolated behaviors, but others must control behavior patterns for them.

    **4.** A teacher should plan to confront an off-task behavior pattern quite differently from the way an isolated off-task behavior is confronted.

**M.** If a student is rewarded for an off-task behavior, the reward is a:

    **1.** positive reinforcer.

    **2.** negative reinforcer.

    **3.** contrived punishment.

    **4.** destructive positive reinforcer.

**N.** Which one of the following is NOT an example of punishment?

    **1.** After daydreaming during the time her teacher was giving directions, Jan feels lost because she doesn't know what to do.

    **2.** Tony is unhappy that his teacher excluded him from a discussion because he repeatedly interrupted other students.

    **3.** Charlie's teacher tells him he can rejoin the group whenever he decides to speak only when he has the floor.

    **4.** Because she started a fight, Betty was required to meet with her teacher after school when she preferred to be socializing with her friends.

**O.** Which one of the following is NOT an example of positive reinforcement?

    **1.** Lloyd talks to Carol in history class instead of being engaged in the learning activity. As a result of their conversation, Carol accepts an invitation to go out with Lloyd.

    **2.** Because Cynthia studied hard, she receives 'A,' as she had hoped, on an exam.

    **3.** Tom enjoys the candy his teacher gave him for paying attention during class.

    **4.** Issac is relieved to find out that his teacher forgot to collect the homework Issac failed to complete.

**P.** Ted's teacher catches him talking and clowning around during time allocated for quietly doing exercises in a workbook. The teacher tells Ted, "Go to the time-out area for 10 minutes. Maybe by then you will have decided to settle down and quietly do your work." Which one of the following ideas did Ted's teacher apply?

   **1.** Positive reinforcement
   **2.** Negative reinforcement
   **3.** Contrived punishment
   **4.** Naturally occurring punishment
   **Q.** A positive reinforcer is destructive when it:
   **1.** encourages an off-task behavior.
   **2.** discourages an on-task behavior.
   **3.** fails to increase the frequency of the target behavior.
   **4.** has undesirable side effects.
**III.** Give an example of a teacher dealing with a student's daydreaming in class via contrived punishment.
**IV.** Give an example of a teacher dealing with a student's daydreaming in class via naturally occurring punishment.
**V.** Give an example of a teacher dealing with a student's daydreaming in class via negative reinforcement.
**VI.** Give an example in which a student's on-task behavior is effectively encouraged by a destructive positive reinforcer. Explain why the positive reinforcer is destructive.
**VII.** Explain how one suggestion associated with Jones' approach might help a teacher more effectively apply Kounin's approach to keeping students on-task.
**VIII.** Explain how one suggestion associated with Ginott's approach might help a teacher more effectively apply Glasser's approach for dealing with off-task student behaviors.


*Reviewing Your Self-Assessment* —————————————————————————

Please compare your response to those of other persons who answered Part I. Discuss the similarities and differences among what you and the others wrote. Here are a few comments regarding the questions raised by Part I of the test:

> The author referred to on-task behaviors as typically "less natural" than off-task behaviors because what students are directed to do in schools (e.g., quietly pay attention, solve computational problems, do calisthenics, and discuss economics) are not what children and adolescents are usually inclined to do. Teachers should, therefore, develop a plan for helping students to be on-task and engaged in learning activities.

The appropriate choices for the multiple-choice items of Part II are: A-3, B-1, C-3, D-3, E-1, F-2, G-4, H-3, I-2, J-2, K-1, L-4, M-1, N-3, O-4, P-3, and Q-4.

You should compare your answers for parts III through VIII with others who took the test. Following are some *sample* responses:

III. Upon discovering Amy daydreaming in class, Mr. Benson tells her, "Write a 500-word composition on what you were daydreaming about and turn it in to me tomorrow."

IV. Allison catches herself daydreaming and realizes that she's missed a critical portion of Ms. Thompson's lecture. Consequently, she does extra work to make up for what she missed.

V. Mr. Damato calls Amanda up to his desk and begins describing what she did correctly and what she did incorrectly regarding a paper she had previously turned in. As he explains, he notices Amanda daydreaming. He abruptly stops his explanation and says, "Here, Amanda! Take your paper to your desk and figure this out for yourself until you can come back and attend to what I'm saying. I'll explain this only when you're ready to listen."

VI. Ms. Byrnes holds a spelling contest between the boys and girls in her third grade class. Keith's diligent studying pays off because he leads the boys to victory. The victory positively reinforces his diligent study habits, but is also destructive because it plants the idea that boys are smarter than girls.

VII. Teachers who heed Jones' suggestions and continually use their eyes to monitor students will be more aware of what is going on. Thus, those teachers will display a higher degree of Kounin's withitness.

VIII. Glasser advised teachers to confer with students who have misbehaved and lead those students to make rational choices about the future courses of their behaviors. Ginott suggested that teachers should describe situations rather than labeling students. Attention to that suggestion from Ginott would help teachers using Glasser's approach to guide students into making rational choices regarding their conduct. Because a teacher focuses on the situation rather than on characterizations of a student, the student is less likely to feel under attack and, thus, is more reasonable in assessing behaviors.

## Supplemental Readings

Azrin, N. H., Hake, D. G., Holz, W. C., & Hutchinson, R. R. (1965). Motivational aspects of escape from punishment. *Journal of Experimental Analysis of Behavior, 8,* 31–44.

Brown, D. (1971). *Changing student behavior: A new approach to discipline* (pp. 1–21). Dubuque, IA: Brown.

Canter, L. (1978). Be an assertive teacher. *Instructor, 88,* 60.

Canter, L., & Canter, M. (1976). *Assertive discipline: A take-charge approach for today's educator.* Seal Beach, CA: Canter and Associates.

Charles, C. M. (1985). *Building classroom discipline: From models to practice* (2nd ed.), (pp. 17–120). White Plains, NY: Longman.

Doyle, W. (1986). Classroom organization and management. In M. C. Wittrock (Ed.), *Handbook of Research on Teaching* (3rd ed.), (pp. 392–431). New York: Macmillan.

Dreikurs, R., Grunwald, B., & Pepper, F. (1982). *Maintaining sanity in the classroom* (2nd ed.). New York: Harper & Row.

Ginott, H. G. (1965). *Parent and child.* New York: Avon Books.

Ginott, H. G. (1972). *Teacher and child.* New York: Avon Books.

Glasser, W. (1965). *Schools without failure.* New York: Harper & Row.

Glasser, W. (1977). Ten steps to good discipline. *Today's Education, 66,* 60–63.

Glasser, W. (1986). *Control theory in the classroom.* New York: Harper & Row.

Jones, F. (1979). The gentle art of classroom discipline. *National Elementary Principal, 58,* 26–32.

Joyce, B., & Weil, M. (1980). *Models of teaching* (2nd ed.), (pp. 413–426). Englewood Cliffs, NJ: Prentice-Hall.

Kounin, J., & Sherman, L. (1979). School environments as behavior settings. *Theory Into Practice, 18,* 145–151.

Krumboltz, J. D., & Krumboltz, H. B. (1972). *Changing children's behavior* (pp. 180–201). Englewood Cliffs, NJ: Prentice-Hall.

McDaniel, T. R. (1986). A primer on classroom discipline: Principles old and new. *Phi Delta Kappan, 68,* 63–67.

Strom, R. D. (1969). *Psychology for the classroom* (pp. 147–208). Englewood Cliffs, NJ: Prentice-Hall.

# part two

# How Do You Get Students to Cooperate?

# How Do You Keep Discipline Problems from Occurring?

# 3

# Creating a Favorable Climate

Chapter 3 is designed to help you:

1. understand that students are more likely to be on-task and engaged in learning activities in a classroom where: (a) A businesslike climate exists so that the task of achieving learning goals is of paramount concern; (b) Transition time is minimized and students are busy; (c) Students are free from the threats of embarrassment and harassment; (d) Expectations for conduct are clearly established.

2. develop organizational techniques that will aid you in establishing a businesslike atmosphere in your own classrooms.

3. discover how transition time can be minimized by: (a) methods for dispensing with administrative tasks; (b) methods for distributing materials and giving directions; (c) the selection of audio-visual aids; (d) the utilization of intra-class groups; (e) planning for students working at differing rates.

4. understand how to take advantage of the beginning of a new school year or new school term in order to establish a classroom environment that encourages student cooperation, on-task behaviors, and engagement.

5. begin thinking about how you can establish a classroom atmosphere in which students: (a) fear neither being embarrassed nor harassed; (b) clearly understand how they are expected to conduct themselves as well as the consequences of their behaviors.

## CREATING A BUSINESSLIKE ATMOSPHERE

### The Advantages of a Businesslike Atmosphere

Why would you want your classroom to have a businesslike atmosphere? I know I want a businesslike atmosphere in my classroom because I want to make life easier for myself. In which classroom situations described by the following four examples would you find it easier to teach?

Ms. Richard's 28 third graders are working in four reading groups when she calls a halt to the activity in order to begin a large group Spanish lesson. Ms. Richard: "Okay, class! Class, listen up. Put your reading things away and get ready. . . . Ilone, please listen to me! Margo, leave Frankie alone; he doesn't like that! Okay, class, put your reading things away and set your desks up in one big group so we can start Spanish." Joey: "Misses Richard, I didn't get a turn to read; you said we were all to have a turn!" Francine: "Get your desk out'a my way! We're supposed to be startin' Spanish." Ms. Richard: "I'm waiting, class. Let's get these desks lined up. . . . You're going to love what we're—Fred, put your reading things away and . . ."

Ms. Morrison's 28 third graders are working in four reading groups when she strikes a small gong situated on her desk. The students look up as she points to the word "Spanish" on a colorful poster displayed on a wall. Ms. Morrison then points to a sketch that symbolizes a large group arrangement for the students. The students immediately put their reading materials away and go about rearranging their desks for a large group session. They communicate with one another in whispers. Within four minutes Ms. Morrison is conducting the Spanish lesson.

As the bell for third period rings at Fort George High, Mr. McMahon enters his room ready to teach Latin. "All right, enough already! Let's get in our seats, we've got a lot of work to do today," he shouts above the din in the room. Some students begin to move to their places, but others continue to be involved in conversation. "Shh, hush up!" is heard from some of the students. Mr. McMahon: "Hey, in here! Knock it off, ladies! Take your homework out and let's begin. . . ."

As the bell for the third period rings at Green Mountain High, Ms. Losavio enters her room ready to teach Latin. The students, who have been milling around and socializing, stop what they've been doing as soon as one student spots her and says, "She's here." Quietly they go to their places. Without a word from Ms. Losavio, they place their homework on their desks.

I assume that you like yourself well enough to prefer to teach in either Ms. Morrison's or Ms. Losavio's situations rather than in those of either

Ms. Richard or Mr. McMahon. Neither Ms. Morrison nor Ms. Losavio appeared to have had to struggle to get students to begin a learning activity as did both Ms. Richard and Mr. McMahon. Are some teachers simply fortunate to operate classrooms where students seem to automatically go about the *business* of learning, while other teachers' struggles fail to achieve even a semblance of order and efficiency? Good fortune, although occasionally playing a role, is undependable. You, like Ms. Morrison and Ms. Losavio, must rely on your own initiatives to establish an efficiently operating, businesslike classroom.

## The Meaning of "Businesslike"

For some people, the term "businesslike" connotes formality in manner and dress. Please do not use such an interpretation in this context. A "businesslike classroom" refers to a learning environment in which the students and the teacher conduct themselves as if achieving specified learning goals takes priority over any other concerns. Surely, even with a businesslike atmosphere, activities other than learning activities take place. Lunch money may be collected, attendance may be taken, school announcements may be heard, visits may be made to the toilet, pleasant socializing may take place, the videotape player may be repaired, the room may be rearranged, and a joke may evoke laughter. However, in a businesslike classroom, such deviations from the business of learning are dispatched efficiently. Engagement in some learning activities may be fun and for other learning activities it may be pure drudgery, but it is *always* considered important, serious business. Purposefulness characterizes a businesslike atmosphere.

## Five Steps Toward a Businesslike Atmosphere

How do you teach your students to consider their engagement in learning activities as serious, important business? How do you establish a smoothly operating classroom with a businesslike atmosphere? First of all, *you* must sincerely believe that the learning activities you plan for your students are vital to the achievement of worthwhile learning goals. Do not expect your students to place any more importance on learning activities than you do. However, telling students that a learning activity is important is likely only to waste time. You communicate the importance of a learning activity by the behavior you model and the attitude you display.

You can begin establishing a businesslike atmosphere in your classroom by: (1) taking advantage of the beginning of a new school year or term to set the stage for cooperation; (2) being particularly prepared and organized; (3) minimizing transition time; (4) utilizing a communication style that encourages a comfortable, nonthreatening environment where students are free to go about the business of learning without fear of embarrassment or harassment; (5) clearly establishing expectations for conduct.


## BEGINNING A NEW YEAR

### Students' Preconceived Notions

Students arrive in your class on the first day of school with some preconceived notions on what to expect and what is expected of them. Even the vast majority of beginning kindergarten students know that they will be required to follow a teacher's directions and that certain antisocial behaviors (e.g., fighting) are unacceptable. Experience has taught older students that screaming, talking out of turn, leaving a classroom without permission, and blatant rudeness are among the things that teachers don't appreciate. Experience has also taught older students that teachers vary considerably regarding: (1) how seriously a teacher takes his or her role of helping students to learn; (2) which specific student behaviors are expected, which are demanded, which are tolerated, which are appreciated, which are recognized, which are unappreciated, which are not tolerated, which are punished, and which are rewarded; (3) consistency of a teacher's reactions to certain student behaviors (i.e., Given a situation, can the teacher's behavior be predicted?).


### Taking Advantage of Initial Uncertainty

Whether you teach pre-kindergarten or college, your students come to you for the first time filled with uncertainties. Some will have developed a distaste for school and are hoping that somehow you might provide them with a different sort of experience. Others will expect from you a continuation of what they perceive to be meaningless, boring, and inane stupidities thrust upon them by previous teachers. Such students feel uncertain only about the particular form your stupidities will take. Fortunately, there are those who have appreciated at least some of their previous contacts with schools and meet you with high expectations.

Because students are uncertain about you at the very beginning of a new school session, they will be watching your reactions, evaluating your attitudes, predicting what the relationships among you and the students will be, assessing their individual places in the social order of the class, and determining how they will conduct themselves. Take advantage of the attention that students will afford you on the first days of a school session to begin establishing on-task and cooperative behavior patterns. During the beginning of a school year or term, you should *strictly* adhere to suggestions (e.g., display withitness, consistently enforce rules, and be highly organized) from this text and from other sources that you choose to incorporate into your teaching. Later, after students better understand what to expect from you, allowing yourself an occasional transgression from the standards you've set for yourself may not harm the smooth operation of your classroom.

## Planning for a Favorable Beginning

Do not simply hope for a favorable beginning; plan for it to happen. At least a week before you prepare for the first class meeting, spend some time alone in your classroom. While there, *visualize* exactly what you want to be going on in that classroom during the middle of the upcoming school session. Picture yourself conducting different learning activities and managing transition times. What traffic patterns for student movement do you want followed? What sounds (e.g., one person talking at a time during large group meetings and soft tones of several students talking at once during small group activities) should be heard? How should non-learning activities (e.g., pencil sharpening, collecting money, and visits to the drinking fountain) be conducted? How should supplies get into and out of students' hands? How will evaluation of achievement occur? What modes of communication will be used? When do you want to spend time planning and completing other work that does not involve interacting with students? Use the Teaching Process Model (Figure 1.1) as a means for organizing your thoughts about your responsibilities. You need to plan your operation so that you can efficiently meet those responsibilities. Anticipate problems that might arise (e.g., supplies that don't arrive and students refusing to follow directions) and simulate and evaluate alternative ways for you to respond to those problems.

Only after you've had a week or so reflecting on exactly how you want your class to operate are you ready to plan for the new school year or term.

Mr. Martin made a checklist that included the following questions for him to answer before planning to meet his middle school social studies class for the first time:

I. *Classroom Organization and Ongoing Routines*
   1. What different types of learning activities (e.g., video presentations, large group demonstrations, small group buzz sessions, and independent project work) do I expect to conduct this term?
   2. How should the room be organized (e.g., placement of furniture, screens, and displays) to accommodate the different types of learning activities and the corresponding transition times?
   3. What rules of conduct will be needed to maximize engagement during the different types of learning activities and to maximize on-task behaviors during transition times?
   4. What rules of conduct will be needed to discourage disruptions to other classes or persons located in or near the school?

5. What rules of conduct are needed to provide a safe, secure environment in which students and other persons need not fear embarrassment or harassment?
6. How will rules be determined (e.g., strictly by me, by me with input from the students, democratically, or some combination of these)?
7. When will rules be determined (e.g., from the very beginning, as needs arise, or both)?
8. How will rules be taught to students?
9. How will rules be enforced?
10. What other parts of the building (e.g., detention room or other classrooms) can be utilized for separating students from the rest of the class?
11. Whom, among building personnel, can I depend on to help handle short-range discipline problems and whom for long-range problems?
12. How do I want to utilize the help of parents?
13. What ongoing routine tasks (e.g., reporting daily attendance) will I be expected to carry out for the school administration?
14. What events on the school calendar will need to be considered as I schedule the class learning activities?
15. What possible emergencies (e.g., fire or student suffering physical trauma) might be anticipated and, considering school policies, how should I handle them?

II. *One-Time-Only Tasks*
1. How will I communicate the general school policies to my students?
2. What special administrative tasks will I be required to complete (e.g., identifying number of students on reduced payment lunch program and checking health records)?
3. What supplies (e.g., textbooks) will have to be distributed?
4. Are supplies available and ready for distribution in adequate quantities?
5. How will I distribute and account for supplies?
6. Are display cards with students' names ready?
7. How should I handle students who appear on the first day, but are not on the roll?
8. What procedures will be used to initially direct students into the classroom and to assigned places?
9. For whom on the student roster might special provisions or assistance be needed for certain types of activities (e.g., students with hearing losses and students confined to wheelchairs)?

III. *Reminders for the First Week's Learning Activities*
1. Do lesson plans for the first week call primarily for learning activities that each have: (1) uncomplicated directions that are simple

to follow; (2) challenge, but with which all students will experience success; (3) built-in positive reinforcers for engagement; (4) all students involved at the same time?

2. Do the first week's lesson plans allow me to spend adequate time observing students, getting to know them, identifying needs, and collecting information that will help me make curricula decisions and design future learning activities?

3. Do plans allow me to be free during the first week to closely monitor student activities and be in a particularly advantageous position to discourage off-task behaviors before off-task patterns emerge, and positively reinforce on-task behaviors so that on-task patterns do emerge?

IV. *Personal Reminders for Myself*

1. Am I prepared to pause and reflect for a moment on what I should say to students before I say it?

2. Am I prepared to use descriptive, rather than judgmental language as I interact with my students?

3. Am I prepared to observe exactly what students are doing and hear exactly what they are saying before making a hasty response?

4. Am I prepared to use a supportive response style?

5. Am I prepared to model a businesslike attitude?

Most of the questions in Mr. Martin's list are dealt with in subsequent sections of this text (e.g., room arrangements in Chapter 6, rules for conduct in Chapter 5, and supportive response styles in Chapter 4). At this time, turn your attention to his three questions under the heading, "Reminders for the First Week's Learning Activities." Read them over once again.

## Learning Activities Conducive to a Favorable Beginning

Only learning activities with easy-to-follow, uncomplicated directions should be used in the early part of a new school session so that: (1) Your students can immediately get to the business of learning without experiencing bewilderment over "What are we supposed to be doing?"; (2) Students will come to expect to understand your directions and, consequently, will be willing to attend to them in the future. If students are confused by your initial directions, they are less likely to bother trying to understand subsequent ones. Later, after students have developed a pattern of attending to the directions for learning activities, you can carefully and gradually introduce more complex procedures to be followed.

Students should find their first engagements with your learning activities to be satisfying. You would like to leave them with the impression, "I did learn something; I can be successful!" The idea, of course, is to make sure engagement is positively reinforced so that a pattern of engaged behavior is developed.

Later in a school session, it will be advantageous for you to have students working on individual levels with some engaged in one learning activity while others are involved in a different learning activity. However, you are advised to get all students involved in the same learning activity in the first stages of a school session. Having all students working on the same task allows you to keep directions simple, monitor the class as a whole, and compare how different individuals approach a common problem. Besides, until you get to know your students, you have little basis for deciding how to individualize. The following are examples of two teachers conducting learning activities that are ideal for students' initial experiences in a new school session:

It is the opening day of a new term at Blackhawk Trail High School. The bell ending the second period rings and the bell to indicate the beginning of third period will ring in 5 minutes. Mr. Stockton, in preparation for the arrival of his third period earth science class, turns on a video player showing a tape on a prominently displayed monitor with the audio volume control turned up rather loudly. As required by school policy, Mr. Stockton stations himself just outside the classroom door between second and third period. As students enter the room, they hear Mr. Stockton's voice coming from the video monitor, "Please have a seat at the desk displaying a card with your name. If no desk has a card with your name, please sit at one of the desks with a blank card. There you will find a marking pen for you to print and display your first name. Once seated at your desk, please take out one sheet of paper and a pen or pencil. You will need them when the third period begins. I would appreciate you clearing your desk top of everything except your name card, pencil or pen, and paper. This message will be repeated until the beginning of third period. After the bell, the directions for today's first lesson will appear on the screen." The message, which is printed on the screen while it can be heard in Mr. Stockton's voice, is repeated continually until five seconds after the third period bell. Mr. Stockton has moved into the room. He moves among the students, gently tapping one inattentive student on the shoulder and pointing toward the monitor. Several times he gestures to the monitor in response to students trying to talk to him.

The message on the video changes. Mr. Stockton's image appears on the screen with this message: "I am about to perform an experiment. It will take six and a half minutes. During that time, please carefully watch what happens. When the experiment is completed, you will be asked to *describe* in writing just what you *observed*. Remember those two words, 'describe' and 'observe.' We will find them to be very important during this course in earth science. . . ."

As the experiment appears on the screen, Mr. Stockton watches the students. The videotape is over after the students are directed to spend seven minutes writing a paragraph describing what they saw. Mr. Stockton circulates around the room reading over students' shoulders as they write. At the end of the 7 minutes, he calls on several students to read their paragraphs. Other students are then brought into a discussion session in which a distinction is made between describing observations and making judgments.

Mr. Stockton feels well about the lesson because all students seem to realize that they had made observations and successfully described them. Mr. Stockton distributes copies of the course syllabus and goes over it item by item. Frequent references to observing and recording experiments, such as the one everyone had just commonly shared, are made as the goals of the earth science course are discussed.

Textbooks are distributed and some administrative tasks are taken care of before the period ends. Mr. Stockton indicates that classroom rules and organizational procedures will be discussed at the very next meeting.

By the way, while the students were viewing the videotape, Mr. Stockton checked the roll and posted the attendance report outside the classroom door for school office personnel to pick up.

Ms. Phegley spent the first two days of the school year just helping her first graders to get accustomed to their new surroundings. She spent the majority of the time getting to know these six-year-olds and teaching them how to follow rules of conduct and some basic routines (e.g., procedures for using the drinking fountain and getting to and from the cafeteria).

On the third day, as the students are seated at their places, Ms. Phegley announces, "Everyone put your hands on your head like this." She puts both her hands atop her head and the students follow along. Ms. Phegley: "Now keep your hands up there until you see me take mine off of my head." Smiling brightly, she surveys their faces with deliberation. Ms. Phegley: "Taped under your table is an envelope containing your very own word." Roger and Ethan begin to reach under their tables. Ms. Phegley: "My hands are still on top of my head. . . . Thank you for waiting. Now, look around the room. What do you see on the wall just above the boards?" "Posters!" "Cards!" "Words!" are some of the replies. Ms. Phegley: "Yes, I agree! There are posters and cards hanging all around the room with words on them. How many are there?" "Too many!" "One, two, three, four . . . ten, there are ten!" "No, more than ten!" Ms. Phegley (interrupting): "I'll tell you how many there are. There are as many words on the wall as there are of you. There's one for each of you. One of those words belongs to Louise, and one belongs to Granville, and one belongs to Marva. . . ." "And one belongs to me!" shouts Mickey. "Which one is mine?" asks Gwynn. "Oh! I know," says Claudia, "the envelopes under our tables will tell us!" Ms. Phegley: "That's right; they will. When I take my hands off of my head that is the signal for you to take the envelope from under your desk and find out which word on the wall it matches. Tamara, look where my hands are. Once you've found your word, you are to go and quietly stand under it. I'll tell you what we'll do next after everyone is quietly standing under his or her own word."

The learning activity continues and eventually culminates with students comparing similarities and differences in their words. Ms. Phegley chose this activity for the first week of school, not only because it helps the students develop some reading readiness skills, but because it gets them used to following her directions and is one with which they could all achieve success. Some students were quicker than others to match the letters and locate where to stand. But this made it easier for those who were slower with this task because it reduced the number of places left to stand and, therefore, the number of comparisons to be made.

## BEING PREPARED AND ORGANIZED

### The Importance of the Third and Fourth Steps of the Teaching Process Model

Both Mr. Stockton and Ms. Phegley, in the aforementioned examples, left their students with the impression that directions are to be strictly followed and learning activities are important business to be taken seriously. Read those two examples once again, and make a list of some of the specific steps that Mr. Stockton took and Ms. Phegley took that helped convey this impression to students. Now, classify each step in your list according to its placement in the Teaching Process Model. For example: (1) Mr. Stockton was operating within the third phase of the Teaching Process Model when he decided to demonstrate an experiment at the very beginning of the class period; (2) Mr. Stockton was operating within the fourth phase of the Teaching Process Model when he videotaped the experiment in preparation for the class meeting; (3) Ms. Phegley operated within the fourth phase when she prepared the posters and hung them on the walls; (4) She was also within the fourth phase of the Teaching Process Model when she taped the envelopes under students' tables prior to meeting her class.

I would guess that a large share of the steps in your list fall within the purview of the third and fourth phases of the Teaching Process Model. The smoothness of the classroom operations and the desirable impressions that were left on students can be credited to what Mr. Stockton and Ms. Phegley did to organize and prepare for their class sessions.

### The Effects of Preparation on Classroom Climate and Efficiency

It took more *preparation* time for Mr. Stockton to demonstrate the science experiment via video presentation than it would have had he conducted the experiment "live." However, this extra effort in preparation made it much easier for Mr. Stockton to start the first class session smoothly and have students engaged in a learning activity while he was free to manage the setting. The video presentation also lent Mr. Stockton's learning activity a professional touch that told students, "This is serious business. The teacher is serious enough to make the extra effort to thoroughly organize and prepare. The same is expected of students." Compare the message such well-prepared sessions send to students to that sent by sessions in which a teacher is prepared only with a piece of chalk and a resolution that "students had better pay attention or else!" Or else what? Such teachers should listen to today's adolescents when they use the popular expression, "Get serious!"

Preparing name cards for students was a simple matter for Mr. Stockton, but it made a major difference in how his initial meeting with students went. Name tags designating seating arrangements provide students with a hint of order in the classroom. Even though Mr. Stockton has approximately 150 students per term at Blackhawk Trail High, because of the name tags, he can call each student by her or his name on the very first day of school. Suppose, for example, that while he is going over the course syllabus, he notices a student's attention drifting away. Because of the name tags, he is readily able to work that student's name into the explanations; such a tactic can serve to cue a student back on-task. "The guy in the green shirt . . ." is not nearly as effective as "Ralph. . . ."

Secondary school teachers typically present information about course expectations at the beginning of a school term. Mr. Stockton prepared a course syllabus for distribution on the first day. Such documents, if professionally prepared, can provide at least three advantages in helping students to be on-task: (1) A course syllabus suggests to students that the coursework is purposeful and gives them an idea of how it will benefit them; (2) A well-organized syllabus gives the impression that the course is well-organized and will be conducted in a businesslike manner; (3) Throughout the term, the teacher can use the syllabus as point of focus (e.g., Mr. Stockton can reference it by saying "Tonight's homework will move you to Section XI on page 9 of your syllabus."); (4) The syllabus provides an outline for the class meetings (e.g., Mr. Stockton's first meeting) in which course expectations are discussed.

When Mr. Stockton was ready to discuss course expectations, he passed out copies of the course syllabus. Ms. Phegley's preparation for placing materials into her first graders' hands was a bit more elaborate. Instead of simply distributing word cards to her students in class, she placed them in envelopes before class started and taped them under table tops where they would be out of the students' sight. What advantages did she gain by going to this extra trouble? Gains reaped by the extra time Ms. Phegley spent in preparation included the following: (1) The first graders were able to discover "their very own" words at the same time without waiting for them to be handed out one at a time; (2) By being taped under the table tops, the word cards were kept out of sight and thus did not become distracting toys before Ms. Phegley was ready for the students to work with them; (3) Having an unknown word located in an unusual place added an air of mystery that helped hold students' attention while Ms. Phegley related the directions for the learning activity; (4) Having the words already distributed before class left Ms. Phegley more freedom during class to supervise and orchestrate the activities.

Generally speaking, the more work you put into your preparation before class, the less work it will take to maintain a smooth operation during class. The benefits of exceptional preparation for highly organized learning activities increase over time for at least two reasons: (1) Materials prepared for one class (e.g., Mr. Stockton's videotape and Ms. Phegley's posters for displaying words) can be reused with or refined for subsequent classes; (2) The businesslike attitude a well-prepared, highly organized teacher models for students has a lasting effect that will help establish on-task and engaged student behavior patterns.

## MINIMIZING TRANSITION TIME

By minimizing transition time, you maximize allocated time. The more allocated time you have available, the more time your students have for being engaged in learning activities (Borg, 1980; Latham, 1984). Of course, making more allocated time available does not necessarily result in greater achievement unless: (1) Learning activities are worthwhile; (2) The additional allocated time actually results in additional engaged time.

Keeping transition time to a minimum has benefits in addition to making more allocated time available. Students' engagement levels are likely to be better when there is a smooth and rapid transition between learning activities than when transition time is extended or when learning activities are interrupted (Kounin, 1977). By efficiently moving from one lesson to another and by streamlining your procedures for dispensing with non-teaching, managerial, and administrative tasks, you can avoid having your students wasting time *waiting* for the business of learning to start. Students waiting to get busy develop their own devices for relieving their boredom (Cangelosi, 1986), such as displaying attention-getting, disruptive behaviors, and daydreaming. The disruptive behaviors tend to extend the transition periods between learning activities and, consequently, amplify the initial cause of the problem. Daydreaming, while not disruptive, makes it difficult for a student to become engaged in the learning activity when transition time stops and allocated time begins. Switching the focus of one's thoughts cannot always occur on cue.

Ideas on how you can minimize transition time are provided by the next five sections.

# DISPENSING WITH ADMINISTRATIVE DUTIES

## Inefficient Use of Classroom Time

The following example would be incredible if it were not indicative of commonplace, everyday occurrences in thousands of classrooms:

Ms. Rolando teaches fourth grade at a school that each day requires her to report to the main office the names of absentees and the number of students planning to eat lunch in the cafeteria that day (categorized by free lunch, reduced payment lunch, and full payment lunch). Students who were absent the previous day are required to display an "admit slip" signed by a school secretary before Ms. Rolando may permit their participation in class. Students appearing after the "second bell" must also possess a "late slip" before being accepted into class. Every Monday, Ms. Rolando is required to check students for head lice and report the names of students displaying symptoms.

On any given Monday morning, the following scene is typical for Ms. Rolando's class:

Twenty-five of Ms. Rolando's 31 students are seated at their desks by the second bell. Four others come in during public address announcements which are followed by the Pledge of Allegiance. Ms. Rolando then begins calling the roll: "Raymond?" "Here." "Melinda?" "Here." "Turner?— Turner! Are you here, Turner?" "Oh! Yes Ma'am, I'm here." "Barbara . . . I see Barbara's absent. . . ." It takes a full 8 minutes to complete the roll call during which time students sit idly or find ways to entertain themselves.

Ms. Rolando then asks, "Which of you on free lunch are eating in the cafeteria today? Okay, keep your hands high! One, two, three, Ralph, is your hand up?—six, seven. Okay, raise your hand if you're on reduced lunch." Turner: "I'm on reduced lunch, but I brought my lunch today. Should I raise my hand?" Ms. Rolando: "You know what I mean! No, Turner, keep your hand down unless you're eating in the cafeteria today." Turner: "What if I just want to get milk today?" Ms. Rolando: "Never mind, Turner, one, two, Willie, put your hand down, you're not on reduced lunch . . . three, four, six, eight. Now, the rest of you who are eating . . ." Six minutes later, Ms. Rolando has her lunch tallies and is ready to check for head lice. She says, "Everybody settle down and stay in your places while I check your heads. . . ." Twelve minutes later, Ms. Rolando discovers that only Pam's name needs to be included on the head lice list.

"Those of you who came in late or who were absent yesterday, bring your passes to me now," Ms. Rolando says as she dispenses with the admit and late slips in four minutes. All this time, her students are waiting for the business of the day to begin. As they wait, they are becoming more and more restless and their moods are changing so that they are becoming less and less ready to become engaged in learning activities.

Forty-four minutes after the second bell, Ms. Rolando starts her math lesson with, "Take out your homework so I can come around and check on who did it and who did not."

## Efficient Use of Classroom Time

Most public school teachers are burdened with administrative tasks that tend to extend transition time and detract from student engagement. However, many teachers cope with this burden with only a minimal loss in allocated time. Ms. Drexler provides an example:

> Ms. Drexler teaches fourth grade at the same school as does Ms. Rolando. She is also required to perform the same morning administrative duties as is Ms. Rolando. The following describes the beginning of a typical Monday morning in Ms. Drexler's class.
>
> Twenty-six of Ms. Drexler's 33 students are seated as the second bell rings and public address announcements begin. As soon as the announcements and the Pledge of Allegiance are completed, Ms. Drexler directs her students to place their math homework papers on top of their desks with "Yes" written in the upper left hand corner of the first page if they plan to eat in the cafeteria that day and "No" if they will not. She then distributes a written-response math quiz which students begin immediately. As they respond to the quiz, Ms. Drexler circulates among the students, filling out a chart which she carries on a clipboard (see Illustration 3.1).
>
> Because Ms. Drexler's chart indicates the lunch status of each student, the simple "Yes" or "No" written on the homework paper is sufficient for her to provide the office with the lunch tallies. As she stops by each student and fills out the chart, she checks for head lice and collects admit slips and late slips from those who are required to have them.
>
> Ms. Drexler checks for homework, completes the head lice check, transfers information from her chart to the form that the main office expects, and takes care of other administrative duties before the students finish the math quiz.

## SAVING TIME WHEN DISTRIBUTING MATERIALS AND GIVING DIRECTIONS

### Inefficient and Efficient Methods

> Mr. Hansen's 28 fifth graders are filing into their classroom just after a recess break. He has planned a learning activity that involves pairs of students working with $250 in play money. Mr. Hansen believes that the

## Illustration 3.1. Ms. Drexler's Chart

| NAME | LUNCH TYPE | YES/NO | ABSENT | TARDY | LICE | HOMEWORK |
|------|-----------|--------|--------|-------|------|----------|
| Amarillo, P. | free | | | | | |
| Bing, D. | full | | | | | |
| Bundy, V. | full | | | | | |
| Cafarell, P. | full | | | | | |
| Church, P. | free | | | | | |
| Costello, A. | part | | | | | |
| D'Armond, R. | full | | | | | |
| Epstein, S. | full | | | | | |
| Gale, R. | free | | | | | |
| Gambino, S. | part | | | | | |
| Grimes, Ma. | part | | | | | |
| Grimes, Mi. | full | | | | | |
| Gustofson, A. | full | | | | | |
| Heidingstelder, L. | part | | | | | |
| Jacobsen, D. | full | | | | | |
| Javier, J. | full | | | | | |
| Johnson, D. | full | | | | | |
| Johnson, C. | free | | | | | |
| Johnson, J. | full | | | | | |
| Luidzinski, M. | part | | | | | |
| Marchand, B. | free | | | | | |
| Mayberry, M. | free | | | | | |
| Nun-Sung, S. | full | | | | | |
| Osborne, B. | full | | | | | |
| Ramad, A. | full | | | | | |
| Sorenson, K. | free | | | | | |
| Sudiaski, J. | part | | | | | |
| Tyler, W. | full | | | | | |
| Tyung, S. | free | | | | | |
| Whitman, V. | part | | | | | |

DATE _____

students will really enjoy and profit from what he has planned and eagerly waits for everyone to be seated so he can explain what to do. Speaking above the mild noise level created by the movement of bodies and a few conversations left over from recess, Mr. Hansen begins, "As soon as everyone's in his place, I want your attention. . . . Okay! Listen up. . . . Hey, Bob, over here! Listen up. . . . Okay, now. Find yourself a partner. . . . Pull your desk next to his. The . . ." "What if it's not a 'him'?" asks Deborah. "That's right. Make that him or her," Mr. Hansen responds. He continues, "When everyone and his or her partner are seated together, I'll pass out some materials and tell you what we'll be doing."

They move around identifying partners. Initially, some have no partners and others have two. Some friendly pushing occurs and comments such as "I wanna be with Allison!" and "I always get stuck with Caesar!" are heard. Thirteen minutes after the start of the period, everyone seems to be with a partner, but the confusion concerns Mr. Hansen. Speaking louder than before, he says, "I have $250 of play money for you and your partner. You will be needing this for the problem you'll have to solve together." While he counts and distributes the money, students begin making remarks: "What are we going to do?" "Oh shoot! This isn't real money!" "Yeah, Mr. Hansen, give us real money!" "Hey! Mr. Hansen, you only gave us $210!"

During the 14 minutes that it takes for each pair to obtain the right amount, some students begin daydreaming, others doodle, and others pick up their conversations from recess. By the time Mr. Hansen is ready to explain the directions for the learning activity, enthusiasm for becoming engaged has waned.

Mr. Jukola wants to conduct the same learning activity with his class of 30 fifth graders that Mr. Hansen was trying to begin in the previous example. However, Mr. Jukola is better prepared than was Mr. Hansen. Before the students return from recess, Mr. Jukola places 15 different numerals (e.g., "62") at each of 15 work stations that he set up in the classroom. Thirty index cards are prepared so that each has a different numerical expression at the top, but the same directions printed below. (Illustration 3.2 is an example of one of these cards. The numerical expressions have been selected so that for each card there is only one other card in the deck that has an equal numerical expression. For example, a card with "$(8 \times 8) - (1/.5)$" would match the card in Illustration 3.2 since $(8 \times 8) - (1/.5) = 62$ as does the expression on the top of the card.)

As the students begin filing into the room, Mr. Jukola gives a card to each and softly announces to about five or six students at a time, "Please follow the directions on the card." Upon entering the room, the students are busy reading and computing. Because Mr. Jukola is not busy trying to provide directions to the entire class, he is able to move among the students and respond to any indications of off-task behaviors.

### Illustration 3.2. One of Mr. Jukola's 30 Index Cards

---

### 60% of $((302+8)/3)$

Go to the work station that is labeled with a number equal to the expression at the top of this card. There you will meet your partner. Next, find the envelope taped under the table top. Remove the envelope and open it. Inside you will find $250 in play money and instructions on what you and your partner should do with it. Good luck!

---

Six minutes after the first student entered the room, all are busy working with their partners. Some started with the learning activity before others arrived as they did not have to wait for directions from Mr. Jukola. The very process for locating their materials and finding out the directions involved them in reading, computing, and acquiring a curiosity about the learning activity (adapted from Cangelosi, 1982).

## Freedom from Having to Speak to the Whole Class

In the first of the last two examples, Mr. Hansen tried to speak to his entire class at once in order to direct students into a planned learning activity. Students who were ready to listen for the directions right away had to wait for everyone else to be situated before finding out what to do. On the other hand, Mr. Jukola had the directions for students to read typed and duplicated on cards and on notes inside sealed envelopes. By not having to tell everyone at once what to do, Mr. Jukola was free to move about the room to help, prod, and encourage individuals. Often, you can achieve smoother, quicker transitions, free of hassles and off-task behaviors, by using modes other than oral presentations to the whole group for communicating directions. Sometimes alternatives to talking about directions are not feasible. However, when directions are complicated or individualized and students are able to read, approaches similar to Mr. Jukola's are usually more time efficient than Mr. Hansen's. In any case, giving directions in a manner that doesn't depend on you having to speak to the class all at once has its advantages: (1) You are freer to supervise and manage the transition time before the learning activity begins; (2) Students do not have to wait for everyone else to be attentive before they begin following the directions; (3) You can save your voice and energy for times when it is more important to speak to the group as a whole; (4) The less you speak, the more attentive students will be when you do speak to them (Cangelosi, 1986); (5) You can more efficiently clear up some students' misunderstanding of the directions. The following two contrasting examples illustrate this fifth advantage:

Ms. McDaniel announces to her 25 science students, "Each of you is to take your scale and individually weigh the five substances beginning with the lightest colored one, then the next lighter one, and so on until you've weighed the darkest colored one last. Any questions?" Xavier: "Then what do we do?" Ms. McDaniel: "I was coming to that." Carmen: "Why do we start with the lightest one?" Ms. McDaniel: "You'll see. Now, plot each weight on the sheet of graph paper. It is marked with the shades of colors on the vertical axis and the weights on the horizontal. Okay, get busy!"

Some students misunderstand the directions and begin weighing the substances according to which one feels lightest in weight, not by shade of color. April beckons Ms. McDaniel to help her, "I don't know what to do." Ms. McDaniel: "What don't you understand?" April: "What to do!" Ms. McDaniel: "I told you to weigh these substances, beginning with the one with the lightest color and. . . ."

Ms. McDaniel repeats the directions several more times before the end of the activity.

Mr. Johnson wants his eighth grade science class to carry out the same activity as did Ms. McDaniel. However, he has a copy of the directions typed on a slip of paper at each work station along with the substances and the graph paper. Students read the directions for themselves, and Mr. Johnson observes how well they are followed. When a student appears to misunderstand, Mr. Johnson simply points to the directive on that student's slip that is not being followed.

Mickey goes over to Mr. Johnson and says, "I don't understand what we're supposed to be doing." Mr. Johnson: "Read the second sentence on the slip just loud enough for me to hear." Mickey: "Line the substances up so that the darkest colored one is fifth, the next darker one is fourth, and so on until the lightest colored one is first." Having already observed that Mickey had not yet done this, Mr. Johnson says, "Do what it says, and then do what the third sentence says."

## Distributing Materials Ahead of Time

Instead of repeating the directions over and over, as did Ms. McDaniel, Mr. Johnson kept referring unsure students back to the directions as they appeared in print.

Distributing materials (e.g., play money or documents) before they are needed for student use can reduce transition time. Mr. Jukola, in this section's second scenario, took advantage of a recess break to distribute materials. Ms. Salley uses time near the end of one learning activity to distribute materials for the next:

> As Ms. Salley's health science students write their answers to questions from a lesson on diseases of the ear, she circulates among them silently reading their answers and placing a closed box containing an otoscope under every other student's desk. She plans for partners to use the otoscope to examine each other's ears after the directed reading lesson. Because she has used this procedure for distributing materials before, the students know they are not to open the boxes without further directions and they know not to ask, "What's this for?"

## Cues for Efficient Routines

Once you have established a consistent, predictable routine for giving directions and distributing materials, student cooperation can be achieved with only a minimal effort on your part. Because certain directions (e.g., "Everyone is to look at the overhead projector screen," "Cluster into small groups of five or six," or "Take out your notebooks") occur over and over, you may want to teach your students to respond to *cues* or signals for beginning certain routine procedures. Here are two examples:

> The variety of learning activities that Ms. Morrison uses in teaching her 28 third graders frequently necessitates the students changing from one type of grouping arrangement to another. To facilitate this transition, Ms. Morrison has several posters clustered together on one wall of the classroom. When she is ready for her students to stop one activity and begin another, she strikes a small gong located near the cluster of posters. Her students have learned that this is the cue for them to stop whatever they are doing and silently pay attention to Ms. Morrison. Once Ms. Morrison has their attention, she uses the posters to give directions for the next learning activity.
>
> She, for example, will point to a part of the poster pictured in Illustration 3.3 to indicate whether or not talking is allowed. Pointing to one of the numerals in Illustration 3.4 indicates the size of the group they are to form. If Ms. Morrison points to "1," the students know to work individually at their places. Pointing to "3" means they work in groups of three; "Class" means there will be a large group session of the whole class.
>
> Mr. Bowie reserves one section of the chalkboard for in-class assignments and another for homework assignments. His industrial arts students know how to find out the assignments without waiting for Mr. Bowie to tell them.

**Illustration 3.3. Ms. Morrison's Poster for Signaling Whether or Not Talking Is Allowed**

## SAVING TIME BY THE CHOICE OF AUDIO-VISUAL AIDS

Ms. Steele announces to her social studies class, "There are seven major features of the Bill of Rights with which I want you to be familiar. Please jot each down in your notebooks as I put it on the chalkboard. Then we'll discuss the feature in some detail." With her back to the class, Ms. Steele lists the first feature on the board. The students try to copy from the board as she writes, but they must *wait* for her to finish writing and move out of their line of vision. Ms. Steele turns around ready to discuss the first feature, but the students are still copying. Some finish sooner than others. Ms. Steele begins her explanation of the feature after most look up from their notebooks, leaving only a few still writing.

With the discussion of the first feature completed, Ms. Steele turns her back again to the class, and repeats the process for the second through the

**Illustration 3.4. Ms. Morrison's Poster for Signaling How to Group for a Learning Activity**

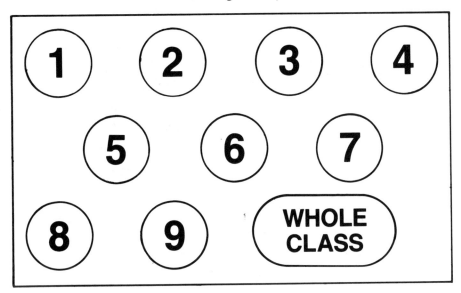

seventh features. By the time she gets to the fourth feature, the chalkboard area that could be readily viewed by the students is exhausted, so she erases the first several features to make room. Erasing is, of course, time-consuming and it prevents her from using the display of the descriptions of those earlier features later in the discussion. During the periods when Ms. Steele was writing on the board, some students amused themselves by daydreaming or whispering among themselves. Some of those students had difficulty getting re-engaged in the discussion each time Ms. Steele faced the class to explain and discuss another one of the seven features.

Mr. Piowaty announces to his social studies class, "There are seven major features of the Bill of Rights with which I want you to be familiar. Please jot each down in your notebooks as I display it on the overhead screen. Then we'll discuss the feature in some detail." Mr. Piowaty observes the students readying their notebooks and then flips on the overhead projector. The first feature is displayed; he watches as the students make their copies. During the ensuing explanation and discussion on the feature, Mr. Piowaty makes notes on the overhead transparency and highlights phrases in the description of the first feature. He does this without ever turning his attention from the class.

The class is cued that it is time to attend to the second feature when Mr. Piowaty replaces the first transparency with one describing the second feature. The process is repeated for the remainder of the features without

Mr. Piowaty ever having to turn away from the class or the students having to wait for either the description of the feature to be written out or for their line of sight to be cleared. Throughout the learning activity, Mr. Piowaty was able to control what the students could view on the screen. Descriptions of features not being discussed were not displayed. However, Mr. Piowaty was able to bring back into view previously discussed features if he wanted to draw comparisons or raise other points about them.

Whenever feasible and practical, you should consider preparing visual displays, and even audio presentations, before you are ready to use them in class. Because he did not have to take students' time writing on the chalkboard with his back to the class, Mr. Piowaty minimized transition time and had a much easier time keeping students engaged than did Ms.

**Illustration 3.5. Ms. Steele Writes on the Chalkboard, Her Back to the Class**

**Illustration 3.6. Mr. Piowaty Illustrates Points on the Overhead Projector While Maintaining Eye Contact with the Class**

Steele. Overhead projectors, videocassette recorders, and microcomputers are only three of the widely available and cost-effective devices that make it easier for you to conduct high-quality, professional demonstrations and presentations that: (1) enhance the businesslike atmosphere of your classroom; (2) require little transition time; (3) make it easier for you to supervise and attend to your students while they are engaged in learning activities.

## SAVING TIME BY THE USE OF INTRA-CLASS GROUPING

*Intra-class grouping* is the subdividing of the students *within* a class into individual work groups for a learning activity. In the first of the next two examples, students waste time waiting their turns to be engaged in a learning activity. In the second example, the teacher uses intra-class grouping to keep students busily engaged.

> Coach McCreary is conducting drills on throwing two-hand chest passes for 13 junior high basketball players. The players are in a single line as Coach McCreary tosses the ball to Jan who is at the head of the line. Jan practices a two-hand chest pass as she throws the ball back to Coach McCreary who exclaims, "Good job, Jan! Next!" Jan returns to the back of the line and the next player has a try. As players take turns, Coach McCreary encourages them, acknowledges properly executed passes, and points out flaws in techniques.

> Coach Adomitis is conducting drills on throwing two-hand chest passes for 13 junior high basketball players. The players are divided into five groups of two and one group of three. Each of the six groups has a ball that is used to throw two-hand chest passes back and forth between players in the group. Coach Adomitis encourages players, acknowledges properly executed passes, and points out flaws in techniques as she circulates among the groups.

While Coach McCreary's students spent more time waiting than practicing, Coach Adomitis kept her students busy due to the way she used intra-class grouping. Intra-class grouping is an especially effective means for accommodating individual differences among students within the same class. Examples of teachers utilizing intra-class grouping are contained throughout this text. For instance, there is the case of Mr. Cefalo on page 138.

## ACCOMMODATING STUDENTS COMPLETING WORK AT DIFFERING TIMES

Mr. Uter distributes a worksheet containing 12 questions for each of his sixth graders. He directs them to use their geography books to help them write a one-paragraph answer to each question. The students get busy with the assignment, which is to be completed in 40 minutes at which time the papers are to be turned in and the questions discussed in a large group session.

After 20 minutes, several students have completed the work, while others are only through the first four questions. Those who finished sit idly waiting for the others. As more students complete the assignment, the noise level in the room increases and becomes disturbing to those still working. The noise bothers Mr. Uter and he finally puts an end to the exercise by saying, "Okay, it looks like most of you are finished. Everybody turn in your papers and we'll discuss the answers."

How could Mr. Uter have planned the assignment so his students' time would be more efficiently utilized? As one of many options, Mr. Uter might have made this a two-part assignment. The first part would consist of the 12 questions to be turned in at the end of the 40 minutes. Time permitting, the second part should be begun in class, but would not be due until the next day (i.e., homework). As a precaution against students rushing through the first part in order to take advantage of the class time for homework, Mr. Uter could make the assignment such that successful completion of the second part is dependent on the first part having been done well. At the end of the 40 minutes, work on either part of the assignment ceases, the first part is turned in, students put the second part away and out of sight, and then the first part questions are discussed in a large group session.

In general, your classroom will operate more efficiently if you sequence your learning activities so that independent tasks need to be finished in class are followed by independent work that has flexible beginning and ending times. Mr. Uter made the mistake of scheduling the large group discussion session immediately after the independent work session without accommodating for some students finishing before others.

## CREATING A COMFORTABLE, NONTHREATENING ATMOSPHERE

### A Frightening Place

You enhance your chances of enjoying a climate in your classroom that encourages on-task, engaged student behaviors by: (1) creating a businesslike atmosphere; (2) being exceptionally prepared and organized, especially near the beginning of a new school term; (3) minimizing transition time by efficiently dispensing with administrative tasks, efficiently distributing materials and giving directions, prudently choosing and preparing audio-visual aids, taking advantage of intra-class grouping, and sequencing learning activities so as to accommodate students finishing work at differing times. However, unless students feel that it is safe for them to wholeheartedly participate in learning activities without being ridiculed, embarrassed, or harmed, the classroom climate will not be as conducive to on-task, engaged behaviors as you would like.

Why would a student ever be fearful of putting forth a concerted effort (i.e., becoming highly engaged) in a learning activity? The reasons are complex and vary from situation to situation; here are some possibilities:

1. School may be such a frightening place for some students that they worry more about protecting themselves than they do about learning.
2. Some students may fear that their efforts to achieve learning goals will be ridiculed by peers who do not value academic achievement.
3. Some students believe that if they put an effort into learning activities and still fail to achieve learning goals, they will either be labeled "stupid" or fail to live up to a previously acquired label of "smart." Consequently, they are afraid to risk failure, so they do not try.
4. Because they feel that a teacher has challenged or embarrassed them in front of their peers, some students consider engaging in learning activities to be tantamount to collaborating with a resented authority figure.

The presence of any of the four aforementioned factors does not excuse misbehavior or off-task behavior. However, as a teacher, you need to understand each and implement strategies for combatting it. Your attention is called to these four factors in this section. Methods for mitigating the influences of these factors are suggested in subsequent chapters.

Why are schools such frightening places for some students? Schools present most pre-kindergarten and primary-grade children with their first regular, daylong experiences away from the comfortable familiarity of their families. Some students from primary grades through high school may be so intimidated by schoolyard bullies that they literally fear for their lives while at school. Pre-adolescent and adolescent students often spend school time fearing that they will fail to gain or maintain the acceptance of peers.

As Dreikurs (1982) and many others have emphasized, students seek peer approval. Achieving the goal of acceptance by a peer group is typically more important in the mind of a pre-adolescent or adolescent than is achieving a learning goal determined by a teacher. Oftentimes, academic learning goals appear long-ranged, whereas a peer-acceptance goal seems immediate and urgent. Consequently, in a case where a student feels that peers do not value achievement in school, a student may fear separation from peers as a consequence of engagement in learning activities.

## Risking Self-Respect

From their earliest moments, most children are inundated with storybook tales, television programs, poems, songs, talk from adults, and other sources that leave them with the following unhappy message: "The degree to which a person is loved, appreciated, and respected by others and the worth of that person are dependent on how well that person performs, accomplishes commendable deeds, and achieves desirable goals." "Rudolph, the Red-Nosed Reindeer," for example, was an object of scorn for his peers until he achieved an act of heroism one Christmas Eve. Then he was loved and respected.

Many well-meaning but misguided parents attempt to motivate their children to achieve by displaying greater signs of love for their children after the children have been successful in an endeavor than they display after the children failed in an endeavor. Consequently, the vast majority of students enter school believing that their own personal worth and self-esteem depend on how well they perform in school. On the surface, such a phenomenon would seem to motivate students to be engaged in learning activities so that they will achieve. In reality, the phenomenon poses one of the greater hindrances to students willingly engaging in learning activities. As a positive reinforcer for on-task behavior, the promise of love and self-respect can be effective over a short term, but it virtually always produces undesirable side effects over time (Ginott, 1972). Thus, destructive positive reinforcement, a term introduced in Chapter 2, fits rewards for achievement or on-task behaviors that communicate to a student the message, "You are a better, more loved person because you have succeeded or behaved as someone else wants you to behave." Similarly, the withholding of love and displays of disrespect following off-task behaviors may briefly serve as a punishment, but, in time, the use of such tactics becomes destructive punishment.

In order to understand why using love and respect as a reward is a destructive positive reinforcer that should be avoided, as should the destructive punishment of withdrawing love and respect, consider the following generalizations: (1) The acquisition and maintenance of love and esteem is one of social man's more basic and compelling drives (Maslow, 1962); (2) Different students achieve learning goals at differing rates and to different degrees (Anderson, 1976; Corno & Snow, 1986). When students are led to believe that the more successful among them will be loved and respected more than the less successful, their ego defense mechanisms will not allow them to participate in what seems to be a game with excessively high stakes and few winners (Lessinger, 1970). Why should anyone other than the more highly apt students be willing to jeopardize his or her self-esteem in a competition in which she or he cannot be best? Students who believe that they are worth less in the eyes of others when they are less than successful in school-related activities are very defensive about engaging in school-related activities. Such defensiveness precludes the attitude of open cooperation that you would like to prevail in your classroom. Here are three examples to illustrate the problem:

> Ms. Davilio would like to find out just how well each of her Spanish-language students has achieved the learning objectives on an instructional unit. A knowledge of how well each has achieved will help Ms. Davilio make wiser decisions regarding what should be retaught, what new objectives should be established, and who needs help with what. Like most teachers, Ms. Davilio uses tests to help her assess student achievement. However, she has difficulty obtaining valid test information on her students' levels of achievement because many of them feel that their personal prestige and Ms. Davilio's fondness for them are tied to their test scores. Consequently, some of these students display such anxiety when taking tests that their scores do not accurately indicate their levels of achievement. Other students do not put forth the effort they should to prepare for tests because, consciously or unconsciously, they do not want to risk "losing face" by trying and failing. There are even other students who attempt to deceive Ms. Davilio into believing that they have achieved more than they actually have by either faking their way through test questions or by directly cheating.

> Maunsell believes that his self-worth depends on his achievements. In time, he begins to resent Mr. Iverson and other teachers who seem to be continually judging him (whereas in reality some of those teachers were only judging Maunsell's achievement, not Maunsell himself). While using Socratic methods for one learning activity, Mr. Iverson asks Maunsell a question. Maunsell suddenly snaps, "Pick on somebody else; you're always trying to make me look bad."

> Ms. Whalen assigns homework to her chemistry class in which students are to attempt to balance some equations. Theresa attempts the problems at home and finds that she has difficulty solving them. Rather than return to school without the equations properly balanced, she feigns illness and does not attend school when the assignment is due. She prefers to miss class and not achieve the objective than to face what she perceives to be a potentially embarrassing situation.

## Disassociating Self-Respect from Achievement

Students would be much less defensive and, therefore, more likely to cooperate if adults did not give them the idea that they risk their self-respect whenever they undertake tasks or are expected to behave in a prescribed manner. The destructive message from an authority figure that leads to student defensiveness is: "I love and respect you when you are successful (or behave properly)." Or in other words, "I do not love and respect you when you are unsuccessful (or misbehave)."

You can mollify a student's defensiveness by communicating: "I am happy when you are successful (or behave properly) because I love and respect you." Or in other words, "I am unhappy when you are unsuccessful (or misbehave) because I love and respect you."

It is not easy for you or any other teacher to effectively communicate that a teacher's job involves judging behaviors and achievement exhibited by students, and that it does not involve judging students themselves. Chapter 4 of this book is designed to help you develop a particular style for communicating with students that, when consistently practiced, eventually breaks through defensive student attitudes and leads to the type of classroom climate where students feel free to enthusiastically cooperate and engage in learning activities. Through appropriate communication techniques, you can: (1) Avoid the characterizations and labeling (e.g., "smart," "dumb," "bright," "slow," and "good") that lead students to be defensive about engaging in learning activities; (2) Gain students' trust so that they understand that they are not gambling with their self-esteem by cooperating with you and engaging in the learning activities you plan; (3) Avoid the resentment and power struggles that occur as a consequence of students feeling embarrassed in the classroom.

## Self-Assessment for Chapter 3

I. Write one paragraph suggesting how the incident described below might influence, both positively and negatively, the businesslike atmosphere of Ms. Schott's class:

> While conducting a questioning strategy session with her class, Ms. Schott notices Ms. Byung-Lee, the school principal, beckoning her to the doorway of the classroom. Ms. Schott calls a halt to the learning activity by telling her class, "Excuse me, class, but I have some business with Ms. Byung-Lee. We'll finish up shortly. While I'm busy, please confine your talk to whispers." After six minutes in which Ms. Schott and Ms. Byung-Lee confer at the doorway, Ms. Schott directs the class, "Okay, now let's get back. . . ."

II. Write two paragraphs explaining why the beginning of a new school year presents a teacher with an especially opportune time for establishing a classroom climate that is conducive to on-task behaviors.

III. Imagine yourself as a teacher about to begin a school year. Answer questions 1 through 9 from Mr. Martin's list on pages 55–56.

IV. Develop a lesson plan for one day in the first week of a school year that fits Mr. Martin's three reminders that appear on pages 56–57. The lesson plan should be one that you could possibly apply within your teaching specialty (e.g., elementary school reading or secondary school physical education).

V. Use two paragraphs to explain why you agree or disagree with the following statement: "The harder a teacher works within the fourth stage of the Teaching Process Model, the less that teacher will have to work within the fifth stage to make learning activities effective."

VI. Think of a teacher you once had who used an inefficient method of taking roll. Think of a second teacher you had who took roll more efficiently. In a paragraph, describe how each took the roll.

VII. List some of the difficulties a teacher makes for himself or herself by taking an unnecessary amount of class time to distribute materials.

VIII. List some of the advantages, relative to keeping students on-task, of directing students into learning activities using ways other than personally speaking to the entire class at once.

IX. Describe two examples in which a teacher uses some sort of audio-visual device (e.g., a chalkboard or videocassette recorder) in communicating information to students during a learning activity. Write the second example so that the teacher's choice of audio-visual device results in a more efficient use of students' time than the choice of audio-visual device in the first example.

X. Write a paragraph explaining how intra-class grouping can sometimes be used to reduce transition time.

XI. Describe an example in which students in a classroom complete an assignment at differing times. Devise and describe a plan for that teacher to use so that students who finish the assignment before others are kept busy with productive activities.

XII. Carlotta is a student who feels more loved after scoring high on tests than she does after scoring low. Explain why such a feeling may eventually discourage Carlotta from enthusiastically engaging in learning activities.

*Reviewing Your Self-Assessment* _____

It would be extremely helpful to your understanding of the topics of Chapter 3 for you to compare your responses to each of the 12 items in the exercise to those of other persons. Discuss with them the similarities and differences among your answers.

## Supplemental Readings

Bowman, R. (1983). Effective classroom management: A primer for practicing professionals. *The Clearing House, 57,* 116–118.

Boynton, P., Di Geronimo, J., & Gustafson, G. (1985). A basic survival guide for new teachers. *The Clearing House, 59,* 101–103.

Cangelosi, J. S. (1986). *Cooperation in the classroom: Students and teachers together* (pp. 13–19). Washington, DC: National Education Association.

Emmer, E. T., Evertson, C. M., & Anderson, L. M. (1980). Effective classroom management at the beginning of the school year. *Elementary School Journal, 80,* 219–231.

Emmer, E. T., Evertson, C. M., Sanford, J. P., Clements, B. S., & Worsham, M. E. (1984). *Classroom Management for Secondary Teachers* (pp. 69–88). Englewood Cliffs, NJ: Prentice-Hall.

Evertson, C. M., Emmer, E. T., Clements, B. S., Sanford, J. P., & Worsham, M. E. (1984). *Classroom Management for Elementary Teachers* (pp. 65–85). Englewood Cliffs, NJ: Prentice-Hall.

Ginott, H. (1972). *Teacher and Child* (pp. 123–144). New York: Macmillan.

Jones, V. F., & Jones, L. S. (1986). *Comprehensive classroom management: Creating positive learning environments* (2nd ed.), (pp. 31–55). Boston: Allyn & Bacon.

McLemore, W. P. (1981). The ABC's of classroom discipline. *The Clearing House, 52,* 205–206.

Morales, C. A. (1978). Discipline: Applicable techniques for student teachers. *Education, 101,* 122–124.

Petreshene, S. (1986, September). Management made easy. *Instructor, XCVI,* No. 2, 70–74.

Petreshene, S. (1986, October). What can you do in 10 minutes? Transition activities that make kids think! *Instructor, XCVI,* No. 3, 68–70.

Rogers, J. F. (1985). Promoting self-discipline: A comprehensive approach. *Theory Into Practice, 24,* 271–276.

# 4

# Communicating with Students

Chapter 4 is designed to help you:

1. develop a descriptive, rather than judgmental, language style in communications with your students so that you: (a) Avoid the characterizations and labeling that lead students to be defensive about engaging in learning activities; (b) Gain students' trust so that they understand that they are not gambling with their self-esteem by cooperating with you and engaging in the learning activities you plan; (c) Avoid the resentment and power struggles that occur as a consequence of students feeling embarrassed in the classroom.
2. understand how to carefully select what to say and when to say it, utilize body language, utilize active listening techniques, and utilize supportive replies so that your students will choose to pay attention to you when you speak.
3. avoid communicating unintended messages that lead your students to misunderstand how you expect them to behave.
4. leave no doubt in your students' minds that each person is responsible for his or her own conduct.
5. emphasize formative, rather than summative, evaluations when communicating with students and parents about students' achievement of learning goals.
6. recognize that the level of professionalism you display in your communications with and about students influences the trust and confidence students have in you.

# USING DESCRIPTIVE RATHER THAN JUDGMENTAL LANGUAGE

## Differences Between Descriptive and Judgmental Language

Research studies indicate that students feel less threatened, less defensive, and more willing to engage in learning activities when working with teachers who consistently use descriptive language than they are when working with teachers who use a more judgmental language style (Van Horn, 1982). *Descriptive language* verbally portrays a situation, a behavior, an achievement, or a feeling. *Judgmental language* verbally summarizes an evaluation of a behavior, achievement, or person with a characterization or label. Judgmental language that focuses on personalities is particularly detrimental to a climate of cooperation (Ginott, 1972).

Teachers use descriptive language in the following two examples:

> Four-year-old Justin shows one of his paintings to Ms. Maeger who exclaims, "The greens and browns in your painting make me think of being outside in a forest!"

> Mr. Zelezak turns to Joe, who has just interrupted Katrina while she was making a comment, and says, "I cannot concentrate on what Katrina is saying while you are talking."

Here are examples of teachers using judgmental language:

> Four-year-old Caroline shows one of her paintings to Ms. Murphy who exclaims, "Why, Caroline, that's a beautiful picture! You are quite a great artist!"

> Ms. Gordon turns to Mindy, who has just interrupted Greg while he was making a comment, and says, "You are very rude for interrupting Greg!"

## The Consequences of Judgmental Language

In order to consistently use a descriptive language style, you must resist even silent thoughts that characterize students with labels such as, "smart," "slow," "good reader," "well behaved," "problem child," "honest," "intelligent," and "underachiever," and the paradoxical "overachiever" (Cangelosi, 1982). Instead of thinking of students according to labels, you should focus on learning tasks, circumstances, and situations.

Ms. Johnson is a fifth grade teacher who fails to separate her judgments about what students do and accomplish from her judgments of students themselves:

Upon returning one of her student's science test papers with a high score, Ms. Johnson remarked, "Whitney, you really proved that you are a good student!" Whitney feels proud as he accepts the paper, but he becomes nervous later when he thinks, "Ms. Johnson won't think I'm a good student if I don't do well on the next test!" Another student with a low test score, who heard Ms. Johnson characterize Whitney as a good student because of his high test score, thinks, "Since I had a low test score, she must think I'm a bad student!"

While orally giving directions to her class, Ms. Johnson notices Ursala talking to a neighbor instead of paying attention. Ms. Johnson tells her, "Ursala, you're always talking when you shouldn't! Why are you such a pain?" Ursala begins to feel uncomfortable in Ms. Johnson's presence as she now believes that Ms. Johnson has little respect for her. Ms. Johnson continues to respond to Ursala's displays of disruptive behaviors with judgmental language. In time, Ursala develops a disruptive behavior pattern as she lives up to what she perceives to be Ms. Johnson's expectations (Rosenthal & Jacobsen, 1968).

In a parent–teacher conference, Ms. Johnson tells Leo's father, "Leo is quite bright, but he tends to be lazy."

## Avoiding Labels

By consistently following their successes with ego builders and following their failures with attacks on their personalities, Ms. Johnson confirms in the minds of her students the belief that personal self-worth depends on success. Even those students who do not care about Ms. Johnson's opinions are impacted by the constant association between achievement levels and character judgments.

Mr. Ramirez is a fifth grade teacher who distinguishes between a student's accomplishments and the value of that student. He does not view a student's display of off-task behavior as a reflection of character flaws. Mr. Ramirez believes that he is responsible for teaching each student to be on-task and to achieve learning goals. He does not include judgment of students' characters among his responsibilities. Following are three examples in which Mr. Ramirez uses descriptive language that helps students realize that he focuses on learning tasks, not on personalities:

Upon returning one of his student's science test papers with a high score, Mr. Ramirez remarks, "Mickey, this paper indicates that you understand the dependence of animal respiration on plant respiration."

While orally giving directions to his class, Mr. Ramirez notices Mary Frances talking to a neighbor instead of paying attention. Mr. Ramirez tells her, "Mary Frances, I would like for you to stop talking and listen to these directions."

In a parent–teacher conference, Mr. Ramirez tells Nettie's father, "Nettie grasped the idea of multiplication right away. However, she does not have all of the multiplication facts memorized because she sometimes does not take the time to complete the drills that I assign in class."

Mr. Ramirez makes a concerted effort to use language that addresses specifically what has or has not been achieved, specific behaviors he expects students to exhibit, and specific behaviors that are unacceptable. He avoids implications that label or characterize personalities. Mr. Ramirez does not hesitate in communicating his feelings about specific behaviors or achievements of students; however, he never allows those feelings to influence the degree to which he respects, cares for, and values students.

## The Fallacy of Labels

Because a student does not comprehend the messages from several readings does not necessarily imply that the student is a "slow learner" or "poor reader." It only means that the student did not comprehend the messages from those readings. The lack of comprehension might stem from a lack of interest in the contents of those readings, from thought patterns that tend to diverge from those of the authors of the readings, from misconceptions regarding the contents of those readings, or from myriad other reasons that do not fall under a general label such as "poor reader." If, however, the student acquires the idea that she or he is a poor reader, then the student is less likely to enthusiastically engage in reading even when he or she is interested in the content, has no misconceptions to overcome, does not think divergently from the author, and suffers no other interferences specific to that particular reading selection. Rather than blaming the lack of reading comprehension on the "poor reader" label, the teacher should focus on a design for helping the student become engaged in learning activities that improve the students' reading comprehension skills.

Because a student readily grasps what is generally a difficult-to-grasp scientific concept does not necessarily imply that the student is especially "bright" or has a "scientific mind." It only means that the student has a grasp of that particular difficult scientific concept. To label such a student "scientifically minded" is to ask her or him to live up to someone else's image and to encourage elitism. To label such a student "bright" is to unwittingly label those who do not grasp the concept "dull" (Cangelosi, 1986).

A student who is misbehaving is not a behavior problem; the misbehavior, not the student, is the problem. The distinction may seem trivial. As a teacher, however, it makes a difference as to whether you perceive the problem to be the behavior or the student. Students who perceive themselves as "behavior problems" cannot do away with the problem without doing away with themselves. Unless such students resort to suicide, they tend to protect themselves by wearing their "behavior problem" label with pride. On the other hand, students who learn that they are "okay" (Harris, 1969), but that they display certain behaviors that are problems, may be willing to alter those behaviors.

## TEACHING STUDENTS TO LISTEN TO YOU

### The Richness of Descriptive Language

Descriptive language is richer in information than is judgmental language. In the next two examples, Mr. Allred's comment is descriptive; Ms. Mustaphos' comment is judgmental. Which comment is more informative to students?

> Mr. Allred and his second graders have just returned to their classroom from the schoolyard where they conducted an experiment on erosion. He announces to the class, "After we finished the experiment, it only took us four minutes to collect our equipment and return to our places here in the room. We didn't disturb any other classes during that time. We will go outside again tomorrow, and conduct an experiment with water."

> Ms. Mustaphos and her second graders have just returned to their classroom from the schoolyard where they conducted an experiment on erosion. She announces to the class, "You are such good boys and girls! I'm so proud of you! Next time we do something like this, I know you'll be just as cooperative."

By listening to Mr. Allred, students gained specific knowledge about what they did and would be doing. They were able to associate how their specific behaviors (e.g., taking only 4 minutes to get situated) impact future plans and opportunities (e.g., they will get to perform another experiment outside the next day). By listening to Ms. Mustaphos, students only found out that their teacher was pleased with them. That is surely important, but Ms. Mustaphos' message did not tell them anything they didn't already know. Hopefully, students already know they are "good." Ms. Mustaphos can't really know that they will be just as cooperative next time, so why did she say that? Was that her attempt to improve the chances that they would be cooperative next time? If so, there was a hint of dishonesty in her statement. Students don't care to listen to teachers who are not being forthright.

### The Judicious Use of Words

In general, students are likely to pay attention to what you say if they have learned that, whenever you speak, you really have something to say. By judiciously using words that inform and by avoiding inane talk, you leave your students with the idea that they miss something by not hearing you when you speak to them.

Unfortunately, students readily learn to be deaf to many teachers because the majority of them are frequently exposed to meaningless talk from adults. The adult talk in the next two examples is all too typical:

> Five-year-old Holly is sitting down drinking a glass of milk. Her father sees her and says, "Don't spill your milk."

Holly's father's words neither taught nor reminded Holly that milk is not to be spilled. She was drinking her milk with no intention of spilling it. She already knew that milk spilling is not allowed. Her father's words taught Holly that he sometimes says uninformative things and that she does not always need to pay attention to him. If, on the other hand, Holly's father noticed her being careless with the milk by swinging the glass around with one hand, he might have said, "Holly, don't you think it would be safer to hold that glass with two hands?" Those words acknowledge that Holly already knows that milk should not be spilled and help her to think of ways to prevent spilling.

> Joshua is working on an individual assignment in Mr. Green's psychology class when he gets up and begins walking across the room. Mr. Green sees him and says, "Joshua, don't get up."

By the time Mr. Green told Joshua not to get up, he was already up and walking. At that time, it was possible for Joshua to sit down, but was impossible for him to have never stood up. Mr. Green was unwittingly teaching Joshua to not pay attention to him by giving a command that he could not possibly obey. Mr. Green could have told Joshua to return to his place. Rather than immediately reacting with the first words that come to mind, it is usually wise for a teacher to pause and carefully frame words before speaking to students.

## Thinking Before Talking

Often, adults send inane messages to children because they react before becoming aware of some relevant circumstances. Here is an example:

> As three-year-old Amanda goes to bed her mother tells her, "Now, don't get up! You stay in bed." Several minutes later, Amanda's mother sees her out of bed and in the hall. She exclaims to Amanda, "I thought I told you to stay in bed! Get back to bed this instant!" Amanda: "But Momma, I have to make pee-pee!" Mother: "Okay, go to the bathroom and then get back to bed."

Had Amanda's mother first observed where Amanda was going before ordering her back to bed, she might have avoided that unnecessary exchange. Over time, Amanda might have learned to better attend to her mother's talk if the circumstances under which she is allowed to get out of bed (e.g., having to go to the bathroom) were initially clarified.

> Mr. Prenn directs his fourth grade class to silently read pages 17 through 21. He notices Maureen talking to Walt and says, "Maureen, this is supposed to be silent reading. You know you're not to be talking." Maureen replies, "I'm sorry, but I was just telling him the page number." Mr. Prenn: "Then that's okay."

Exchanges such as the one between Maureen and Mr. Prenn cannot always be avoided. However, if they become common occurrences, they condition students to ignore listening to what a teacher is saying. If Maureen was only telling Walt the page numbers, the talking would have self-terminated without Mr. Prenn's intervention. Had he first waited to see if the talk would quickly stop, he could have avoided the exchange of useless words.

Sometimes, teachers and other adults teach students to be "deaf" to them by acting as if they are terminating a self-terminating behavior. Here is one example:

> Peabody Junior High teachers are expected to stand in their doorways to enforce hall rules which include "no running." Mr. Adams notices Carol and Mark running toward the room across the hall from his door. Just as the two students get to their room, they hear Mr. Adams yell, "Stop that running!" They were about to stop running, not because of what Mr. Adams yelled, but because they were at their destination.

The aforementioned incident was relatively harmless, but a more positive impact on how well students listen to Mr. Adams could have been realized had he either said nothing about the running or acted decisively to prevent such running from recurring. Mr. Adams's words only served to remind the students that adults say a lot of meaningless things.

Why are adults sometimes so unthinking in their use of language? If they understood their reasons, they might learn to be more careful in their use of words. Here is a hypothesis as to why Mr. Adams chose such an ineffectual approach that may ultimately lead students to ignore his words:

> From his location in his classroom doorway with a hall crowded with students, Mr. Adams is really not in an advantageous position to enforce the hall rules. If he leaves his post to effectively deal with Carol's and Mark's running, he no longer will be serving as a reminder to the scores of other students in the hallway to follow the rules. He realizes that his mere

presence is a cue to many students. Mr. Adams may not really find Carol's and Mark's running offensive enough for him to exert enough time and energy to deal with it effectively. They were only running, not fighting. On the other hand, he doesn't simply ignore the self-terminating running because he feels obliged to announce to anyone in earshot that he is doing his duty. If Carol and Mark collide with something and injuries result, he can at least say, "I told them to stop running."

## More and More Useless Words

Students also begin to learn to ignore teacher talk when teachers act as if they are initiating a self-initiating behavior. For example:

> Mr. Chapman's fourth graders eagerly begin working on a learning activity he has just explained to them. He then says, "Okay, get to work."

The unnecessary words that interrupted their engagement lead Mr. Chapman's students to place less importance on what he says. As a teacher, you should limit what you say to only what you intend to be heard.

Students may begin tuning a teacher out when that teacher makes judgments that only the students can make. Ms. White makes judgments for her students in the following example:

> Ms. White is introducing a learning activity to her fifth graders. She says, "You're going to love this! This'll be more fun than what we've been doing! You won't want to stop after we begin to. . . ."

How long will Ms. White go on? Whether or not the students will enjoy the activity, find it fun, or will want to stop is something for them to individually judge for themselves. Probably some will enjoy the activity, while others won't. Shouldn't Ms. White get on with the directions and quit trying to sell the activity to them? If the activity is truly enjoyable for the students, they will find this out when she stops talking and they become engaged. If Ms. White thinks *she* will enjoy the activity, she should quickly pass that information to the students by telling them, "I'm going to enjoy this; I hope you will also." The students would probably like to know how she feels. But she only wasted time and words by trying to inform them of their own feelings.

## Speaking Only to Intended Listeners

> Mr. Brunoski is sitting at his desk as his business law students silently read the passages from the text that he assigned. Mr. Brunoski notices that Ali is doing his chemistry homework instead. From his place at the front of

the room, Mr. Brunoski says, "What do you think you're doing, Ali?" Ali: "I wasn't doing anything!" Mr. Brunoski: "Well, you sure weren't reading your business law! Put that stuff away, before I confiscate it. Do the reading like everybody else." Ali: "Yes, sir."

Ali needed to be engaged in the reading and that was the message that *he,* not the others in class, needed to hear from Mr. Brunoski. Shirley, for example, stopped reading her assignment when Mr. Brunoski spoke out. She then had to wait for the exchange between Mr. Brunoski and Ali to cease before becoming re-engaged. Students other than Ali had to either ignore what Mr. Brunoski said or become disengaged in the learning activity. Had Mr. Brunoski dealt with the situation similar to Ms. Lowe's handling of the following one, students would be more inclined to listen to him in the future:

> Ms. Lowe is sitting at her desk as her business law students silently read passages from the text that she assigned. Ms. Lowe notices that Woody is doing chemistry homework instead. Ms. Lowe walks over to Woody, squats down directly in front of him, and makes eye contact with him. She whispers, "Woody, it is time for you to be reading from your business law text." She stands, pivots, and returns to her desk as Woody puts away the chemistry homework and appears to read the business law text.

Ms. Lowe made it clear that what she had to say was meant only for Woody. Other students didn't need to stop their work to find out that Ms. Lowe's message didn't apply to them. Ms. Lowe doesn't speak to the entire class unless she expects all of them to listen. Her students are conditioned to stop and listen when she addresses them because they haven't had to block out her voice when her message was for someone else.

## Body Language

In the example, Ms. Lowe effectively used body language to let her class know to whom she was speaking and to gain Woody's attention before speaking. As Jones (1979) and other researchers have discovered, how you position your body when speaking to students has a major impact on what messages students receive. Because Ms. Lowe got out of her seat, got near Woody, and spoke to him shoulder to shoulder and eye to eye, Woody was likely to listen to Ms. Lowe and realize that she meant business.

Teachers sometimes make the mistake of saying one thing to students, but communicating another as a consequence of their body language. Here is an example:

> At the chalkboard, Ms. Nagle is writing some sentences that she has directed her students to classify as either simple or compound. As she

writes with her back to the class, she is disturbed by loud talking from the class. "No more talking!" she says without pausing from her writing task. The students quit talking momentarily, but soon the noise level increases again. Continuing to write, but now looking over her shoulder toward the class she shouts, "I've had it with all this noise! I said, 'No more talking!'"

Ms. Nagle's students don't really take what she said very seriously. Her voice provides a hint of stress and indicates to them that she is not really in control. Her body language indicates that she is willing to continue with the learning activity although she hasn't obtained their cooperation. Because she doesn't bother to face them and command their attention, many of them don't attend to her demand that there be "no more talking." Do you think Ms. Terrell, in the following example, will have more success in getting her students to follow her directions than did Ms. Nagle?

At the chalkboard, Ms. Terrell is writing some sentences that she has directed her students to classify as either simple or compound. As she writes with her back to the class, she is disturbed by loud talking from the class. Ms. Terrell puts the chalk down on the chalk tray, pivots, and directly faces the class. She pans her eyes across the class, making eye contact with one student and then another. Momentarily, she feels they are ready to listen and she says, "The talking is disturbing me and those of you who are trying to analyze these sentences." She pauses and observes them briefly before turning around to continue with the task at hand.

## Speaking Only to the Attentive

Ms. Terrell obtained her students' attention *before* trying to speak to them. Here is a rule for you, as a teacher, to follow: *Speak to people only when they are ready to listen.* Sometimes, students may not be ready to listen to you because they do not think you understand them well enough to tell them anything that they would consider important. In other cases, they may be preoccupied by thoughts with which they must dispense before attending to your message.

## LISTENING TO STUDENTS

You effectively communicate with students, not only by sending them messages, but also by receiving their messages. Students will become bored with your monologues sooner than they will with verbal interchanges with you. They are more likely to be attentive to what you are saying when you say it within a conversation with them rather than as part of a speech to which they are expected to listen passively.

Listening to students, observing their actions, and reading what they write are opportunities for you to learn what they think, believe, feel, know, understand, misunderstand, value, are willing to try, and are unwilling to try. A reasonably accurate understanding of your students' thoughts and attitudes is vital to your ability to identify students' needs, decide learning goals, design learning activities, and evaluate how well learning goals are achieved. You also need to understand students' thoughts and attitudes in order to decide what messages you should communicate and when and how each message should be communicated. By listening to them, you will discover how to get students to listen to you. Consider the following two contrasting examples:

Except for Billy, Ms. Lye's kindergarten students are following her directions by putting away the math manipulatives with which they've been working and by gathering around her in the reading corner to hear a story. Billy has just thrown himself on the floor and is screaming, "I'm hungry! I wanna eat my candy!" Ms. Lye goes over to Billy who is now yelling and crying incoherently. He flails his arms and legs and seems out of control. Ms. Lye grabs him and says, "Stop that, Billy! Get hold of yourself. What's the matter with you anyway?" Billy continues crying and unintelligibly screaming something about "candy." Ms. Lye is on her knees with Billy. Speaking loudly to be heard above the screams, she says, "That's enough! You know you can't have any candy right now! You haven't even had lunch yet! Please calm down. I know you will like this story; you can sit on my lap while I read it." Billy doesn't even hear her as he continues the tantrum.

Except for Lois, Ms. Medlyn's kindergarten students are following her directions by putting away the math manipulatives with which they've been working and by gathering around her in the reading corner to hear a story. Lois has just thrown herself on the floor and is screaming, "I'm hungry! I wanna eat my candy!" Ms. Medlyn goes over to Lois who is now yelling and crying incoherently. She flails her arms and legs and seems out of control. Ms. Medlyn gets down on her knees and gently, but firmly, takes Lois by the shoulders and turns her so that the two are face to face. Without speaking, Ms. Medlyn observes and listens for some indications of what's on Lois' mind. Soon, she catches the word "candy" among all the sounds emanating from Lois. Speaking loudly, calmly, and distinctly and maintaining direct eye contact, Ms. Medlyn says, "You may have some candy. Do you want candy?" Hearing the word "candy" seems to strike a chord with Lois and she momentarily gains a semblance of composure. Ms. Medlyn seizes the opportunity to say, "As soon as you get control of yourself, we will talk about getting some candy." "But, I want my candy!" Lois says as she again starts to get upset. "Oh! You have some candy? Where is your candy now?" Lois: "I left it." Ms. Medlyn: "You left it where?" Lois: "I don't know." Ms. Medlyn: "May I help you find it?"

Lois is now relatively calm as she answers, "Yes." "Okay, I will. You put away your math things and after I finish reading the story, we'll talk about finding your candy."

Lois was too upset to follow Ms. Medlyn's initial directions to the class. However, because Ms. Medlyn actively listened to Lois' seemingly incoherent communications, she was able to detect a key to obtaining Lois' attention. By saying something that Lois wanted to hear, Ms. Medlyn was able to help Lois be calm enough to hear what Ms. Medlyn had to say. Ms. Medlyn did not try to get her own message across (i.e., put math materials away and prepare for the story) until Lois was able to receive that message. Please note that Ms. Medlyn never promised Lois anything she was not prepared to deliver. When, in order to get Lois' attention, she said, "You may have some *candy*," she was not telling Lois that she would give her candy or that Lois could eat candy before the math materials were put away, the story was heard, and lunch was eaten.

## USING SUPPORTIVE REPLIES

### Accepting Feelings

Ms. Leonard is walking among her algebra students as they individually work on factoring polynomials. Paul tells her as she passes near his desk, "I can't figure these out! They're just too hard for me." Ms. Leonard replies, "Paul, these should be a piece of cake for a smart guy like you! Just do them like the example we did on the board. They're really simple. Let me show you. First, begin by. . . ."

Ms. Leonard tried to encourage Paul and help him build his confidence. What impact do you think her response had on Paul's thinking? Ms. Leonard's response denied Paul's feelings. He said the problems were hard; she said they were simple. She indicated that such problems were easy for smart people like him. Will he conclude that he is dumb? Will he conclude that when Ms. Leonard discovers that he can't do them, and is therefore not smart, she will no longer like and respect him? As Ms. Leonard tries to explain the algebraic process to Paul, he may not attentively listen because he feels she didn't hear him. In his mind, Ms. Leonard doesn't understand the difficulty and frustration he is experiencing. Ms. Leonard's response to Paul's expression of frustration was an example of a *nonsupportive response* because the response did not indicate that the listener (e.g., Ms. Leonard) understood and accepted the feelings of the speaker (e.g., Paul). Expressions of feelings receive a *supportive response* when the listener indicates that the expression has been understood and accepted (Gordon, 1974; Rogers, 1969).

## Relieving Frustration

Ms. Palcic uses a supportive response in the following example:

> Ms. Palcic is walking among her algebra students as they individually work on factoring polynomials. Bruce tells her as she passes near his desk, "I can't figure these out! They're just too hard for me." Ms. Palcic replies, "Factoring polynomials can really be difficult. I see that you're having trouble with these. Read this number five to me. . . ."

Before trying to help Bruce with the factoring problems, Ms. Palcic let him know that she understood what he was going through and that he was perfectly fine, although he was experiencing difficulties with the problems. Frustration can be quite incapacitating and sometimes a person must relieve his or her frustration before addressing the source of the frustration. Having another person's empathy can sometimes serve to relieve frustration. Here are two contrasting examples that may be familiar to many married couples:

> Theresa tells her husband, "I feel so tied down! The children have been off-the-wall all day long and I'm just sick of being with them!" "Oh, come on! You know you love those kids," replies her husband. Theresa: "I never get a chance to get away from them and be with other adults." Her husband: "Now, didn't I take you out to dinner Tuesday? And Saturday, I'll stay home so you can go out and do whatever you like. You'll feel better."

> Eva tells her husband, "I feel so tied down! The children have been off-the-wall all day long and I'm just sick of being with them. I never get a chance to get away from them and be with other adults." Her husband: "I don't know how you manage to do what you do all day. I got a taste of what you're talking about last Saturday, and you are putting up with it practically everyday!"

Eva's husband's reply was supportive. He let Eva know that he heard her, and it was okay to feel as she did. Theresa's husband, with his non-supportive reply, found flaws in Theresa's statement and attempted to propose a solution to the problem before indicating that he understood the problem. Theresa, like Eva, needed understanding and the knowledge that her husband did not think less of her for feeling the way she did.

Here are two contrasting examples that are especially common.

## Defusing Conflict

In the first example that follows, the parent uses a nonsupportive response, while the parent's response in the second is supportive.

Mr. Drake is driving his four-year-old daughter, Krisilen, home from school when they approach an ice cream shop. Krisilen: "I want some ice cream! I want some ice cream!" Mr. Drake: "No you don't! You haven't had your supper, and you never have sweets before supper." Krisilen: "Momma let me have some gum before supper one time!" Mr. Drake: "Don't argue with me; you're not getting any!" They drive past the ice cream shop, but Krisilen continues to mutter, "I *do* want it."

Mr. Fisher is driving his four-year-old daughter, Allison, home from school when they approach an ice cream shop. Allison: "I want some ice cream! I want some ice cream!" Mr. Fisher: "Yes, I bet you do. Ice cream would really taste good right now! It's too bad we haven't had supper yet." They drive past the ice cream shop. Allison: "Can I watch 'Sesame Street' when we get home?"

Both Krisilen and Allison simply expressed a desire for ice cream. Neither actually asked for it. In his supportive reply, Allison's Dad acknowledged that Allison wanted ice cream before he reminded Allison of the rule. Instead of recognizing her desire for ice cream, Mr. Drake argued with Krisilen and perpetuated a conflict that need not continue. By acknowledging students' feelings with supportive replies, you can often avoid arguments and dispense with excuses for not being on-task. In the first of the next two examples, Mr. Layton's nonsupportive reply leads to a useless argument. In the second example, Ms. Malone's supportive reply avoids an argument while clearly communicating an expectation.

Adrian to Mr. Layton, his physical education teacher: "Do I have to dress out today? I feel so stupid in these baggy gym shorts. My legs are too skinny!" Mr. Layton: "Why, Adrian, you look good in shorts. You have nice legs. Of course you want to dress out! Do you want to mess up your regular clothes?" Adrian: "I don't have nice legs!" Mr. Layton: "They're not skinny by any means." Adrian: "I don't mind messing up my clothes."

Frank to Ms. Malone, his physical education teacher: "Do I have to dress out today? I feel so stupid in these baggy gym shorts. My legs are too skinny!" Ms. Malone: "You don't like the way you look in those gym shorts? I wish I didn't have to wear these shorts either. Better hurry and get dressed; we're starting volleyball on time today."

## AVOIDING UNINTENDED MESSAGES

### The Risk of Misinterpretation

As a teacher, you deal with many students at once. Because of this, the interpretations some students make of what you say and what you do are likely to differ from those of other students. Obviously, you are continually risking being misinterpreted. Unintended messages, unwittingly communicated to students by teachers, can cause many of the misunderstandings about expectations that lead students to be off-task. Miscommunicating with your students cannot be completely avoided. However, you can reduce the frequency with which you send unintended messages to students by: (1) modeling a businesslike attitude; (2) avoiding disrupting your own learning activities; (3) avoiding destructive positive reinforcers; (4) avoiding destructive punishments.

Here is an example of a teacher failing to display an adequate businesslike attitude with her students and consequently sending the message that engagement in learning activities does not hold highest priority:

> Ms. Coonley is conducting a lecture-discussion for her eleventh grade health science class when her principal, Ms. Rodriguez, appears in the classroom doorway and beckons Ms. Coonley to her. Ms. Coonley tells her class, "Excuse me, I have some business with Ms. Rodriguez. Please be quiet until I'm through." Ms. Rodriguez then engages Ms. Coonley in a 9-minute conversation about a meeting to be held that night. In the meantime, the students' thoughts turn to other things beside the contents of the health science lecture-discussion. When Ms. Rodriguez leaves, Ms. Coonley turns to her class and says, "Okay, let's get back to our discussion. Where were we?"

## Modeling a Businesslike Attitude

In the following example, Mr. Chenier's businesslike attitude tends to convince students that what goes on in class is of primary importance:

> Mr. Chenier is conducting a lecture-discussion for his eleventh grade health science class when his principal, Ms. Meador, appears in the classroom doorway and beckons Mr. Chenier to her. Mr. Chenier turns to Ms. Meador and says, "Just a moment, Ms. Meador, Phil is just responding to a comment about the sensibility of taking decongestants." Phil takes about 30 seconds for his response while Mr. Chenier listens intently. Mr. Chenier: "Class, keep Phil's thought in mind while I quickly check with Ms. Meador." Ms. Meador then tries to involve Mr. Chenier in a conversation about a meeting that night, but Mr. Chenier instead uses 40 seconds to arrange to speak with her at another time. Mr. Chenier apologizes to the class for the interruption and the class continues. The students had little time to have their thoughts drift from the topic.

## Avoiding Disruptive Teacher Behavior

Teachers fail to model businesslike attitudes when they disrupt their own learning activities. Such disruptions carry the unintended message, "Disruptive behavior is acceptable." Consider the following two contrasting examples:

> Mr. Miller's third grade students are busy with a science assignment in which each student reads about a problem and writes out a proposal for a solution. The room is quiet when Robert and Chad begin talking to one another from their places in the back of the room. Mr. Miller, seated at his desk in the front, notices them and in a loud voice announces, "This work is supposed to be done on your own. I don't want any talking until everyone is finished. Chad and Robert, cut the talking out right now." All of Mr. Miller's students looked up and listened during Mr. Miller's announcement. Some turned to see what Chad and Robert were doing when he mentioned their names. Some continued to watch them for a while to see if they'd talk again.

> Ms. Toney's third grade students are busy with a science assignment in which each student reads about a problem and writes out a proposal for a solution. The room is quiet when Andrew and Julius begin talking to one another from their places in the back of the room. Ms. Toney quietly and discreetly walks over to them, catches their eyes and whispers in a very businesslike tone, "Get back to work." Only the students very near Andrew and Julius notice Ms. Toney's actions.

Mr. Miller disturbed his entire class and caused them to be off-task in order to help Robert and Chad back on-task. Ms. Toney, on the other hand, remembered that her task was to conduct the learning activity. Thus, she took care of the disruptive talking without becoming a disruption herself.

## Avoiding Destructive Positive Reinforcers

Please reread the section entitled "Destructive Positive Reinforcers" that appears in Chapter 2.

The side effects of destructive positive reinforcers are often unintended messages such as "Homework is unimportant" (as in the case of the Ms. Coco example from Chapter 2), or "A student is worthy of more respect for knowing an answer" (as in the Mr. Breaux example from Chapter 2). The use of positive reinforcers to encourage on-task behaviors is dealt with throughout the remainder of this text. Whenever considering a positive reinforcer, you should reflect on the possibility of side effects that may lead to unintended messages.

Please reread the section entitled "Destructive Punishment" from Chapter 2.

## Avoiding Destructive Punishment

Punishment that leads to unintended messages is destructive. Consider the following two examples:

> In class, Mr. Fabian directs Virgil, "Please read your answer for number six from the assignment." Virgil: "I didn't get to my homework." Mr. Fabian: "You didn't *get* to your homework! And why not?" Virgil: "Well, we had a basketball game last night and. . . ." Mr. Fabian: "Oh! That's right. You're a hot-shot basketball player. You're too important to do your homework. You think you'll ever make a living playing basketball?" Virgil feels embarrassed in front of his peers as Mr. Fabian continues.

> Ms. Jennings notices Vern, one of her third graders, playing with some string instead of reading the passage she just assigned. She comes up behind Vern and raps him on the head with her knuckles. Vern winces in pain. His head still hurts as he returns to the assigned reading.

The embarrassment he felt may have served to discourage Virgil from again being caught without his homework. The pain suffered by Vern may teach him not to play with string where Ms. Jennings will see him. Thus, both examples of punishment may have effectively discouraged some particular types of off-task behaviors. However, might they also be destructive because they communicated unintended messages? The embarrassment may have taught Virgil not to trust Mr. Fabian and it distracted from the businesslike atmosphere of the classroom. After all, the business at hand did not involve whether or not Virgil was a "hot-shot." Unfortunately, Ms. Jennings' actions let Vern know that violent behavior is acceptable within the confines of the classroom. Vern learned an effective, but uncivil, means for getting someone's attention and convincing another to do what you want.

The use of punishment is dealt with in Part Three of this book. Possible side effects should always be considered before punishment is selected as a means for discouraging off-task behaviors.


## BEING RESPONSIBLE
## FOR ONE'S OWN CONDUCT

Canter (1978), Dreikurs (1982), Ginott (1972), Glasser (1965), Gordon (1974), and most other purveyors of thought on classroom discipline emphasize that each and every individual is responsible and held accountable for his or her own behaviors. Except for the relatively unusual cases where one person physically accosts another, one person cannot *make* another do something. Once students realize this, they are disarmed of virtually all of their excuses for misconduct. In order to lead students to understand that only they are in control of their own conduct, you should consistently use language that is free of suggestions that one person can control another. In other words, purge your language of statements such as these: "Be careful of what you say or you'll make Mia feel bad." "He made me lose control." "You made Allen cry." "Fred, don't get Tommy into trouble." "She got me so mad." "Vernon just can't get along without Martha." "She makes me happy."

Such language should be replaced with: "Be careful of what you say or Mia may think you don't enjoy her company." "I didn't maintain control when I saw what he did." "Allen was so unhappy with what you said, that he cried." "Fred, don't encourage Tommy to do something he shouldn't." "I got so mad when I thought of what she did." "Vernon depends on Martha for help." "I'm happy to be with her."

Remind students that they control their own behaviors when they say such things as: "I did it because everybody wanted me to." "She hurt my feelings." "Make me happy."

## FORMATIVE VERSUS SUMMATIVE EVALUATIONS

### Two Reasons for Evaluating Student Achievement

What is the sixth step in the Teaching Process Model? There are two reasons why you, as a teacher, evaluate students' achievement of learning goals: (1) You need assessments of your students' progress relative to specific objectives *during* an instructional unit to help you make decisions regarding how to design learning activities, when students are ready for certain learning activities, and which learning activities should be repeated; (2) You are expected to provide periodic judgments on how well students have done as a result of instructional units that have been completed. Judgments of achievement that are made as students progress through a unit and are used for the former of the aforementioned purposes are referred to as *formative evaluations*. Judgments of achievement that are used for the latter purpose are referred to as *summative evaluations*. (Cangelosi, 1982).

Are grades on reports sent to parents a result of formative or summative evaluations? Grades result from summative evaluations. In which one of the following two examples is the teacher communicating a formative evaluation?

> Jay asks Ms. Motta, his basic chemistry teacher, "Do you think if I sign up for advanced placement chemistry, I'll do okay?" Ms. Motta: "I don't know. That's really up to you. But I am confident that you understand almost everything we've covered in basic chemistry."

Larry asks Mr. Jones, his basic chemistry teacher, "Why did you give us so many problems to work on for homework? You usually don't give half that many." Mr. Jones: "You seem to conceptualize the formulas very well, but you've been making a lot of computational errors. The only way I know for you to overcome that difficulty is to practice and practice."

Mr. Jones indicated that he used his evaluations of what Larry did and didn't do well to influence the design of a learning activity. Thus, Mr. Jones' evaluation was formative. Effective teachers design learning activities in light of ongoing, frequent formative evaluations that are regularly communicated to students (Rosenshine & Stevens, 1986). Summative evaluations occur periodically (e.g., at the end of a learning unit), but they need not occur as frequently as do formative evaluations. However, when students and their guardians think of teacher evaluations, they are nearly always thinking of the summative variety (because they're thinking of grading).

## Emphasizing Formative Evaluations

The grade consciousness that many students and their guardians display can interfere with how well teachers are able to communicate formative evaluations to students. Consider this scenario:

Mr. Wedington wants to find out exactly which steps in a long division process his fifth graders can do and on which steps he needs to provide help. To find this out, he meets with each student individually and has the student think aloud while working out a long division computation. It is Stephanie's turn to demonstrate her skill with the process. Mr. Wedington: "Stephanie, I want to watch you divide 753 by 12. Write it out here on your paper and tell me what you are thinking as you go through the steps." Stephanie writes down "12 ÷ 753" but stops and says, "I don't know the answer." Mr. Wedington: "Neither do I. But I do know *how* to find the answer. I'd like you to begin to find the answer." Stephanie: "I can't while you're watching me!" Mr. Wedington: "Why not?" Stephanie: "Because I'll make a mistake and you'll count off." Mr. Wedington: "This has nothing to do with your grade. I just want to see how you divide, so I can help you divide better." Stephanie writes "6" as a partial quotient above the "5" in "753." Quickly, she asks, "Is that right?" Mr. Wedington: "Tell me why you decided to put '6' there." Stephanie begins to erase the "6" as she exclaims, "Oh! It's not right!" Mr. Wedington gently grabs her hand and stops her from erasing her correct response. Stephanie: "Oh! We're not allowed to erase. . . ."

All Mr. Wedington wanted to do was to diagnose Stephanie's skill with long division so he would be in a better position to help. But Stephanie was so used to having teachers grade what she tries, that she just doesn't understand that Mr. Wedington is trying to help her, not grade her.

What can you do to help students overcome their defensiveness regarding being evaluated and gain the cooperation you need to conduct ongoing formative evaluations? Here are three suggestions: (1) Use descriptive rather than judgmental language; (2) Clearly distinguish for your students those relatively infrequent tests that you use to make summative evaluations from the nearly continual observations and tests used for formative evaluations; (3) Do not collect data for summative evaluations during learning activities.

Descriptive language helps convince students that you evaluate only their levels of achievement of specific learning goals and that you do not evaluate *them.*

Frequent assessments that are used to keep students apprised of their progress throughout learning units, but that do not influence their grades, help students to conceptualize, and thus cooperate in, formative evaluations. Those less frequent assessments that do influence students' grades should be distinguished as extraordinary events for which their engagements in your learning activities and formative evaluations have prepared them.

You, like many teachers, probably value student-centered learning activities in which students respond to your questions (e.g., with Socratic methods), solve problems, or have discussions. Sometimes, students are reluctant to engage in such activities because they feel they're being graded. A comment of one seventh grader is typical: "Sure, Mr. Burke says, 'We learn by our mistakes.' But when we make mistakes, he's right there to take off points!" Here are two examples of conversations that discourage students from feeling free to ask questions, try out answers, and make mistakes during learning activities:

> Byron: "Mrs. Thomas, I was surprised to get only a 'C' in sociology. My test scores weren't that bad." Ms. Thomas: "Well, I had to take into account your participation in class. You really struggled, missing a lot of questions."

> Sam: "Thanks for the 'A'." Mr. McHale: "You got it because you've been so sharp in class lately. You really do a good job of contributing to discussions."

## GRADES AS A FORM OF COMMUNICATION

Although formative evaluations should be emphasized more than summative evaluations, summative evaluations must still be periodically communicated to students and their guardians. Grades and report cards are common vehicles for such communications. Unfortunately, many teachers use grades for other purposes. Here are some examples:

> Ms. Carter bases 40 percent of her students' history grades on attendance. She believes this will motivate students to come to class.

> Mr. Albright lowers a student's reading grade by one letter for every 10 demerits the student receives during a term. A student gets demerits for exhibiting disruptive behaviors in class.

When teachers make grades directly contingent on attendance, effort, level of cooperation, or other factors different from student achievement of academic learning goals, the meaning communicated by grades is lost. Is a "B" in history an indication of how well a student has achieved the goals specified by the history course syllabus, or is the "B" a reflection of effort, willingness to cooperate with the teacher, faithfulness to assignments, or what? There are far more effective ways to motivate students to be on-task than *artificially* rewarding on-task behaviors with high grades and *artificially* punishing off-task behaviors with low grades. Specific suggestions for positively reinforcing on-task behaviors and punishing off-task behaviors, without distorting the meaning of grades, are included throughout the remainder of this text. In general, there is no need for you to artificially manipulate grades as long as you: (1) Make sure your learning activities provide students with effective means for achieving the stated learning goals; (2) The summative evaluations that you use to determine grades are based on assessments that are valid indicators of how well students achieved those same learning goals.

## COMMUNICATING WITH GUARDIANS

### Focusing on Formative Evaluations

You should, but may not always, be able to depend on help from students' guardians to help secure students' cooperation. Often, you may want to discuss formative evaluations with guardians in order to help them to understand what you're trying to get their children to accomplish and how they can help. Sometimes communications are thwarted by guardians who think all teacher evaluations are summative. In this scenario, Mr. Perkins attempts to gain Rolando's mother's cooperation; he must keep steering the conversation away from summative and toward formative evaluations.

> Mr. Perkins does not have the time to confer with guardians of his fifth graders as frequently as he would like. He does, however, maintain con-

tact by routinely phoning one or two guardians each school day. In this way, he is able to speak with a guardian of each student at least once every three weeks. It normally takes two conversations before a guardian understands that Mr. Perkins' intentions are to inform them about *what* his or her child is doing and not to either praise or criticize the student. Here is an account of Mr. Perkins' first conversation with Rolando's mother:

Mr. Perkins: "Hello, Ms. Mitchell. This is Sal Perkins, Rolando's teacher. If you're not too busy right now, I'd like to take three or four minutes to let you know *what* Rolando's working on in fifth grade. If this is an inconvenient time, I can call back later." Ms. Mitchell: "I can talk now, but what kinda trouble is that boy giving you? You just let me know, and I'll lay it on him." Mr. Perkins: "Rolando's not giving me any trouble. I just wanted to let you know about some things Rolando is working on in school." Ms. Mitchell: "Is he going to pass? How are his grades?" Mr. Perkins: "We're just beginning a lesson on how to use math to find the best prices when shopping." Ms. Mitchell: "That sounds interesting. Do you think he'll learn it?" Mr. Perkins: "Yes, and he should improve both his reading and math skills as we start examining newspaper ads." Ms. Mitchell: "It'd be good for him to do more reading. He'd rather watch TV. I'm always telling him, 'Turn off that boob tube, and go do some reading.' But he just keeps watching." Mr. Perkins: "You've just given me an idea! Let's use his liking for TV to build his interest in relating math and reading to shopping. I'll assign Rolando to make a record of price-related information that is communicated in TV commercials. We'll use his notes during our math lessons." Ms. Mitchell: "I'll make sure he has his pad and pencil with him whenever he's in front of the television." Mr. Perkins: "That'll be a help. Thank you." Ms. Mitchell: "Anything else?" Mr. Perkins: "He'll be working on expanding his writing vocabulary and using dictionaries for another week." Ms. Mitchell: "How's his writing?" Mr. Perkins: "Each day this week, I'll give him a list of between five and ten new words and ask him to write sentences using them for homework. It should take him about 20 minutes a night to look up the words in his dictionary and write the sentences." Ms. Mitchell: "I'll see that he does it." Mr. Perkins: "Thank you. I'll call again in about three weeks and we can further discuss what Rolando is doing in school." Ms. Mitchell: "That would be very nice. Thank you for calling."

## Conferences

Conferences between guardians and teachers are more common in elementary schools than they are for secondary schools. Each elementary teacher is involved with fewer students, with greater responsibilities for each, than is the typical secondary school teacher. It is quite common for elementary schools to periodically devote entire school days for conferences between teachers and guardians. This practice is less common for secondary schools, but there are times when even secondary teachers must find time for conferences with individual guardians. Following are suggestions for you to consider whenever you meet one of your student's guardians for a scheduled conference:

1. Prepare an agenda for the conference that specifies: (a) the purpose of the meeting (e.g., to communicate summative evaluations relative to achievement of learning goals for the previous nine weeks or to develop a plan to increase the rate at which the student completes homework assignments); (b) a sequence of topics to be discussed; (c) a beginning and ending time for the conference.
2. Except for special situations, invite the student to attend and participate in the conference. (Healthier, more open attitudes are more likely to emerge when the student, as well as the guardian and you, is involved.)
3. Schedule the meeting in a small conference room or other setting where distractions (e.g., a telephone) are minimal and there is little chance for outsiders to overhear the conversation.
4. Provide a copy of the agenda to each person in attendance. During the meeting, direct attention to the topic at hand by referring to the appropriate agenda item and by using other visuals (e.g., report card or test).
5. During the conference, concentrate remarks on descriptions of events, behaviors, and circumstances. Focus on needs, goals, and plans for accomplishing goals. Completely avoid characterizations and personality judgments.
6. During the conference be an active listener so that you facilitate two-way communications between you and those at the meeting and, thus, increase the likelihood that: (a) You get your planned message across; (b) You learn from the others at the meeting and pick up ideas for working more effectively with the student.

## Written Communications

Besides conferences with guardians, which out of necessity are infrequent, some teachers send home weekly or monthly newsletters that are designed to apprise guardians of what their children's classes are doing. An example is on the page opposite.

By taking the time to write such form letters, you foster the goodwill and understanding of students' guardians. Their understanding of what you, as a teacher, are trying to accomplish with their children will serve you well when you need to call on them to help you deal with behavior problems.

**PARENTS' NEWSLETTER FOR AMERICAN
HISTORY II,**
### 3RD PERIOD
From Jake Bertolli, Teacher
Vol. 1, No. 24, Week of March 16–20

**Looking Back**

Our last letter mentioned that we had begun a unit on late
19th century industrialism in the United States. I think a majority of the class were a bit bored with the material dealing with
some of the major personalities (e.g., Carnegie and Rockefeller)
that influenced industrialization in that era. However, I was quite
pleased with the enthusiasm nearly everyone showed for the lessons on worker–management issues, especially when we studied
the problems that led to the enactment of child labor laws. Based
on my statistical analysis of the results, the test the class took last
Friday seemed to provide a pretty accurate indicator of what most
students achieved during the week. The class average on the test
was 37.3, slightly higher than I had anticipated.

**This Week**

This week we will be discussing the rise of trusts in this country and move into the presidency of Woodrow Wilson. The relationship between the economic climate in the United States and
the fighting of World War I will be a major focus of the class. One of
the goals of the lesson is to help your daughter or son to understand how one event (e.g., a corporation in the U.S. decides to
expand) influences another (e.g., strategic plans for a battle in
Europe).

Homework assignments will include: (1) Read pp.588–661
from the textbook for Thursday's class; (2) Watch the show from
8:30 to 9:30 on Channel 7, Tues. night, and be prepared to discuss
its content on Wednesday; (3) Complete a worksheet, to be distributed Thursday, and attach it to the test to be given on Friday; (4)
Prepare for Friday's test.

**Looking Forward**

Next week, we will compare what we learned about the rise
of industries and corporations near the turn of the century to
today's world economic situation. In subsequent weeks, we'll
return our attention to the 1920s and examine some causes of
war and ways to achieve peace.

## PROFESSIONAL CONFIDENCE
## AND STUDENTS' RIGHTS

### Violations of Trust

What, if anything, bothers you about the behavior of the teachers in the next three scenes?

> Two teachers, Mr. Bates and Ms. Saddler, are talking in the 45th Street Sixth Grade Center faculty room. Mr. Bates: "How's it going?" Ms. Saddler: "There must be a full moon! The kids are a bit nutsy today. Just hope you never have Arla Neville. She can't follow what's going on, so she entertains herself by bugging me. Why do I have to have all the retards?"

> Bill Kresie, a high school coach and social science teacher, meets one of his friends, Vickie Dobson, in the grocery store. Mr. Kresie: "Hi, Vickie." Ms. Dobson: "Well, hello, Bill. What've you been up to?" Mr. Kresie: "Same old stuff. How about you?" Ms. Dobson: "Well, you know my daughter, Christine. . . ." Mr. Kresie: "Yes, lovely girl. How's she doing?" Ms. Dobson: "She just broke up with Ronald Boher and has taken up with Don Palmer." Mr. Kresie: "Really! Good move on her part. Ronald's a real loser. He went out for football, you know, and showed no guts at all. I had Don in American history. Bright, bright kid!"

> In a parent-teacher conference with Gary Mastoroni's father, Ms. Mauger tells him, "You know Gary is doing quite well. I wish all my students were like Gary. If I could get Elmo Thompson to cooperate like Gary, I'd jump for joy!"

Trust between a teacher and a student is an important ingredient in establishing a classroom climate that is conducive to cooperation, on-task behaviors, and engagement in learning activities. Teachers violate that trust when they gossip about students or share information obtained through their role as teachers with people who need not be privy to that information. Ms. Saddler, in the first of the three aforementioned examples, was frustrated and obviously needed to talk about her difficult day. Her behavior was understandable, but was it professional? Was it excusable? Her baneful use of the label "retards" displayed Ms. Saddler's disregard for at least some accepted professional standards. If all the teachers at 45th Street Sixth Grade Center understand that the faculty room is a place for teachers to vent some of their frustrations and what is said does not leave the faculty room, then Ms. Saddler's comments may never get back to students. Once students acquire the idea that teachers gossip about them, they are far less likely to feel comfortable in trusting those teachers. Mr. Kresie and Ms. Mauger can hardly hope that their comments about students will not be spread by the outsiders to whom they spoke.

## Privileged Information

Surely, there are times when you, as a teacher, should communicate information and express your judgments about students' achievement levels and behaviors to others. Who should be privileged to those communications? Typically, the following are considered to have a right and need to know:

1. For most cases, the *student* needs to be kept apprised of his or her own status regarding achievement of learning goals and evaluations of personal behaviors.
2. The student's *guardians* often need to be aware of their child's level of achievement and behaviors for two reasons:
   A. Guardians who understand just what their children are and are not accomplishing in school are in an advantageous position to serve as partners to teachers to help their children cooperate and achieve.
   B. Guardians are legally responsible for their children's welfare. They do, after all, delegate and entrust some of their responsibilities to teachers. They should know how the school is impacting their children.
3. *Professional personnel (e.g., a guidance counselor or another of the student's teachers) who have instructional responsibilities for that student* sometimes need to know about the student's achievement and behaviors so that they are in a better position to help that student.
4. *Professional personnel (e.g., the principal, subject area supervisor, or curriculum director) whose judgments impact the curricula and conduct of the school* sometimes need to be aware of an individual student's achievements or behaviors so that they will be in an advantageous position to make school-level decisions.
5. Because a school often acts as an agency that qualifies students for occupations, other institutions, or for privileges (e.g., scholarships), it may sometimes be necessary for a *representative of an institution to which a student has applied* to have knowledge of evaluations of that student's achievements and behaviors. However, school personnel should seriously consider following a policy that they release information on an individual student's achievements or behaviors to such representatives only with that student's and his or her guardians' authorization.

## Self-Assessment for Chapter 4

I. Following is a list of statements by teachers. Label each that is strictly *descriptive* with a "D," each that is *judgmental of a person* with a "JP," and each that is *judgmental of a behavior, achievement, or situation* with a "J."

    A. "Xavier, you are very polite."
    B. "Xavier, that was a very polite thing for you to do for Richard."
    C. "Xavier, you allowed Richard to go first."
    D. "I am having trouble concentrating because of the noise in here."
    E. "All that noise in here shows that some people are inconsiderate."
    F. "Your score on this test makes you one of my best students."
    G. "Your score on this test was the highest in the class."
    H. "You did better on this test than anyone else in the class."
    I. "Pushing Ryan like that is not acceptable behavior."
    J. "Pushing Ryan like that is a violation of class rules."
    K. "I am angry because you pushed Ryan like that."
    L. "Pushing Ryan like that makes you tough; I'll show you who is tough!"

II. Write two paragraphs suggesting how the tactics Ms. Price alludes to in the following example can backfire on her and eventually encourage students to be off-task in her class:

> Ms. Taylor asks Ms. Price in the faculty lounge, "How do you get your students to do their homework?" Ms. Price: "I embarrass the hell out of them in front of their buddies, if they come to class unprepared. I can make them feel like less than nothing for not doing what I assign."

III. Students sometimes don't bother to listen to teachers because they've learned that adults often speak to them without really having anything of consequence to say. Categorize each of the following examples of teachers talking to students as either *inane* or *informative*:
    A. "Karl, your milk is dripping down the side of your glass."
    B. "I am really enjoying myself!"
    C. "I expect you to behave while we're visiting the library."
    D. "You really had a good time!"
    E. Mr. Ballam notices one student in his class of 28 looking around during a written-response test. Mr. Ballam announces to the class, "Keep your eyes on your own paper."
    F. "Until we get back to the room, remain close enough to touch your partner."

IV. Marcia, a sixth grader, comments to her teacher, "I don't want to take this test. I'll just flunk it." Provide a *supportive* response Marcia's teacher could make and also provide a *nonsupportive* response. In both responses, let Marcia know that she is expected to take the test as scheduled.

V. This chapter's section "Avoiding Unintended Messages" gives four examples of teachers unwittingly miscommunicating with students. Develop and describe in a paragraph five more realistic examples of such unfortunate events.

**VI.** Circle each of the following comments that suggest that maybe individuals are not completely responsible for their own conduct:
- **A.** "Marla had trouble regaining her composure after Davalon spat on her."
- **B.** "Evelyn's clowning in class is due to her lack of attention at home."
- **C.** "He made me so ashamed!"
- **D.** "Fred, your behavior will embarrass your mother!"
- **E.** "I'm embarrassed!"
- **F.** "Study hard and make me proud."
- **G.** "I'll be very pleased to see you do well."
- **H.** "He made me hit him."
- **I.** "I was running so I wouldn't be late."

**VII.** Label each of the following teacher-made decisions as either *formative* or *summative*:
- **A.** Mr. Jones decides to give Brenda a "C" in physical education.
- **B.** Ms. Tempelton judges that her learning unit on China went very well.
- **C.** Ms. Blackstone decides that she should spend another day on an inductive activity for discovering a formula for the area of a triangle.
- **D.** Ms. Collier decides not to allow Marcus to use paints for the rest of the week.
- **E.** Mr. Larusso decides to cut the homework assignment in half.
- **F.** Ms. Banker decides that Juanita has made satisfactory progress.

**VIII.** Write a one-page essay that presents positions both for and against the following policy:

> A grade a student receives in a course should *only* reflect how well that student has achieved the specified goals of that course.

**IX.** Write a paragraph explaining the advantages you, as a teacher, gain by maintaining a routine flow of information about your class to students' guardians.

**X.** Describe two examples in which teachers' gossip about their students results in a loss of their students' trust.

---

*Reviewing Your Self-Assessment* ⎯⎯⎯⎯⎯⎯⎯⎯⎯⎯⎯⎯⎯⎯⎯

Compare your responses to Part I of the exercise to the following: A-JP, B-J, C-D, D-D, E-JP, F-JP, G-D, H-J, I-J, J-D, K-D, L-JP.

Compare your response on Part II to those of others who answered that item.

Here is a set of responses to Part III: A-informative, B-informative, C-inane, D-inane, E-inane, F-informative.

Compare your responses to Part IV to those of others. Here is a possibility for a *supportive response:* "Yes, you seem nervous about taking the test and it starts in only 40 seconds." Here's a possible *nonsupportive response*: "Oh, come on, Marcia! You'll do just fine! Just relax; you'll see."

Discuss your examples and those of others for Part V.

For Part VI, the following should be circled: B, C, D, F, H.

For Part VII, A, B, and F are summative and C, D, and E are formative.

Discuss your responses and those of others for parts VIII, IX, and X.

### Supplemental Readings

Cangelosi, J. S. (1982). *Measurement and evaluation: An inductive approach for teachers* (pp. 367–384). Dubuque, IA: Brown.

Ginott, H. (1972). *Teacher and child* (pp. 35–120). New York: Macmillan.

Gordon, T. (1974). *T.E.T.: Teacher effectiveness training.* New York: Peter H. Wyden.

Harris, T. A. (1969). *I'm OK–you're OK: A practical guide to transactional analysis.* New York: Harper & Row.

Paley, V. G. (1986). On listening to what children say. *Harvard Educational Review, 56,* 122–131.

Rogers, C. R. (1969). *Freedom to learn.* Columbus, OH: Merrill.

Wolfgang, C. H., & Glickman, C. D. (1986). *Solving discipline problems: Strategies for classroom teachers* (2nd ed.), (pp. 26–62). Boston: Allyn & Bacon.

# 5

# Establishing Procedures and Rules for Conduct

Chapter 5 is designed to help you:

1. distinguish functional rules from specific procedures and understand how to use a combination of the two for managing a classroom.
2. distinguish between necessary and unnecessary classroom rules of conduct.
3. understand how the existence of unnecessary classroom rules of conduct encourages off-task student behaviors.
4. understand why a failure to enforce existing rules, both necessary and unnecessary, encourages off-task student behaviors.
5. be thoughtful about your methods for establishing rules (i.e., when, by whom, and how).
6. apply the Teaching Process Model to help students comprehend rules, know how to follow them, and predict the consequences of not following them.
7. begin to develop a plan for establishing classroom rules of conduct and specific procedures for: (a) maximizing on-task behaviors; (b) increasing safety and security; (c) preventing activities within your class from disturbing others outside of your class; (d) maintaining acceptable standards of decorum among students, school personnel, and visitors to the school campus.

## STATING FUNCTIONAL RULES

### Semantics

*Classroom rules of conduct* are formalized statements that provide students with general guidelines for the types of behaviors that are required and the types of behaviors that are prohibited. Some teachers attempt to soften the restrictive nature of rules by stating them as a list of what behaviors are allowed (e.g., "You may talk when recognized."). These teachers would like to avoid both negative statements (e.g., "Do not talk without first being recognized.") and imperative statements (e.g., "Remain silent until you are recognized."). Telling students what they *may* do might be preferable to negative and imperative statements in normal conversations with students. However, negative statements and imperative statements are quite appropriate for formal rules that are written into a classroom's bylaws for conduct.

Stating classroom bylaws of conduct as a list of what may be done, rather than what should and should not be done, suggests that nothing is allowed unless it is included on the list of rules. Statements such as "You may talk when recognized" literally communicate nothing. "You may talk when recognized" does not imply not to talk when unrecognized. Why should you be concerned with semantics? You should be concerned because, if you are going to have formalized classroom rules of conduct, you and your students should be prepared to take them very seriously. Word rules so that they denote exactly what is intended. A list of "do's and don'ts" will communicate more accurately than a list of what is permitted. After all, permissible behaviors are far too numerous to include in any list. Mr. Redden's imprecisely worded rule, indicating what may be done, contributes to the unnecessary confrontation in the following example:

> Mr. Redden's sixth graders are working on individual assignments at their places when Don quickly gets up and exits the room. In 4 minutes he re-enters and Mr. Redden asks, "Where have you been, Don?" Don: "To the bathroom." Mr. Redden: "It wasn't time for you to go to the restroom." Don: "Why not?" Mr. Redden: "Read rule number six on the bulletin board." Don: "It says, 'You may go to the restroom during the last 5 minutes of the class period." Mr. Redden: "There's still 20 minutes left." Don: "But, the rule doesn't say we can't go before the last 5 minutes." Mr. Redden: "Don, you know what the rule means. . . ."

Don probably did know what the rule meant, but he is right; the rule did not say what it meant. You need not attempt to use legal language when stating rules, but by being reasonably accurate and to the point, you may encourage students to take rules seriously.

### Focusing on the Rule's Purpose

Classroom rules of conduct may also be stated so narrowly that they become nonfunctional. Consider the following example:

> "All students are to remain seated during group-administered tests until the teacher has given the signal that all of the papers have been collected," is included among the rules of conduct for Mr. Blanton's eighth grade classroom. Thau is taking one such test, sitting between Nikita and Kay, both of whom have finished the test and are waiting for the others. Kay rises up and leans over Thau and hands Nikita a pencil. Mr. Blanton notices the disturbance and motions Kay up to his desk where he asks, "Kay, what is the rule about getting out of your seat during a test?" Kay: "I was only returning the pencil I borrowed from Nikita. And besides, I never left my desk." Mr. Blanton: "How is that possible?" Kay: "I leaned way over and managed to keep my knee on my seat." Mr. Blanton: "That's the same as leaving your desk." Kay: "Not if my knee was still touching. . . ."

The time Mr. Blanton wasted with that inane conversation with Kay should have been more purposefully spent. It is ridiculous to argue over whether or not Kay left her seat. The concern should be with preventing disturbances to students, such as Thau, who are still taking the test. Mr. Blanton's rule to "stay in your seat" is too narrow to serve the purpose of "not disturbing others who are still taking the test." Kay focused on remaining in her seat when she should have been more thoughtful about not disturbing Thau. Mr. Blanton's rule is not stated in *functional* terms. A rule stated in functional terms focuses on the purpose or function for having the rule in the first place. Examples of rules stated in functional terms include: "Be careful not to distract others while they are being tested." "Allow others an opportunity to speak without being interrupted." "Do nothing that would risk you or another person being injured, harmed, or made uncomfortable." "Respect the property of others."

### The Number of Functionally Stated Rules

A minimum number of functionally stated rules (e.g., less than 10) are generally preferable to a large number of narrow rules, each applicable to specific situations (e.g., "Do not sharpen your pencil while the video player is running"), for the following reasons: (1) A few rules are easier to remember than many rules; (2) Each rule in a small set of rules is more likely to appear important than is each rule in a large set of rules; (3) Functional rules appeal to the common sense of students and lead students to be thoughtful about their behaviors (e.g., "Would handing this pencil to Nikita disturb Thau?"); (4) Functional rules focus attention on purposeful

**Illustration 5.1. Kay Manages to Stay in Her Seat as She Disturbs Thau**

behaviors (e.g., how to be considerate) rather than on disfunctional techni-
calities (e.g., whether or not a student was seated). Teachers may sometimes fall into the trap of establishing too many narrowly focused rules
instead of fewer than 10 basic functional rules because they confuse rules
of conduct with *routine procedures applicable only to specific situations* (e.g.,
during group testing or while videotapes are being viewed).

## PROCEDURES FOR SMOOTHLY OPERATING
## CLASSROOMS

Routine procedures, like rules, should communicate expectations for behavior. Unlike a rule, however, a *routine procedure* applies only to a particular type of activity and does not define a general standard for conduct.
Rules or bylaws for classroom conduct should be written down and promi-

nently displayed in the classroom. Except for particularly complex activities, procedures are usually learned through participation and need not be displayed in written form. *Procedures* are simply the mechanisms by which students move through transition periods and learning activities. Well-designed, efficient procedures are necessary for a smoothly operating classroom. Here is a sample of the types of routine classroom activities for which procedures need to be established: (1) students arriving in the classroom at the beginning of a school day or class period; (2) roll being taken; (3) administrative duties being completed (e.g., collecting lunch money); (4) collecting assignments; (5) students desiring to speak aloud in class; (6) going to lunch; (7) sharpening pencils; (8) getting a drink; (9) going to the bathroom; (10) taking things from the storage area; (11) moving from a teacher-led large group activity to a small group discussion session; (12) cleaning up after using a learning center; (13) leaving the room during class; (14) returning to class following an absence; (15) taking tests; (16) retaking tests; (17) borrowing materials; (18) requesting individual help; (19) setting up conferences outside of class hours; (20) having a guest in the classroom (e.g., guest lecturer, visiting parent, supervisor, or observer from a college); (21) using the computers; (22) visiting the library; (23) turning in reports; (24) fire and disaster drills; (25) listening to announcements; (26) leaving the room at the end of the school day.

The list, of course, could go on and on. It may be helpful for you to begin with some general categories and list specific activities for which procedures are to be determined under each category. Categories might include: (1) room use; (2) use of supplies; (3) large group learning activities; (4) small group learning activities; (5) individualized learning activities; (6) transitions between learning activities; (7) administrative duties.

In order to help you think further about establishing routine procedures for your own classroom, classify each of the 26 types of activities from the given sample according to the aforementioned seven categories. Modify, delete, and add categories to fit your needs and begin developing your list of types of activities for which procedures will need to be determined.

## NECESSARY RULES OF CONDUCT

### Four Purposes for Rules

As a youth, Mr. Tuft learned that hats are not to be worn indoors. He remembers his father yelling at him, "Take that hat off of your head! What kind of a place do you think you're in? There're ladies present!" He remembers his parents laughing at "Old Mr. Busby" for forgetting to take his hat off when he visited their home. When Mr. Tuft became a teacher, it seemed natural for him to establish a rule prohibiting the wearing of hats in the classroom. He didn't give it much thought.

Mr. Tuft frequently finds himself interrupting his own learning activities in order to enforce his no-hat-wearing rule.

Teachers, as well as school administrators, sometimes establish *unnecessary* rules of conduct. A *necessary classroom rule of conduct* is one that serves at least one of the following purposes (Cangelosi, 1986):

1. To maximize on-task behaviors and minimize off-task, especially disruptive, behaviors
2. To secure the safety and comfort of the learning environment
3. To prevent the activities of the class from disturbing other classes and persons outside of the class
4. To maintain acceptable standards of decorum among students, school personnel, and visitors to the school campus.

## Justification of a Rule

Which one, if any, of the four purposes does Mr. Tuft's no-hat-wearing rule serve?

Ordinarily, students wearing hats does not interfere with their being on-task. Of course, you can think of exceptions, such as a student wearing an outlandish hat. But such exceptions can be covered under general functional rules, such as "Dress for class so that your apparel is not a source of distraction that makes it difficult for others to concentrate on their work."

Mr. Tuft's no-hat-wearing rule could hardly be justified as serving the second of the four purposes for rules of conduct. Hat wearing is unrelated to the safety and security of most classroom situations. Again, there are exceptions. For example: (1) A hat dislodged from a student's head during a volleyball game could cause someone to slip; (2) During contact drills, football coaches would be negligent if they didn't require their students to wear helmets. Such exceptions can be effectively handled under *procedures* for specific learning activities (e.g., expectations regarding dress for volleyball games could be included in the teacher's directions for playing volleyball).

Classroom rules are established for the third of the four purposes out of consideration for persons who are not in the class, but who are on or near the school campus. Even a lively on-task discussion can be disturbing to a neighboring class. Establish rules such as "Be considerate of other classes by holding down your voices," and procedures for specific activities, such as "While we are walking past those houses on the way to visit the science center, stay on the sidewalk and away from people's lawns." Prohibiting the wearing of hats does not seem to serve the third purpose for having rules for conduct.

If Mr. Tuft can justify his no-hat-wearing rule at all, he'll probably relate it to the fourth purpose. Maintaining acceptable standards of decorum among students, school personnel, and visitors to the school campus is surely necessary to the development of a healthy, businesslike climate. Common courtesy is a critical ingredient in a smoothly operating classroom. However, Mr. Tuft and other teachers should be cautious that they do not use this fourth purpose as an excuse for imposing their personal biases and tastes on students.

## Politeness and Courtesy

The bases for this fourth purpose are: (1) Impolite interactions among students and teachers lead to ill feelings that diminish the likelihood of cooperation in the classroom; (2) Polite interactions among students and teachers help maintain a classroom that is conducive to cooperation; (3) The community within which a class exists expects that class to exhibit certain standards of courtesy. One of the problems you, as a teacher, face with this fourth purpose is how to decide what behaviors are polite and which are impolite. In all probability, your students come to you from a variety of backgrounds and subcultures. While hat-wearing in a building may be distasteful to one, it may be in vogue to another, and required by the religion of yet another. One approach is to define *politeness and courtesy as behavior that is exhibited as the result of thoughtful consideration for the rights and feelings of others.* Such a liberal definition, as opposed to conventional dictionary definitions (e.g., "Showing good manners, cultured, refined"), focuses on thoughtfulness toward others, rather than on one group's opinion on what constitutes "good" taste.

This approach can also lead to some difficulties:

During a discussion on nutrition in Ms. Oskoei's health class, Julie says, "There was something in the newspaper yesterday about some scientists saying we should be careful not to eat too much red meat." Dick: "I don't give a shit what any scientists say, I'm not gonna stop eating meat." Ms. Oskoei: "Dick, please don't use words like that while we're having class."

After class, Ms. Oskoei meets with Dick privately and says, "Which one of our classroom rules did you violate today?" Dick: "I don't know." Ms. Oskoei: "I have one in mind that I think you did violate and I want you to read through the list and guess at which one I have in mind." Dick begins to read the list of rules that are displayed on the wall. Dick: "I don't know. Are you talking about the fourth one?" Ms. Oskoei: "Please read it aloud." Dick reads, "Before you act or speak, think of how your actions and words influence others. Act and talk in ways that others appreciate and not in ways they find offensive." Ms. Oskoei: "Yes, that is the one." Dick: "Because of what I said! Aw! Everybody says 'shit.' That doesn't hurt anybody." Ms. Oskoei: "I agree with you. It's no big deal. But there are people, including me, who just don't like to say or hear that word during class. Since you are quite capable of substituting words that others don't find offensive to express yourself, I'll expect you not to violate rule number four again." Dick: "But Misses Oskoei, we talk about bowel movements and urine in health class. Why is that okay?" Ms. Oskoei: "The fact is our society considers it okay to talk about those things on television, such as in laxative commercials, but our society doesn't allow the word 'shit' to be spoken on television. Unless our society changes its opinion about such words, people are going to feel uncomfortable hearing them spoken in formal, businesslike settings like our classroom. I'm sorry, but I'm one of those people. Right or wrong, we violate rule number four by using words like 'shit' when other words that don't offend anyone can be used instead." Dick: "It doesn't seem right that something is okay one place, but not in another." Ms. Oskoei: "It's like belching. Most everyone has a good healthy belch now and then. But most people in our society find other people's belching to be disgusting. Dick (laughing): "So belching is a violation of rule four also." Ms. Oskoei: "A public display of belching, when it could be avoided, would indeed be a violation of rule number four."

Did Dick violate the classroom rule of conduct that is related in the example? Whether or not Dick's use of a word that is socially unacceptable to many people violated the rule depends on whether or not others found his expression offensive. Ms. Oskoei did indicate to him that she, for one, found the term offensive. If you feel that Dick was within his rights in saying what he pleases as long as no one is really hurt or prevented from being on-task, then you may not want to include any rules for the fourth purpose dealing with standards of decorum. For that view, rules may only be necessary for the first three purposes. On the other hand, if you find it important to uphold community standards of courtesy in your classroom, then establish rules for the fourth purpose. However, please proceed with care. You want to make sure that you do not allow unnecessary rules to be established under the guise of maintaining acceptable standards of decorum. The mistake of establishing unnecessary rules can cause you more problems than the mistake of failing to establish necessary ones.

## THE CONSEQUENCES OF UNNECESSARY RULES

When considering whether or not a particular rule should be included among the rules of conduct for your classroom, ask yourself, "Which of the four purposes for having rules does this one serve?" If the answer is "none," then that rule is *unnecessary* and should not be included. If you do include unnecessary rules, you will be faced with three unpleasant consequences:

1. You will be responsible for enforcing a rule that does not have a defensible rationale. Thus, you put yourself in the position of teaching students to submit to unjustified regulations.

2. Once your students realize that one of the rules you enforce serves no important purpose, they will tend to generalize that other rules must be unimportant also.
3. Students who are penalized for resisting unnecessary rules are likely to become disenchanted with school. Such students are often distracted from the business of learning because time that could be allocated for learning activities is used to deal with rule violations.

Of course, you could choose to enforce only the necessary rules and ignore the unnecessary ones that appear on the books. This is inadvisable. Unenforced rules, even unnecessary ones, teach students that rules need not be taken seriously. It is more difficult to teach students to be on-task when they feel they can be selective about which rules to follow and which rules to ignore.

## WHEN TO DETERMINE RULES AND ROUTINE PROCEDURES

Some teachers prefer to determine all rules for conduct and a large share of routine procedures at the very beginning of a school year or term. Others establish both rules for conduct and routine procedures as the need for them becomes apparent. There are advantages of establishing rules and many of the routine procedures at the outset of a school term: (1) Because expectations are formally communicated from the beginning, some off-task behavior patterns will not have time to emerge; (2) Students are more receptive to learning rules and procedures at the beginning of a school term than they are once they've become accustomed to a situation; (3) The sooner students know about rules and procedures, the more time they will have to practice following them.

There are advantages of establishing rules and routine procedures throughout the school term: (1) Waiting to establish some rules avoids prescribing rule-breaking behaviors for students who were positively reinforced for breaking rules in previous classes; (2) Students are more likely to understand a rule or a procedure when it is established in response to a need that has just become apparent; (3) Students are more likely to appreciate the importance of individual rules and procedures that are established gradually, rather than being thrust on them all at once.

You will probably want to use some combination of the two approaches by establishing several functional rules of conduct and some basic routine procedures at the outset, and then developing a more comprehensive list over time. The younger your students, the more time you will need to take establishing and teaching rules and procedures at the very beginning of a school year.

## WHO SHOULD DETERMINE RULES

Do rules more effectively serve their four purposes when teachers determine them or when students themselves agree on them? Should you use an authoritarian process, a democratic process, or some combination of the two to establish rules? That question is addressed by numerous research studies (Evertson & Emmer, 1982; Glickman & Wolfgang, 1979). Considering the conclusions from a number of these studies, it appears that there are four ways for you to establish rules. How well each method works depends more on how you go about implementing the method, than it does on the method itself. The four methods are:

1. You decide upon all rules, making sure that each is functional, necessary, and not confused with a routine procedure.
2. You determine all rules yourself, but your determinations are influenced by the recommendations of students.
3. Rules are proposed and voted upon by students. You are responsible for establishing the structure for democratic decision making, providing leadership to encourage the establishment of necessary, functional rules, and ensuring that every student has the opportunity to participate in decisions.
4. Some combination of the other three methods is used. Typically, you impose a few fundamental guidelines for behavior, and students participate in decisions about more specific rules that fall within the purview of those guidelines.

## TEACHING RULES TO STUDENTS

Establishing rules for conduct and routine procedures for activities is one thing. Teaching students to follow those rules and procedures is quite another. Students must first learn what the rules and procedures are and how to follow them; then, they must become willing to follow them. The Teaching Process Model applies to the teaching of rules and procedures just as it does to the teaching of academic subjects. Examples in which teachers successfully establish, teach, and utilize rules and procedures are provided in the next section.

## TEACHERS WHO EFFICIENTLY USE
## RULES AND PROCEDURES

Ms. Williams autocratically establishes some basic routine procedures and functional rules of conduct for her second grade class at the very beginning of the school year. She plans to spend a major share of the first two weeks teaching rules and procedures.

At the beginning of the second day of the new school year, Ms. Williams announces to all 27 of her students, "There are four rules that you are required to follow whenever you are at school. Here is the first one." Ms. Williams displays a bright orange poster with "RESPECT THE RIGHTS OF OTHERS" boldly printed and a drawing of a cluster of happy faces. Touching each word on the poster as she says it, Ms. Williams continues, "Respect the rights of others! That is our first rule. I will hang this reminder for you right here on the wall. Connie, please help me with this." Quickly, the bright orange poster is permanently displayed. "Now read this with me as I point to each word," Ms. Williams directs the class. Together the class recites with her, "Respect the rights of others." Ms. Williams: "What does it say, Allen?" Several students, including Allen, shout out, "Respect the rights of others!" Ms. Williams: "I'm sorry; there were too many people talking for me to understand Allen. Allen?" Allen: "It says, 'Respect the rights of others.'" Ms. Williams: "Thank you. Now, I want everybody to quietly think to themselves what the rule means before we discuss it." Ms. Williams waits 30 seconds, and says, "Okay, let's share our ideas on what it means to respect the rights of others. We'll begin with Reginald." Reginald: "Well, respecting others is being nice to them." Ms. Williams: "And what are some of the ways that we can be nice to others . . . ?"

The discussion over the first rule continues, until Ms. Williams is satisfied that her students have a reasonable understanding of the types of behaviors this rule requires and the types it forbids. Ms. Williams then teaches her students the procedures she will use for dealing with violations of rule number one; they are as follows.

Ms. Williams has made arrangements with Mr. Demery who teaches another second grade class at her school to combine their two classes for 40 minutes every afternoon just prior to dismissal. During that 40-minute period some type of activity that the students find especially enjoyable is conducted. One day there may be supervised recreation in the playground, gym, or auditorium. Another day, the children may view a videotape or play games in the computer lab.

Only Mr. Demery supervises the combined classes for the first 20 minutes of these sessions. Ms. Williams reserves that first 20 minutes to individually meet with any of her students who have violated rules or failed to follow procedures. At these conferences, Ms. Williams and the students work out a plan for preventing such violations or failures in the future. Ms. Williams supervises the second half of these 40-minute periods to allow Mr. Demery to work out plans with any of his students who violated rules or failed to follow procedures.

In teaching her students the procedures for dealing with violations of the first rule, she does not, of course, attempt to relate all the details of the arrangement with Mr. Demery. In time, the students will learn this for themselves. She does tell them, "Any time I recognize someone not respecting the rights of another, I will simply tell them, 'Meet with me to discuss the first rule when it's time to join Mr. Demery's class,' We won't discuss it until that time comes."

On the third day of the new school year, Ms. Williams introduces the second rule with a bright green poster with one happy face and the message "RESPECT YOUR OWN RIGHTS." Ms. Williams' experiences have taught her to urge students to be more assertive in protecting their own rights and not allowing themselves to be abused. She uses role-playing learning activities to teach this rule. The following is an example of one such lesson.

Ms. Williams announces to her class, "Ron and Frankie will perform a skit to help us better understand the second rule. Imagine that they're out in the schoolyard waiting for the first bell to ring. Ron will be playing the part of Joe, who is a fourth grader. Frankie will be Bob, a second grader. Okay, fellows, you're on!" Holding his lunch pail, Bob walks near Joe. Joe grabs Bob by the shoulder and says, "Hey! Where you going, Buddy?" Bob: "Just to my room." Joe lets go of Bob and asks, "You wanna be my friend?" Bob: "I guess so." Joe: "Good! I'd like to be your friend too. Whatcha got in the box?" Bob: "My lunch." Joe: "Let me look at it. You might have something for me." Bob: "Naw! I gotta get to my room." Joe (holding up his fist to Bob): "Look! You'd better let me check out your lunch or you'll be sorry." Ms. Williams interrupts the skit at that point saying, "Thank you. Let's stop the drama for a few minutes to discuss what we've seen. I want each of you to think of what Bob can do so that he won't break the second rule." A discussion ensues in which suggestions are made as to how Bob can protect his rights from Joe's bullying behavior. Later, Ms. Williams has Ron and Frankie act out two different endings to the skit. In one, Bob violates the second rule by allowing Joe to take his lunch. In the second, Bob protects his rights.

On subsequent days, Ms. Williams introduces and teaches two other rules: "GIVE EVERYONE A CHANCE TO LEARN" and "FOLLOW PRO-CEDURES."

Ms. Williams' third rule is primarily concerned with preventing disruptive behaviors during learning activities. This particular rule serves as a general guideline that leads to many of the procedures governing both transitional and allocated time. The following episode illustrates this relationship.

In the second week of the school year, Ms. Williams directs her students to individually complete a language arts exercise at their places. As they work, students begin to yell out for Ms. Williams to help them or to interrupt her while she is helping another. Other students grow impatient waiting for Ms. Williams to get to them and they begin talking among themselves. The noise becomes disturbing to some who are trying to complete the tasks.

Having observed the chaos, Ms. Williams develops a procedure for this type of learning activity and decides to teach it to her students the next time she directs them into a learning activity that requires them to work individually at their places. She prepares to implement her plan and the lesson begins as follows.

Ms. Williams: "Class, may I have your attention please?" She looks directly into students' eyes until everyone appears to be ready to listen. Ms. Williams: "Thank you very much. Do you remember what happened the last time we worked out of our writing workbook?" Because Ms. Williams had previously established a procedure for speaking in a large group arrangement, students raise their hands to signal Ms. Williams that they would like to answer her questions. No one yells out a response. Ms. Williams: "Sadi, what do you remember happened?" Sadi: "It got very noisy and you couldn't get around to help all of us." Other students provide more detail as Ms. Williams conducts a discussion in which the problems with which she wants to deal are articulated by the students. Finally, Ms. Williams says, "It seems to me that we didn't give everyone a chance to learn the last time. We need a procedure so we won't break the third rule when we need to use our workbooks again. I'll explain the procedure now." She takes a bag from the storage closet and holds it up for the class to see. Ms. Williams: "In here is something to help us to give everyone a chance to learn when we are working at our places." Barbara: "Is it candy? Are you going to give us candy for being good?" Ms. Williams looks at Barbara sternly and raises her finger to her lips. Barbara receives the message and does not pursue her question. Ms. Williams pulls a device from the bag that the students have never before seen. The device consists of a holder with a clip that can be attached to a student's desk (see Illustration 5.2). The holder contains three flags—a red, a blue, and a yellow. Each flag can be rotated up or down. Ms. Williams gives each student one device for his or her desk and teaches them the following procedure for working quietly at their places.

As long as a student is progressing through the assignment and does not want to be disturbed, that student is to display the yellow flag. When a student wants to be helped, a red flag should be displayed. When a student has completed the work and is also willing to help others, she or he should display a blue flag. Ms. Williams quietly moves from one student displaying a red flag to another directing those displaying blue flags to quietly provide help also.

Ms. Williams chose this seemingly elaborate flag raising procedure over a more conventional "raise your hand" procedure because she believed that: (1) The formality of the flags would help teach students just how seriously she expects them to follow the procedure; (2) Students who want help could simply display their red flags and could continue to work without having to hold their hands up; (3) It provides a quiet, efficient method for utilizing the help of students who finish the assignment before others.

**Illustration 5.2. Ms. Williams' Students Using Her Flag Raising Procedures**

Because of her arrangement with Mr. Demery, Ms. Williams has a very useful structure for dealing with rule violations and failure to follow procedures. Rules and procedures that are not enforced are counterproductive. How Ms. Williams conducts the conferences to work out plans to prevent repeat offenses is, of course, quite a critical factor influencing the effectiveness of her rules and procedures. The question of how to deal with students after they have violated a rule or failed to follow a procedure is addressed in chapters 7, 8, 9, and 10.

The following is an example of a teacher who allows students' suggestions to influence her decisions regarding procedures:

Ms. Clifford tells her seventh grade class, "I have received three separate complaints from other teachers that their lessons were disturbed by some of us who were making trips to the library. If those reports are true, then we were in violation of our rule against bothering people outside our group. We still need to make trips to the library. I wonder if I need to develop a procedure that guards against our bothering other classes." Some students raise their hands. Ms. Clifford: "Dale?" Dale: "The trouble is three or four of us go at once. Maybe you should allow only one to go at a time." Ms. Clifford: "I will seriously consider that. Jim?" Jim: "Find who's causing the trouble and don't let them ever go to the library again." Yolanda: "But we really weren't doing anything wrong! Mrs. Crooks, she's always trying to get us in trouble." Ms. Clifford: "That's not relevant. I really don't care about what has already happened. I just want to make sure we don't disturb others in the future." Jean: "Do we really need a special procedure if we just promise to keep quiet from now on?" Ms. Clifford: "That's what I'd like to decide. How many of you think we need a special procedure for going to the library? Raise your hands. One, two, three, . . . most of you believe we need one. Okay, I would like each of you to take out a sheet of paper and suggest what I should do in two or three sentences. Please do not put your name on the paper. I'll take your papers home tonight and consider your suggestions. I'll have a decision for you tomorrow."

The following scenario of a teacher using a democratic process for determining procedures was first reported in *Cooperation in the Classroom: Students and Teachers Together* (Cangelosi, 1986):

> Mr. Cooper has 12 hand-held, battery-operated calculators available in his classroom for use by his 32 eighth graders. The calculators are kept in a box on a supply table in the back of the room. Except for certain learning activities designed to improve students' computational skills and certain tests for assessing those computational skills, students generally have free access to the calculators. Class treasury funds are used to maintain a supply of calculator batteries.
>
> Mr. Cooper begins to notice that calculators are left on when not in use and that students fail to return them quickly to the box after using them. Students are beginning to complain that they have trouble obtaining a working calculator when needed. To address the complaints, Mr. Cooper calls a "class community meeting." Whenever such meetings are held the students know that they operate under *Robert's Rules of Order* (Robert, 1970) and they can raise issues of common concern. At this meeting, Mr. Cooper describes the recurring difficulty with calculator use; he proposes that the problems be resolved.
>
> After a discussion, the group agree that procedures governing the use of calculators will be formulated. Roy moves and Gertrude seconds a motion indicating that anyone who leaves a calculator on or doesn't immediately return one to the supply box will never again be allowed use of the calculators. After some discussion, the motion is amended to change the penalty from banning calculator use for life to a week for the first offense,

two weeks for the second, and so forth. Mr. Cooper and several students speak against the motion for now, arguing that other proposals that do not restrict calculator use should be considered. They base their argument on two points: (1) Work would be impaired if the calculators were not available to all students; (2) Such a rule would sometimes place Mr. Cooper in the position of trying to find out who left a calculator on or failed to return one to the box.

The motion fails 14 to 15 with 2 abstentions and 1 student absent. Amanda then proposes that students be allowed to use calculators only while standing at the supply table. She argues that they should be able to use them without removing them from the area and that the machines could be secured to the table. The motion is defeated after students argue that the table area would become congested and that they need calculators at their desks. After further discussion, the following motion finally passes.

The batteries will be removed from the calculators and those batteries will be held in storage. Four unused batteries will be distributed to each student from those already in storage and from additional ones purchased from the class treasury. Each calculator will be marked with an identification numeral and kept in the supply box without batteries. A student may obtain a calculator by checking it out, writing his or her name, time, date, and the calculator's numeral on a checkout-checkin sheet left on the supply table. To use the calculator, the student installs his or her own batteries, which are to be removed and retained by the student upon returning the calculator. Students will be required to maintain their own supply of batteries just as they do their pencils and paper. Batteries will be kept on hand for sale at a profit for the class treasury.

The motion seems a bit complicated, but Mr. Cooper helps students work out the necessary details that make the written version appear complex. Once the procedure is in effect for a week, students acquire behavior patterns and follow the procedure with little thought given to the complex written description that appears in the minutes of the class community meeting.

## SCHOOL-WIDE DISCIPLINE POLICIES

Your classroom rules of conduct and procedures should not be in conflict with school-wide policies. Unfortunately, students in many departmentalized schools (e.g., most high schools) have to deal with rules for one teacher that are inconsistent with those for another (Cangelosi, 1980). Many schools have rules that are unnecessary, according to the definition presented herein. Banning hats, prohibiting boys from wearing earrings, and regulating boys' hair length are typical examples of school-wide regulations that are difficult to justify under the four reasons for classroom rules of conduct. Your job as a teacher is more difficult when you are required to enforce unnecessary rules.

More and more, schools are moving toward a uniform discipline policy that allows teachers to establish their own classroom rules of conduct, but provides two major advantages over having no school-wide policy at all. First of all, the school-wide discipline policy can establish general guidelines for individual teachers' classroom rules for conduct. Ideally, these guidelines are flexible enough to allow for autonomy while providing enough directions to prevent teachers from being in conflict with one another. Secondly, the school-wide discipline policy can establish a support service for enforcing individual teachers' classroom rules of conduct. Here is an example:

> A month prior to the opening of a new school year, the faculty of Caseyland High School meets for 5 days to develop policies and plans for the year. One agenda item is to agree on: (1) guidelines for teachers to follow in establishing classroom rules of conduct; (2) how the school administration can support teachers' enforcement of their rules of conduct.
>
> After sharing ideas and working with a consultant on student discipline, Caseyland High's teachers and administrators agree to the following:
>
> 1. Each teacher is responsible for establishing rules of conduct for his or her own classes. Those rules should address only the following purposes: (a) maximizing on-task behaviors; (b) increasing safety and security; (c) preventing class activities from disturbing others outside that class; (d) maintaining acceptable standards of decorum.
> 2. Assistant Principal Coombs will serve as the chief administrator of the school-wide discipline program.
> 3. Teachers should write out rules as they are established and share them with Ms. Coombs so that she is in a better position to provide support services for teachers enforcing those rules.
> 4. The school will maintain a time-out room to which teachers may send students to wait until the beginning of the next period of the day. No one teacher may send more than two students to the time-out room during any one period. A paraprofessional will supervise the time-out room.
> 5. There will be an in-school suspension program in which students who have been officially suspended from a class spend that class time in a special supervised classroom. There they work on individualized assignments for the class they are missing. The following steps lead to an in-school suspension.
>
>> 1. Because of an alleged rule violation, a teacher chooses to write up the violation on a form supplied by Ms. Coombs' office.
>> 2. The student takes a copy of the form to Ms. Coombs' office where an appointment is set up with the student and Ms. Coombs.

3. If the appointment cannot be arranged before the student is scheduled to return to the class for which she or he was written up, then
the student spends the period when that class next meets in the in-
school suspension classroom until the conference can be held.
4. At the conference, the student and Ms. Coombs attempt to work out
a plan for returning to class.
5. The plan, which is designed to prevent a recurrence of the incident
leading to the write-up, is forwarded by Ms. Coombs' office to the
teacher. If the teacher agrees to the plan, the student is readmitted
and is no longer on in-school suspension.
6. If the teacher does not agree to the plan, then a meeting of the three
parties (i.e., the student, the teacher, and Ms. Coombs) is held to
work one out.
7. If one still cannot be agreed upon, the student's guardians are
brought into another session to try to arrange a plan. In the meantime, the student remains in in-school suspension.

It should be noted that the plan may involve the teacher altering behaviors as well as the student. If it appears that no reasonable plan will be
worked out in the very near future, arrangements are made for the student
to be transferred out of that class.

## Self-Assessment for Chapter 5

I. In a short paragraph, explain the differences between a classroom
rule of conduct and a routine procedure.
II. In a short paragraph, explain why the literal meaning of the following statement fails to communicate anything about expected conduct: "You are allowed to come into the room after the first bell."
III. Which of the following rules or procedures are stated in functional
terms?
A. When you have been recognized to speak (e.g., to answer or ask
a question) during a large group meeting, speak so that everyone
in the room can hear you.
B. Do not chew gum in the classroom.
C. Avoid doing anything that dirties, mars, or damages the class-
room, its furniture, and its equipment.
D. Sit straight with both feet on the floor.
E. Use expressions like "thank you," "pardon me," and "please."
Refer to adults as "sir" and "ma'am."
F. Do not bring toys to school.

**G.** Do not distract others while they are thinking.

**H.** Be considerate of others' feelings.

**IV.** Using two short paragraphs, describe two alternative procedures you would consider for routinely "checking" your students' homework.

**V.** According to this text, what is the difference between a *necessary* and an *unnecessary* rule of conduct?

**VI.** Obtain a list of the rules of conduct established by a teacher you know. In your opinion, which ones are necessary?

**VII.** Decide whether you agree or disagree with the following statement: "The mistake of establishing unnecessary rules can cause a teacher more problems than the mistake of failing to establish necessary rules."

Provide a rationale for your decision in a paragraph.

**VIII.** What are the advantages and disadvantages of establishing all rules and procedures at the very beginning of a school term?

**IX.** What are the advantages and disadvantages of having students democratically determine rules of conduct?

**X.** Design a school-wide discipline policy for the type of school in which you are or will be teaching.

## *Reviewing Your Self-Assessment*

Compare your responses to those of others who also engaged in the exercise. Discuss the similarities and differences in detail. For item III, statements A, C, G, and H are stated in functional terms.

## *Supplemental Readings*

Brophy, J. E., & Putnam, J. G. (1979). Classroom management in the elementary school. In D. L. Duke (Ed.), *Classroom management: The seventy-eighth yearbook of the National Society for the study of education* (pp. 182–216). The University of Chicago Press.

Cangelosi, J. S. (1986). *Cooperation in the classroom: Students and teachers together* (pp. 28–37). Washington, DC: National Education Association.

Emmer, E. T., Evertson, C. M., Clements, B. S., & Worsham, M. E. (1984). *Classroom Management for Secondary Teachers* (pp. 15–38). Englewood Cliffs, NJ: Prentice-Hall.

Jones, V. F., & Jones, L. S. (1986). *Comprehensive Classroom Management: Creating Positive Learning Environments* (2nd ed.), (pp. 396–416). Boston: Allyn & Bacon.

Lasley, T. J. (1985). Fostering nonaggression in the classroom: An anthropological perspective. *Theory Into Practice, 24,* 247–255.

# 6

Designing and Conducting
Engaging Learning Activities

Chapter 6 is designed to help you:

1. distinguish between students being intrinsically motivated to be engaged in learning activities and students being extrinsically motivated to be engaged in learning activities.
2. begin to develop ideas for designing learning activities in which students are intrinsically motivated to engage because those learning activities focus on problems which students have a felt need to solve.
3. develop techniques that encourage students to be on-task when you are giving directions.
4. develop techniques that encourage students to be engaged during the following types of learning activities: (a) lecture sessions; (b) discussion sessions; (c) questioning sessions; (d) independent work sessions; (e) homework assignments; (f) video, film, or guest lecture presentations.
5. develop ideas for creating classroom arrangements that facilitate students being on-task and engaged in learning activities.

## INTRINSIC AND EXTRINSIC MOTIVATION

### Student Disinterest

"School is boring." "History is awful! Names, facts, dates—Who cares?" "My teacher says geometry is supposed to teach us logical thinking, but all we do is memorize somebody else's proofs." "Why do we have to learn this? Nobody ever uses it!" "Why can't we study about something we care about?" "The best thing happened today! There was a fire drill and so we didn't have to go to reading!" "Tomorrow, we don't have to study science 'cause we're going on a field-trip." These all too familiar sounding comments, of course, were made by students. Many suggest that students do not cooperatively engage in learning activities because they find the activities uninteresting and of no immediate value to them (Wittrock, 1986). Teachers need not be entertainers and learning activities should probably be more work than fun for students. However, there are designs for learning activities that stimulate students' enthusiasm for engagement. Such designs are based on strategies for *motivating* students to be on-task.

## Intrinsic Motivation

Students are *intrinsically motivated* to be engaged when they choose to participate in a learning activity because they perceive value in participating in an activity that will directly benefit them. The intrinsically motivated student recognizes that by experiencing the learning activity he or she will satisfy a need. Here are two examples of students who are intrinsically motivated to get engaged in a learning activity:

> Casey wants to stay healthy and avoid illness. He believes that a proper diet will help him stay in good health. Thus, when his seventh grade teacher directs his class to read a chapter on nutrition, Casey willingly completes the assignment.

> Samantha believes strongly that people should not hunt and kill wild animals. When her English teacher gives a lecture on how to write creatively, Samantha listens intently because she wants to become a more effective writer so that she will be in a better position to convince others, through her writing, not to hunt.

Students learn to recognize the value of learning activities from having been positively reinforced as a *direct* result of being engaged.

## Extrinsic Motivation

Students are *extrinsically motivated* to be engaged when they choose to participate in learning activities, not because they recognize value in experiencing the activity, but because they desire to receive rewards that have been artificially associated with engagement or because they want to avoid consequences artificially imposed on being off-task. Here are two examples of students who are extrinsically motivated to be engaged in learning activities:

James' seventh grade teacher directs his class to read a chapter on nutrition. James completes the assignment because he wants to make high grades in school in order to please his dad. James believes that reading the chapter on nutrition will enhance his chances of raising his grades.

Roy listens intently while his English teacher lectures on creative writing because he fears that if he doesn't listen, he will be embarrassed by not knowing answers when asked questions in class.

Students become extrinsically motivated to be engaged by having their engaged behaviors positively reinforced with rewards that are not directly related to the learning activity itself. Similarly, *contrived* punishments following off-task behaviors can teach a student to be extrinsically motivated to avoid being off-task.

Honor roll, academic scholarships, academic competitions, letter jackets for students with high grade point averages, and honor societies are just some of the attempts by teachers and school administrators to provide incentives for being engaged in learning activities. Typically, such attempts do not extrinsically motivate those students who are in greatest need of motivation because such rewards are only vied for by students who have a history of academic success and, thus, feel they have a reasonable chance of winning. Teachers can, however, design into learning activities extrinsic motivators for all students. Here are two scenarios:

To motivate her 28 second graders to study spelling words, Ms. Malaker holds team spelling tournaments. The class is divided into four teams, The "Protectors," "Gobots," "Starriors," and "Bird People." On Monday, the Protectors stand in line at the front of the classroom. Ms. Malaker calls out the word "harp." The first Protector says, "H." The second says "U." Ms. Malaker: "No, that's not it." The second Protector exclaims, "Oh, shoot!" and looks in anticipation to the third Protector who says, "A." The fourth one says "R." The fifth says "R." Ms. Malaker: "No." The sixth says, "P." Ms. Malaker: "Very well, the Protectors got 4 right and 2 wrong. Four minus 2 leaves 2. So the Protectors have 2 points so far. The second word is 'tap.' The seventh Protector says, "T." The first says "A" and the second "P." Ms. Malaker: "That's 3 right and 0 wrong. So, that's 3 more points, giving the Protectors a total of 5 points. The next word is 'biggest'. . . ."

The Gobots have their turn on Tuesday, the Starriors on Wednesday, and the Bird People on Thursday. On Friday, each of the seven members of the team with the highest number of points receives a free pass to the zoo.

Ms. Malaker prefers this type of spelling contest to traditional spelling bees for three reasons: (1) Even the least skilled spellers can contribute and be rewarded for a winning effort; (2) To compete, team members must listen to one another as letters are called out; (3) Students are not eliminated from the spelling drill for missing a letter as they are in traditional spelling bees.

Mr. Landry meets individually with each of his 26 fifth graders once every 2 weeks. He spreads the conferences over a 2-week period so he is not overloaded at any one time. During a conference, Mr. Landry and the student agree on a set of goals and rewards the student will receive if the goals are accomplished.

During such a conference with Mindy, they review how well previous goals were accomplished, and begin establishing new goals. Mr. Landry shows Mindy a page from their science text and says, "I would like for you to choose an experiment from this section. Figure out how to do it, set it up, and demonstrate it for the class on Wednesday. You'll get 20 science points for doing it at all and another 15 for following the steps exactly the way they are in the book. Do you agree?" Mindy: "Okay, I'll try." Mr. Landry hands Mindy a test paper. "You scored 14 on this pretest. Monday, we'll have the posttest. You bring that pretest score up at least 10 points to a 24 or better and you get a 'B.' Bring it up more than 20 points and you get an 'A'." Mindy takes notes on the goals and the rewards as they go on to other subjects and other goals.

## The Preferred Type of Motivation

Ms. Malaker's and Mr. Landry's methods for extrinsically motivating students to be engaged in their learning activities were, of course, superior to not motivating students at all, but inferior to having students intrinsically motivated (Pratt, 1980). Students can be intrinsically motivated to engage in learning activities only if those learning activities are clearly designed to help students achieve objectives that are clearly based on students' needs (i.e., The Teaching Process Model is followed). But even when there is an obvious connection among student needs, learning objectives, and learning activities, students will not normally be intrinsically motivated. You, the teacher, must include in your design for learning activities a plan that leads them to be intrinsically motivated. So-called "problem-solving" learning activities are designed to stimulate students' interest and intrinsically motivate engagement (Cangelosi, 1986).

## PROBLEM-SOLVING LEARNING ACTIVITIES

### The Non–Problem-Solving Approach

The following example is purely fictitious; it never happened and, hopefully, never will:

Mr. Doe, an industrial arts teacher, conducts a high school carpentry class so that he first covers a unit on hammering nails into wood. The second unit is on sawing lumber. Subsequent lessons include measuring planks, squaring corners, joining ends, selecting materials, sanding, inserting screws, the care of a drill, safety, and using a drill press. Mr. Doe's students study and practice the skills from each unit in isolation from one another.

What do you think of Mr. Doe's fictitious course? It is organized ridiculously. *Real* industrial arts teachers don't teach skills in isolation from one another. Typically, carpentry teachers have students undertake a project on which they learn necessary skills as they apply them to the task. Projects may be individualized, such as one student building a bookcase, another a doghouse. In some cases, the entire class may focus on one large project, such as the construction of a portable classroom building. Unlike Mr. Doe, real industrial arts teachers provide students with learning activities that teach students special skills and the integrated applications of those skills to real-life problems (e.g., how to build something people care about having).

Unlike the previous one about Mr. Doe, the following example is taken from an actual event.

Mr. Ullrich conducts a math unit on equivalent fractions for his sixth graders by: (1) lecturing on the importance of understanding fractions; (2) explaining the rules for expressing fractional equivalents; (3) demonstrating several examples on the chalkboard; (4) assigning exercises; (5) providing individual help with exercises; (6) assigning homework from the textbook; (7) reviewing the homework in class.

Mr. Ullrich's learning activities were fairly standard for academic subjects. Like the Mr. Doe's fictional lesson, techniques (e.g., finding fractional equivalents) and ideas are often taught in isolation from their real-world applications. Mr. Ullrich lectured students on the importance of what they were to learn, but do you really think his students will be intrinsically motivated to be engaged in the learning activities on fractions because of what he said? Had Mr. Ullrich followed the example of most industrial arts teachers and designed his unit so that it focused on problems with which students are concerned, then students would have discovered the value of learning about fractions for themselves.

## The Problem-Solving Approach

Here is an example of a teacher using a problem-solving approach to teach sixth graders about equivalent fractions:

Ms. Olson has observed her 24 sixth graders at Westside Elementary long enough to understand the kind of things that interest them. In planning a math unit on equivalent fractions, she decides to take advantage of: (1) the interest that some of the students have in the basketball season; (2) a class social for which they are planning to bake three cakes; (3) physical education activities in which students are running various distances for time.

She begins by assigning 6 students to the "basketball" group, 9 to the "cake" group, and 9 to the "running" group. While the other 18 are working on assignments, she meets with the basketball group and has the following conversation.

Ms. Olson: "How do you think our Westside boys' basketball team is doing this year?" Mary: "We've won three." Gene: "Yeah, and lost two." Antoine: "Yeah, but we would've won those if it wasn't for the refs." Ms. Olson: "What's your favorite NBA team, Alphonse?" Alphonse: "The Utah Jazz!" Antoine: "Aw, I like the Lakers." Ms. Olson: "Who's doing better this year, the Jazz or Westside?" Antoine: "The Jazz may be better, but we win more." Mary: "You're crazy! The Jazz have won a lot more games." Antoine: "Well sure! They play more." Marcia: "Yeah, they also lose more." Ms. Olson: "Okay, wait a minute. We have a game today. Antoine, your math assignment is to report Westside's won-loss record to the class tomorrow. Alphonse, your job is to look up the Jazz's record in the morning paper and report it to the class." Mary: "What for?" Ms. Olson: "We're going to figure who's having a better year, Westside or the Jazz."

In a similar fashion, Ms. Olson meets with the cake group. She directs some of those students to report figures from recipes that are designed to serve seven. The recipes will be used to bake cakes for Ms. Olson and the class of 24.

Her meeting with the running group leads them to report times for different distances they are to run at physical education that afternoon.

The following day, Ms. Olson uses the group's data to confront the class with a number of problems, including: (1) Which team is doing better, Westside in their 5 games or the Jazz in their 44 games? (2) According to the recipe for seven, how much flour should the class get to have enough cake to serve 25? (3) Do we run faster in a 30-meter race or in a 60-meter race? Ms. Olson uses inductive questioning techniques to help her students to discover that such questions or problems can be efficiently solved by the use of equivalent fractions.

Later in the unit, Ms. Olson explains the rules for expressing fractional equivalents, demonstrates examples, and assigns and reviews exercises. At no point does she have to tell students how important it is for them to be able to skillfully use equivalent fractions. They have already discovered that for themselves.

According to Webster (1979), a *problem* is a perplexing or difficult question that needs to be answered or something difficult that must be worked out. Because problems suggest difficulties, people are often inclined to think of problems as undesirable. However, the existence of problems serves as a strong motivator for human endeavor. A perfectly satisfied person, one who recognizes no problems, lacks motivation to change, and thus, to learn. Why would anyone want to learn to read unless she or he had a felt need to receive a written communication? Why would someone want to learn how to drive nails unless there is something he or she wants to build or repair? Do people ever write unless they have something to communicate? Who, outside of schools, ever works with equivalent fractions without first being confronted with a problem she or he is motivated to solve?

## Intrinsic Motivation via the Problem-Solving Approach

Students can be *intrinsically* motivated to engage cooperatively in learning activities when those activities focus on problems the students have a felt need to solve. Learning activities, such as those typically conducted by industrial arts teachers and the one in the atypical example used by Ms. Olson, that are initiated by confronting students with real-world problems are known as *problem-solving learning activities*. Apparently, the goals of many teaching units do not lend themselves to problem-solving learning activities. For such situations, you need to utilize extrinsic motivators to ensure student engagement. However, when well-organized problem-solving activities are used, obtaining students' cooperation and engagement is usually a much easier task for a teacher. Following are 10 examples of teachers using problem-solving learning activities; the first one was initially reported in *Cooperation in the Classroom: Students and Teachers Together* (Cangelosi, 1986):

> Ms. Piscatelli designs a 2-week unit to help her high school history students better understand the activities of the U.S. Congress in the first third of the twentieth century. Ms. Piscatelli observes her students so as to identify current issues that concern them. She decides to focus on the following current problems: (1) Should marijuana be legalized? (2) What should the federal government do about unemployment? (3) What should Congress do to ensure the rights of ethnic minorities? (4) Does the United States need an Equal Rights Amendment? (5) What should the federal government do about abortions? (6) What stand should the federal government take on combating pollution?
>
> The learning activities include the following:
>
> **1.** Ms. Piscatelli assigns each class member to one of six task groups. One group, consisting of five students, is directed to examine how Congress

handled the prohibition of alcohol in the first third of the twentieth century and then relate those lessons of history to the current question about marijuana. The group is to report on Congress' rationale for repealing prohibition and to identify both similarities and differences between the question of alcohol prohibition then and marijuana prohibition now. Each of the other five task groups examines one of the other problems in a similar manner.

2. Each task group is provided with an organizational structure within which to operate, a list of resources from which to acquire information, a list of deadlines for specific subtasks, and directions on how findings are to be reported to the rest of the class and to Ms. Piscatelli.

3. To obtain an overall picture of the climate within which the Congress operated in the first third of the twentieth century, and thus be better able to compare those problems to current problems, all students are assigned to read a chapter from the text that deals with the period from 1901 to 1935.

4. Each task group reports to the class according to the schedule.

5. After each task group reports, class members who are not members of that task group discuss the report and propose a solution for solving the current problem.

Mr. Byers involves his fourth grade students in a project to build a scale model of the schoolyard in order to teach them about ratios and proportions.

Ms. Groves discovers that 12 of the juniors in her literature class read below the third grade level. Realizing that 9 of them want to pursue a driver's license, she provides them with the state driver's manual and uses it as a textbook for improving their reading skills. While they focus on learning how to pass the test for a driver's license, they steadily improve their reading levels.

Mr. Gervin takes advantage of his fifth graders' desire to decide upon their own rules for classroom conduct to teach them principles of democratic government.

Ms. Robique's suggestion to her kindergarten students that they make greetings cards for their parents is met with considerable enthusiasm. That enthusiasm helps keep them engaged in a learning activity designed to teach them to form manuscript letters while working on greeting cards.

Ms. Jones' students discover the rules of multiplying signed numbers while trying to figure out how drivers can avoid speed traps.

While some second grade students manage a classroom store and others make purchases from it, they acquire, as a result of their teacher's planning, some needed computational and reading skills.

Mr. Orborson realizes that his seventh graders have an avid interest in television, but virtually no interest in history. In order to stimulate their interest in history, he designs a learning activity in which they are assigned to analyze certain TV shows for historical accuracy. For example, one student is to compare the dress of the actors on two "Old West" shows to the dress of persons from that era who appear in history book photographs.

While caring for and feeding the inhabitants of the classroom aquarium, preschoolers polish their counting and grouping skills.

Mr. Cefalo often combines intra-class grouping techniques with problem-solving learning activities in order to accommodate the variety of achievement levels and interests displayed by the 34 tenth graders in his English class. As part of a unit designed to improve students' creative writing abilities, he groups students into pairs and assigns each pair a topic on which information is to be gathered and reported upon in writing. Mr. Cefalo utilizes what he has learned about the students to design the assignment. Herb, for example, is an avid motorcycle racing fan who has not displayed either much ability or desire to write. Ron, on the other hand, displays both a knack for and interest in writing, but knows hardly anything about motorcycle racing. Therefore, Mr. Cefalo pairs Herb with Ron and directs them to write a report on motorcycle racing as it exists in the local community.

Mr. Cefalo figures that Herb will tend to be engaged in the activity because his knowledge of motorcyle racing is needed by Ron. Ron, who already possesses quality writing skills, should be challenged by the problem of having to write about an unfamiliar topic. Because of the diversity regarding interests and achievement levels between Herb and Ron, both contribute to the completion of the task.

## IDEAS FOR GIVING DIRECTIONS

### Explicitness, Specificity, and Directness

Whenever you are conducting a learning activity that is designed to stimulate your students to reason, appreciate, discover, or create, then it may be quite appropriate for you to be indirect and inexplicit with what you say to them. For example:

During a problem-solving learning activity, Ms. Southworth is trying to help her junior high students discover the principles of physics that make it possible for airplanes to fly. At one point in the lesson, Judy asks, "What would happen if the wings of the plane were curved on the bottom like they are on top?" Ms. Southworth: "That's a good question. Let's think about it. In that case, would the air pass over the top surface faster or slower than it would over the bottom surface?" Judy: "I guess that. . . ."

Ms. Southworth knew the answer to Judy's question, but instead of giving the answer, she responded with another question. This indefinite, evasive communication was appropriate in *this* type of situation because Ms. Southworth's objective was to get Judy to reason, not simply to know the answer. However, when instead of stimulating thinking, you are providing students with *directions* for an upcoming learning activity, your communications should be extremely *explicit, specific,* and *directly to the point.*

You generally give directions during transition periods, just before the start of a learning activity. Directions must be explicit, precise, and concise so that transition time is minimized and allocated time is not wasted because students failed to follow the directions for the learning activity. In which two of the next four examples are teachers' directions clear and to the point? In which two will student engagement in the upcoming learning activity be impaired because the directions don't precisely communicate what is to be done?

Ms. Aldomat is holding a gymnastics class on the basketball court of the Saddle Hill School gym. Just as her 18 third graders complete their routine warmup–stretching exercises, Ms. Aldomat briskly walks directly to a point on the middle of one foul shot line of the basketball court. There, she pivots, faces her students, and blows her whistle for an instant. She holds her hand high above her head with the palm facing the students. The students have learned from previous class periods that the whistle signals an end to one activity and Ms. Aldomat's hand signal means to line up in front of her to wait for directions. As the students quickly move toward her, she says, "Line up on the half-court line, one arm's length apart facing me." She watches them intently as they line up facing her. As soon as everyone is in position, she drops her hand and points to Jenny who is standing first on their left-hand side of the line. Ms. Aldomat: "Jenny, please do four cartwheels directly forward and then wait on the baseline behind me facing us." Jenny obliges. Ms. Aldomat: "Thank you. Stay there, Jenny." She continues speaking to the group, "When I say 'start,' I want the rest of you to begin taking turns doing four cartwheels and waiting on the line as Jenny did. We'll begin on this end with Frank. As soon as Frank starts his third cartwheel, Freda goes, then Tamara, and so on down the line. Remember to watch the person to your left. You go as soon as he or she begins the third cartwheel. Ready, start!"

As the students take their turns, Ms. Aldomat positions herself so that she is just out of the way of the student who is about to begin. That helps signal the students to wait for their turns. If a student is late starting, she says nothing, but simply gestures with her hand.

**Illustration 6.1. Ms. Aldomat Provides Her Students with Explicit, Specific Directions**

    Ms. Duncan is holding a gymnastics class on the basketball court of the Westdale School gym. Just as her 18 third graders complete their routine warmup–stretching exercises, Ms. Duncan announces, "Okay, okay, that's enough. All right, listen up now. Let's do something else now." The last student stops stretching and the students gather around Ms. Duncan as she says, "We're going to practice our cartwheels now." "Good! Good!" Rhonda yells, jumping up and down. Tommy: "I hate cartwheels! Can't we jump on the tramp?" "Yeah! Yeah! Let's jump on the tramp, Miss Duncan," exclaims Dustin. Ms. Duncan: "We'll do the tramp another time, but it's time to work on cartwheels. Here's what we'll do. Go over to the middle of the court and. . . ." Several students run over to the center circle of the basketball court. The others, not knowing what to do, hesitate before rushing over themselves. Ms. Duncan reluctantly follows and says, "I didn't say to go yet. Now listen. I'm only going to say this once. Form a line." The students line up in somewhat of a semicircle as they tend to bunch themselves around the center court circle. Ms. Duncan: "Spread out. Come on! You know what I mean." Finally, the students are positioned and ready to hear Ms. Duncan who says, "Now, one at a time, I want you to do several cartwheels. We'll start over here on the end with Justin and then go on to the next one after Justin is about halfway through. Okay, let's go."

Mr. Boudreaux wants to lead his third-period English students through the literal, interpretative, and analytical stages of reading poems. After completing a brief lecture on reading poetry, he directs the students into the next learning activity by distributing copies of Edwin A. Robinson's poem "Richard Cory" and saying, "I want you to carefully read this wonderful poem and be prepared to discuss it when everyone is finished." Some of the students are beginning to read the poem as Mr. Boudreaux continues to provide direction. Mr. Boudreaux: "Now wait, don't start yet. Anthony, pay attention! Thank you. Okay, now as I was about to tell you, when you come across a word in the poem that you don't know, look it up in the dictionary and write down the definition." Denise: "Where should we write them?" Mr. Boudreaux: "Just on a sheet of paper. No! I've got a better idea. Write them on the back of your copy of the poem. Then you'll have them together for our discussion. Any other questions? Good! Let's get started."

Mr. Rice wants to lead his third-period English students through the literal, interpretative, and analytical stages of reading poems. After completing a brief lecture on reading poetry, he distributes a three-page document to each student containing: (1) directions on the first page; (2) the poem "Richard Cory" by Edwin A. Robinson on the second page; (3) a list of questions for discussion on the third page. Watching their faces closely and seeing that everyone has the document, Mr. Rice raises his hand signaling the students that he expects their attention. Mr. Rice: "Thank you. Let's go through the directions on the first page." Seeing that Blanche is thumbing through the pages, he gently taps her desk top and whispers, "First page." Confident that everyone appears to be attentive, he reads the following directions aloud, occasionally pausing to clarify or emphasize points:

"After receiving the signal to start, you have 14 minutes to:

1. Take out your pocket dictionary.
2. Read the poem 'Richard Cory' on the next page. As you read it, circle with your pen each unfamiliar vocabulary word. Look it up in your dictionary. Decide for yourself which of the meanings given in the dictionary Robinson meant for that word. Get the number of the page from your dictionary where that word appears. Jot that page number just over the word on your copy of the poem. Be ready to explain your choice of definitions to the class.

3. Read through the questions on the third page of this document.
4. Reread the poem. But, this time, read it so that you are prepared to discuss the answers to the questions with the class.
5. After the 14 minutes are up, we will have a two-part class discussion. The first part will focus on word meanings from the poem. The second part will focus on the questions from the third page."

"Richard Cory" is rather brief; the third page consists of the following questions:

1. What is meant in the poem by the following?

"... he was always human when he talked" (line 6)
"... he glittered when he walked" (line 8)
"And went without meat and cursed the bread" (line 14)

2. Was Richard Cory a happy man? Why or why not?
3. How did others think of him? Did they think he was happy? What lines from the poem support your answer?

## Nine Points About Directions

Ms. Aldomat's and Mr. Rice's explicit directions more efficiently communicated exactly what students were to do during learning activities than did either Ms. Duncan's or Mr. Boudreaux's. Ms. Aldomat and Mr. Rice took advantage of the following:

1. The students of teachers who display *businesslike attitudes* are more likely to efficiently follow directions than those of teachers who seem lackadaisical and less organized. Both Ms. Aldomat and Mr. Rice appeared to know exactly what tasks students were expected to complete and had well-organized plans for accomplishing those tasks.
2. As Jones (1979) pointed out, teachers' *body language* is a powerful medium for communicating expectations to students. By briskly walking to the point where she wanted to give directions, deliberately positioning herself, and directly facing students, establishing eye contact with shoulders paralleling the students', Ms. Aldomat communicated that her directions were to be heard and strictly followed.
3. Because giving directions is a frequent, routine occurrence in a classroom, teachers can minimize transition time, streamline communication procedures, display a more businesslike attitude, and reduce the amount of teacher-talk in classrooms by establishing *signals* or *cues* that instantaneously communicate certain recurring expectations to students. Nonverbal signals are particularly effective. From their prior experiences in her class, Ms. Aldomat's stu-

dents knew exactly how to respond to her whistle, her hand over her head, and even her body language. Similarly, Mr. Rice had conditioned his students to appropriately react to certain signals.

4. Speaking to students who are not attentively listening is not only a waste of time and energy, it also encourages inattentive behavior patterns. By deliberately *gaining at least the appearance of everyone's attention before providing directions,* teachers communicate the seriousness of the directions and increase the chances that the directions will be followed. Both Ms. Aldomat and Mr. Rice achieved eye contact with students to check on whether or not students were ready to listen and to signal that they expected to be heard before beginning to speak. Had students' attention not been obtained very quickly, then they would have resorted to more decisive methods for dealing with student inattentiveness (e.g., methods for dealing with off-task behaviors that are suggested in subsequent chapters of this text).

5. Students who have learned that their teacher tends to *say things only once* tend to listen the first time the teacher speaks. Ms. Duncan said, "I'm only going to say this once," but she probably repeated herself anyway, because her initial directions were so vague.

6. Students are more likely to listen carefully to the directions of teachers who *restrict their remarks to exactly what students need to know* to successfully engage in the upcoming learning activity. Neither Ms. Aldomat nor Mr. Rice mixed uninformative, inane words with directions, as did Mr. Boudreaux who included, "Okay, now as I was about to tell you. . . ."

7. When teachers are providing directions, they are not conducting a discovery lesson or any other sort of higher cognitive level learning activity. Efficiently communicated directions in which transition time is minimized *do not normally allow time for students to debate the pros and cons of what is to be done.* Unlike Ms. Duncan, Ms. Aldomat never provided students with an opening for arguing about the upcoming learning activity. She had Jenny demonstrate the cartwheels before the class even knew they would be doing cartwheels instead of jumping on the trampoline.

8. Students are far more likely to follow directions that *provide very specific guidelines for exactly what is to be done* than they are for ambiguously worded general directions. Ms. Aldomat told her students, "Line up on the half-court line, one arm's length apart facing me," rather than, "Form a line." She directed students to do "four" cartwheels instead of "several." Mr. Rice's time limit of "14 minutes" communicates something more specific to students than "in a while," "several minutes," "when everyone is finished," "10 minutes," or "15 minutes." Numbers like 10 and 15 appear rounded and less specific. Unlike Mr. Boudreaux who told his students only

to be prepared to discuss the poem, Mr. Rice provided very specific guidelines for how to prepare for the discussion.

9. The *more senses (e.g., seeing and hearing) through which directions are communicated*, the more likely students are to understand them. Besides telling her students what to do, Ms. Aldomat had Jenny demonstrate what was to be done. Mr. Rice's students heard and read his directions. If students had questions about the directions or appeared to misunderstand them, Mr. Rice could simply point to the relevant statements on the first page of the document he distributed.

## IDEAS FOR LECTURE SESSIONS

### Student Engagement During Lectures

For students to be engaged in a lecture-type learning activity, they must be attentively listening to what the teacher is saying. Taking notes and attempting to follow a teacher-prescribed thought pattern may also be components of student engagement for many lecture sessions. Such engagement requires students to be cognitively active, while physically inactive. This is not readily achieved for students of any age and virtually impossible to sustain with younger students. Lectures that continue uninterrupted for more than five minutes are ill-advised learning activities for primary grade students. Older students' attention can be maintained somewhat longer, but it is not easy. In the first of the next two examples, the teacher is not likely to maintain even older students' attention during her lectures. In contrast, the teacher in the second example utilizes lecture techniques designed to obtain and maintain student engagement.

Ms. Haenszel has prepared a lecture designed to help her junior high math class understand, know, and apply the arithmetic mean statistic (i.e., averaging numbers). The 28 students quietly sit at their desks, 12 of them poised with paper and pencil for note taking, as Ms. Haenszel begins from her station near the chalkboard at the front of the room. Ms. Haenszel: "Today, class, we are going to learn about a statistic for averaging data. It is called the arithmetic mean and many of you are probably already familiar with it. Here's the definition." She turns to the chalkboard and writes as she says, "The arithmetic mean of N scores equals the sum of the scores divided by N." She keeps her side to the class so that she can easily look over her shoulder at the class and still see what she writes on the board. Continuing, she says, "For example, to compute the mean of 30, 25, 20, 30, 40, 30, 60, 10, 0, and 15, we would first add all the numbers to find the sum. Let's see, . . . that adds up to 260. Now, there are 10 scores, so we divide 260 by 10 and get 26.0. The mean in this case is 26.

The arithmetic mean is a very important statistic. For example, if we had a second set of data, say 25, 18, 15, 20, 70, 10, 10, 8, 30, and 15, and we wanted to know whether the second set of numbers totalled more or less than the first, then we could compare their means to find out. In the second case, the sum is . . . 221. And 221 divided by the number of scores, which, like the first ones, is also 10 is 221 divided by 10 which is 22.1. So the arithmetic mean of the first group of scores, although containing a zero and no number as large as 70, is, on the average, bigger. This is because 26.0 is greater than 22.1."

Mr. Dwyer has prepared a lecture designed to help his junior high math class understand, know, and apply the arithmetic mean statistic. The 31 students are quietly seated at their desks as he begins by distributing copies of the form appearing in Illustration 6.2.

Facing the class from a position near the overhead projector, Mr. Dwyer says, "In the blank by 'Question to be answered,' please write, 'Do the people in this classroom on row two or row four have the bigger feet?'" He flashes on the overhead projector so that the question he just told them to write is displayed. Mr. Dwyer: "Now, I've got to figure a way to gather data that will help me answer that question. I know! We'll use shoe sizes as a measure. Everybody write his by the first 'Data for _____' blank." He flips an overlay off of the transparency and "Data for row two:" appears on the screen.

**Illustration 6.2. Students' Form to Accompany Mr. Dwyer's Lecture**

### AN EXPERIMENT

Question to be answered:

Data for _____

Data for _____

Treatment of _____

Treatment of _____

Results:


Conclusions:

Mr. Dwyer: "Starting from Jason in the back and moving up to Becky in the front, those of you in row two call out your shoe size one after another so we can write them down on the form." He writes down the following numbers in the appropriate space on the transparency as the six students in row two give their sizes: "5.5, 6, 8.5, 6, 7.5, 9.5." Briskly moving his attention to row four, Mr. Dwyer flips over another overlay on the transparency and exposes "Data for row four:" on the screen. Mr. Dwyer, "Let's get the info from row four so we can fill this one in also. Row four, start in the back as we did with row two." The process continues until "5, 10, 5, 6.5, 7, 7.5, 8, 7.5" for row four are displayed by the overhead.

Mr. Dwyer: "Now, how should I use these numbers to help us answer the question?" Several students raise their hands, but Mr. Dwyer says, "Thank you. But let me try to figure this one out for myself. It's easy enough to compare one score to another." Pointing to the appropriate numerals on the transparency, he continues, "David's 10 from row four is larger than Jason's 7.5 from row two. But, I don't want to compare just one individual's number to another. I want to compare this whole bunch of numbers—" (he circles row two's numbers with his pen) "—to this bunch." (He circles row four's numbers.) Mr. Dwyer: "I guess we could add the numbers for row four, add them up for row two, and then compare the two sums." A couple of students begin to say, "But Mr. Dwyer—" Motioning them to stop speaking, he says, "Let me think. We'll add them up and compare. What's the sum from row two, Terri?" Terri: "43." Mr. Dwyer: "Thank you. And what about for row four, Jamie?" Jamie: "56 and a half." "Thank you. So row four has the bigger feet since 56.5 is greater than 43," Mr. Dwyer says as he writes, "56.5 > 43." Mr. Dwyer: "I'll pause briefly now, to hear what you have to say. Vanessa?" Vanessa: "That's not right. It won't work." Mr. Dwyer: "You mean 56.5 isn't greater than 43!" Vanessa: "No, there're more feet on row four." Mr. Dwyer: "No, all the people on row four have two feet just like those on row two. I counted. Now that we've taken care of that problem, and established that everyone on both rows has the same number of feet, comments or questions from anyone else?—Yes, Jeremy." Jeremy: "That's not what she meant. You know what she means. She's telling you that there're more *people* on row four. So what you did was not right." Mr. Dwyer: "Let me see if I now understand Vanessa's point. She's telling me that we don't want our indicator of how big the feet are to be affected by how many feet, just the size of the feet. We've got to figure out a way to compare two groups when one has more people than the other. I'm open for suggestions. Jon?" Jon: "You could drop two of the numbers from row four and that would make them both have six." Mr. Dwyer: "That seems like a possible solution. Let's hear one more suggestion, maybe one that doesn't make us lose any of the data we collected. Alice?" Alice: "Divide by how many you have in a group, anytime one group is bigger than the other." Mr. Dwyer: "And what will that do for us?" Alice: "It'll even up the sizes." Mr. Dwyer: "Oh, I see. Dividing by the number of data points makes the sums fairer to compare. So what Alice suggested is to divide the sum of row two by six and the sum of row four by eight."

Flipping over another overlay, he displays the two lines each with "Treatment of _____" on the screen as it appears on the students' forms. He writes in, "Row two data: Sum of 6 shoe sizes = 43. 43/6 = 7.17." On the next line he writes, "Row four data: Sum of 8 shoe sizes = 56.5. 56.5/8 = 7.06." "So!" he exclaims, "Vanessa was right. Row two really does seem to have bigger feet than row four! That is, of course, if you want to use this particular statistic as the way to decide. This statistic is well known as the VAJJ and the formula for it is as follows." He changes to a clear transparency and writes, "VAJJ = (sum of numbers)/ (number of numbers). For example, the VAJJ for the ages of the five people that live in my house = (4 + 6 + 9 + 32 + 40)/5 = 18.2."

Emory raises his hand and Mr. Dwyer recognizes him. Emory: "Why do you call the statistic a VAJJ?" Mr. Dwyer: "It's called a VAJJ after its inventors, Vanessa, Alice, Jon, and Jeremy. They just invented it today." The class breaks into laughter. Mr. Dwyer: "It is also known, according to math books, as the 'arithmetic mean.' " Switching to a clean transparency, he writes out, "The arithmetic mean of a group of N numbers = the sum of the numbers divided by N."

## Thirteen Points About Lectures

Please consider the following thoughts when designing lectures:

1. Students are more likely to be engaged during a lecture session if the teacher has *provided clear directions for behavior*. Students need to have learned how to attend to a lecture. Questions about how to take notes, if at all, should be answered before the lecture begins.
2. Some sort of *advanced organizer to direct students' thinking helps students to actively listen* during a lecture. A written outline of topics to be covered or problems to be addressed, such as the form that Mr. Dwyer distributed, can be useful in keeping students engaged.
3. *Signals, especially nonverbal ones, can efficiently focus students' attention* during a lecture. Mr. Dwyer utilized at least two such signals. He directed students to a particular item on the form and had them write specific things down from time to time during the lecture. This helped students stay on track, preventing some mind-wandering. His use of the overhead projector also helped maintain students' focus. Turning the projector on signals students to look. Turning it off signals students to focus their eyes elsewhere. The use of transparency overlays controls what students see.
4. Lectures are useful learning activities for teachers who want to

have a group of students concurrently follow a common thought pattern. Lectures, such as Mr. Dwyer's, that are designed to do more than just feed information to students, run the risk of becoming discussion or questioning sessions. Thus, *some means for staying on track should be considered* when planning a lecture. One method is to have signals worked out with students so that they clearly discriminate between times when the teacher is strictly lecturing and when discussion or questions are welcome. Mr. Dwyer divided his lecture into two parts. In the first part, he presented the problem to be addressed, collected data, and focused thoughts on how to manipulate the data. During this first part, he had students speak, but they did not enter into a discussion session or raise questions. They simply provided him with data that he used in the lecture. Between the first and second parts of the lecture, Mr. Dwyer conducted a brief discussion session in which the students discovered the formula for the arithmetic mean. After the discussion, when he was again lecturing, he did entertain Emory's question, but he had set the students up to ask such a question in order to achieve a nice transition into the formal statement of the formula. Mr. Dwyer let his students know when their comments and questions were welcome by saying such things as, "But let me try and figure this one out myself . . ." and "I'll pause briefly now, to hear what you have to say. . . ."

5. At least three advantages can be gained by videotaping lectures ahead of time and playing them for students in class: *(a) Videotaped lectures avoid some of the interruptions in thought that occur when students make comments or ask questions; (b) The teacher can more attentively monitor students' behavior and effectively respond to indications of disengagement; (c) Kinks and mistakes in the presentation can be corrected and improvements made before the lecture is played for the class.* With videotape and other record-and-play devices (e.g., video laser discs), teachers can easily start, interrupt, replay, terminate, modify, and repeat presentations.

6. Students are more likely to follow lectures that *utilize professional quality media.* Students can hardly be engaged when the learning activity requires them to read, see, or hear something that is unintelligible. No doubt, school budgets and lack of preparation time present major limitations on the quality of the media used with lecture presentations.

7. Entertaining is not teaching. However, lectures that interject a bit of humor or contain other *attention-getting devices do help keep students more alert* than a straight monologue that only provides information. Care must be taken that the attention-getting devices don't become a distraction and focus students' thoughts away from the lesson.

8. *Students are more likely to alertly follow a lecture in which the lecturer maintains eye contact with those students.* This, of course, was one of the advantages Mr. Dwyer's use of the overhead had over Mr. Haenszel's use of the chalkboard.

9. Reading from lecture notes while stationed behind a lectern is a sure formula for student daydreaming and mind-wandering, and a major cause of student disengagement. *Teachers can deal more effectively with mind-wandering and daydreaming behaviors when they move about the room as they lecture.*

10. *Students who hear their names are usually alerted to listen to what is being said.* Thus, many teachers purposefully interject the names of individual students into their lectures. For example, during a lecture in a Spanish class, a teacher might say, "Suppose George wanted to tell Louise that her hair had just caught on fire. He could begin by. . . ."

11. To be engaged in lectures, students need to do more than just passively sit and listen. They need to be actively listening, trying to follow the teacher's thought patterns. Mr. Dwyer realized this, so he appeared to be thinking and reasoning aloud. *Teachers can facilitate engagement by verbally walking students through cognitive processes that lead to information and answers.* Such an approach is akin to the spirit of problem-solving learning activities alluded to in a prior section of this chapter.

12. As teachers lecture, they should frequently monitor their students' comprehension of what is being said. *Planned breaks in a lecture, in which students are asked questions, can provide the teacher with formative evaluation information that should guide subsequent stages of the lecture.*

13. Sometimes, students become disengaged during a lecture because the teacher used an unfamiliar word, expression, formula or symbol. The teacher continues, assuming the students understand; the students are no longer listening because they are busy trying to figure out the unfamiliar word, expression, formula, or symbol. *Teachers should make themselves aware of knowledge and skills that are prerequisite to following a planned lecture and to teach for those prerequisites before giving the lecture.*

## IDEAS FOR DISCUSSION SESSIONS

### Student Engagement During Discussions

For students to be engaged in a discussion-type learning activity, they must attentively listen to what classmates say and be willing to make comments and raise questions that are relative to the topic of discussion.

Discussions can be conducted in small intra-class groups or in large group meetings of a whole class.

As part of her efforts to help her 26 second graders develop both their skills and interest in reading, Ms. Torres directs the class to silently read a three-line story entitled "Making Things" from page 97 of one of their readers. In 35 seconds, everyone is finished and Ms. Torres begins a brief questioning session that leads into a large group discussion.

Ms. Torres stands in front of the class holding her copy of the reader open to page 97 in one hand and her bookmark held hand high over her head with her other hand. Ms. Torres: "Please put your bookmark on page 97, close your book, and keep it on your desk." She demonstratively follows her own directions with her copy of the reader as she watches the class do the same. Ms. Torres: "I would like for everyone to think about the answer to the question I'm about to ask. What was the reading about?" Most of the students raise their hands. Ms. Torres recognizes Gail who says, "Making things." Ms. Torres moves about the room as she asks, "What did Gail say? Doris." Doris: "She said, 'making things.'" Ms. Torres: "Why would anyone want to make things? Jamal." Jamal: "It's fun." Ms. Torres: "Todd?" Todd: "You don't have to pay for them." Ms. Torres: "Put your hand up if you never, ever like to make anything." No hands are raised. Ms. Torres: "It looks like we agree that we sometimes like to make things. We are about to have a *discussion* on making surprises for other people. Who remembers what we do when we have a class discussion?" About half the class raise hands. Ms. Torres says, "First we'll hear from Veda, then Morris, and Simon." Veda: "Only one talks at a time." Morris: "You hafta raise your hand to talk." There's a pause, so Ms. Torres motions to Simon who says, "That's what I was going to say." Ms. Torres: "Tell me, who calls on people who raise their hands to talk? Jessie." Jessie: "The last one that talked." Ms. Torres: "Thank you. Remember in a discussion, I don't call on you. Whoever has the floor calls on the next person to speak."

Ms. Torres: "Let's talk about making things, but not just anything. Let's talk about making things to surprise someone with something he or she likes. We'll begin the discussion with Marvell. Marvell, you have the floor to start the discussion on making surprises for others to enjoy." Fourteen students eagerly raise their hands beckoning Marvell to call on them. Marvell: "I like to make drawings and surprise my Momma. She hangs them up on the wall. Okay, Lydia." Lydia, who is seated near to where Ms. Torres is standing, begins, speaking directly to Ms. Torres, "My brother lost the pick for his guitar, so I cut out a piece of this stuff and wrapped it up in a box for him." As Lydia speaks, Ms. Torres moves to a point across the room from her so that most of the other students are positioned between Ms. Torres and Lydia. This encourages Lydia to project her voice and speak to the class rather than to Ms. Torres only. The discussion continues for 12 minutes with Ms. Torres continually moving about the classroom, occasionally motioning students to speak up and politely reminding them of the topic.

After the discussion, Ms. Torres conducts an activity in which students take turns reading aloud from a three-page story entitled "Surprise Pancakes." Ms. Torres then divides the class into four subgroups. Each subgroup is assigned a section of the room for them to meet sitting on the floor in a circle. After all four subgroups are in place, Ms. Torres says to all of the subgroups at once, using body language and gestures to help her students understand her directions, "Austin, you are the discussion leader for this group. Veda, you're the leader there. Marvell, here. Zeke, there. Your group is to think of five things we could make to bring home as a surprise for our parents. The surprises have to be something that we could all make here at school. Okay, you have nine minutes to decide and we've already used four seconds."

Ms. Torres moves from one group to another. Stopping to listen to the discussion in Veda's group, Jo asks her, "Is it okay if we cook something, like the kids did in the story?" Ms. Torres: "What do the rest of you think about cooking something?" Veda: "I didn't think we could, but. . . ." Seeing that Veda's group is again talking to one another, Ms. Torres quickly moves to Austin's group where Mary Jo and Freda are involved in a private conversation about cats. The other five appear to be on-task. Ms. Torres: "What have you decided we should make so far?" Austin answers, as Mary Jo and Freda continue their conversation, "Greg thinks we should make up a song." Zane: "That's stupid!" Ms. Torres: "Freda, what do you think about us making up a song?" Freda: "What?" Ms. Torres: "Explain your idea to Freda one more time, Greg." Ms. Torres sees that the subgroup, including Mary Jo and Freda, are listening to Greg, so she moves over to another subgroup.

After nine minutes, the alarm of the chronograph on Ms. Torres' wrist rings and she says, "Time's up. Just stay in your places and we'll have each group give us its list." She positions herself by a chalkboard and makes a list of the 16 "things to make" as they are told to her. Only one subgroup had exactly five suggestions, the others had one, three, and seven respectively. Several suggestions appear in the list more than once. Ms. Torres: "We will leave this list on the board until tomorrow when we decide which ones we will actually make as surprises for our parents. Right now, I would like for you to return to your places and open your readers to page 101." Once the students are in their places with their books open and ready to listen, Ms. Torres says, "What is the name of the story beginning on page 101? Barton." Barton reads, "Things to Make at School." Ms. Torres: "Thank you. Class, I want you to take this reader home tonight and read 'Things to Make at School.' We will discuss it tomorrow before we decide on which things from our list we will make."

## Six Points About Discussion Sessions

Thoughts for you to keep in mind when planning discussion sessions include:

1. How efficiently the time allocated for a discussion session is utilized partially depends on how clearly the *directions for the discussion communicate the exact procedures to be followed*. If a teacher consistently follows the same procedures for all discussions, students learn from repeated experiences to automatically follow those procedures without elaborate directions. Ms. Torres needed only to remind her students of the procedure for speaking to the group. In prior sessions, she probably had to spend more time teaching that procedure. In subsequent sessions, she may not need to remind them anymore.

2. Student talk is likely to stray from the topic of a discussion unless that *topic is specified and the purpose of the discussion is understood*. Ms. Torres led into the large group discussion with a questioning session in which she controlled the subject about which students talked. She had her students thinking about "making things" before she began the discussion that was to specifically deal with "making things to surprise someone he or she likes." The small discussion groups were directed to complete a specific task.

3. The focus of a discussion is more likely to be maintained when students perceive that the discussion is purposeful. *The purposefulness of discussions can be appreciated by students when the teacher uses lead-in activities to set the stage for the discussion. The outcomes of the discussion are used in activities subsequent to the discussion.* The readings and the questioning session had Ms. Torres' students focusing on the topic prior to the discussion. She used the list produced during discussions the following day.

4. Students have a tendency to direct their comments to the teacher. *Seating arrangements in which students are facing one another and the teacher is not a focal point to encourage students to speak and listen to one another.* Ms. Torres moved about so that most of the class was between her and whoever had the floor during the large group discussion.

5. With only a minimal disruption to discussions, teachers can silently use *hand signals to remind individuals to attend to a speaker or to motion a speaker to direct comments to the group, speak up, or slow down.*

6. By *using the comment of one student to involve another,* teachers model active listening behavior while encouraging participation. Ms. Torres, for example, asked Freda about Greg's idea.

## IDEAS FOR QUESTIONING SESSIONS

### Student Engagement During Questioning Sessions

For students to be engaged in a questioning-type learning activity, they must attentively listen to each question asked by their teacher, attempt to formulate answers to that question, and either express their answers in a manner prescribed by the teacher or listen to others express their answers. *Recitation* is one type of questioning session which teachers use to help students memorize. Here is an example:

> Ms. Caldaron asks her fourth graders, "What is the capital of Mississippi? Eva." Eva: "Jackson." Ms. Caldaron: "What is the capital of Louisiana? Vincent." Vincent: "New Orleans." A number of students eagerly raise their hands and Ms. Caldaron calls on Rosalie who says, "Baton Rouge." Ms. Caldaron: "That is correct. Baton Rouge is the capital of Louisiana. Now, what about the capital of. . . ."

Generally more interesting and helpful to students than recitations are *higher level questioning sessions* that are designed to stimulate students to think, discover, and reason. Here is an example:

> Mr. Becnel is conducting a higher level questioning session for the purpose of helping his 28 eighth graders understand how writers use facts to support their opinions. He displays an overhead transparency listing eight statements taken from a magazine article the class has just read. The list, as it appears on the transparency, is given in Illustration 6.3.
>
> Mr. Becnel to the class: "The eight statements on the screen are from the reading. Notice that some of the statements are marked with 'O's, others with 'X's." Can anyone tell me why the 'X' statements belong together and why the 'O' statements belong together? How are the 'X' statements like each other, but different from the 'O' statements?" Jamal, Tracy, and Sidney eagerly have their hands up; they raised them even before Mr. Becnel had completed his questions. Without pausing after his questions, Mr. Becnel calls on Sidney. Sidney: "The ones with the 'X's have numbers in them." "No, no!" cries Jamal. Tracy is waving her hand trying to get Mr. Becnel's attention and three other students raise their hands. Mr. Becnel: "Easy, Jamal. Let's give Sidney a chance. Does the fourth one have a number in it?" Sidney: "No." Mr. Becnel: "But, is it an 'X' statement?" Sidney: "Yes." Mr. Becnel: "Then what can you conclude?" Sidney: "My idea's not right." Mr. Becnel: "I agree that you've managed to disprove your hypothesis. Jamal?" Jamal: "The ones with the 'O's are things that everyone doesn't agree on." Mr. Becnel: "What do you mean? Give us an example." Jamal: "My aunt doesn't think fishing is

**Illustration 6.3. List of Statements Used in Questioning Sessions Conducted by Mr. Becnel, Mr. Mongar, Ms. Kranz, and Ms. Dzildahl**

X   "There are about 20 varieties of barracuda."

O   "Barracuda are fearless."

X   "Some of the barracuda of the Southern Atlantic weigh over 60 pounds."

X   "Some people eat sun-cured barracuda meat."

O   "Barracuda meat is not as tasty as more commonly eaten fish."

O   "Fishing for barracuda is an exciting sport."

X   "Barracuda have numerous sharp teeth."

O   "Barracuda are ferocious."

exciting. She hates fishing. And who knows if barracuda are fearless. Did anyone ever ask a barracuda?" Mr. Becnel: "Can't the same thing be said for the 'X' statements?" Sidney: "No, because each of the 'X' ones we can know for sure." Mr. Becnel: "For example?" Sidney: "You can weigh a barracuda and count his teeth." Murray: "Not me! I'm not gonna count no monster's teeth!" Laughter erupts in the class. Mr. Becnel: "Barracuda are monsters. Is that an 'X' statement or an 'O' statement? Okay, Jamal." Jamal: "That's an 'O' statement, because that's just what Murray thinks. Some people may think they're pretty." Mr. Becnel: "Statements of what some people think, but that can't be determined as true or false, are statements of what? What is the word for ideas we don't all agree to—for all the 'O' statements?" Tracy: "Opinions! 'O' for opinions." Mr. Becnel: "Are all the 'O's statements of opinions?" Jamal: "Yes." Sidney: "What do the 'X's stand for?" Mr. Becnel to Sidney: "Think of a word for something we can absolutely know to be true. It doesn't begin with 'X,' but it fits all of our exed statements." Sidney: "Theories?" Tracy and Jamal eagerly raise their hands. Mr. Becnel: "But do we know all theories to be true?" Tracy: "Facts." Mr. Becnel: "Who agrees with Tracy?" Sidney, Jamal, and two others raise their hands. Mr. Becnel: "I agree also. All of the exed statements are called what?" Jamal: "Facts."

As the questioning session continues, the relation between the author of the reading's use of facts and her use of opinions is discovered by a number of Mr. Becnel's 28 students.

What did you think of Mr. Becnel's use of questioning or Socratic methods for stimulating students to reason? The session was probably very valuable to Jamal, Sidney, and Tracy. However, what about the other 25 students; what did they learn? Mr. Becnel seemed to know how to effectively utilize questioning strategies, but only a relatively small portion of his class seemed involved. For high-level questioning sessions to be effective for all students, each student must attempt to answer the questions posed by the teacher. It is unnecessary for all students to express their attempted answers to the teachers, but they should at least have the chance to formulate answers in their minds. Because Mr. Becnel called on Sidney immediately after asking his first set of questions, most students did not have enough time to even try to answer the questions. They quit thinking of their own answers in order to hear Sidney's answer and the ensuing discussion.

In the example, Mr. Becnel, like most teachers, did not allow enough time to elapse between the end of his question and when he accepted a student's answer to the question. The average time teachers, as a group, wait for students to respond to their in-class questions is less than two seconds (Arnold, Atwood, & Rogers, 1974). After experiencing a few sessions like Mr. Becnel's in which they are asked questions that they don't have the opportunity to answer, most students learn to not even attempt to formulate their own responses. Some will politely listen to the responses of the few, others entertain themselves with off-task thoughts, and others, if allowed, entertain themselves with disruptive behaviors.

Mr. Becnel should not discard Socratic methods. High-level questioning sessions are the only type of learning activities for helping students achieve certain types of learning objectives (Joyce & Weil, 1980). What Mr. Becnel should do is reorganize his questioning sessions and apply techniques that lead *all students* to address *all questions* raised. Such techniques are illustrated by the next three examples.

Mr. Mongar is conducting a high-level questioning session for the purpose of helping his 28 eighth graders understand how writers use facts to support their opinions. He displays an overhead transparency listing eight statements taken from a magazine article the class has just read. The list, as it appears on the transparency, is given in Illustration 6.3.

Mr. Mongar: "I am going to ask you some questions, but I don't want anyone to answer aloud until I call on someone. Just answer the questions in your mind." Mr. Mongar asks them to consider the differences and similarities, if any, between the "X" statements and the "O" statements. Two students eagerly raise their hands and say, "Oh, Mr. Mongar!" Mr.

Mongar is tempted to call on them and positively reinforce their enthusiasm, but he resists and they sit quietly after seeing his stern look and gesture. He waits, watching the students' faces. Finally, he says, "Tom, do you have an answer?" Tom nods. Mr. Mongar: "Good! How about you, Linda?" Linda: "Yes." Mr. Mongar: "Fine. Are you ready, Thelma?" Thelma: "No, I don't know." Mr. Mongar: "I'd like for you to just think aloud. What are your thoughts about how the 'X' statements and 'O' statements are different." Thelma: "I don't see any difference; they're all about barracuda." Mr. Mongar: "That's an important similarity among all the statements. Now, I'd like some volunteers to share their answers with us. Okay, Rita." Rita: "Well, it seems to me that. . . ."

Ms. Kranz is helping her 26 eighth graders understand how writers use facts to support their opinions, and as did Mr. Mongar and Mr. Becnel, she distributes to each student a list of eight statements taken from a magazine article the class has just read. (The list, as it appears on the handout, is given in Illustration 6.3.)

Ms. Kranz: "At the bottom of the handout you just received, each of you is to write one paragraph describing why you think the 'X' statements go together and why the 'O' statements go together. How are the 'X's alike, but different from the 'O's? How are the 'O's alike, but different from the 'X's?" As the students think and write out answers, Ms. Kranz moves about the room, reading what students write from over their shoulders. Some students write nothing until Ms. Kranz comes by their desk and silently motions for them to write. After noticing that everyone has written something, she asks, "Would you please read to us what you wrote, Pete?" Pete reads, "The ones with the 'X's are more specific. The other ones, with the 'O's, are general." Ms. Kranz: "Judy, please read yours." Judy: "I don't think this is right, I wasn't—" Ms. Kranz interrupts and says, "I would appreciate you just reading exactly what you wrote." Judy: "The 'O' statements are more critical of barracuda than the other ones are. The 'X' statements are more straight-forward." Ms. Kranz: "Crystal, I'd like for you to compare what Pete read to what Judy read. Is there anything about Judy's answer that is similar to Pete's?" Crystal: "It seems that. . . ."

After the discussion on her first set of questions, Ms. Kranz raises follow-up questions and again has the students silently write out answers. Because she reads some responses as she circulates around the room, she can select the responses to be read that will better stimulate discussion and help make points she wants made.

After subdividing her class of eighth graders into five groups of five or six each, Ms. Dzildahl distributes to each group the list of eight statements used by the other teachers.

She directs each group to decide on the differences and similarities between the "X" and the "O" statements, and gives them 11 minutes to prepare and present their decisions to the rest of the class. Ms. Dzildahl moves from one group to the other and monitors them as they work.

## Six Points About Questioning Sessions

Here are some thoughts for you to keep in mind when designing learning activities in which you raise questions for your students to answer:

1. Unlike recitation sessions, student engagement during high-level questioning sessions requires students to take time to ponder and think about questions posed by teachers before expressing answers. Consequently, *students are unable to be engaged in high-level questioning sessions unless their teachers provide for periods of silent thinking between when questions are asked and answers expected.*

2. Having all students write out their responses to questions posed by a teacher has at least four advantages over having only students who are called on express answers: *(a) Students have to organize their thoughts to write out answers, thus providing an additional learning experience; (b) Allowing time for students to write serves as a silent period for all students to be thinking about how to respond to questions; (c) Written responses makes it possible for teachers to preview students' answers and decide which ones should be read to the class; (d) Having written responses available to read avoids some of the stammering and grasping for words that are typical of students answering aloud in front of their peers.*

3. *By directing a question at a particular student before articulating the question, a teacher may discourage other students from carefully listening to that question.* Mr. Becnel, Mr. Mongar, Ms. Kranz, and Ms. Dzildahl all posed most of their questions before designating someone to answer aloud. None of them, for example, phrased his or her questions like, "Johnny, is this an 'X' or an 'O' statement?" If they had, students other than Johnny may not have bothered to hear the question.

4. Teachers need to move quickly from one student to another so that as many students as possible express answers aloud. However, with high-level questions, some students' answers are complex and need to be discussed in detail; answers are not simply "right" or "wrong." In order to involve more students, maintain a single focus, and yet have some particular answers fully discussed, *teachers should use the responses of some students to formulate subsequent questions for other students.* Mr. Becnel applied this technique by using Murray's characterization of barracuda as "monsters" in his next question for the class. Ms. Kranz asked Crystal to compare Pete's response to Judy's.

5. *Students are more likely to engage in questioning sessions in which: (a) Questions relate to one another and focus on a central theme or problem rather than appearing isolated and unrelated; (b) Questions are specific rather than vague.* Mr. Becnel's questions all focused on the relation between facts and opinions as used in a particular selection that the entire class read. Vague questions, such as, "Do you understand?"

hardly focus thought as well as, "Is the statement 'Barracuda are monsters' an 'X' or an 'O' statement?"

6. *Learning activities conducted prior to questioning sessions can serve to maintain the focus of the questioning session. Also, students learn the importance of engaging in questioning sessions when the sessions culminate in some sort of problem resolution that is applied in subsequent learning activities.* Mr. Becnel used the reading of the passage on barracuda to set the stage for the questions. He should use what the students discovered about how the author supported opinions with facts in a follow-up assignment. Subsequent activities might include: (a) an assignment in which students read a new passage and analyze it, pointing out where the author supported opinions with facts; (b) directing students to write an opinion piece in which they use facts to support their points.

## IDEAS FOR INDEPENDENT WORK SESSIONS

### Student Engagement During Independent Work Sessions

Engagement in an independent work session requires a student to complete some assigned task without disturbing others also working on the task. Typically, students work individually with the teacher available for help (e.g., the case described on pages 120–124 in which Ms. Williams introduced the "colored flags" procedure to conduct a language arts independent work session). When you plan for such sessions, two potential problems should be taken into account: (1) How can you efficiently provide the individual help that students may need to remain engaged with the task? (2) How do you accommodate students' completing the task at differing times?

The first problem was experienced by Mr. Dupont-Lee in the example beginning on page 22. The second led to the disruption of Mr. Uter's learning activity in the example beginning on page 75. Ms. Evans solved these problems for the independent work session described in the next episode:

Ms. Evans distributes a copy of the following to each of the 34 students in her Spanish I class:

1. Please take out your translation notebook, pencil, textbook, and Spanish–English dictionary.
2. Translate into English each of the six sentences under the heading "A orillas del lago" on page 63 of your text by the following procedure:
   A. Look at the entire sentence. Lightly circle, with your pencil, each word whose meaning you don't remember in English.

**B.** Look up the meaning of each word you circled in your dictionary and write down the "short" meaning in your notebook.

**C.** Locate the verb in the sentence.

**D.** Determine the tense of the verb. If you need help in determining the tense, turn your text to page 39 and follow the directions for "Verb Tenses."

**E.** Write a *literal*, word-by-word translation of the sentence in your notebook.

**F.** Write an *interpretative* translation of the sentence right under the literal one in your notebook.

**3.** In 17 minutes we will go over the translations of the six sentences.

**4.** If you finish the six sentences before 17 minutes are up, please begin your homework assignment which appears in the usual place on the chalkboard.

Ms. Evans reads through the directions with the students and the students begin the task at their desks. Soon several students raise their hands and Ms. Evans walks over to Brad who tells her, "I can't do these." Ms. Evans immediately notices that Brad has all of his materials out with the text and notebook open to the appropriate pages, but that he has neither circled any words nor written anything down. She says, "I'll be back to see what you've done in 70 seconds. In the meantime, do this." She points to line 2-A on his copy of the directions. Ms. Evans goes over to Anna Mae who says, "What's 'lugar' mean?" Ms. Evans says nothing, but points to the words 'Lightly circle, with your pencil, each word whose meaning you don't remember in English' in line 2—A of the directions. As Anna Mae circles 'lugar,' Ms. Evans picks up Anna Mae's dictionary, hands it to her, and moves to another student.

## Four Points About Independent Work Sessions

By keeping the following thoughts in mind, you may improve the chances that your students enjoy high levels of engagement during the independent work sessions that you plan and conduct:

1. By *clearly defining a task in the first place*, teachers avoid many of the nagging questions about what to do that can be observed in many classrooms during independent work sessions. Ms. Evans' extra effort to specify her directions beforehand prevented her from wasting allocated time repeating or clarifying directions.

2. So as to efficiently provide real help (Jones, 1979) to all students when they need it in order to remain engaged in an independent work session, teachers must *avoid spending too much time with any one student*. For students with adequate reading skills, having steps for task completion spelled out in writing allows the teacher to quickly

refer students to what they need to do to help themselves. Ms. Evans used this technique and avoided lengthy exchanges with students. For students who cannot read (e.g., some kindergarteners), tasks for independent sessions should be kept extremely simple. If there are, for example, three steps in the completion of a task, the teacher might consider conducting three separate brief independent work sessions, devoting a session to each step.

3. To avoid having early finishing students idly waiting for others to complete the task, teachers should *sequence independent work sessions so that they are followed by other independent activities with flexible beginning and ending times.* The homework assignment Ms. Evans directed her students to begin after they translated the sentences could easily be interrupted when the class is ready to go over the translations and then completed later.

4. *Establishing some sort of formal routine for requesting help* minimizes the time students spend waiting and maximizes the time they have for working on the task. Ms. Williams' "colored flags" procedure, described on pages 123–124, provide an example of such a formal routine.

## IDEAS FOR HOMEWORK ASSIGNMENTS

### Student Engagement in Homework

Unlike most other types of learning activities, students typically must allocate their own time for engaging in homework assignments. Students doing homework may sometimes have parents or guardians nearby signaling them on-task. However, parental supervision of students' homework varies extremely according to circumstances in homes, the ages of students, and a myriad other factors. Engagement in a homework assignment usually requires students to: (1) understand directions for the assignment; (2) schedule time away from school for the assignment; (3) resist outside-of-school distractions while completing the assigned task; (4) deliver a report of the completed work in class by a specified deadline.

Many teachers find it so difficult to have students diligently complete homework assignments, that they have given up and no longer expect students to do homework. But for most academic subjects, homework is a critical form of learning activity that provides students with their only opportunities for *solitary* thinking, studying, practicing, and problem-solving. The crowded social setting of a classroom is not very conducive to the type of concentrated, undisturbed thinking in which individuals must engage to achieve certain cognitive learning objectives (e.g., being creative or analytical). To teach your students to complete homework you assign, you must make sure that engagement in this relatively unsupervised type of learning activity is positively reinforced. In the first and third of the next four examples, Mr. Davis and Ms. Salsevon try both contrived positive reinforcement and contrived punishment to extrinsically motivate students to do homework. Ms. Hanzlik and Mr. Sampson, in the second and fourth examples, utilize intrinsic motivation because the positive reinforcers for doing homework and the punishment for not doing it are naturally occurring.

Mr. Davis directs his 28 third graders to complete the 25 multiplication computations from Excercise 8–6 of their math workbook for homework. The next day, he collects the workbooks and returns them with a smiling face sticker on the homework of each student who had at least 20 correct answers. Four students who did not even attempt the exercise are verbally reprimanded in front of the class.

Ms. Hanzlik carefully examines the 25 multiplication computations from Exercise 8–6 of her third graders' math workbooks. She selects the 12 computations from the 25 that she thinks will provide her students with practice in each of the possible problem areas typically encountered by students attempting this particular computational process. The next day she collects the work and does a quick error pattern analysis on it (Ashlock, 1976). The papers are returned to the students with a clear indication of exactly those steps in the computational process they did correctly and those they did not. Because she had carefully selected the computations, she is able to provide more helpful feedback with fewer computations than she would have on all 25 computations or on randomly assigned ones.

While the rest of the students are going over her error pattern analysis, correcting their mistakes, and beginning on another assignment, Ms. Hanzlik calls the four students, Tim, Gail, Mary Jo, and Phil, who did not complete the assignment aside to speak with them. Ms. Hanzlik: "I'm sorry you didn't give me the opportunity to help you learn how to do this kind of multiplication." Phil: "I would've done it, but—" Ms. Hanzlik interrupts Phil, saying, "It doesn't make any difference why you didn't do it. Let's just figure out when you can get this done so I can analyze it and get it back to you before you leave school today. I need to do that for you before you can continue to learn math." Gail: "I forgot—" Ms. Hanzlik: "Please, just let me think of how I can help you.—I know! Here's what we'll do. I'll let you do those 12 problems right after lunch today. That's when the rest of the class will be baking pumpkin bread. You can finish it then, and I'll go over it right after school and get it back to you just in time for you to catch your buses."

As part of a unit on writing library papers, Ms. Salsevon directs her eighth grade English class to choose a topic, find at least four references from the library on that topic, develop an outline for writing a report on the topic, and write an essay of five to eight pages following the outline. The assignment is due in two weeks and, in the meantime, procedures for using the library, using references, outlining, and writing essays will be covered in class. The students are told that 40 percent of their grade for the unit will be based on whether or not this homework assignment is turned in on time. The other part of the grade will be from the exam to be given at the end of the unit.

As part of a unit on writing library papers, Mr. Sampson provides his 26 eighth grade English students with a list of topics and assigns the following homework: "Examine the list of topics. Pick three topics that interest you more than the others. For each of the three, write one paragraph explaining why that topic is more interesting to you than some of the others. Bring your paragraphs to class tomorrow."

The next day, Mr. Sampson asks each student in class, "What three topics did you write about?" If the student lists three, then Mr. Sampson asks the student to read her or his favorite paragraph to the class. The nine students who do not have the assignment completed exactly as Mr. Sampson had directed are not asked to read to the class. After the last of the 17 students has read, Mr. Sampson collects the papers and makes the following announcement, "Based on what you read and what I read in these papers, I will assign each of you a topic for a project to be completed in the next two weeks."

The next day, Mr. Sampson distributes a slip of paper to each student with the name of the topic to which he or she is assigned. Those who had followed Mr. Sampson's directions with the previous homework assignment are given the more popular, favored topics for their projects than are those who did not write paragraphs expressing their preferences. Mr. Sampson announces to the class, "For homework, go to the library and find four references about the topic for your project. Write out the title of each reference, its author, and one sentence on what the reference is all about. Bring your list to class tomorrow." Six students raise their hands. Mr. Sampson calls on Allison. Allison: "What's a 'reference'?" Mr. Sampson: "Good question! What did you want to say, Jessie?" Jessie: "I don't know what we're supposed to do." Mr. Sampson: "Allison doesn't know what a 'reference' is and Jessie doesn't know what to do for homework because I haven't explained these things to you yet. We're going to spend the rest of the today's class explaining just how to do tonight's homework assignment." The rest of the day's English period is devoted to learning activities on how to find and report on references in the library.

The next day, the learning activities focus on the lists of library references that the students bring to class. Some time is spent in explaining how to develop outlines for writing library papers. The homework assignment for the next day involves refining the reference lists and developing the first drafts of the outlines. This inextricable association between homework assignments and in-class learning activities continues throughout the unit until writing the final draft of the library paper is assigned for homework.

Students' grades for the unit are determined strictly by their performances on the in-class examination given at the end of the unit. However, items on the exam require students to refer to how they used library references for their project, refer to their outlines, refer to their final library paper, and attach a copy of both their outlines and the library paper.

## Eight Points About Homework Assignments

Your students are more likely to complete homework assignments on time if you keep the following thoughts in mind when planning those assignments:

1. Students do not automatically know how to schedule their time for homework, efficiently study, nor present homework as a teacher expects it. Thus, teachers should plan learning activities, especially early in a school term, to *teach students how to budget time for homework and exactly what procedures to follow for completing homework.*
2. *Simple, uncomplicated homework assignments are more likely to be followed than complex ones.* Unlike Ms. Salsevon, Mr. Sampson divided a rather complex, multi-step assignment into numerous simple assignments.
3. Students tend to delay the completion of assignments until just before it is due. Thus, *for long-range assignments, teachers should set short-range deadline dates for completion of intermediate steps that eventually lead to final completion.* Rather than simply require the library paper to be completed at the end of the two-week period, Mr. Sampson had students complete specific tasks leading to the final paper throughout the two-week period.
4. Some teachers are guilty of assigning homework just because it's expected and, consequently, the assignment does not tie in very well to in-class learning activities. These teachers' students learn to consider homework as a useless waste of their time. Using homework as punishment or withholding homework assignments as a reward are highly destructive forms of punishment or positive reinforcements that teach students to resent having to do homework. *All homework assignments should clearly be an integral part of an overall plan of learning activities designed to help students achieve worthwhile goals.*
5. *Student behavior patterns of diligently doing homework assignments are encouraged when their efforts are positively reinforced by feedback provided by their teachers.* Mr. Davis' students only found out whether their final answers on their homework were right or wrong. On the other

hand, Ms. Hanzlik's students were provided with helpful information on exactly how to execute the computations as a result of their homework efforts.

6. Ms. Salsevon attempted to motivate her students to complete a homework assignment by making students' grades contingent on whether or not the assignment was completed on time. Mr. Sampson, on the other hand, treated the assignment as a learning activity, not a test. However, Mr. Sampson made it clear that the homework assignment helped the students achieve exactly the same learning goals that the graded examination would test. *Students can learn the importance of diligently doing homework when there is a clear link between the homework they are assigned and the test they take.* In order to help students identify this association earlier rather than later, some teachers give tests that require students to complete tasks that are nearly identical to those assigned for homework. They do this early in a school term and, until students develop behavior patterns of doing homework, they virtually always test after every homework assignment.

7. Mr. Sampson tied each homework assignment in his unit on writing library papers to in-class learning activities. Students who failed to complete homework as specified by his directions felt clearly disadvantaged in the class period when the assignment was due. *By utilizing homework in the class session in which it is due, students failing to complete the assignment can experience naturally occurring punishment by being unable to fully participate in class. Similarly, students who have completed the assignment on time can be positively reinforced by the success they experience in class.*

8. If the potential for guardians to encourage or supervise their children's homework is ever to be realized, *teachers, at the very least, must keep those guardians apprised of what in the way of homework is expected of their children.* Some teachers have successfully entered into written agreements with guardians indicating the guardians' willingness to supervise or at least encourage children to do homework.

## IDEAS FOR VIDEO, FILM, AND GUEST LECTURE PRESENTATIONS

Engaged behavior for students during media or guest lecture presentations is similar to that expected during lectures presented by teachers. This type of learning activity is alluded to here only to remind you of three things:

1. Video, film, and guest lectures should be treated like any other learning activity and be an integral part of a planned unit of instruction.

2. You should plan the presentation with the guest lecturer to make sure that the speaker understands your expectations and that he or she communicates his or her expectations to you. In turn, you prepare your students beforehand to live up to those expectations.
3. Videotape, films, and other types of "canned" presentations should be previewed in advance for quality and content.

The following relates an unfortunate incident in which a teacher failed to heed the last of the three aforementioned principles; fortunately the occurrence is extremely rare:

> Planning to show the videotape *Nuclear Energy: Savior or Destructor* to his science class, Mr. Donaldson inserts the cassette he rented into the VCR and takes a seat in the rear of the room. To his surprise the very beginnings of *Patricia's Hot Night* shows on the screen before he rushes to the front of the room to stop the tape. Mr. Donaldson isn't sure if a video rental store worker carelessly put the tape in the wrong case or if one of his students pulled a prank.

## CLASSROOM DESIGNS THAT ENHANCE STUDENT ENGAGEMENT

In order for you to implement some of the ideas presented herein for conducting engaging learning activities, you must be able to easily and quickly move about in your classroom. Your classroom's acoustical characteristics need to be such that students can hear what you intend for them to hear without disturbing reverberations and background noise. Students can hardly be engaged in a learning activity in which visual presentations (e.g., overhead transparencies, videos, or chalkboards) are used if they cannot comfortably see what is displayed. Transition time can hardly be minimized when major rearrangements of furniture are required between learning activities. Furthermore, it is difficult for you to take one or several students aside and hold a conference if there is no convenient area for doing so while still supervising the rest of the students.

Questions regarding optimum classroom size and ideal room shape have been extensively studied (Loo, 1977). Classroom acoustics can be vastly improved by the installation of special FM equipment (Berg, 1986). Unfortunately, teachers typically have virtually no control over the size and shape of their own classrooms nor over any equipment that is permanently installed in them. Teachers are assigned rooms that they did not design to accommodate groups of students whom they did not select. In spite of poor circumstances, many teachers make the most of things by carefully and creatively arranging their classrooms.

In her first year as a literature and Spanish teacher at Vanguard High School, Ms. Del Rio is assigned room 129 for homeroom and for teaching two remedial classes with 23 and 27 students respectively, one American literature class of 30, and two Spanish I classes with 29 and 30 students respectively. Room 129's initial arrangement and the way Ms. Del Rio utilizes it for the first month is depicted in Illustration 6.4.

Ms. Del Rio is quite pleased that her room is equipped with three microcomputers. The school placed them in her room for delivering computer assisted instruction (CAI) in Vanguard's special remedial reading programs, but she utilizes these computers in her other three classes as well. Because she stresses problem-solving and student-centered learning activities, she finds room 129's initial arrangement inconvenient. It is difficult for her and the students to move about. She laments, "I have to negotiate an obstacle course to provide individual help to students located near the center of the room. I jab myself at least twice a day on the corners of these desks!" She feels she is unable to conveniently and smoothly move in the vicinity of students as they begin to drift off-task. Furthermore, the arrangement does not provide for separation between sound-producing group activity areas (e.g., where lectures and videos are presented) and quiet areas (e.g., where individual reading or CAI is going on).

Dissatisfied with the inflexible arrangement, Ms. Del Rio makes a list of the accommodations she wants her room to provide:

1. Quick and easy access for her between any two points in the room.
2. A designated "quiet area" for students to engage in individualized work (e.g., silent study or CAI).
3. A designated large group activity area for an entire class to congregate for discussions, lectures, tutorial sessions, and media presentations.
4. Small group activity areas for task groups to conduct their business.
5. Storage space for equipment and materials to be kept out of sight.
6. A secure teacher's desk in a location with a favorable vantage point.
7. A silent reading room and minilibrary that can comfortably accommodate several students at a time.
8. A time-out room for isolating students.
9. A private room in which Ms. Del Rio can hold uninterrupted conferences with individuals (e.g., a student with his or her guardians) when a class is not in session.

Ms. Del Rio doesn't believe she can possibly build all the features on her wish list into her classroom, but she does begin modifying room 129 to more closely resemble her ideal classroom. In the third month of the school year, she manages to have the school administration exchange the 30 traditional student desks for 10 6.5' by 2.67' elliptically shaped tables and 30 folding chairs. Her arrangement with three students per table is diagrammed in Illustration 6.5. Although she would prefer students having their own desks rather than sharing tables, this new arrangement provides

# Illustration 6.4. Room 129's Initial Arrangement

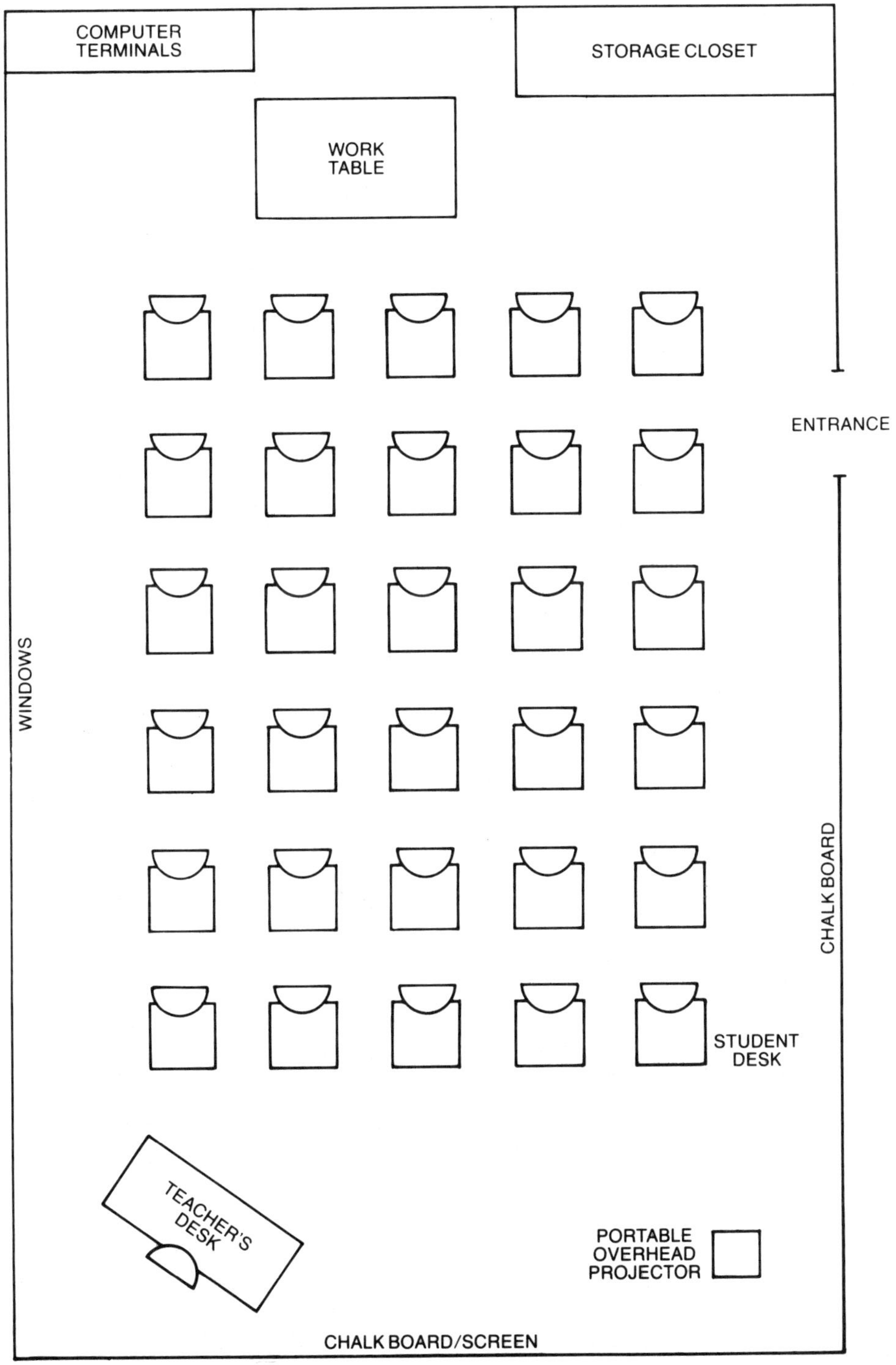

COMPUTER TERMINALS

STORAGE CLOSET

WORK TABLE

ENTRANCE

WINDOWS

CHALK BOARD

STUDENT DESK

TEACHER'S DESK

PORTABLE OVERHEAD PROJECTOR

CHALK BOARD/SCREEN

## Illustration 6.5. Ms. Del Rio's 1st Rearrangement of Room 129

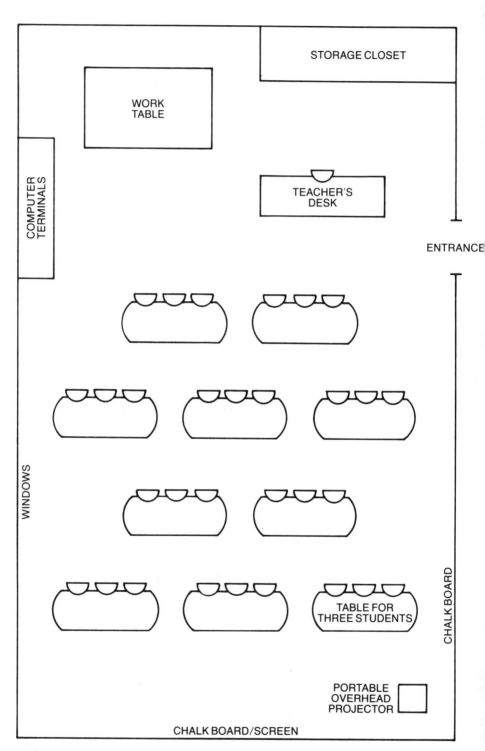

# Illustration 6.6. A Small Group Activity Arrangement in Room 129

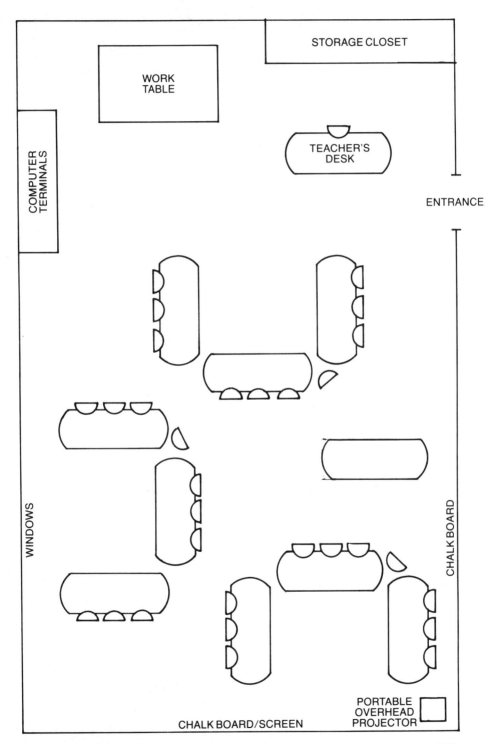

**Illustration 6.7. Ms. Del Rio Provides for More Area in Rear of Room 129**

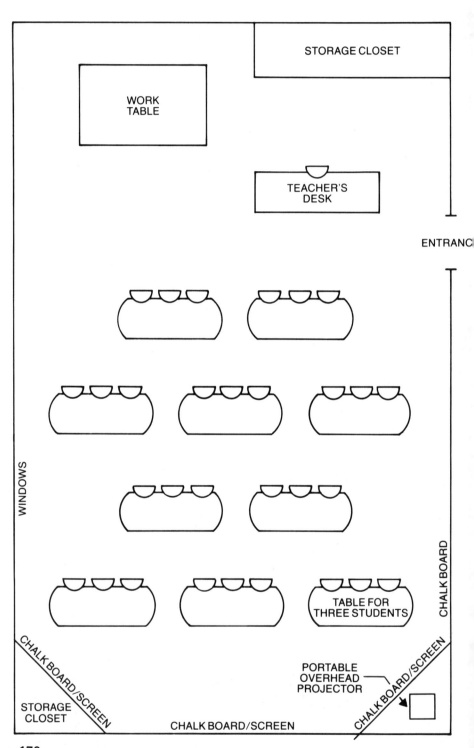

**Illustration 6.8. Room 129 at the Beginning of Ms. Del Rio's Second Year**

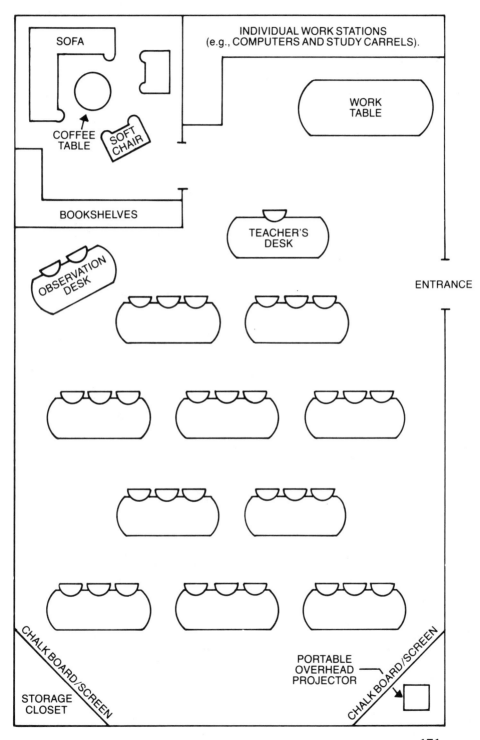

**Illustration 6.9. Room 129 as Ms. Del Rio Finally Left It**

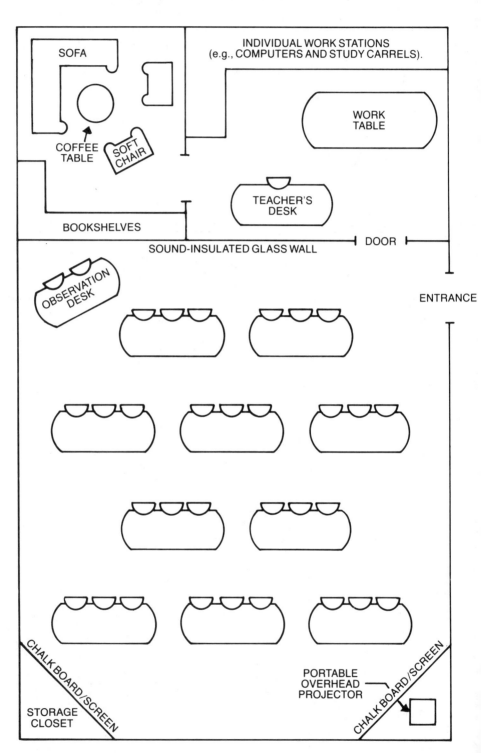

**Illustration 6.10. Room 9, P.S. 157 When Mr. Hawkoos First Took It Over**

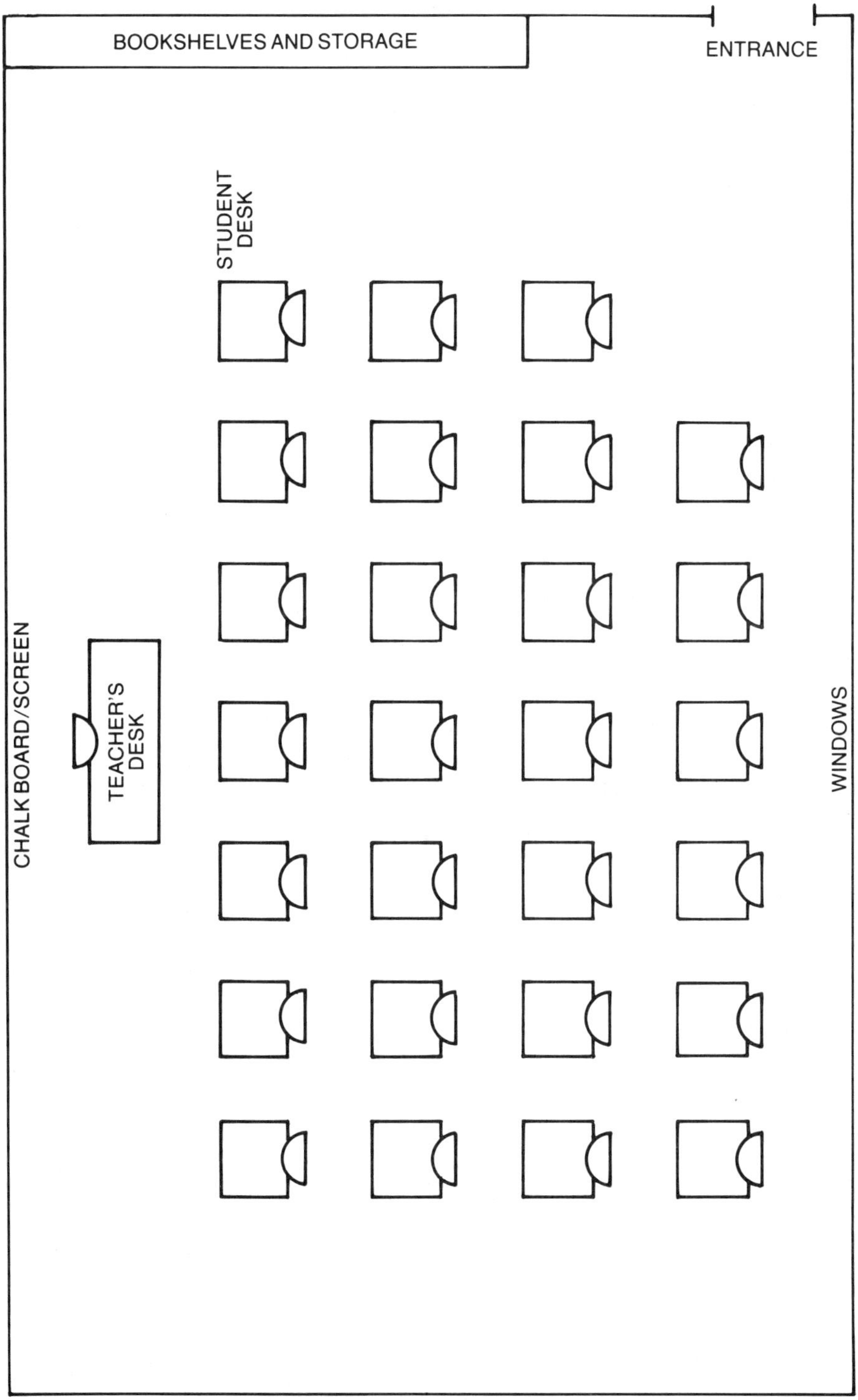

# Illustration 6.11. Room 9 in P.S. 157 After Mr. Hawkoos' Alterations

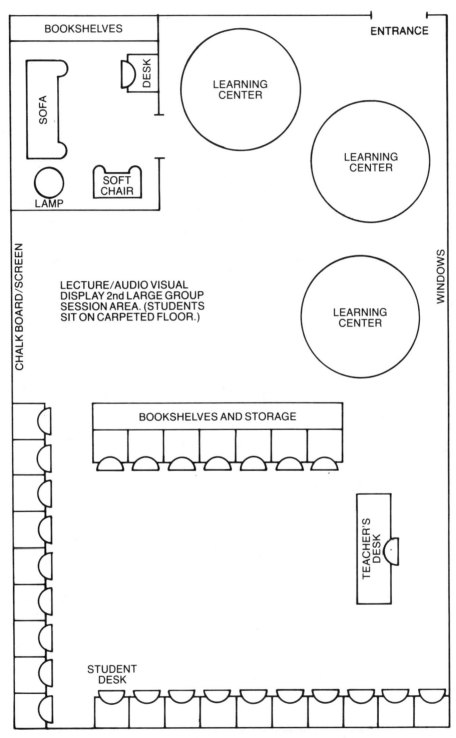

more work areas in the back of the room and makes it easier for her to move about the room from one student to another. For small group discussions, she can quickly have students rearrange tables and chairs to follow the pattern given in Illustration 6.6.

Ms. Del Rio needs the storage space provided by the large closet in the back of room 129. However, she also needs more area in the back of the room for the quiet work section. To remedy that situation, she gets one of the school's custodians to install a closet with a chalkboard and projection screen on the doors in each of the two corners in the front of the room. She had observed that these two front corners had been dead space. With this latest modification, depicted by Illustration 6.7, room 129 has more viewable board and screen areas, storage space is maintained, and additional floor areas are available in the back of the room.

During the summer break after her first year, Ms. Del Rio calls on the generosity and skills of some of her students and their guardians. They partition off an 8' by 10' area in the back of room 129 to serve as a combination minilibrary, reading room, time-out room, conference room, and out-of-class-hours escape room for Ms. Del Rio to work undisturbed. Used book shelves, a coffee table, a sofa, and two chairs, all labeled "surplus" in the school district's warehouse, furnish the new room. While the volunteer carpenters are walling in the 8' by 10' room, Ms. Del Rio mentions that it would be nice to have study carrels in the quiet area in the back of the room. Mr. Singleton, a cabinetmaker by profession, custom-builds the carrels to her specifications. Illustration 6.8 depicts how room 129 appears on the first day of Ms. Del Rio's second year at Vanguard.

Ms. Del Rio finds it much easier to keep students on-task the second year at Vanguard than she did the first. The additional year's experience plays a major role as do the modifications to room 129. However, sometimes the noise from the learning activities in the front of the room is disturbing to the individualized activities in the rear. The problem is mitigated as a result of the tour of her room and presentation she makes for Vanguard's Home and School Association. Members are so impressed with her initiative that they appropriate funds for installing two doors and a sound-insulated glass wall in room 129. The project is completed over the Christmas break and room 129 appears as in Illustration 6.9.

Ms. Del Rio would have continued to improve room 129 had she not accepted a position for the following year at Rose Park High. Room 244 that she will be assigned at Rose Park is similar to the one depicted in Illustration 6.4.

Illustration 6.10 is a diagram of room 9 in Public School Number 157 where Mr. Hawkoos is assigned to teach 27 third graders. Utilizing tactics similar to those used by Ms. Del Rio, Mr. Hawkoos' room 9 is modified as diagrammed in Illustration 6.11.

## Self-Assessment for Chapter 6

I. Following are examples of students whose engaged behaviors are either intrinsically or extrinsically motivated; place an "I" by each example of intrinsic motivation and an "E" by each example of extrinsic motivation:

A. Clyde carefully listens to the questions his teacher raises in class to avoid the embarrassment he feels when he's called on and doesn't provide an acceptable response.

B. Lynnae's mother tells her she can adopt a new kitten only if she does well on her next spelling test. Because of this, Lynnae diligently works on her spelling homework.

C. To impress her coach, Carmen spends extra time during basketball practice running up and down the bleachers.

D. To build up her endurance, Noel spends extra time during basketball practice running up and down the bleachers.

E. Because he wants to someday visit Europe, Damien diligently works on the exercise his French teacher has assigned.

F. Casey carefully listens to and watches his teacher as she shows him how to write his name. He is anxious to write it himself on the Mother's Day card he's prepared.

G. In order to avoid being criticized by her teacher, Marnae carefully follows directions when completing a writing assignment.

H. To increase the chances that her teacher will display her essay on the bulletin board, Nadine carefully follows directions when completing a writing assignment.

I. Convinced that by learning arithmetic he can increase his chances of purchasing a better bicycle for less money, Anthony raises questions in class about how to complete a computation.

II. Write three or four paragraphs describing the associations between: (A) positive reinforcement and whether motivation is intrinsic or extrinsic; (B) whether punishment is contrived or naturally occurring and whether motivation is intrinsic or extrinsic.

III. Develop two overall unit plans for teaching a four-year-old how to count from 1 to 20. Design the first plan so that it does *not* use problem-solving learning activities. Design the second plan so that it does utilize problem-solving learning activities.

IV. In a paragraph, compare, with respect to advantages and disadvantages for keeping students engaged, problem-solving to non-problem-solving learning activities.

V. Develop one specific lesson plan for teaching one objective within one of your own teaching specialties. Describe in one or two paragraphs how you would provide your students with *directions* for that learning activity.

   VI. Design a lecture-type learning activity within one of your teaching specialties. In one or two paragraphs, describe your plan for conducting the lecture.

  VII. Describe a discussion-type learning activity within one of your teaching specialties. In one or two paragraphs, describe your plan for conducting the discussion.

 VIII. Design a high-level-questioning-type learning activity within one of your teaching specialties. In one or two paragraphs, describe your plan for conducting the questioning session.

   IX. Design an independent-work-type learning activity within one of your teaching specialties. In one or two paragraphs, describe your plan for conducting the independent work session.

    X. Design a homework-type learning activity within one of your teaching specialties. What is the assignment?

   XI. Examine a classroom used to teach students within one of your teaching specialties. Make a detailed sketch of the room arrangement. Decide how you would rearrange the room to make it more conducive to students being on-task. Sketch your modified arrangement.

*Reviewing Your Self-Assessment* _____

Check your responses to Part I against the following: A-E, B-E, C-E, D-I, E-I, F-I, G-E, H-E, I-I.

Compare your response to Part II to those of others. The responses should include the following points: (1) When a behavior is positively reinforced by a naturally occurring reward, one tends to be intrinsically motivated to repeat that behavior; (2) When a behavior is positively reinforced by a contrived reward, one tends to be extrinsically motivated to repeat that behavior; (3) When a behavior is followed by naturally occurring punishment, one tends to be intrinsically motivated to avoid that behavior; (4) When a behavior is followed by contrived punishment, one tends to be extrinsically motivated to avoid that behavior.

Compare your response to Part III to those of others. In general, the problem-solving learning activities focus on concerns that students have prior to engaging in the activity. The non-problem-solving learning activities focus more on what is to be learned than on utilizing what is learned to address questions, concerns, or tasks which interest students.

Compare your responses to Part IV to those of others. In general, students tend to be intrinsically motivated to engage in problem-solving learning activities because they discover they can accomplish some of the things that are important to them via engagement in the learning activities. Because problem-solving learning activities tend to be more student centered and indirect than more traditional styles of teaching, students may initially perceive them to be weird and unstructured. Consequently, they may tend to be off-task until they are taught on-task behaviors for this seemingly new type of activity. Problem-solving learning activities should not be thrust all at once on students who are not used to them.

Compare the directions you prepared for Part V to those prepared by others. Also, analyze them to see how many of the nine ideas about directions enumerated on pages 142–144 were taken into account.

Compare the lecture plan you prepared for Part VI to those of others. Also, analyze the plans to see how many of the 13 ideas from pages 147–149 were utilized.

Compare the plan for the discussion-type learning activity you prepared for Part VII to those of others. Also, analyze the plans to see how many of the six ideas from page 152 were utilized.

Compare the plan for the high-level-questioning-type learning activity you prepared for Part VIII to those of others. Also, analyze the plans to see how many of the six ideas from pages 157–158 were utilized.

Compare the plan for the independent-work-type learning activity you prepared for Part IX to those of others. Also, analyze the plans to see how many of the four ideas from pages 159–160 were utilized.

Compare the homework assignment you prepared for Part X to those of others. Also, analyze the plans to see how many of the eight ideas from pages 163–164 were utilized.

Compare your classroom rearrangement, in response to Part XI, to those of others. Which features, from Ms. Del Rio's list of nine on page 166, were you able to incorporate?

## Supplemental Readings

Berg, F. (1986). *Listening for the hard of hearing students.* San Deigo, CA: College Hill Press.

Charles, C. M. (1983). *Elementary classroom management* (pp. 104–140, 184–199). White Plains, NY: Longman.

Clark, L. H., & Starr, I. S. (1981). *Secondary and middle school teaching methods* (4th ed.), (pp. 41–59, 167–222). New York: Macmillan.

Emmer, E. T., Evertson, C. M., Sanford, J. P., Clements, B. S., & Worsham, M. E. (1984). *Classroom management for secondary teachers* (pp. 4–14). Englewood Cliffs, NJ: Prentice-Hall.

Evertson, C. M., Emmer, E. T., Clements, B. S., Sanford, J. P., & Worsham, M. E. (1984). *Classroom management for elementary teachers* (pp. 4–14). Englewood Cliffs, NJ: Prentice-Hall.

Johnson, D. R. (1982). *Every minute counts: Making your math class work* (pp. 7–16). Palo Alto, CA: Seymour.

Johnson, D. R. (1986). *Making minutes count even more: A sequel to every minute counts* (pp. 2–54). Palo Alto, CA: Seymour.

Loo, C. M. (1977). *The differential effects of spatial density on low and high scorers on behavior problem indices.* A paper presented at the annual meeting of the Western Psychological Association, Seattle, WA.

Tobbin, K. (1986). Effects of teacher wait time on discourse in mathematics and language arts classes. *American Educational Research Journal, 23,* 191–200.

Walker, J. E., & Shea, T. M. (1984). *Behavior management: A practical approach for educators* (3rd ed.), (pp. 148–149). St. Louis, MO: Times Mirror/ Mosby.

Zumwalt, K. K. (Ed.). (1986). *Improving teaching: 1986 ASCD yearbook.* Alexandria, VA: Association for Supervision and Curriculum Development.

# part three

# How Can You Solve Discipline Problems?

# How Should You Deal with Students' Failure to Cooperate?

# 7

# Approaching Off-Task Behaviors Systematically

Chapter 7 is designed to help you:

1. deal with student off-task behaviors by applying the Teaching Process Model rather than by reacting without careful consideration of how to teach students to supplant off-task behaviors with on-task behaviors.
2. understand the rationale and begin developing some ideas for how to implement each of the following suggestions for responding to student off-task behaviors: (a) either respond decisively to an off-task behavior or ignore it altogether; (b) distinguish between teaching students to be on-task and "character building"; (c) distinguish between isolated off-task behaviors and off-task behavior patterns; (d) control the time and place for dealing with off-task behavior; (e) provide your students with dignified ways to terminate off-task behaviors; (f) avoid playing detective; (g) utilize the help of colleagues; (h) utilize the help of guardians; (i) utilize alternative lesson plans; (j) do not use corporal punishment; (k) know your rights and limitations; (l) maintain your options; (m) know your students and know yourself.

## DEAL WITH OFF-TASK BEHAVIORS VIA THE
## TEACHING PROCESS MODEL

### A Mechanism for Focusing

Ms. Blythe is lecturing to her eighth grade class when Jane, one of her 26 students, begins looking around as she taps her pencil against her desk. Ms. Blythe finds Jane's behavior annoying and judges it to be a potential distraction to others in the class. Without much thought, Ms. Blythe interrupts her own lecture and from the front of the room complains to Jane, "Will you stop that? Can't you ever do what you're supposed to?"

Ms. Guevarra is lecturing to her eighth grade class when Jeanne, one of her 26 students, begins looking around as she taps her pencil against her desk. Ms. Guevarra finds Jeanne's behavior annoying and judges it to be a potential distraction to others in the class. Within the span of three seconds and without interrupting her lecture, the following thoughts pass through Ms. Guevarra's mind: "Jeanne needs to pay attention and quit making that noise. This is not a chronic behavior for Jeanne and I've never had to deal with it from her before. I will get her to stop and return her attention to the lecture. How should I accomplish this? I'll continue to lecture, but I'll move near her and make eye contact. If that doesn't get her attention or she continues to tap, I'll gently touch her tapping hand. If that fails, I'll think of another tactic."

Continuing her lecture, she walks to a point near Jeanne. Jeanne ceases looking around and appears to attend to the lecture, but she keeps tapping her pencil. Ms. Guevarra gently grabs Jeanne's hand. Jeanne stops tapping and hardly any of the other class members even notice the silent communication between Ms. Guevarra and Jeanne. Ms. Guevarra continues to monitor how well Jeanne and the other students attend to the lecture.

Unlike Ms. Blythe, Ms. Guevarra systematically dealt with an off-task behavior as she would deal with any other student learning need. She approached Jeanne's off-task behavior using the same steps of the Teaching Process Model that she would use to teach a learning unit in science, social studies, physical education, or any other content area of the curricula. In only a matter of seconds she:

1. *identified a student need* when she decided that Jeanne should stop tapping and pay attention;
2. *determined a learning objective* by deciding that she would somehow get Jeanne to stop tapping and become engaged in the lecture session;
3. *planned a learning activity* when she decided to stand by Jeanne, make eye contact, and gently grab Jeanne's hand as she continued with her lecture;

4. *prepared for the learning activity* by moving into position to carry out her plan. (This whole incident happened so fast that Ms. Guevarra had virtually no need to prepare for the rather simple learning activity in this example. Admittedly, a point is stretched here to remind you of all six steps of the Teaching Process Model. In more complicated examples of teachers dealing with off-task behaviors, preparation for the learning activity may be quite elaborate.)

5. *conducted the learning activity* by actually standing by Jeanne, trying to make eye contact, and gently grabbing her hand; and

6. *evaluated how well the learning objective was achieved* by observing Jeanne to see if she would again begin to tap and look around.

Ms. Blythe's response to Jane's off-task behavior appeared to be an unthinking reaction to being annoyed. Instead of focusing on the problem of getting Jane back on the track of engaged behavior, Ms. Blythe disrupted the engagement of the rest of the class, and attacked Jane's personality with an irrelevant, rhetorical question. Such tactics may get Jane to stop tapping and look forward, but she would be a very unusual adolescent if she were able to listen to and think about the substance of Ms. Blythe's lecture immediately after being asked, "Can't you ever do what you're supposed to?" Jane was probably thinking about what she considered to be Ms. Blythe's insulting and embarrassing attack on her in front of her peers.

Of course, Ms. Blythe's approach to Jane's off-task behavior was quite understandable. Teachers are continually faced with the problem of orchestrating a group of young people who can manage to display very annoying behaviors. Students *ought* to behave cooperatively without teachers having to apply creative tactics to lead them to do what they *should* do on their own. It's no wonder that Ms. Blythe sometimes reacts thoughtlessly to her students' displays of disruptive behaviors. However, although Ms. Blythe's tactics were understandable, they're also ineffectual. To overcome the temptation to respond to students' annoying behaviors with ineffective displays of emotion, you, as a teacher, would do well to train yourself to be constantly mindful of the Teaching Process Model. By having your thoughts organized according to the six steps of the Model, you will likely be ready to systematically respond to students' displays of off-task behaviors, even the annoying ones, as did Ms. Guevarra.

## More Elaborate Applications

In the next two examples, teachers deal with off-task behaviors systematically by applying the Teaching Process Model. Unlike the two previous examples, the students' off-task behaviors with which these teachers must deal are behavior patterns rather than simply isolated incidences. Consequently, in the next two examples, the teachers' tactics are more elaborate than those used by Ms. Guevarra.

Al, one of Ms. Reid's fourth graders, is engaged in a small group learning activity with four other students playing "geography bingo." The game leader calls out, "The largest continent." Paul exclaims, "Bingo! It's Asia and I've got it right here for bingo!" Al stands up and yells at Paul, "You stupid ass-hole! I had that one too! I could've got bingo!" With those words, Al shoves Paul down and upsets the other students' game cards. Ms. Reid arrives on the scene, firmly grabs Al by the arm, and briskly walks him to a point just outside the classroom door. Looking directly into Al's face, she calmly says, "Wait here while I check to see if Paul is hurt." Without giving Al a chance to speak, she unhesitatingly turns and walks back to where the incident occurred as other students gather around Paul who, though still lying on the floor, is beginning to communicate his plans for retaliation. Ms. Reid interrupts Paul, saying, "I'm sorry that Al pushed you down, but I'm happy that you are not hurt." Helping Paul to his feet, Ms. Reid continues speaking without giving anyone else a chance to complain about Al or giving Paul a chance to make further threats. Ms. Reid: "Blaine and Carol, I would appreciate you helping each other pick up this mess and getting the bingo game started again. Let's go with just four players this time. Everyone else, please return to your work. Thank you for cooperating." Ms. Reid quickly returns to Al standing in the doorway and says, "Right now, I don't have time to work with you on your misbehavior during geography bingo. Now, I have a class to teach and it's time for you to work on geography. We'll just have to wait until tomorrow morning to discuss this matter. When your bus arrives tomorrow morning, you come immediately to the classroom and meet me at my desk. Will you remember, or should I phone your house tonight to remind you? Al: "I'll remember." Ms. Reid: "Fine! Now, you still have 13 minutes to work on geography. Go get your geography book and bring it to me at my desk." At her desk, Ms. Reid directs Al to complete a geography exercise at a work table located away from the rest of the class. The exercise is a drill on the same geography skills that the bingo game was designed to develop.

At the end of the school day, when Ms. Reid experiences her first solitary moments after the students have been dismissed, she thinks to herself: "I bought myself some time to figure out what to do about Al's outbursts in class. That was a real chance I took grabbing him. With his temper, he might've turned on me. This is the third or fourth time something like this has happened while Al was involved in a group activity. What makes him so aggressive? Well, that's not what I have to worry about right now. My job is to prevent this from happening again. I'll exclude him from any small group activity for the time being. Today, I hope he didn't think the geography book exercise was a punishment. I don't want to teach him to hate geography. But, he's got to understand that antisocial behavior isn't tolerated in my classroom! Look at me, I'm getting myself all worked up just sitting here by myself. What do I do? I could just explain my dilemma to him and ask him to think of a solution.

**Illustration 7.1. Ms. Reid Has Her Class Back On-Task Before Dealing with Al's Misbehavior**

That tactic worked really well with Grayson. But Grayson is a different chemistry than Al. Al's not ready for that yet. He's too defensive; he'd be telling me how it wasn't his fault. I'd love to know more about his home situation and find out why he's so defensive. But I don't have time to worry about that; I've got a more immediate problem to solve. Okay, here's what I'll do:

1. I don't want to give him a chance to argue and be defensive when we meet tomorrow, so I will not even try to explain the reasons for the way I'm dealing with the problem. I'll simply tell him what we're going to do and not defend the plan.
2. I will assign him to work by himself away from others in the class when he would normally be involved in some small group acitivity. His independent assignment will be over content similar to the small group activity in which others will be engaged.
3. I'll watch for indicators that he is modifying his antisocial behavior pattern and is becoming more willing to cooperate in group activities.
4. Gradually I'll work him back into group activities as I see encouraging indications that there will be no more trouble. I'll avoid involving him in any sort of competitive activities for a long time.

Okay, how shall I present this plan to him tomorrow? What will I do if he doesn't show up tomorrow? I'd better prepare for that possibility. . . ."

Mr. Mitchelson routinely assigns his eleventh grade literature class homework that takes students from 45 to 90 minutes to satisfactorily complete. Assignments might involve the students in reading a short story, writing an essay, or preparing a reference report. For the first several months of the school session, Mr. Mitchelson finds that only a few students take the time and effort to complete the assignments to his satisfaction. His discussions with the students indicate that they view the assignments as busy work that holds little value for them. Most of them fake their way through the assignments barely doing enough to keep them out of trouble with Mr. Mitchelson. In response to this concern Mr. Mitchelson begins to incorporate some of the principles of problem-solving learning activities, and he makes certain that students recognize the relation between these homework assignments and problems which they feel a need to solve. Gradually, nearly every student is consistently satisfactorily completing the homework.

However, Wilma is one of the exceptions. Even though Mr. Mitchelson's assignments are now meaningful to the students, Wilma rarely completes homework. The fact that Mr. Mitchelson is now using in-class learning activities that depend on completion of homework assignments compounds Wilma's difficulties because her failure to complete homework makes it nearly impossible for her to participate. When queried about homework, Wilma consistently indicates that she tries, but just can't get the assignments finished. Mr. Mitchelson is convinced that Wilma has the ability to satisfactorily complete the work. He decides to do something to help her to consistently choose to do homework. As he plans the learning activities for teaching her this on-task behavior pattern, he thinks: "I could subtract points from her grade for not getting in assignments on time, but her literature grade should reflect how well she achieves course goals, not how faithfully she finishes work. I want to base grades on test scores. But of course, if she continues not finishing homework, there's no way she'll achieve the goals and consequently she'll get poor grades anyway. Maybe I should just let her go and she'll learn her lesson by failing the course, that would work nicely as naturally occurring punishment. But what is my purpose as a teacher, to teach her some life-long lesson about being responsible or to help her achieve course goals? I'm not going to take on the problem of trying to change her life, just teach her literature by trying to get her engaged in my learning activities. No, I won't just let it go. The next time she doesn't complete an assignment, I could refer her to Mr. Taylor. But even though he's the counselor, I don't think he'd be much help. Scratch that one. What if I set up a contingency contract with her, working out a system in which privileges depend on completion of homework? Let me save that one for later if other things don't work out. What if I required her to remain after school to complete unfinished work? Then she'd miss her bus which is fine with me. That would be a nice naturally occurring punishment. But then I'd have to stay with her and I don't want to do that to myself. Of course, I've got to stay after school for 45 minutes anyway, but I need that time for other things and unless I stood over her, she'd still fail to get the work done. Scratch another good idea. What I really need to do is find out why she doesn't finish these assignments. She doesn't have a job or anything; she must have the time. Grace says she normally turns in her math homework. Let's see, tomorrow's schedule calls for her to turn in a report expressing why she thinks the people Charly works with in *Flowers for Algernon* are not his friends. And then most of the class has 'free reading time' scheduled at the library. If she doesn't have the report as assigned, I'll require her to finish it in class. There'll only be about five others in the room at that time, and I can observe her working on the assignment."

The next day, Wilma has only the introductory paragraph to her report. In that one paragraph, the purpose of the report is accurately stated. As planned, Mr. Mitchelson directs her to complete the report by the end of the 55-minute class period. Wilma sits and stares at her paper for 10 minutes without writing. Mr. Mitchelson goes to her and looks over her shoulder. She asks, "Mr. Mitchelson, is my introduction okay?" "You've stated the purpose with clarity," he replies and moves away. Several minutes later, she comes to Mr. Mitchelson and the two have the following conversation: Wilma: "Were the factory workers Charly's  friends or not?" Mr. Mitchelson: "What do you think?" Wilma: "I don't know." Mr.

Mitchelson: "You say you don't know what you think?" Wilma: "Well, I don't think the workers were very nice to Charly. Am I wrong?" Mr. Mitchelson: "You can't be wrong. It's a matter of opinion. There is no way to be right or wrong in this case. As you said in your introduction, the purpose of this report is to express your opinion on whether or not the workers were Charly's friends. If you say what you believe, then you are correct whether or not anyone else agrees with you." Wilma: "Oh!"

Wilma returns to her seat and writes for 5 minutes before returning to Mr. Mitchelson with one more line written. "Is this right, Mr. Mitchelson?" she asks. . . .

After the school day, Mr. Mitchelson continues thinking about ways to help Wilma choose to complete assignments: "Wilma really seems reluctant to express her opinions. She finally completed her report in class, but in the meantime she drove me nuts seeking my approval on each line before she'd write the next. She appears afraid to complete one step in an assignment before having the previous step okayed. Either that or she doesn't trust others and me to accept her opinions. Now that I think about it, just about all of the assignments she doesn't do require her to give her opinion. I think Wilma needs to learn that I'm receptive to and value her opinions. It will take some time for her to become convinced of that. In the meantime, as an intermediate step I should help her get in the habit of completing homework. For now, I'll implement the following plan:

1. I'll privately tell her just what I've decided and that I expect her to complete every assignment.
2. I'll make sure that for at least a week, I won't give her assignments in which she is to express her own opinions. For example, with the *Flowers for Algernon* report, instead of directing her to report on why she thinks the people with which Charly works are not his friends, I'll modify it so she's asked to write about somebody else's opinion on whether or not they were Charly's friends. Maybe the assignment for her would be to interview a classmate and report his or her opinion on the question.
3. If Wilma completes these modified assignments every day for a week, I'll gradually begin giving her assignments where she's to express her own opinions. I'll be careful never to judge her opinions; I'll judge only the processes by which she arrives at those opinions. If she doesn't complete all of the first week's assignments, then I'll re-evaluate the situation, consider other causes, and maybe move to a contingency contract plan to positively reinforce doing homework.

I need to really evaluate how well this works before deciding whether or not to change my strategy."

### Staying Calm and Organizing Thoughts

In the last three examples, Ms. Guevarra, Ms. Reid, and Mr. Mitchelson viewed the problem of eliminating off-task behavior as they would view the problem of helping a student to achieve any other learning objective. By applying teaching techniques to the task of helping students choose on-task behaviors instead of off-task behaviors, they were able to focus their time, energy, and thoughts on the important issues confronting them. Ms. Reid, for example, did not try to moralize about the evils of fighting with Al. She realized that telling Al about the evils of fighting, something he's likely to have heard already, would serve nothing. Teachers, such as Ms. Blythe, who do not systematically focus on the behavior to be altered tend to compound difficulties by dwelling on irrelevant issues (e.g., whether or not Jane can ever do what she's supposed to do). Teachers who fail to focus on the goal of getting and keeping students on-task and engaged in learning activities sometimes feel offended when students are disruptive and do not pay attention. These teachers sometimes deal with their own hurt feelings by retaliating against students rather than focusing on getting the students to behave as they should.

The Teaching Process Model, of course, provides you with a way of organizing your thoughts about teaching students to behave as they should. As you apply this model, you will, as Ms. Guevarra, Ms. Reid, and Mr. Mitchelson did, need to design strategies or learning activities for dealing with off-task behaviors. The remainder of this chapter provides you with 13 suggestions for devising strategies. Chapter 8 focuses on ways for you to develop strategies that help students supplant off-task behavior patterns with on-task behavior patterns. Chapter 9 is concerned with ideas for dealing with nondisruptive off-task behaviors; Chapter 10's concern is disruptive behaviors.

## EITHER RESPOND DECISIVELY TO AN OFF-TASK BEHAVIOR OR IGNORE IT ALTOGETHER

Ms. Hillyard is busy explaining some rules for capitalizing words to her class of 31 fifth graders. "Now, who can tell me which words in this sentence should begin with a capital letter?" she asks, as she begins to write on the chalkboard, "my friend eddie said 'looking for ghosts' was a—" Just then, she hears some students talking among themselves. Looking over her shoulder, she sees Don, Abby, and Lyle involved in a conversation. "Hey you chatterboxes, stop talking and pay attention," she says as she finishes writing the sentence, "—funny movie." The three students continue talking. They hardly heard Ms. Hillyard's message for them as she failed to get their attention before speaking. Ms. Hillyard continues her explanation for several more minutes before once again trying to quiet Don, Abby, and Lyle by saying, "Okay, I told you to knock it off already. This time I mean no more talking!" She continues her lesson as they continue talking.

It would be inadvisable for Ms. Hillyard to have ignored her students' inappropriate talking; however, ignoring the misbehavior in the example would not have been as destructive as was her weak, halfhearted response. Not only were her efforts in dealing with the three students' off-task behaviors ineffectual, but Ms. Hillyard's actions displayed to the class that they need not seriously consider her directions (e.g., "Stop talking and pay attention"). In general, an indecisive, perfunctory attempt at dealing with one incident of off-task behavior compounds a teacher's difficulties in effectively dealing with subsequent incidents of off-task behaviors. Here is why:

1. When a teacher demonstrates that he or she is aware of off-task behaviors, but does not make the effort to effectively lead the students to supplant the off-task with on-task behaviors, students tend to generalize that the teacher is not serious about expecting them to be on-task. Such an attitude tends to detract from the businesslike climate that should prevail in a classroom.
2. A teacher (e.g., Ms. Hillyard) who only tells students how to behave without taking action to lead students to follow what is said conditions students to not bother to listen. Some teachers will repeat demands for students to be on-task (e.g., "Pay attention") over and over without students complying until the teacher finally gets angry and upset. Such a practice conditions students to not listen until the teacher becomes angry and upset.
3. Halfhearted efforts that are nonproductive or counterproductive waste a teacher's valuable energy and time.

If you're confronted with an off-task student behavior, but are not at the time in a position to apply a strategy that has a reasonable chance of working, then you should at least delay your response until help can be obtained or until you can design and apply a suitable strategy.

In the next example, Mr. Clark's response to students' off-task behavior is more decisive than was Ms. Hillyard's.

Mr. Clark is busy explaining some rules for capitalizing words to his class of 31 fifth graders. "Now, who can tell me which words in this sentence should begin with a capital letter?" he asks, as he begins to write on the chalkboard, "my friend eddie said 'looking for ghosts' was a—" Just then, he hears some students talking among themselves. He stops writing, pivots and faces the class to see Jim, Oral, and Mavis carrying on a conversation. Walking directly over to the three, he picks up the book, paper, and pencil off of Jim's desk and says, "Jim, please take these over to that empty seat over there. Mavis, you take your stuff and work from that desk in front of Mike." Confident that his directions will be followed, he quickly returns to the front of the room and continues his explanation.

## DISTINGUISH BETWEEN TEACHING STUDENTS TO BE ON-TASK AND "CHARACTER BUILDING"

### A Teacher's Responsibilities and Capabilities

In the example in which Ms. Reid utilized the Teaching Process Model to deal with Al's disruptive behavior, Ms. Reid focused on helping Al to terminate an in-class, antisocial behavior pattern. Ms. Reid recognized that she is responsible for keeping her students engaged in learning activities that are designed to get students to achieve worthwhile learning goals. She believes that developing Al's character and teaching him to be an upstanding moral human being are outside of the realm of both her responsibilities and capabilities. Her method for stopping the clash between Al and Paul and quickly getting everyone re-engaged in the learning activity was effective at least partially because she focused on her responsibilities as a teacher.

Sometimes when a teacher understandably reacts in anger to an annoying off-task student behavior, that teacher loses sight of where a teacher's responsibilities begin and end. Here is an example:

> While her first graders are working in intra-class reading groups, Ms. Blanchard sees Todd yank Celia's hair so hard that she falls over backwards and begins crying. Ms. Blanchard yells to Todd, "Come here, boy!" Todd comes over as all the other students stop their work to watch. "How would you like me to pull your hair? You think you're tough! I can be a lot tougher than you! I'll make you sorry for ever being a bully! Suppose I let Celia pull your hair! Would you like that? Well, would you?" Todd: "I didn't pull that—" Ms. Blanchard: "You didn't what? Wait until one of the big second or third graders picks on you! You'll learn not to be so mean!"

### Focusing on the Task

Ms. Blanchard's anger clouded her focus and, instead of taking effective action to prevent a recurrence of such intolerable misbehavior, she got off-track trying to get Todd to be sorry for *being* "mean."Rather than deal with the incident, she focused on Todd's "meanness." In the following example, reported in *Cooperation in the Classroom: Students and Teachers Together* (Cangelosi, 1986), Mr. Wagoner helps a student substitute engaged behavior for off-task behavior without allowing himself to be sidetracked into thinking he's building character:

> Libba, an eleventh grader, stops at a convenience store on her way to school. She buys three cans of beer and consumes them before her 8:45 A.M. homeroom period. Neither her homeroom nor her first period history teacher notices anything strange in her behavior. However, as second period begins, she appears tipsy to Mr. Wagoner, her science teacher. Mr. Wagoner directs two students to begin setting up an experiment that he plans to demonstrate to the class. While they are doing this, he subtly beckons Libba to the doorway and out in the hall. Detecting the odor of alcohol on her breath, he says, "It's your business if you want to mess up your own life. But it's my business to teach you science, and I can't teach it to you when you're in that condition. When we've completed this conversation, you go back to your desk. Just keep quiet and concentrate on facing straight ahead. Did you hear me?" Libba: "Yes, sir." Mr. Wagoner: "Fine. Tomorrow morning come to this room at 8:15. We'll discuss the matter then. Can you remember to be here or should I remind you with a call tonight?" Libba: "I'll remember; I'll be here."
>
> At 8:15 the next morning, Libba makes her appointment and Mr. Wagoner tells her, "If you ever come into my class again while under the influence of alcohol or any other drug, I will immediately send you to Ms. Swindle's office. I will inform Mr. Giradeau that I refuse to teach you in that condition. And I will inform your parents of the situation. Do you understand?" Libba: "Yes, but I'm not the only—" Mr. Wagoner (interrupting): "I am not talking with you about others, only you. I don't discuss your problems with other students, and I won't discuss theirs with you. Do you understand?" Libba: "Yes!" Mr. Wagoner: "Yesterday while you were 'out of it,' we were analyzing this experiment that is described here in my teacher's manual. I want you to take my manual home tonight and analyze the experiment as it is described on pages 79 through 84. Bring in your results, and I'll be happy to give you feedback on them as soon as I find the time. That should catch you up with the rest of the class. You won't be behind anymore. Okay?" Libba: "Okay." Mr. Wagoner: "See you in class. Keep smiling."

## DISTINGUISH BETWEEN ISOLATED OFF-TASK BEHAVIORS AND OFF-TASK BEHAVIOR PATTERNS

Different strategies are used for learning activities that teach students to terminate isolated off-task behaviors than for off-task behavior patterns. Off-task behavior patterns are usually more difficult to terminate than isolated incidents. However, teachers usually have the luxury of taking time to plan strategies for dealing with patterns; whereas, isolated off-task behaviors should typically be dealt with as they occur. You can effectively utilize behavior modification principles (e.g., extinction and shaping) that are covered in Chapter 8 to teach students to eliminate off-task behavior patterns. You need to be mindful of behavior modification principles when dealing with isolated off-task behaviors in order to guard against off-task behavior patterns developing out of the isolated incidents. If an isolated off-task behavior is positively reinforced, then an off-task behavior pattern may emerge.

## CONTROL THE TIME AND PLACE
## FOR DEALING WITH OFF-TASK BEHAVIOR

Once Ms. Reid stopped Al and Paul from fighting in the example beginning on page 186, she attended to getting the class re-engaged in learning activities and arranged for a more convenient time to take measures for preventing recurrences of Al's disruptive behaviors. She wanted to wait to speak with Al: (1) after she had time to collect her thoughts and develop a plan of action; (2) at a time and place in which she wouldn't be burdened with having to supervise other students; (3) when and where no other students would be around so Al would feel free to communicate with her without concern for what his peers were thinking; (4) after they both have had time to cool off.

Like Ms. Reid and Mr. Wagoner in the example beginning on page 194, you will be more effective dealing with off-task behaviors if you manage to control the times and places for interacting with students over their misbehaviors. Typically, students are more concerned with the images they portray for their peers than they are with what you or any other teachers are trying to do for them. Consequently, you are more likely to achieve a productive interchange about preventing recurrences of off-task behaviors in a private conference with a student than you will when both of you are worried about others in the vicinity. Do not make the mistake of making a major issue out of one student's off-task behavior in front of other students in order to exhibit the undesirability of the off-task behavior. Such strategies usually lead to feelings of embarrassment and resentment that detract from the cooperative, businesslike climate you want existing in your classroom.

## PROVIDE STUDENTS WITH DIGNIFIED WAYS
## TO TERMINATE OFF-TASK BEHAVIORS

Ms. Fabian is conducting a writing lesson in which her third graders are taking turns writing three-word sentences on the chalkboard. "Okay, Valerie, it's your turn. Please put your sentence on the board," she says.

Valerie just looks away and doesn't get up from her desk. Ms. Fabian: "Valerie honey, please write your sentence on the board." Valerie: "I don't have one." Ms. Fabian: "Here, we'll help you. I'll give you two of the three words and you use them in a three-word sentence. How about, 'John loves'? You find a third word and make a sentence that starts 'John loves'. Valerie: "No!" Ms. Fabian feels threatened by Valerie's refusal. She fears that if she allows Valerie to win the struggle of wills in front of the class, others will also refuse to follow her directions. Ms. Fabian: "Valerie, you had better be up and writing on the board before I can count to five!" Valerie: "I won't." Ms. Fabian: "I'm counting! One, two, three, four, Valerie, you'll be sorry . . . five! Okay, young lady, you had your chance, now we'll see that you'll learn to do what you're told!" Valerie: "Okay, okay! I'll write your sentence." Valerie gets up and walks to the front of the room. Ms. Fabian: "It's too late now. I already counted to five. You had your chance!" Valerie: "I said, I'll write the sentence." Ms. Fabian: "Not until I receive an apology. You tell me you're sorry for your rudeness and you apologize to the class for wasting their time." Valerie faces the class and says, with her head down and a sheepish grin across her face, "Sorry!" Ms. Fabian: "And what do you say to me?" "I'm sorry, Misses Fabian," she mutters with glaring eyes. Ms. Fabian: "That's more like it!"

Ms. Fabian's mishandling of Valerie's off-task behavior left Valerie feeling stripped of her dignity in front of her peers. What could Ms. Fabian ever expect to gain by insisting that Valerie apologize? Did the apology reestablish Ms. Fabian's authority after her counting-to-five strategy failed? The apology might have temporarily helped Ms. Fabian to feel better about herself, but unfortunately, such power games only create an atmosphere of unhealthy competitiveness between teacher and students. Such competitiveness precludes the development of dignified, businesslike attitudes that are so vital if a classroom is to be characterized by cooperative student engagement.

If you expect dignified behaviors from your students, you need to avoid doing anything that leads them to fear that their dignities are in jeopardy. Thus, your strategies for dealing with their off-task behaviors, even rude and annoying ones, should provide them with face-saving ways to supplant off-task behaviors with on-task behaviors. This is not always easily done. When students behave rudely, it is tempting for teachers to respond with clever comebacks or put-downs. Not only does this practice destroy a healthy classroom climate, it can easily backfire on a teacher as it did in the following example:

Mr. Sceroler is urging his eighth grade class to get their homework in on time as he says, "There's nothing I can do if you don't have the work for me to see." Ronald from the back of the room, in a barely audible tone, quips to the student next to him, "He could always go jack off!" Having overheard the comment, Mr. Sceroler yells at Ronald, "What was that you said?" Ronald begins to grin and look around at his classmates. "You were trying to show off for us and now you can't say anything! What did you say?" Ronald whispers with his head down, "Nothing." Mr. Sceroler, seeing Ronald back down, begins to feel confident as he continues, "What was that? Speak up. What did you say?" Now facing Mr. Sceroler, Ronald says in a loud voice, "I said I didn't say nothin'!" Mr. Sceroler retorts, "You can't even use decent English. Of course you didn't say anything. You aren't capable of saying anything, are you?" Some class members laugh. Enjoying the audience, Mr. Sceroler smiles. Ronald, very concerned with what his classmates are thinking, suddenly stands up and shouts at Mr. Sceroler, "I said you could always go jack off, but then I forgot, you don't have a dick!"

By trying to outwit Ronald instead of providing him with a face-saving way of getting back on-task, Mr. Sceroler turned a self-terminating incident into a most unfortunate confrontation with unhappy consequences for all concerned. Since Mr. Sceroler initially heard Ronald's rude remark, why would he ask him, "What was that you said?" Ronald tried to end the incident by not replying, but Mr. Sceroler persisted and left Ronald with only the choice of either lying about what he said or repeating what would surely be interpreted as an obscenity. Had Mr. Sceroler not been such an insecure adult, intent on proving his superiority over an adolescent, he might have left Ronald a dignified way to return to on-task behavior by either ignoring the original remark or by politely directing Ronald to visit with him at a more convenient time.

## AVOID PLAYING DETECTIVE

You also encourage competitiveness between you and your students by playing detective, as Mr. Brubacher does in the following example:

Some students in Mr. Brubacher's biology class begin regularly amusing themselves by covertly screeching "Whoop-whoop!" while he speaks to the class. At first, he tries laughing the disruptions off with comments like, "There's a bird in here, and I've got a hunting license!" But after a couple of days, Mr. Brubacher no longer finds any humor whatsoever in the rudeness. To the delight of his students, he vows to catch the pranksters and put an end to the whoop-whooping. Unsuccessfully, he tries to identify the source of the annoying sounds. More and more students get into the act and are becoming bolder and more creative in devising ways to emit the sound without getting caught.

In the next example, Ms. Fisher deals with an ongoing disruptive behavior from an unidentified source as did Mr. Brubacher. However, unlike Mr. Brubacher, Ms. Fisher refuses to play the detective game with her students.

> After a day in which Ms. Fisher's students amused themselves by covertly screeching, "Whoop-whoop!" when she spoke to the class, she thinks to herself:
>
> "I wish I knew who's responsible for that horrible whoop-whooping. But, I'm not going to play their little game with them, so I'm not going to even try to find out. I really don't care who's doing it; I just won't tolerate it any more. They know that noise annoys me, so I shouldn't try to act as though it doesn't. Tomorrow, I'll be ready with an alternative lesson plan if they try the whoop-whooping while I'm explaining things to them.
>
> The next day, Ms. Fisher is lecturing on the digestive system, when "Whoop-whoop" is heard and some of the students begin to laugh. Abruptly, Ms. Fisher stops the lecture and silently and calmly displays a transparency on the overhead with the following message: "I cannot explain the digestive system to you while that noise is going on. I simply won't try to do what you won't allow me to do. But I am responsible for seeing that you learn this material. So please open your book to page 179. Study pages 179 through 191. Most of what we planned to talk about today is covered in those pages. Do not forget that we have a test over the unit objectives scheduled for Monday. Good luck!"
>
> Ms. Fisher believes that most of her students would prefer attending to her explanations than only depending on reading the text. Thus, she believes that if she continues to abruptly move to her alternative lesson plan each time her lectures and explanations are disrupted, enough peer pressure will be exerted to stop the unidentified sources of the "whoop-whooping."

## UTILIZE THE HELP OF COLLEAGUES

Refer to Mr. Martin's checklist for preparing for the opening of a new school year on pages 55–57. Item 11 under "Classroom Organization and Ongoing Routines" is "Whom, among building personnel, can I depend on to help handle short-range discipline problems and whom for long-range problems?" In the example beginning on page 120, Ms. Williams has an arrangement with Mr. Demery, a fellow teacher, that allows the two of them to more effectively deal with off-task behaviors than they could working alone. You would do well to seek out a few teachers in your school on whom you can depend to (1) Work out cooperative arrangements for handling discipline problems as did Ms. Williams and Mr. Demery; (2) Share ideas and provide counsel on how to teach students who get off-task to be on-task.

Dealing with off-task behaviors is one of the more difficult jobs with which anyone is confronted. Do not play "macho teacher" and be too embarrassed to seek help. Routinely share ideas with trusted colleagues and seek help when confronted with particularly difficult situations. Ms. Reid, in the example in which she arranged some think-time for herself before confronting Al's antisocial behavior, may have used some of that time to confer with another teacher or an instructional supervisor who has experience dealing with similar problems. Of course, it is assumed that you will seek the help of other professionals like yourself without violating the professional trust that exists between you and your students.

## UTILIZE THE HELP OF GUARDIANS

### The Myth of the Good Teacher

In *Assertive Discipline: A Take-Charge Approach for Today's Educator,* Canter and Canter (1976) assert (and we quote with permission):

> Today's teachers must contend with . . . the "Myth of the Good Teacher." This myth basically goes as follows: "A 'good' teacher should be able to handle all behavior problems on her own, and within the confines of the classroom." This means if you are competent, you should never need to go to your principal or the child's parents for assistance. . . . No one teacher, no matter how good she is, or how much experience or training she has, is capable of working successfully with each and every child without support. There are many students today whose behavior is so disruptive that a teacher must have assistance from both the principal and the parent(s) in order to deal effectively with the child and his behavior.
>
> This "myth" places a burden of guilt upon teachers who encounter problems with their students. According to the myth, if they were "really good" they wouldn't have these problems. These guilt-ridden, inadequate feelings tend to keep teachers from asking for the help they need with certain students. (pp. 6–7)

Canter and Canter (1976) advise you to, "Ask for assistance from the student's parents," insisting that, "You have the right to ask the parents or principal for whatever assistance you deem necessary, in order to maximize your potential influence with a child!" The potential for success of a number of the strategies for dealing with off-task behaviors related in examples throughout this book depends on teachers eliciting the cooperation of student guardians; the following are included among these examples: (1) The Alpine Junior High "assertive discipline" program (see pages 32–33) provided for guardians to sign a form indicating their willingness to comply with the stipulations of the program; (2) Ms. Reid (see pages 186–188) was ready to bring Al's guardians into the picture and she communicated that to Al by asking him, "Will you remember, or should I phone your house tonight to remind you?"

Undeniably, guardians have a responsibility for helping teachers teach their children to cooperate in school. Often, however, obstacles to utilizing the help of guardians are difficult to overcome. The guardians of some children, for one reason or another, are simply not available to help. The reasons may or may not be understandable, but an unavailable or unapproachable guardian can hardly be utilized, leaving you to seek other alternatives for help in working with their child. The "Myth of the 'Good' Teacher" leads some misdirected teachers to contact guardians only as a last resort, when it is too late to efficiently deal with a discipline problem.

## Assertiveness

Some teachers, burdened by the myth, approach guardians so apologetically that their lack of assertiveness precludes the effective communications necessary for the teachers to acquire constructive parental help. Canter and Canter (1976) state:

> Many teachers feel threatened and overwhelmed by parents, especially if the parents are pushy or manipulative. Thus, many teachers have difficulty in being assertive with parents; they do not clearly and firmly let the parents know what they want or need from them, nor do they stand up for their rights. As a result, all too often we hear teachers being woefully nonassertive. For example, when calling parents:
>
> - *They apologize for bothering parents:* "I'm really sorry to bother you at home with this . . ."
> - *They downgrade the problem:* "We had a 'small' problem with your son today." (In reality he had a violent tantrum which disrupted the entire class for 20 minutes.)
> - *They belittle themselves:* "I just don't know what to do with your son." (Yes, you do! You need the cooperation of the parents to discipline him at home for his tantrums.)
> - *They do not clearly state their needs:* "I know you are busy, working and all, but if you could find the time I'd appreciate it if you talked to your son about his tantrums." (You want her to discipline her son at home— period!)
> - *They downgrade the consequences of the child's behavior:* "I don't know what will happen if he doesn't change his behavior in class." (Yes, you do! He will need to be suspended.)

Often teachers confuse being assertive with being hostile. They are afraid that if they are assertive, the parent will be offended and go to the principal. However, hostility means that you express wants and needs in a manner which offends others or violates their self-dignity. The difference between nonassertive, hostile, and assertive communications with parents can best be illustrated by a direct comparison of the different responses.

*Situation:* You call the parents to discuss the behavior problems of their child. During the conference, the parents become angry and unfairly blame you for their child's problems at school.

- *Nonassertive Response:* You sit there and passively take the criticism without expressing your concerns and feelings.
- *Hostile Response:* You get defensive and tell the parents off, blaming them for their child's problems.
- *Assertive Response:* You listen to the criticism. You express your recognition of their feelings. *Again,* you express that you called them to arrange some constructive cooperation between you, which will help their child's behavior.

*Situation:* A child comes to school dirty and unkempt. You call the parents to express your concern about the child's cleanliness, and request that he come to school better kempt. The parents balk at your request, as they have in the past.

- *Nonassertive Response:* You listen to the parents and don't press your demands.
- *Hostile Response:* You tell the parents that it is a disgrace the way they send their child to school, and they should be ashamed of themselves.
- *Assertive Response:* You firmly repeat your demand, and let the parents know that in the best interest of their child you will contact the appropriate agency, if the situation does not improve.

*Situation:* You call the parents to ask their cooperation in following through at home on the contract you have with their child, as a result of the behavior problems he has in your class. The parents are very reluctant to do so.

- *Nonassertive Response:* You give up and don't press your wants.
- *Hostile Response:* You tell the parents how inadequate they are, and that they had better learn to discipline their child.
- *Assertive Response:* You firmly repeat your demands, and let the parents know the consequences if their child continues to do poorly in school.

As you have seen, in the assertive responses of each situation, the teacher stated her position and stuck to it. It was firm, not passive, not hostile. You, as a teacher, need to let the parents know where you stand and then allow them to *choose* whether to cooperate with your wishes. When you are nonassertive (passive), you allow the parents to control you. You feel lousy and don't receive the support or action you need to help the child. When you are hostile, you put down the parents. They will become threatened and, again, you will not get what you want and need from them.

We have found that teachers can learn to be more assertive and, thus, more effective in their relations with parents. The model we utilize is simple, easily learned and implemented.

1. Assert yourself and contact parents as soon as you see that there is, or possibly will be, a situation with the child where you will need the parents' cooperation.

2. Know what you want from your meeting or conversation with the parents. (Goal)
3. Plan how you will achieve the goal. (Objectives)
4. Know why you want parents' cooperation and assistance. (Rationale)
5. Be prepared to explain what you feel will occur if the parents are not cooperative (Consequences)
6. Have documentation to support your comments. (pp. 156–160)

Of course, eliciting the help of guardians to address a student's off-task behavior problem is much easier when you have already established an efficient line of communication with those guardians prior to being confronted by the problem. Mr. Perkins, from the example beginning on page 102, and Mr. Bertolli who routinely publishes the *Parents' Newsletter for American History II, 3rd Period,* an example of which is on page 105, have made it easier for themselves to utilize the help of guardians by keeping guardians apprised of their goals and expectations. Knowing guardians before a discipline problem arises also gives you an advantage in deciding how to handle the problem. Ms. Jackson, in an example for you to read when you get to page 251 of this text, deals with the problem of three students showing up in her class high on marijuana. Because prior to the incident she had communicated with the students' guardians, she is able to develop her strategy for preventing a recurrence of the misbehaviors in light of what she knows about what kind of help or hindrance she can expect from each individual set of parents. As you will see when you read the example, she decides to involve two of the students' guardians, but not the guardians of the third.

## UTILIZE ALTERNATIVE LESSON PLANS

When implementing a planned learning activity, you should, of course, expect students to cooperate with you and become engaged. By being confident that they will be on-task, you communicate your expectations and, thus, increase the chances that they will be on-task and engaged. However, you also need to be prepared for the possibility that all students' cooperation is not as forthcoming as you expected. In the example beginning on page 186, Ms. Reid gets Al engaged in an alternate geography learning activity after his behavior excluded him from the geography bingo plan. Ms. Fisher, in the example beginning on page 198, is prepared to deal with a recurrence of her students' "whoop-whooping" with an alternative learning activity that communicates that she is both completely serious about them learning the digestive system and completely serious in her demands for courteous cooperation in her classroom.

A well-designed, appropriate learning activity should not be aborted simply because things don't go quite as smoothly as planned. Do not give up on your well-thought-out ideas. However, being prepared with alternative plans can sometimes save the day when students' off-task behaviors render your original plan unworkable.

## DO NOT USE CORPORAL PUNISHMENT

### Corporal Punishment

In Chapter 2 a distinction is made between naturally occurring punishment and contrived punishment. *A punishment for a person's behavior is naturally occurring if an aversive stimulus is experienced by that person as a direct consequence of that behavior. Punishment that is intentionally and artificially imposed following a behavior is contrived punishment.* Examples illustrating the difference between the two types of punishment are provided by pages 38–40.

*Corporal punishment is a form of contrived punishment in which physical pain or discomfort is intentionally inflicted upon an individual for the purpose of trying to get that individual to be sorry he or she displayed a particular behavior.* Naturally occurring punishment, even if it is physically painful or uncomfortable, is *not* considered corporal punishment. The pain Henry experiences in the following example is *not* corporal punishment for his behavior because the pain *is* a direct consequence of that behavior itself:

> Ignoring Lakeland Elementary School's "no running in the halls" rule, Henry sprints toward the cafeteria trying to be first in line. He trips and falls suffering a painful bruise on his elbow.

Each of the following is an example of corporal punishment:

> For repeated violations of the school dress code, Bonnie is sent to Mr. Bailey, the assistant principal, who administers three swats to Bonnie's buttocks with his infamous "board of education." In accordance with local school district policy, Mr. Bailey's secretary witnesses the punishment as a "protection against accusations of abuse."

> John is busily carving a picture with the point of a compass in his school desk top when Ms. Salsberry, his fifth grade teacher, surprises him from behind by twisting his ear and asking, "Do you think this will help you remember not to abuse your desk?" John shrieks in pain.

> While supervising her pre-kindergarten class on the playground, Ms. Barfuss notices Raymond running toward a street full of traffic. Ms. Barfuss chases him down and slaps his thigh twice with her hand and says, "No, Raymond! Don't go in that street. You could be killed!" Raymond's leg stings for about 50 seconds after the incident.

Mr. Keller notices two eighth graders taunting a sixth grader just outside his classroom. He yells to them, "Come here, you two bullies!" Meekly they approach him. Mr. Keller grabs the two boys by the backs of their necks and bangs their heads together.

Ms. Loycano's third graders are supposed to be quietly working problems in workbooks when she notices Theresa and Eva involved in a conversation. "Would you two please come up here?" Ms. Loycano asks. Theresa: "What in the shit for?" Ms. Loycano responds, "I don't enjoy hearing that kind of language in the classroom, Theresa. You stay in here when the rest go to lunch and we'll help you remember how to speak in here." When the other students leave, Ms. Loycano is ready for Theresa with a bar of soap and wet towel which she uses to literally wash out the inside of Theresa's mouth.

As she is conducting a group discussion on citizenship for her fourth graders, Ms. Xavier notices Lyman starting to pass a note to Becky. Ms. Xavier: "Let's see the note, Lyman." "I don't got no note!" Lyman says as he quickly sits on the note. Ms. Xavier walks over to Lyman and says, "Stand up." Rather than stand, Lyman squirms in his desk and the note falls to the floor. Ms. Xavier grabs it and with a smile says, "I think I'll read it to the class!" Lyman stands up and screams, "No!" as he kicks Ms. Xavier on her shin. "Ouch!" she screams as she kicks him back. "Boy, that'll teach you to never think of touching me again!" she yells.

Do not confuse corporal punishment with other uses of physical force. The following are *not* examples of corporal punishment:

Mr. Triche is conducting his eighth grade math class when a student, not in his class, enters his room and exclaims, "Please Mr. Triche, hurry! Andy and Todd are beating up Bennie!" Mr. Triche dashes out of his room and follows the alarmed student to the site of the assault. Andy and Todd are kicking Bennie as he lies on the floor. Mr. Triche puts a headlock on both offenders and pulls them off Bennie. Andy and Todd struggle in an attempt to free themselves, but Mr. Triche's grip holds firm. Mr. Triche directs the student who had alarmed him to seek first aid for Bennie from a nearby teacher. Maintaining his headlocks, he forcibly escorts Andy and Todd to the school office where he turns the matter over to the principal.

Ms. Marlin is delivering a history lecture to her high school class when she notices John listening to music through the earphones he's wearing. Ms. Marlin: "Would you please put your walkman away until class is over?" John: "What for?" Ms. Marlin: "Because I don't want you in here unless you are going to pay attention to the lesson." John: "You can't make me leave!" Ms. Marlin walks over to John and says, "John, let's have this discussion out in the hall. We can settle it without the others having to listen to us." John: "I ain't going out there with you." Ms. Marlin puts her hand on John's arm and says, "There's no reason to turn this into a major incident; just come with me and everything will be all right." John stands up and yells, "Don't touch me, you old bitch!" and shoves Ms. Marlin toppling her over backwards. Standing over her, he begins to throw a punch at her, but before he can, she kicks him viciously in his groin. As John drops to the floor in pain, Ms. Marlin scrambles to her feet, quickly moves away from John, stands in the doorway and gives the following orders to the class: "Everyone but John, get out in the hall immediately! Cynthia, you run to the Office, tell them what happened and get us some help." Before John can rise from the floor, enough students are already moving out of the room and into the hall so that the path between him and Ms. Marlin is blocked.

Mr. Triche used physical force for the sole purpose of terminating the assault on Bennie. Although Andy and Todd probably experienced pain as a consequence of his force, the purpose of the force was not to inflict that pain. The purpose was to get them under control in order to end the assault and get them to the principal. Similarly, Ms. Marlin's rather violent response to John's attack should not be considered corporal punishment because the purpose of the response was to protect herself and restore order. Had she continued to strike out at John after she had successfully immobilized him, then she would have been administering corporal punishment. On the other hand, Mr. Bailey, Ms. Salsberry, Ms. Barfuss, Mr. Keller, Ms. Loycano, and Ms. Xavier administered corporal punishment because their physical force was applied with the intent of providing students with physically painful or uncomfortable experiences that would cause them to regret their misbehaviors.

## Arguments For and Against Corporal Punishment

Should corporal punishment ever be used in schools? If so, under what circumstances should it be used and how should it be applied? These two questions continue to be debated as they have been for at least the past 200 years. In some school districts corporal punishment, as it is defined herein, is absolutely prohibited; in others it is encouraged (Van Dyke, 1984). Everyone seems to at least publicly agree that students need to be protected from abusive corporal punishment in which either serious physical trauma results or in which it is applied thoughtlessly. However, many researchers suggest that all corporal punishment is abusive because of its deleterious effects on both the long-term welfare of students and on the educational environment of the school (Rose, 1984; Welsh, 1985). The National Education Association, the American Federation of Teachers, the Council for Exceptional Children, and the American Psychological Association are only four of the many prominent professional organizations that have issued statements adamantly opposing the use of corporal punishment in schools (National Education Association, 1972, Reardon & Reynolds, 1979; Wood, 1982).

There is a ban on the practice in the public schools of some countries and states (e.g., New South Wales in Australia and New Jersey in the U.S.). Yet, the widespread, but inconsistent, practice of corporal punishment continues to prevail in both public and private schools in the United States and elsewhere. Van Dyke (1984) estimates that nearly 1.5 million times per year corporal punishment is inflicted in over 77,500 U.S. schools.

Supporters of corporal punishment as a response to off-task school behavior in at least some circumstances provide the following arguments:

1.  There is the saying, "Spare the rod and spoil the child."
2.  The *Bible* (e.g., Prov. 13:24, 12:15, 23:13) supports corporal punishment as a means of moral development.
3.  What else works?
4.  Some students do not understand anything else.
5.  Teachers need to be able to protect themselves.
6.  Corporal punishment builds character and, for boys, masculinity.
7.  There are harsher, more dangerous forms of punishment, such as sustained psychological embarrassment.
8.  Students want corporal punishment. It provides the firm guidance that students need to feel secure.
9.  It leads students to respect teachers and to have respect for authority.
10. Parents want their children disciplined at school.
11. Unlike many other ways of handling off-task behaviors, corporal punishment can be immediately administered and finished with so that the student can quickly return to the business of being engaged in learning activities.
12. Using corporal punishment for one student's off-task behavior may deter others from modeling that off-task behavior.
13. Judicial courts in the United States have consistently upheld the right of school officials to utilize corporal punishment (Kerr & Nelson, 1983).
14. The abuses of corporal punishment can be prevented by allowing its application only under clearly specified, strictly controlled circumstances. Different school districts have developed their own guidelines. The following is a sample of rules from the guidelines of a variety of districts:
    A.  Corporal punishment shall only be used as a last resort, after other more desirable means have failed.
    B.  Corporal punishment may be administered only to students whose parents have provided the school with written permission.
    C.  Corporal punishment may only be administered by the school principal or his or her designee.
    D.  Corporal punishment shall be prescribed only for those who will profit from it.

    **E.** No student is required to submit to corporal punishment providing that he or she is willing to accept the alternative noncorporal punishment that is prescribed by the school discipline official.

    **F.** To give those involved a cooling off period, no corporal punishment may be administered within one hour from when the violation that is to be punished occurred.

    **G.** Whenever corporal punishment is administered, at least two professional adults must be present.

    **H.** Corporal punishment may be administered only for certain student offenses as specified in the "Disciplinary Code Handbook."

    **I.** Corporal punishment may be administered to boys only.

    **J.** The severity of corporal punishment is strictly limited.

The arguments provided by those opposed to any form of corporal punishment in schools seem more compelling:

    **1.** Opposition to corporal punishment is *not* opposition to firm, strict discipline. "Sparing the rod" does not mean "spoiling the child" if other, more effective means for handling misbehaviors are employed.

    **2.** Research does not support the notion that corporal punishment is an effective tool in teaching students to supplant off-task behaviors with on-task behaviors (Bongiovanni, 1979).

    **3.** Corporal punishment is an extremely destructive form of contrived punishment. Even when it serves to discourage one misbehavior, the long-range side effects can be far less desirable than the original misbehavior (Hyman & Wise, 1979). Welsh (1985) reports that no one has ever demonstrated the utility of spanking a child and, "When spanking does work, it is not unlike whacking your watch with your hand to make it tick. This crude procedure may work for a while, but the long-term consequences of hitting one's watch is likely to be detrimental to the delicate mechanism. Our research suggests that the watch analogy also holds for whacking children." The association between children experiencing corporal punishment and their development of aggressive or violent behavior patterns is both well-documented and well-publicized (Azrin, Hake, & Hutchinson, 1965; Azrin, Hutchinson, & Sallery, 1964; Bandura, 1965; Delgado, 1963; Ulrich & Azrin, 1962; Welsh, 1985).

    **4.** Corporal punishment shatters any semblance of a businesslike classroom climate in which mutual respect, cooperation, and seriousness of purpose prevail (Cangelosi, 1986; Kohut & Range, 1979; Strike & Soltis, 1986; Sulzer-Azaroff & Mayer, 1977). The sanctity of the learning environment is violated whenever any sort of violent behavior is tolerated. Corporal punishment is not only tolerated violence, it is condoned violence that is modeled by school personnel.

5. Research findings indicate that school personnel who rely on corporal punishment tend to be less experienced, more closed-minded, more neurotic, less thoughtful, and more impulsive than their counterparts who do not use corporal punishment (Rust & Kinnard, 1983).

## Corporal Punishment, A Poor Choice

Assuming that it is legal to use corporal punishment in your school, under what circumstances should you either administer it yourself or refer students to another who is authorized to administer it? Although it is still commonly used and may sometimes seem to be a swift, decisive way of dealing with certain off-task behaviors, there are no circumstances in which you should depend on corporal punishment. How can one possibly resolve the inconsistency between using corporal punishment and being a professional educator once the following have been considered: (1) the availability of more effective alternatives to dealing with off-task behaviors (e.g., see subsequent chapters of this text); (2) the long-range side effects of corporal punishment; (3) its corrupting influence on the businesslike air of respect and cooperation that contribute so much to maintaining students on-task and engaged in learning activities?

## KNOW YOUR RIGHTS AND LIMITATIONS

There are, of course, some school districts in which you would surely find yourself with legal problems for ever doing anything that even resembled applying corporal punishment. In other districts, you may be required to explain why you failed to use corporal punishment in certain circumstances. When addressing off-task behavior problems, you need to be mindful of the limitations of your rights and responsibilities as a professional teacher. Those rights and responsibilities vary considerably according to the location of your school. Unfortunately, there is probably no way for you to fully protect yourself from legal suits stemming from circumstances that arise in your school. Mr. Triche was commended by his principal, fellow teachers, and by Andy's parents for the way he handled the delicate situation described in the example on page 204. Neither Todd nor Andy was injured in the incident and, according to virtually everyone involved, he prevented Bennie from being seriously injured. In spite of this, a suit that led to two years of expensive litigation was brought against Mr. Triche for his actions in this incident. How do you protect yourself from this kind of action? There is no foolproof method, but being aware of schoolboard and school policies and principles of accepted professional practice can help, as can a habit of being reflective before taking a course of action. Mr. Triche did not, in fact, violate any law or school policy by his actions and he did think about what to do before acting. Repeatedly, he indicates that he does not regret handling the situation as he did. However, he does regret having to fight a legal battle as a consequence of doing the right thing.

Fortunately, legal actions against teachers who fulfill their responsibilities and who do not exceed the limits of their authority when dealing with discipline problems are unlikely occurrences. Before having to wrestle with a sticky situation, find out just what kind of backing you can expect from your school administrators and supervisors. Know, for example, if you have the right to bar a student from your classroom until some contingency you've specified has been met. Come to an agreement on these matters with your principal before the start of a school year.

## MAINTAIN YOUR OPTIONS

Three clichés, the second one particularly disgusting, may help make the point of this section: "Don't back yourself into a corner," "Don't draw your gun unless you're prepared to use it," and "Hold on to your last card." Once you're aware of the extent of your authority, do not exhaust it. If, for example, you tell a student, "Either sit down immediately or you're out of this classroom for good," you have committed yourself to what, in most situations, is the extent of any teacher's authority. If the student doesn't sit down immediately, you have left yourself little recourse. Did you really want things to go that far? Before ever exhausting your options regarding a situation, seek the help of supervisors.

## KNOW YOURSELF
## AND KNOW YOUR STUDENTS

Routinely take time to examine your own motives for the methods you use with students. Why do you handle things the way you do? How far are you willing to go with a plan? How much time and energy are you willing and able to spend on solving a particular problem? What are you willing to risk? To effectively handle off-task behaviors, you must provide yourself with honest answers to these questions. For some off-task behavior problems under certain circumstances, you should tell yourself that your priorities lead you to be unwilling to spend the time and energy necessary to effect solutions. In each of these instances, implement only the first step of the Teaching Process Model by recognizing that there is a student need with which you are not prepared to deal.

Be receptive to individual differences among your students. Measures that effectively deal with the off-task behavior of one student may be disastrous with another. Be conservative in attempting new ideas with students you don't know well until you have found the ideas to be work-able with familiar students. On the other hand, don't give up on an idea because it doesn't work for all students all of the time.

The better you understand yourself and your students, the more effec-tively you will be able to respond to displays of off-task behavior with decisiveness, sensitivity and flexibility.

## Self-Assessment for Chapter 7

I. Ms. Odle follows the Teaching Process Model to plan and conduct a two-week learning unit on drug, alcohol, and tobacco abuse for her fifth grade class. She had completed step one some time ago when she determined that her students needed to become aware of the physio-logical and psychological effects of using such substances and in light of that need, she determines the objectives for the unit and, thus, completes step two. For steps three, four, and five she plans, pre-pares, and conducts learning activities that include, among other things, small group discussions, guest lecture presentations, poster projects, and formative tests. Near the end of the two-week period, she administers a comprehensive test, the results of which help her complete step six in which she makes a summative evaluation about what students gained from the unit.

Ms. Odle also utilizes the Teaching Process Model to deal with students' off-task behaviors as they occur during time allocated for the unit's learning activities. Following are two such episodes; for each, please specify in writing just what she did for each of the six steps in handling the off-task behavior:

Ms. Odle is sitting in the back of her classroom as Mr. Boisvert speaks to the 27 fifth graders on some of his experiences as a counselor at a drug rehabilitation center. She is disturbed by the general lack of attentiveness to Mr. Boisvert's lecture. Some students are huddled, whispering to one another and giggling; very few appear to be en-gaged in the learning activity. Their lack of attentiveness coupled with Ms. Odle's display of interest encourage him to address Ms. Odle instead of the students. Ms. Odle thinks to herself: "They should be listening to him. He's taking time from his busy schedule to share some very important ideas; the least we can do is to courteously listen. I'm going to do something to get them re-engaged in Mr. Boisvert's lecture. But what? I'd like to avoid dramatizing the fact that the stu-dents aren't listening. He might find that embarrassing and there's no need to let him know that I know that they don't find his talk engag-ing. I know!—But, I've got to wait for the opportune moment in his talk. . . ."

". . . and its seems that most of the kids I see just don't think that much of themselves," Mr. Boisvert is saying as Ms. Odle stands up from her place in the back of the room and interrupts, "Excuse me, Mr. Boisvert. You've just made such an important point; I want to make sure everyone understands it." She walks to the front of the room, thinking to herself, "Maybe if I stand up front, just a little behind him, he'll quit directing his remarks to me and I'll be in a position to maintain eye contact with the class. They're more likely to at least pretend to be attending, if they see me watching them. They know me well enough!" Arriving at a point by Mr. Boisvert, but looking directly at the class, she asks him, "Would you please explain a little more about what it means for a kid not to think much of him or herself?" As Mr. Boisvert continues, Ms. Odle positions herself slightly behind him and to one side where she can monitor the class with her best "be quiet, eyes ahead, sit up straight and listen, or else life in here as you now know it will cease to exist" look on her face. For the remainder of the talk, Ms. Odle observes for indications of how well her tactics are working.

For some time, Ms. Odle has believed that Treva should break her habit of making a joke out of what other students say during learning activities. Ms. Odle hadn't decided to do anything about this off-task behavior pattern until a couple of days into the learning unit on substance abuse when Treva went into her "drunken stupor" act in response to another student's very serious comments about the effects of alcohol. After school that day, Ms. Odle thinks to herself, "It wouldn't be so bad if Treva didn't wait for some of the more serious, thought-provoking moments in our discussions to start the class laughing. Then it's hard to get them back into a serious, thoughtful vein. Besides, she's conditioning some students to keep their mouths shut out of fear that their words will be twisted into a joke. I'm going to help Treva reduce the frequency of her clowning. But how should I approach it . . . ?"

Ms. Odle designs and implements a plan for: (1) identifying the positive reinforcers (e.g., the attention she receives from others laughing at her) for her clowning; (2) taking steps to prevent her clowning in class from being positively reinforced (e.g., just prior to discussion session one day, Ms. Odle showed the class a short film that she thought would bring home the point that "taking drugs is never funny"); (3) providing positive reinforcers for an appropriate alternative behavior (e.g., making sure attention is drawn to Treva when she makes serious, on-task comments in class); (4) gathering data for deciding how well the plan is working.

II. For each of the following statements, write a half-page essay that either argues for or against the statement:

A. "Although it is not generally advisable to ignore the off-task behaviors of students, ignoring an incident of off-task behavior is preferable to dealing with it halfheartedly."

B. "Teaching students to be on-task differs from molding students' characters."

C. "If a teacher simply terminates a student's disruptive behavior in class and doesn't take measures to prevent recurrences until after class, other students in the class will think that they too can get away with disruptive behaviors."

D. "Students are very concerned with what their peers think of them. Thus, humbling a student in front of the class for disruptive behavior is an effective means of preventing such disruptions in the future."

E. "Sometimes it is better for a teacher to fail to identify the perpetrators of a classroom disruption than to play the game of 'detective' with students."

F. "Experienced teachers who apply sound classroom management principles do not need the help of colleagues, supervisors, or parents in dealing with off-task behaviors."

III. Design a learning activity for helping students within your teaching specialty achieve a particular learning objective. Now, develop an alternative learning activity that you might use in case students do not cooperate with your first plan.

IV. The following selections, identified by authors' names, from the supplemental readings section at the end of this chapter deal with corporal punishment: Hyman (1978), Hyman & Wise (1979), N.E.A. (1972), Rust & Kinnard (1983), Van Dyke (1984), Wolfgang & Glickman (1986). Try to locate and read as many as you can.

*Reviewing Your Self-Assessment* _____

Check your response to Part I to see if it contains generally the same ideas as the following sample response:

Ms. Odle followed the Teaching Process Model in responding to her students' inattentiveness during Mr. Boisvert's guest lecture presentation. She: (1) identified student needs by deciding that the students ought to be politely paying attention to the talk; (2) determined a learning goal by deciding that she would do something to get them to silently attend to the lecture; (3) determined a learning activity by deciding to discreetly interrupt Mr. Boisvert at an opportune moment and apply her "I mean business" body posture technique; (4) prepared for the learning activity by moving into position; (5) conducted a learning activity by saying what she did and standing as she did in front of the class; (6) evaluated how well the goal was achieved by deciding how well her tactics worked.

She also utilized the six steps in dealing with Treva's disruptive behavior pattern by: (1) determining a student need when she decided that Treva should break her habit of inappropriate joking; (2) determining a learning goal by deciding to do something to help Treva reduce the frequency of clowning in class; (3) designing a learning activity by developing a plan for getting Treva to extinguish her behavior pattern of clowning in class; (4) preparing for at least one component of the learning activity by arranging to have the film on "taking drugs is never funny" to be shown; (5) conducting a learning activity by carrying out her plan with such activities as showing the film; (6) evaluating how well Treva is progressing by utilizing the data she gathers.

Please have others read your responses to parts II and III and you read their responses. Discuss the differences and similarities among yourselves.

Discuss with others your beliefs about corporal punishment in light of the selections you read for Part IV.

## *Supplemental Readings*

Bell, L. C., & Stefanich, G. P. (1984). Building effective discipline using the cascade model. *The Clearing House, 58,* 134–137.

Canter, L., & Canter, M. (1976). *Assertive discipline: A take-charge approach for today's educator* (pp. 155–178). Seal Beach, CA: Canter and Associates.

Cunningham, A. R. (1983). The deportment chart: A student management tool that could help a classroom teacher. *The Clearing House, 56,* 421–422.

Duke, D. L., & Jones, V. F. (1984). Two decades of discipline—Assessing the development of an educational specialization. *Journal of Research and Development in Education, 17,* 25–35.

Hyman, I. A. (1978). A social science review of evidence cited in litigation on corporal punishment in the schools. *Journal of Child Psychology, 30,* 195–199.

Hyman, I. A., & Wise, J. H. (Eds.). (1979). *Corporal punishment in American education.* Philadelphia: Temple University Press.

Kohut, S., & Range, D. G. (1979). *Classroom discipline: Case studies and viewpoints.* Washington, DC: National Education Association.

National Education Association. (1972). *Report of the task force on corporal punishment.* Washington, DC: Author.

Rich, J. M. (1984). Discipline, rules, and punishment. *Contemporary Education, 55,* 110–112.

Rogus, J. F. (1985). Promoting self-discipline: A comprehensive approach. *Theory Into Practice, 24,* 271–276.

Rust, J. O., & Kinnard, K. Q. (1983). Personality characteristics of the users of corporal punishment in the schools. *Journal of School Psychology, 21,* 91–105.

Strike, K., & Soltis, J. (1986). Who broke the fish tank? And other ethical dilemmas. *Instructor, 95,* 36–39.

Swick, K. J. (1985). *Parents and teachers as discipline shapers.* Washington, DC: National Education Association.

Van Dyke, H. T. (1984). Corporal punishment in our schools. *The Clearing House, 57,* 296–300.

Welsh, R. S. (1985). Spanking: A grand old American tradition? *Children Today, 14,* 25–29.

Wilcox, R. T. (1983). Discipline made gentle. *The Clearing House, 57,* 30–35.

Wolfgang, C. H., & Glickman, C. D. (1986). *Solving discipline problems: Strategies for classroom teachers* (2nd ed.), (pp. 164–180). Boston: Allyn & Bacon.

Woolridge, P., & Richman, C. L. (1985) Teachers' choice of punishment as a function of a student's gender, age, race, and IQ level. *Journal of School Psychology, 23,* 19–29.

# 8

# Modifying Off-Task
# Behavior Patterns

Chapter 8 is designed to help you:

1. begin to develop ideas for designing learning activities to teach students to supplant off-task behavior patterns with on-task behavior patterns.
2. understand how the following principles of behavior modification influence the development of behavior patterns: (a) extinction; (b) alternative behavior patterns; (c) reinforcement schedules; (d) shaping; (e) cuing; (f) generalization and discrimination; (g) modeling; (h) satiation.

## SYSTEMATIC TECHNIQUES
## FOR CHANGING HABITS

### The Formation and Elimination
### of Behavior Patterns

Theories associated with behavioristic psychology provide explanations for how behavior patterns are formed; they also provide a basis for strategies used to teach students to terminate off-task behavior patterns in favor of on-task behavior patterns. The ideas of positive reinforcement, punishment, and negative reinforcement (introduced in Chapter 2), coupled with the behavior modification principles of extinction, alternative behavior patterns, reinforcement schedules, shaping, cuing, generalization, discrimination, modeling, and satiation, are particularly powerful forces for you to understand and utilize in dealing with your students' off-task behavior patterns.

Behavior modification principles are continually influencing both the formation and elimination of your students' behavior patterns. Taking advantage of these principles to help students break off-task habits and acquire on-task habits is, of course, preferable to having them operate completely out of your control. You get the behavior modification principles that are explained in this chapter to work for you by: (1) consciously considering their influence when planning learning activities and when interacting with students; (2) being very systematic when applying them to off-task behavior problems.

## The Need for Systematic Observations

Being systematic is particularly valuable in evaluating how well a behavior modification plan is working. For example:

> Jana, one of Mr. Washington's first graders, habitually yells out to him while he is busy working with other students. Mr. Washington decides to apply both the principles of extinction and alternative behavior patterns in devising a scheme to deal with Jana's disruptive behavior pattern. After some thoughtful consideration, he decides that Jana's yelling is positively reinforced by the attention it gains her. Thus, he plans to ignore her whenever she yells for him, and to provide her with special attention when she acts in a more appropriate fashion. He tries his plan, but he doesn't systematically gather data on how the plan is working. Instead, he only depends on his informal perceptions which leave him with the impression that the frequency of Jana's yelling is increasing, not decreasing. Illustration 8.1 depicts what appears to be happening according to Mr. Washington's unsystematically formed impression.

Mr. Washington dropped his plan after three days because it did not seem to be succeeding. However, had he been a bit more systematic about maintaining records, he might not have given up so quickly. If, for exam-

## Illustration 8.1. Mr. Washington's Perception of the
## Frequency of Jana's Yelling

| 3 days prior to program | 2 days prior to program | 1 day prior to program | 1st day of program | 2nd day of program | 3rd day of program |
|---|---|---|---|---|---|
| JHT JHT JHT | JHT JHT JHT | JHT JHT JHT | JHT JHT JHT JHT | JHT JHT JHT JHT JHT JHT JHT JHT | JHT JHT JHT JHT JHT JHT JHT JHT JHT JHT |

ple, he had kept a tally sheet with him and marked down every time Jana yelled, a somewhat different picture may have emerged (Illustration 8.2).

Is such a discrepancy between perceived frequency of yelling and actual frequency likely? Research results suggest that such differences are quite likely (Cangelosi, 1982). Compare the tallies perceived by Mr. Washington from Illustration 8.1 to the actual tallies of Illustration 8.2 and speculate as to what may have caused the discrepancies. Prior to the day that Mr. Washington began implementing his behavior modification plan, Mr. Washington's perceptions were quite accurate. Data collected before any sort of intervention (e.g., Mr. Washington's application of behavior modification principles) are referred to as *baseline data*. The actual baseline data differ very little from what Mr. Washington thought. According to both Mr. Washington's perception and the systematically collected tallies, Jana's screams increase in frequency right after the plan is implemented. Does this surprise you? Jana's screaming had gained her attention in the past. When Mr. Washington began ignoring her, she could be expected to at least initially attempt with greater vigor what had previously worked.

It is after the plan had been in operation for a couple of days that Mr. Washington's perceptions appear distorted. How might that phenomenon be explained? It may be that Mr. Washington's expectations changed when he began implementing his plan. Jana's yelling is an annoying habit that he wants her to terminate. He's developed a plan that *ought* to work; he *expects* it to work. Expecting the plan to work, Jana's every yell appears to echo louder, more annoying than her yells before he was working to stop the yelling.

### Illustration 8.2. Jana's Actual Frequency of Yelling

| 3 days prior to program | 2 days prior to program | 1 day prior to program | 1st day of program | 2nd day of program | 3rd day of program |
|---|---|---|---|---|---|
| JHT JHT JHT | | JHT JHT |||| | JHT JHT JHT ||| | JHT JHT JHT JHT JHT | | JHT JHT JHT JHT | | JHT | |

| 4th day of program | 5th day of program |
|---|---|
| //// | /// |

## APPLYING THE PRINCIPLE OF EXTINCTION

### The Principle

*Whenever the positive reinforcers for a person's voluntary behavior pattern are removed or cease to exist, the person will begin to discontinue that behavior pattern.* This phenomenon is know as the *principle of extinction*. Students begin to break habits when they discover those habits are no longer rewarding. One voluntarily establishes a particular behavior pattern only in the presence of positive reinforcers. The removal of those reinforcers will, in time, extinguish that behavior pattern. Both desirable (e.g., on-task) and undesirable (e.g., off-task) behavior patterns are extinguished either by conscious design or by an unplanned change in a situation.

### Unintentional Extinction

Here is an example of an unplanned extinction of a behavior pattern:

> Ruth, a sixth grader, begins stopping by her school's library to browse and pick up books. During some of her initial visits, Ruth helps Ms. Tolbert, the librarian, shelve books and do other chores. Ms. Tolbert enthusiastically expresses her appreciation and carries on lively conversations with Ruth as they work together. Ruth enjoys Ms. Tolbert's companionship and feels that her efforts are appreciated. Ruth begins coming every day after school to help. After about a month, Ms. Tolbert becomes accustomed to Ruth's presence and help and is less attentive to her. Ms. Tolbert appears less interested in talking with Ruth and she expresses her appreciation for Ruth's help less often than she did before. Soon Ruth's after-school library visits become less frequent until she no longer shows up at all.

From the description of the example, it appears that Ruth's help in the library was initially positively reinforced by the appreciation Ms. Tolbert expressed and the companionship she provided. Ruth was motivated to continue to help in the library after school as long as that behavior pattern was positively reinforced. The principle of extinction was unwittingly applied by Ms. Tolbert when she ceased providing the positive reinforcement for Ruth's habit.

### Intentional Extinction

You can sometimes take conscious advantage of the principle of extinction to teach students to eliminate certain off-task behavior patterns by: (1) specifying the exact behavior pattern to be extinguished; (2) identifying the positive reinforcers for the behavior; (3) developing a plan for eliminating the positive reinforcement; (4) in light of baseline data, establishing a realistic time schedule for reducing the frequency of the behavior; (5) implementing the plan; (6) evaluating how well the pattern is being broken. Here is an example of a teacher planning to use the principle of extinction to help students break an off-task behavior habit:

> Ms. Goldberg, a mathematics teacher, has been using a procedure in which each student's grade is determined by the number of points accumulated during a semester. A student has two means for gaining points: (1) Half of the total possible points are based on test scores; (2) The rest of the points are awarded for homework that, when turned in on time, is scored according to the number of correct responses.
>
> Ms. Goldberg begins to notice that increasingly more students receive high marks on homework, but low marks on test papers. Under her system, these students are still able to "pass" the course. She analyzes the situation, collects some baseline information, and realizes that these students are simply copying their homework from others. Understanding that her grading system positively reinforces this habit of copying instead of actually doing homework, she decides to alter her grading procedure so that those positive reinforcers are eliminated. She plans to continue to assign homework, but not to allow the number of correct responses on the homework to any longer influence the semester grade. Instead, she will use the homework as strictly a learning activity that provides students with practice and feedback relative to the skills that they will be asked to display on the tests. The tests will be the sole source of data for determining semester grades.
>
> After explaining her new grading procedure to the class, she implements it and closely monitors for evidence that students are still copying homework. She compares that evidence to her baseline data and assesses whether or not the test scores seem to improve as the homework copying seems to diminish.

Please note that extinction is not the only method for helping students to eliminate off-task behavior patterns. Other methods (e.g., punishment, cuing, or satiation) are surely more appropriate whenever the positive reinforcers for an off-task behavior pattern either cannot be identified or cannot be efficiently controlled.

## ALTERNATIVE BEHAVIOR PATTERNS

Students, like all living persons, are always behaving in some manner. Sleeping, running, remembering, watching television, doing homework, waiting in line, thinking about schoolwork, thinking about an embarrassing moment, worrying about appearance, listening, talking, being angry, and daydreaming are only a minute portion of the cognitive, affective, and psychomotor behaviors that contribute to a person's behavior complex at any given moment. Because students are always displaying some type of behavior, *whenever one behavior problem is extinguished an alternate or replacement behavior pattern emerges.* Consequently, when you are trying to help a student terminate one undesirable off-task behavior pattern, you should guard against that student replacing the current pattern with an equally undesirable, or even less desirable off-task behavior pattern. Ms. Goldberg, in the aforementioned example, needs to guard against students replacing "copying homework" behavior with "cheating on tests" behavior.

When you apply the principle of extinction, you should specify a suitable alternative behavior pattern that you plan to have positively reinforced. Ideally, the alternative on-task behavior pattern is incompatible with the off-task one that is to be extinguished. Ms. Goldberg, in the example, would be wise to make sure that she provides feedback on her students' efforts on their homework that clearly enhances their chances on improving test scores. Students who don't make the effort to do their homework problems, either correctly or incorrectly, find out that they have placed themselves at a grave disadvantage on tests. Thus, she would be positively reinforcing the alternative on-task behavior pattern of doing one's own homework.

In the next example, a teacher directly deals with an off-task behavior pattern, not by applying the principle of extinction, but by positively reinforcing an alternative behavior pattern that is incompatible with the off-task pattern.

> Jerry habitually litters the area where his teacher, Mr. Archer, conducts shop class. Mr. Archer places Jerry in charge of the daily clean-up crew that is responsible to see that the work area is clean before any class session can be dismissed. The work crew is directed to begin their duties five minutes before the scheduled end of a period. As soon as the area is clean, the class is free to leave. The promise of leaving early and the responsibility of being in charge of the crew are positively reinforcing to Jerry's alternative pattern of cleaning up. Cleaning up is incompatible with the original off-task pattern of littering.

## APPLYING THE PRINCIPLE OF SHAPING

> Abby hardly ever speaks up in Mr. Arata's class. Mr. Arata sets a goal to get Abby to voluntarily answer questions, make comments, and raise questions during group learning activity sessions. During a lecture-discussion session on protecting endangered wild animals, Mr. Arata notices Abby bringing her hand up to stroke her hair. Mr. Arata quickly says to her, "Yes, Abby, what did you want to say?" Abby: "Nothing." Mr. Arata:

"I thought I saw you raise your hand. You looked like you disagreed with the way the location of the dam was decided." Abby: "No, I agree with the process." Realizing that most of the others also agree, Mr. Arata tells the class, "Those of you who agree with Abby raise your hands." Most of the students lift their hands. Mr. Arata: "Danny, why do you agree with Abby?" Danny: "Well, I think she's right because . . ." A faint grin drifts across Abby's face.

During the ensuing weeks, Mr. Arata controls class discussions so that any move Abby makes that indicates that she is beginning to open up in class is followed by positive reinforcers. Mr. Arata has discovered that while Abby does not enjoy being the center of attention, she does enjoy having what she believes affirmed by others. He uses this knowledge to design the positive reinforcers for any contribution she makes to class discussions.

Mr. Arata attempted to apply the principle of shaping to help Abby develop an engaged behavior pattern of talking during discussion sessions rather than failing to speak up and contribute to discussions. The emergence of a student's behavior pattern is due to *shaping* when the following occurs: *(1) Some seemingly random action by the student (e.g., Abby stroking her hair) that has some characteristic similarity to the behavior to be learned (e.g., Abby raising her hand to speak up in class) is positively reinforced; (2) Subsequent actions by the student that are more like the behavior to be learned than previous actions are positively reinforced; (3) Subsequent actions by the student that are less like the behavior to be learned than previous actions are not positively reinforced.*

Here is an example of a kindergarten teacher who applies the principle of shaping to help her students develop a habit of using courteous, thoughtful language:

> When Ms. Harris' students speak to her, she makes a concerted effort to provide them with intense eye contact and displays of interest as long as they are speaking positively about others and using expressions such as "thank you," "please," "excuse me," and "if you don't mind." When they speak unkindly of others, use demanding tones, or fail to use the aforementioned type of expressions, then she uses fewer active listening techniques and appears less interested in what they are telling her. At the beginning of any conversation, she searches for any, even accidental, display of thoughtfulness in the student's conversation. She makes sure that the student recognizes her appreciation of that display.

The classic example of shaping that has been publicized numerous times is presented once again here to help you remember the principle:

> Students in a college class decided to use shaping to play a practical joke on their professor. They would appear very attentive to the professor's lecture whenever he made any movement toward the doorway of the

lecture hall. Any movement away from the door or any failure to move at all was met with inattentiveness. After a week, the professor found himself lecturing from the doorway.

## MAINTAINING DESIRABLE BEHAVIOR CHANGES

### Reinforcement Schedules

How long a behavior pattern (either on-task or off-task) persists is largely dependent on the scheduling of positive reinforcers. Two types of reinforcement schedules are of particular concern in dealing with off-task behaviors in the classroom: (1) *Fixed;* (2) *Intermittent.*

### Fixed Schedules

*Fixed schedules of positive reinforcement* can be either *fixed intervals* or *fixed ratios. Fixed interval schedules* provide for a positive reinforcer to routinely occur after a set amount of time elapses in which a prescribed behavior has been displayed. *Fixed ratio schedules* provide for a positive reinforcer to routinely occur after a prescribed behavior has been displayed to a specified degree or with a specified frequency. Students on fixed positive reinforcement schedules should always be able to predict how and when they will be rewarded for displaying the prescribed behavior. Teachers use fixed schedules of positive reinforcement in the next two examples. In the first, the schedule is fixed interval; the second is an example of fixed ratio.

> Ms. Mecke makes arrangements with a local theater chain to provide enough movie passes for her to carry out a strategy she has devised to help her manage her class. Each day, she checks to see whether or not students have completed all required work and cleaned up their work areas. Those students who have maintained a perfect record for a school week are given a movie pass. Each student begins on Monday morning with a fresh record and the opportunity of receiving a pass on Friday.

> Nearly every time Mr. Schwartz asks a question in class, David blurts out an answer. Mr. Schwartz speaks to David about the problem, but David has difficulty controlling his desire to share his thoughts on whatever topic is raised. Finally, Mr. Schwartz and David work out the following agreement: For every sequence of questions that Mr. Schwartz raises for the class, Mr. Schwartz will call on David to answer every fifth question providing that David has sat quietly through the previous four questions and listened to others give their responses.

Ms. Mecke's students knew exactly what they would have to do for five consecutive days in order to receive a movie pass on Friday. David understood that he had to display quiet listening behavior through four straight questions and answers before he could be rewarded with a chance to speak out in class. The agreement that Mr. Schwartz and David worked out is a rather simple form of a *contingency contract*. Contingency contracts are commonly associated with fixed schedules of positive reinforcers. You enter into a contingency contract with a student by agreeing to provide some sort of rewards or privileges in return for the student displaying some sort of prescribed behavior. *Contingency proclamations* are similar except that the prescription is imposed upon the student by the teacher rather than the two having cooperatively worked out the arrangement. An example of a formalized contingency contract appears in Illustration 9.2 on page 240–241.

## Intermittent Schedules

Fixed schedules of positive reinforcers are particularly powerful in motivating students to initiate a behavior pattern. However, *intermittent schedules* are far more powerful in getting students to retain behavior patterns once the pattern has been started (Martin & Pear, 1983). With an intermittent schedule, the student whose behavior pattern is being positively reinforced cannot accurately predict when rewards will occur. An intermittent schedule of reinforcement is irregular; the reinforcers do not occur with fixed regularity. Most unplanned reinforcement schedules are intermittent; this is the case in the following example in which an undesirable behavior pattern emerges:

> Fourteen-year-old Michelle begins consuming wine. Although the taste does not appeal to her, it causes her to feel light-headed and, temporarily, she feels relieved from the pressures and anxieties of being an adolescent. Her drinking is positively reinforced by this feeling of relief. A week later, she is feeling down and drinks again. However, this time, she feels no high, so she drinks more until she feels better. On other occasions, she feels no relief, only terribly sick, after drinking. She continues to drink in the hope that it will make her feel better; sometimes it does and sometimes it doesn't. She can't predict how much she must drink to feel better or even if any one drinking bout will provide her with any relief at all.

The intermittent positive reinforcement schedule for Michelle's drinking will likely lead to a permanent habit unless some incompatible, alternative behavior pattern is positively reinforced. The classic example of an intermittent schedule is that of the unpredictable rewards associated with gambling behavior. Gambling, of course, can become quite compulsive.

## Planned Schedules of Reinforcement

A planned schedule of positive reinforcers that is commonly used in conjunction with shaping provides for a generous fixed schedule during the stage in which the behavior pattern is to be initiated, a meager fixed schedule after the pattern has been exhibited for a time, and an intermittent schedule to maintain the pattern until the student becomes intrinsically motivated to continue the pattern without outside intervention. Here is an example:

Mr. Devlin experiences difficulty in getting Milan to complete reading assignments. Milan tends to display disruptive behaviors during in-class reading assignments. After giving the matter considerable thought, Mr. Devlin decides to use shaping to teach Milan to choose to read books. One day, Mr. Devlin sees Milan pick up a magazine, thumb through it, and put it down. Mr Devlin: "If you read any one article in that magazine, you can tell me about it during the Braves game tomorrow night. I have an extra ticket." Milan: "You mean you'd take me to see the Braves!" Mr. Devlin: "If you read the article." Milan: "It's a deal!" After the game, Mr. Devlin hands Milan a short story on baseball and says, "When you get through reading this, maybe we can talk about it at another game."

In time, Milan reads more, but Mr. Devlin schedules payoffs farther apart and makes them contingent on more ambitious readings by Milan. Eventually, Milan learns to enjoy reading without the anticipation of an extrinsic reward. The extrinsic motivation that stemmed from a desire to attend baseball games is eventually replaced by the intrinsic motivation derived from Milan's enjoyment of reading.

## CUING

Ms. Setzer's second graders are working in pairs as the noise level in the classroom begins to rise to an unacceptable level. Saying nothing, Ms. Setzer calmly walks over to the light switch and blinks the lights once. The noise level drops to an acceptable level.

Mr. Weaver is vocally giving directions to his chemistry students as they work at laboratory tables. As they follow his directions, they become somewhat noisy in their efforts to help one another. As Mr. Weaver continues to speak, he gradually lowers his voice so that it is no longer audible to those in the noisy room. The students begin signaling one another to quiet down and the noise level drops below Mr. Weaver's volume.

Five minutes ago, Ms. Petterson assigned Tyrone and his sixth grade classmates some exercise problems to work in class. After working one, Tyrone is doodling and gazing around the room. Ms. Petterson walks over to Tyrone and silently looks at his paper. Tyrone's attention returns to the exercise problems.

*A cue is a signal that stimulates a person (e.g., a student) to exhibit a previously learned voluntary behavior pattern.* From the example, it appears that Ms. Setzer had conditioned her students to lower their voices in response to the blinking light cue. Similarly, students responded to Mr. Weaver's lowering his voice as a cue to quiet down. Ms. Petterson's proximity to Tyrone cued him back on-task.

Teaching students to respond to cues, especially nonverbal ones, is invaluable to an efficient, smoothly operating classroom. Recall how Ms. Morrison used posters in her classroom as cues to facilitate smooth transitions between learning activities in the example that begins on page 69. As suggested by a number of the examples provided in chapters 9 and 10 (e.g., Mr. Legget's method of dealing with Rosalie's habitual mind-wandering in the example beginning on page 235), efficient cues can sometimes be worked out with students to signal them that they are exhibiting an off-task behavior and should immediately replace that behavior with a previously agreed on alternative behavior. Krumboltz and Krumboltz (1972) state, "Cuing seems to work better under some circumstances than under others. When cues are verbal, they are sometimes confused with nagging but there is an important distinction. Nagging is persistent unpleasant urging or scolding by finding fault. Cuing is a simple nonhostile direction when the child needs a reminder or when he needs help in learning."

## GENERALIZATION AND DISCRIMINATION

### The Idea

The communication style that Ms. Sowel uses with her seventh graders in the next two examples should not be emulated in any respect. However, her conversations with two students are presented to introduce the ideas of generalization and discrimination.

> Betty is busily trying to write an essay in Ms. Sowel's class. She frowns, crumples her paper and tosses it on the floor. Ms. Sowel turns to Betty and says, "Young lady, pick up that paper right now! Do you throw trash on your living room floor at home?" Betty: "No, ma'am. I'm sorry." Ms. Sowell: "Well, if you don't throw trash on the floor of your living room, then you shouldn't throw it on the floor of your classroom either!"

> As Ms. Sowel's seventh grade English students file into her room, Roy shoves Hildreth from behind. Hildreth spins around face to face with Roy and says, "Look mother-fucker, don't start any of your shit with me!" Ms. Sowel dashes to Hildreth, turns him to her by his shoulders and loudly exclaims, "Maybe that filthy language is tolerated around your home, but it will not be tolerated in my classroom!"

## The Principle of Generalization

Ms. Sowel, in her crude manner, attempted in the first example to help Betty exhibit in the classroom a behavior pattern (i.e., disposing of trash in a proper container rather than the floor) that Betty practices at home. Ms. Sowel wanted Betty to *generalize* a behavior pattern from one situation to another. *Students generalize by responding to a new set of stimuli in a manner similar to the way in which they have been conditioned to respond to a different, but similar, set of stimuli.* Students tend to generalize between two situations and, thus, respond similarly in both situations because they focus on commonalities instead of differences. You teach students to generalize between two situations by providing them with cues that remind them of what is common to both situations.

## The Principle of Discrimination

By throwing paper on her classroom floor, although she wouldn't have done so at home, Betty, displayed that she was *discriminating*, rather than generalizing, between the stimuli presented by the classroom and that presented by her home. Ms. Sowel attempted to get her to generalize her disposal-of-trash behavior at home to the classroom. In the second episode, Ms. Sowel made a poorly conceived attempt to get Hildreth to *discriminate* between his home—where, according to Ms. Sowel's rude remark, a type of language is acceptable—and her classroom, where that type of language is unacceptable. *Students discriminate by responding to a new set of stimuli in a manner dissimilar to the way in which they have been conditioned to respond to a different, but similar, set of stimuli.* Students tend to discriminate between two situations and, thus, respond differently in one situation than they do in the other because they focus on differences rather than commonalities. You teach students to discriminate between two situations by providing them with cues that remind them of what is different about the two situations.

## Discriminating Between the Principles of Generalization and Discrimination

In the next four examples, Vern, Stephen, Amanda, and Alyson appear to be generalizing:

> Whenever Vern watches television at his house, he relaxes, never trying to follow what is being said very closely. Vern's teacher shows his class a videotaped lecture on the Declaration of Independence. Although Vern's teacher indicated that they would be tested on the content of the video, Vern is very relaxed as he watches the video monitor and does not follow what is said very closely.

Eight-year-old Stephen tells his mother, "Sidney took my ball away from me at school today!" "What did you do about it?" his mother asks. "I slugged him and took it back," he replies. "Good!" his mother says. "You have to take care of yourself." A few days later, Stephen's four-year-old brother grabs a book that Stephen is reading. Stephen hits his brother and grabs back the book.

Amanda diligently works on her history assignments and she reads some unassigned history books. Afterwards, she obtains a grade of "A" in history. Amanda begins diligently working on her science course and seeks additional work in science.

Alyson notes that her mother is more responsive to her requests when she says "please." She asks her teacher, "May I please play with a puzzle?"

Shauna, Mickey, Nancy, and Chris appear to discriminate in the next four examples:

Whenever Shauna watches television at her house, she relaxes, never trying to follow what is being said very closely. Shauna's teacher shows her class a videotaped lecture on the Declaration of Independence. Although the medium is similar to the television in her home, Shauna realizes that she will be tested over the content of the video. Shauna takes notes and listens closely as she watches the video monitor.

Mickey speaks openly about his sexual fantasies to his buddies, but he never mentions them to his father.

Nancy always does homework for Mr. Clancy's class, but she rarely does it for Ms. Taylor's class.

Twelve-year-old Chris tries to win and uses his hardest "slam" when playing table tennis against Amy, his older sister. However, when he plays table tennis against his five-year-old brother, he just pats the ball back to him and never "slams."

## APPLYING THE PRINCIPLE OF MODELING

Marilyn is a student in Mr. Bomgars' class when he asks the class, "If y equals 6 divided by the quantity of x minus 3 where x is a real number between 0 and 3, what happens to y as x approaches its minimum? George." George: "Well, I think—" Interrupting George, Mr. Bomgars says, "*You* 'think'! That must be a new experience for you! I've never known you to think before!" A few class members roar with laughter. The next day, a friend tells Marilyn, "I'm late for a meeting, I'd better hurry."

Marilyn in a loud voice says, "You hurry! How can you hurry while carrying around that stomach?"

As part of a problem-solving learning activity for her ninth grade class, Ms. Rogers assigns Sandy to a task group with Ed and Diane. Initially, Sandy has little motivation for working on the task and solving the problem. However, as she associates with Ed and Diane who enthusiastically and diligently work on the project, Sandy gains an interest in working on the task herself.

Several days after Scott's mother spanks him, he hits his younger sister.

Phil and Dudley are confronted by a pusher on their school's grounds with an offer to buy some dope. Phil declines the offer with, "No, I don't use the stuff." Dudley pulls out some money and says, "Okay, I'll try it." As soon as Dudley completes the transaction, Phil pulls out his own money and tells the pusher, "Yeah, I'll have some too."

Three times a week, Ms. Shelly makes an hour available to her fifth graders to silently read any selection they make from a large collection of trade books available in her classroom. During the "free silent reading" periods, Ms. Shelly catches up on paperwork. Only about half of Ms. Shelly's students enthusiastically read during "free silent reading" periods.

Three times a week, Ms. Loyacono makes an hour available to her fifth graders to silently read any selection they make from a large collection of trade books available in her classroom. During the "free silent reading" periods, Ms. Loyacono always silently reads books of her own choosing. Virtually all of Ms. Loyacono's students enthusiastically read during "free silent reading" periods.

Like Marilyn, Sandy, Scott, Phil, Ms. Shelly's students, and Ms. Loyacono's students in the aforementioned examples, *individuals are modeling behavior when they initiate behavior patterns because they observed others displaying similar behaviors.* Modeling is a form of generalization in that modeling occurs because of an "if the behavior is okay for him or her, then it's okay for me" logic. Because children and adolescents tend to follow the examples set by others, modeling is a particularly powerful means for teaching behavior patterns to students. However, you should guard against using the destructive and ineffective tactic of comparing one student's behavior to that of another. If, for example, Tom is told, "Why don't you behave more like Bill? Bill never gives me trouble!" Tom is likely to resent Bill and begin protecting his own ego by acting as un-Bill-like as he can. You effectively use modeling either by quietly serving as an example of the behavior pattern you want students to follow or by grouping students who need to learn to follow the behavior pattern with those who already display it. In the examples at the beginning of this section, Ms. Loyacono applied the former method and Ms. Rogers applied the latter.

## APPLYING THE PRINCIPLE OF SATIATION

Andy is distributing literary magazines to the rest of the eleventh graders in Ms. Elkins' literature class. Andy places a magazine in front of James who hands it back to Andy and says, "Hey, I don't take anything from you!" "You gotta take it now 'cause you already put your nigger hands on it!" replies Andy. James leaps to his feet and the two square off at each other. Some of the other students, along with Ms. Elkins, step in and take charge and, without further incident, Ms. Elkins sends them both to the dean's office.

Andy and James have been at each other's throats since school began two months ago. Ms. Elkins does not want to have them suspended, as they usually conscientiously engage in learning activities and are both progressing nicely toward the learning goals Ms. Elkins has set. Except for antagonizing each other, neither tends to display disruptive behaviors. However, this latest incident is just one more in a continuing series of confrontations between the two. Ms. Elkins refuses to conduct her class under the fear that Andy and James will break out in a fight. She decides to try one more tactic before recommending suspensions.

Her plan calls for Andy and James to work closely and be assigned tasks in which the success of one depends on the success of the other. Initially, she assigns them to work on a joint project on which they will receive the same grade. Ms. Elkins believes that while working together, they will become so saturated with antagonizing each other that they might eventually choose to cooperate instead. She knows she is gambling, but she considers the current situation to be intolerable and suspension undesirable.

In the example, Ms. Elkins attempted to apply the *principle of satiation which states that if an established learned behavior is allowed to continue unchecked, the person exhibiting that behavior may soon become tired of the pattern and elect to terminate it.* If, as in the case of Andy and James, immediate naturally occurring punishment is a consequence of the behavior pattern, the satiation principle may be applicable. Of course, if the naturally occurring punishment is very severe, one may not be able to afford to apply the satiation principle. You wouldn't, for example, apply the satiation principle in dealing with a child who habitually ran out in a busy street. You might consider satiation as a method for terminating off-task behavior patterns only if: (1) Naturally occurring punishment is a consequence of the behavior pattern; (2) The naturally occurring punishment is not too severe; (3) You are willing to tolerate the off-task behavior pattern long enough for the satiation principle to take effect.

## Self-Assessment for Chapter 8

I.  Below is a list of 11 ideas or principles from behavioristic psychology that can be used in the design of learning activities to help students supplant off-task behavior patterns with on-task behavior patterns. Classify each according to one of the following: (1) focuses on *terminating an existing behavior pattern*; (2) focuses on *developing a new behavior pattern*; (3) can focus on *either* terminating an existing pattern or developing a new one.
   A. Positive reinforcement
   B. Punishment
   C. Negative reinforcement
   D. Extinction
   E. Alternative behavior
   F. Shaping
   G. Cuing
   H. Generalization
   I. Discrimination
   J. Modeling
   K. Satiation

II.  In several sentences describe an example in which a student is on-task because she or he generalizes between two situations.

III.  In several sentences describe an example in which a student is off-task because she or he generalizes between two situations.

IV.  In several sentences describe an example in which a student is on-task because she or he discriminates between two situations.

V.  In several sentences describe an example in which a student is off-task because she or he discriminates between two situations.

VI.  In two paragraphs, describe an example in which a teacher: (1) identifies an off-task behavior pattern exhibited by a student; (2) identifies an alternative on-task behavior pattern for that student to develop; (3) devises a plan for applying the principle of extinction to help the student eliminate the off-task pattern and for positively reinforcing the alternative pattern.

VII.  Rewrite your description of the example for Part VI, but this time write it so that, unknowingly, the teacher uses a *destructive* positive reinforcer for the alternative behavior pattern.

VIII.  Describe an example in which a teacher uses the principle of shaping to help a student develop an on-task behavior pattern.

IX. Describe an example in which a teacher *unwittingly* uses the principle of shaping to lead a student to develop an off-task behavior pattern.

X. Milton is a seventh grader who habitually fails to bring the required workout uniform to physical education class. Describe three scenarios: one in which his teacher uses contrived punishment to deal with this off-task behavior pattern, another in which the teacher uses naturally occurring punishment, and another in which the teacher uses negative reinforcement.

*Reviewing Your Self-Assessment* ———————————————————

Check your responses for Part I against these: B, D, and K focus on terminating existing behaviors; A, C, E, F, and J focus on developing new behaviors; G, H, and I could be either. Cuing could be either because cues can be used to remind students to initiate a behavior or to remind them to stop behavior they are exhibiting. Generalization could be either because students can either generalize that what is okay under one circumstance is okay under another, or they could generalize that what is not okay in one situation is also not okay in another. Discrimination could be either because students can recognize that because a behavior is okay in one situation does not mean it's okay in another, or they can recognize that inappropriate behavior for one set of circumstances may be appropriate for another set.

Discuss with your colleagues the differences and similarities among your responses to parts II through X.

## Supplemental Readings

Brown, D. (1971). *Changing student behavior: A new approach to discipline.* Dubuque, IA: Brown.

Homme, L. (1973). *How to use contingency contracting in the classroom.* Champaign, IL: Research Press.

Kerr, M. M., & Nelson, C. M. (1983). *Strategies for managing behavior problems in the classroom* (pp. 3–79). Columbus, OH: Merrill.

Krumboltz, J. D., & Krumboltz, H. B. (1972). *Changing children's behavior.* Englewood Cliffs, NJ: Prentice-Hall.

Presbie, R. J., & Brown, P. L. (1985). *Behavior modification* (2nd ed.). Washington, DC: National Education Association.

Walker, J. E., & Shea, T. M. (1984). *Behavior management* (3rd. ed.), (pp. 24–121). St. Louis, MO: Times Mirror/Mosby.

Wolf, M. M., Hanley, E. L., King, L. A., Lachowicz, J., & Giles, D. K. (1970). The timer game: A variable interval contingency for the management of out-of-seat behavior. *Exceptional Children, 37,* 113–117.

# 9

## Dealing with Nondisruptive Off-Task Behaviors

Chapter 9 is designed to provide you with some ideas to use for developing your own techniques for effectively handling both isolated incidents and patterns of nondisruptive off-task student behaviors. In particular the following types of nondisruptive off-task behaviors are addressed: (1) mind-wandering and daydreaming; (2) refusing to participate in class activities; (3) failing to complete homework assignments; (4) failing to bring materials; (5) being under the influence of debilitating drugs during class; (6) being absent or tardy; (7) cheating on tests.

### NONDISRUPTIVE OFF-TASK BEHAVIORS

Nondisruptive off-task behaviors can easily be disregarded by teachers. Such behaviors (e.g., daydreaming) do not interfere with the learning activities of the class as a whole; a student only interferes with his or her own learning by exhibiting nondisruptive off-task behaviors. A student usually suffers only minor consequences from one isolated incident of nondisruptive off-task behavior. However, there are three reasons why you should not generally disregard nondisruptive off-task behaviors, even isolated ones:

1. Whenever students are off-task, they are failing to benefit from your planned learning activities and consequently are diminishing their chances of achieving learning goals. Since, as a teacher, you are responsible for helping students achieve learning goals, it follows that you are responsible for helping students be on-task.
2. Off-task behavior patterns begin with isolated off-task behaviors that are positively reinforced.

**3.** Students exhibiting nondisruptive off-task behaviors tend to fall behind in a lesson. Once students miss one part of a learning activity, they are likely to not understand subsequent parts (even if they become re-engaged). These students may well become bored, frustrated, and disruptive.

The efficacy of the solutions you prescribe for any off-task behavior problem is dependent on your understanding of the students, the peculiarities of the situation, and yourself. Please keep in mind that the examples of teachers dealing with off-task behaviors that are given in this chapter and the next are *only* examples. The teachers' methods in these scenarios worked or didn't work (examples of teachers' mishandling situations are also included) because of individual characteristics of the involved persons and circumstances. You and other teachers can learn from them, but you must develop your own unique style for handling the unique cases you confront.

## MIND-WANDERING AND DAYDREAMING

### Detection and Response

Mind-wandering and daydreaming may be the most common forms of student off-task behaviors. Mind-wandering is an ". . . *uncontrolled* coursing of ideas through our heads and mental pictures of something not present. . . ." (Dewey, 1933). Daydreaming is similar to mind-wandering except that the daydreamer cognitively controls the thoughts and images (Klinger, 1978). Although traditionally children have been reprimanded, embarrassed, and punished for allowing their thoughts to deviate from school tasks while involved in imaginative episodes, daydreaming seems to serve a critical purpose in cognitive development (Gold & Cundiff, 1980). There appears to be a direct relation between the frequency at which individuals daydream and their level of creative achievement (Lyerly, 1982). Mind-wandering and especially daydreaming *per se* shouldn't be discouraged by teachers, but students need to learn to control mind-wandering and time their daydreams so that engagement in learning activities isn't disrupted.

Because teachers cannot directly observe mind-wandering and daydreaming as they can other off-task behaviors (e.g., inappropriate talking), it is difficult to detect this form of student disengagement from learning activities. Shrewd and concerned teachers learn to read body language, recognize vacant looks in students' eyes, and use questioning techniques to detect incidences of students quietly drifting out of touch with learning activities.

Mr. Minchot is explaining to his ninth grade science class how Darwin and Wallace each arrived at his theory of natural selection. Most of the class listens intently. Amelia sits straight up staring directly at Mr. Minchot as she imagines herself along a river bank galloping high on a horse. Mr. Minchot, pleased with his class's silence, continues unaware of Amelia's disengagement.

Ms. Searcy is explaining to her ninth grade science class how Darwin and Wallace each arrived at his theory of natural selection. Most of the class listens intently. Amy sits straight up staring directly at Ms. Searcy as she imagines herself along a river bank galloping high on a horse. Ms. Searcy, who watches her students' faces as she lectures, notices the blank look in Amy's eyes. Suspicious that Amy is not engaged in the lesson, she pauses and asks, "What do you think about that, Amy?" Amy: "About what?" Ms. Searcy: "About what I said." Amy: "I don't know what you said." Ms. Searcy: "You don't know what I said! Were you daydreaming?" Amy: "Yes, ma'am." Ms. Searcy: "Amy, the daydreamer, off in a world of her own! All right! Let's listen from now on." Amy: "Yes, ma'am. I will."

"Off in a world of her own! Amy, the daydreamer!" Amy thinks to herself as she stares directly at Ms. Searcy and nods her head as if agreeing with what Ms. Searcy is saying. Amy keeps pondering those words; she likes the sound of "a daydreamer, off in her own world."

Ms. Smith is explaining to her ninth grade science class how Darwin and Wallace each arrived at his theory of natural selection. Most of the class listens intently. Anita sits straight up staring directly at Ms. Smith as she imagines herself along a river bank galloping high on a horse. Ms. Smith, who watches her students' faces as she lectures, notices the blank look in Anita's eyes. Suspicious that Anita is not engaged in the lesson, Ms. Smith pauses and asks the class, "Why do you suppose Darwin waited so long before publishing his theory? Anita?" Anita: "What's the question?" Ms. Smith: "Please repeat the question for those of us who missed it, Michael." Michael: "You asked why Darwin took so long before publishing his stuff." Ms. Smith: "Thanks, Mike. What's your opinion, Debbie?" Debbie gives her opinion and the lecture discussion continues. Ms. Smith subtly observes Anita to see if her strategy worked.

If Amelia continues to enjoy her daydreaming during Mr. Minchot's lecture, she may soon develop a pattern of daydreaming in his classes. The beginning of a lecture may serve as a cue for Amelia to daydream. Ms. Searcy disrupted her own learning activity to belabor Amy's behavior and destructively characterize Amy as a "daydreamer." Amy may now begin to think of herself as a "daydreamer" who romantically lives in a "world of her own." Ms. Smith's one question for Anita, hopefully, cued her back on-task without disrupting the rest of the class and without positively reinforcing the daydreaming.

## Strategies

Mr. Cavallaro's second graders are working on independent computational exercises. He circulates among them, checking on their engagement. Richard stares off into space; Mr. Cavallaro doesn't believe Richard is thinking about the exercise problems. Mr. Cavallaro moves into Richard's line of vision and makes eye contact. Richard seems to return to work. However, Mr. Cavallaro begins noticing more and more students appear to have wandering minds. Convinced that their attention spans are inadequate for the exercise to efficiently continue uninterrupted, he calls for their attention, directs them to stop their computing, and takes them outside where he conducts a 5-minute session of calisthenics. After the exercises, they return to the classroom and complete the computations.

Mr. Legget detects that a number of his seventh grade English students frequently allow their minds to wander off the topic at hand during learning activities. By watching students' faces and raising questions, he determines that this form of disengagement is particularly prevalent during large group sessions in which he lectures and conducts discussions. He decides to attempt a strategy with Rosalie, who appears to habitually daydream, and to evaluate how well it works with her. If successful, he will try the strategy with others and eventually develop a plan for the entire class. In a one-to-one conference with Rosalie, they both recognize the problem and agree to the following plan.

Mr. Legget is to provide Rosalie with a tiny, flat rubber image of a frog that can easily be attached to and removed from Rosalie's desk top. Mr. Legget will keep a statue of a frog facing the class on his desk. During large group learning activities, Rosalie is to attach the rubber frog to her desk top. Everytime she sees the frog on her desk "looking" at her, she is to glance at the frog on Mr. Legget's desk and be reminded that it is not the time to daydream.

The success of the plan depends on the frog cuing Rosalie to discriminate between when daydreaming is appropriate and when it is not. She does not attach the frog to her desk at times when daydreaming is appropriate. After a 2-week trial, Rosalie and Mr. Legget both agree that the frequency at which she daydreams during large group learning activities is significantly lower than it was before they started the program. The time frame for the plan is extended.

Pleased with Rosalie's success, Mr. Legget initiates a similar strategy with Mike. However, it seems that Mike tends to stare upward and not see anything when he daydreams; the plan fails. Mr. Legget decides to use a sound cue approach with Mike and they agree that Mr. Legget will watch for signs that Mike's attention is drifting. When he believes Mike's thoughts have wandered, he will wait for an appropriate point in the lecture or discussion and rap a pencil, which he always carries, against the backside of the ring he wears. Upon hearing the unique sound, Mike is to remind himself to focus his thoughts on the lesson.

The plan works fairly well with Mike, and Mr. Legget experiments with other cues for other students. Some work well, others do not. After a month, Mr. Legget is having trouble keeping up with what cues whom. Finally, he calls a class meeting to relate a plan for the entire class to combat daydreaming and mind-wandering during lectures and discussions. The plan calls for him to trigger the beeper on the chronograph he wears on his wrist anytime he detects at least three students drifting off.

While deciding on his approach, Mr. Legget had considered placing a small gong on his desk and striking it whenever he deems that a "stay with us" cue is needed. The gong, he thought, would have a dramatic effect. However, because he can't carry the gong with him, he rejected it to retain the mobility afforded by the beeper on his chronograph. After implementing his plan for 2 weeks, he evaluates its success. He decides that, although it doesn't seem to help some students, it is worthwhile continuing because it is working for others.

## REFUSING TO PARTICIPATE IN CLASS ACTIVITIES

Here are four examples of teachers effectively dealing with students' disengagement during in-class learning activities; in these examples reasons other than mind-wandering or daydreaming interfere with the students' in-class participation:

Ms. Webb has just directed her first grade students to carry out assignments in five-member task groups. Five classmates, Sophonia, Scott, April, Heather, and Louis, are assigned to work together and plan a mural for the classroom. Scott, April, Heather, and Louis move to their work area and begin discussing the project. Sophonia remains at her desk on the other side of the room. Ms. Webb observes the situation for a minute, collects her thoughts, and discreetly goes to Sophonia and says to her in a soft voice, "You are not working with your group. Can I help you?" Sophonia: "No, I'm okay." Ms. Webb: "Why did you decide to stay here instead of working with your group?" Sophonia: "Because of Scott; he makes me mad." Ms. Webb: "Why did you get mad?" Sophonia: "He calls me 'dummy'!" Ms. Webb: "I understand why you would get mad. I don't like it when someone calls me 'dummy.'" Ms. Webb reads Sophonia's expression and believes she has received the supportive communication. Hoping that Sophonia has dealt with her feelings, Ms. Webb confidently says, "Now, hurry and get with your group. We need your ideas so that we'll have the best mural possible!" As Sophonia moves toward her task group, Ms. Webb decides to be especially attentive to Sophonia's and Scott's group, thinking that her presence will reduce the chances that Scott will call Sophonia "dummy." As Ms. Webb continues to supervise the activities in the room, she thinks to herself, "What, if anything, should I do if I hear Scott call Sophonia 'dummy'?"

**Illustration 9.1. Mr. Sabid Discreetly Wakes Derald and Hands Him a Note**

Mr. Sabid directs his French class to translate 12 sentences before the end of the class period; he plans to collect their work and provide them with feedback on it the next day. As other students begin the work, Derald puts his head down on his desk and falls asleep. Mr. Sabid thinks, "I could just let him go and require him to complete those translations before he leaves school today. But I'd rather stop his sleeping in class before it becomes a distraction to others. I wonder what's going on with him today. It's not like him to do this. Well, for whatever reason, I'm not going to allow him to develop a habit of sleeping in my class. I know! I'll write a note to him. A note won't be disturbing to the others, nor will it call attention to him." Mr. Sabid writes:

Derald:
    If I do not receive your complete translations before I leave today at 4:30, I will not be able to provide you with feedback on them in tomorrow's class. If

you don't finish them by the end of the period, turn them in to me at 4:20 P.M.
today in room 143. I will be working in there then.

Mr. Sabid

Quietly, Mr. Sabid walks over to Derald, inconspicuously shakes him
until he opens his eyes, and hands him the note. Mr. Sabid immediately
walks away, not giving Derald an opportunity to make a comment to him.
If Derald does not either complete the work by the end of the class or meet
Mr. Sabid with the work at 4:20, Mr. Sabid plans to contact Derald's
parents.

Mr. Burns-Whittle notices that one of his fifth graders, Jamie, is just
sitting at his desk instead of working on the assigned in-class word recognition exercise. Mr. Burns-Whittle discreetly goes over to Jamie, makes
eye contact, and signals him to begin working. Jamie just looks away
without taking the cue. Mr. Burns-Whittle then whispers directly to Jamie,
"I would like you to begin the exercise now." Assuming Jamie will begin,
Mr. Burns-Whittle confidently walks away. A minute later, he sees that
Jamie has still not begun. He beckons Jamie to meet him just outside the
room in the hall. There, he softly asks Jamie, "Why have you not begun
your work?" Jamie: "Because I don't want to." Mr. Burns-Whittle: "I
understand that you don't want to do this exercise, but I suggest that you
get it over with now so you won't need to worry about it later today."
Jamie: "I'm not going to do it." Mr. Burns-Whittle: "Jamie, do you know
what the word 'option' means?" Jamie: "No." Mr. Burns-Whittle: "An
option is a choice. It's an opportunity to choose. Right now, you have an
option. You have a choice to make. . . . What did I just say?" Jamie: "I
have a choice." Mr. Burns-Whittle: "You have the option of going to Ms.
Cook's office and waiting there for me until 2 o'clock when I have the time
to work with you. Or, you have the option of quietly returning to your
desk and completing the assignment. Which option do you choose?"
Jamie: "I don't want to go to Misses Cook's office." Mr. Burns-Whittle:
"So, give me your choice. I have to get back to our class." Jamie: "Okay, I
won't go to Misses Cook." Mr. Burns-Whittle: "Whatever you say, Jamie.
You've made your choice."

Jamie returns to his place and reluctantly begins working. Mr. Burns-
Whittle thinks, "If he doesn't continue working, I'll send him to the office
and instruct them to have him wait for me until I get there at 2 P.M. That'll
give me time to think through what to do."

Mr. Cobb is a junior high school social studies teacher who does not
design learning activities around problems that students have a felt need to
solve. Throughout his years as a teacher, Mr. Cobb has had difficulty with
students habitually failing to participate in class activities, failing to complete homework assignments, failing to bring materials to class, and skipping his classes. Consequently, he finds it necessary to initiate the follow-

ing plan for each of his social studies classes that meet five days a week for 55 minutes per meeting.

The last 30 minutes of each Wednesday's meeting and the entire 55 minutes of each Friday's meeting are designated as "option times." Each class member has the opportunity to spend each option time period in exactly one of the following ways:

**Option 1:** in a supervised "study hall" in which the student is required to individually and silently work on school-related tasks of his or her choice.

**Option 2:** in a "free activity" in which the student does as he or she pleases (e.g., watches a videotape, listens to records, socializes, plays games, goes to the library, or attends supervised study hall) within a predetermined set of specific guidelines.

**Option 3:** working under Mr. Cobb's direction, completing certain tasks (e.g., filing, collating papers, cleaning the classroom, duplicating materials, or performing classroom maintenance) within a predetermined set of specific guidelines.

The specific guidelines that pertain to the plan are printed in a book of classroom regulations that every student has. Mr. Cobb provides each student with the opportunity of signing a contingency contract similar to the contract that appears in Illustration 9.2. Students who do not sign such a contract automatically exercise option 1 during each option time. Those that sign will exercise either option 2 or 3 during option times depending on how well they have fulfilled the contingencies of their contract during any given week.

Although some of Mr. Cobb's colleagues criticize his plan because it takes away so much time from regularly scheduled class, Mr. Cobb continues to use it. He believes that the plan's overall impact leads to a richer participation in learning activities because students are more diligent with in-class activities, homework, and attendance. His data indicate that each student lost far more than 85 minutes of class time per week prior to implementation of the plan simply because of time Mr. Cobb spent dealing with student disengagement.

## FAILING TO COMPLETE HOMEWORK ASSIGNMENTS

### Meaningful Homework

While conducting a learning activity within a unit on modern poetry for one of her high school English classes, Ms. Ramsen provides definitions and explanations of the following concepts: rhythm, meter, iamb foot, trochee foot, anapest foot, and dactyl foot. Ronny, Stacy, and most of the

# Illustration 9.2. Mr. Cobb's Contingency Contract

## CONTINGENCY CONTRACT

Contract Period:

Beginning                                Ending

We the undersigned,                              (here
referred to as "Teacher") and                        (hereafter referred to as "Student") do hereby enter into a contract
with the following provisions:

The teacher will maintain a record of option credits* for the
student in a ledger book (hereafter referred to as "the ledger")
during the contract period according to the following schedule:

**ATTENDANCE** (10 credits per day maximum):
10 credits for each regularly scheduled social studies class at
which the student attends for a complete 55 minutes. 5 credits for each such class that the student attends for less than
the 55 minutes.

**HOMEWORK** (10 credits per day maximum):
Homework assignments completed and returned by the deadline established by the teacher will be rated for completeness
and effort on a scale of 1 to 10 by the teacher. Homework
received after the deadline will be rated for completeness and
effort on a scale of 1 to 5.

**IN-CLASS ASSIGNMENTS** (10 credits per day maximum):
In-class assignments completed and returned by the deadline established by the teacher will be rated for completeness
and effort on a scale of 1 to 10 by the teacher. In-class assignments received after the deadline will be rated for completeness and effort on a scale of 1 to 5.

**HAVING MATERIALS IN CLASS** (5 credits per day
maximum):
5 credits are earned each day that the student has all of his/
her materials (e.g., books, pens, and paper) for full class
participation.

The student may choose to exercise option 2** during option
times on a Wednesday by forfeiting 50 of his/her option credits.
Otherwise the student is required to exercise option 3** on the
Wednesday. The student may exercise option 2 during option time
on a Friday by forfeiting 100 of his/her option credits. Otherwise

# Illustration 9.2. (*Continued*)

the student is required to exercise option 3 on Friday. The student must have a ledger balance of at least 50 option credits before a Wednesday class period begins and 100 option credits before a Friday class begins to be in a position to choose option 2 on that day.

The student's option credit balance shall not in any way influence decisions which the teacher makes (e.g., course grades) other than whether or not the student may choose option 2 on Wednesdays and Fridays.

Nothing in this contract shall supersede classroom, school, or school system policies and regulations.

This contract may be voided before its ending date by mutual agreement of both the student and the teacher.

---

*Option Credits are defined on page 6 of "Classroom Regulations."
**Options 2 and 3 are defined on page 8 of "Classroom Regulations."

Teacher                                    /    date

Student                                    /    date

Witness                                    /

Witness                                    /

other students listen to Ms. Ramsen and record the definitions in their notes. Ms. Ramsen then assigns homework in which they are to read and analyze several poems, classifying them according to rhythm and meter. The assignment specifies exactly what is expected. At the end of the period, Ronny complains to Stacy, "How can Ramsen expect me to do this when I don't even know what she's talking about? Iambs! Trochees! She must be crazy! Those definitions don't make any sense to me. She didn't teach them to us!" Stacy: "No one understood her today; I don't know how to do the homework." That night as Ronny struggles through Ms. Ramsen's assignment, the concepts introduced in class that day begin to come clear to him. After analyzing several poems, the differences between an iamb foot and a trochee foot are apparent.

For many learning objectives, in-class learning activities serve only to provide direction, stimulate thinking, and explain assignments, while actual student objective achievement occurs after class when students individually think, practice, and work out problems on their own. In many circumstances, the most efficient time for students to conceptualize, memorize, or polish skills is when they are working on out-of-class assignments. Unfortunately, some teachers don't keep the eight ideas listed on pages 163–164 in mind when designing homework assignments. They assign homework only because it is the thing to do. Mr. Davis' students, in the next example, are given busy work which has little relevance to student attainment of any goal that fulfills any of their needs.

Mr. Davis to his history class: "For tonight's homework, complete Exercise 5–3 beginning on page 83 of your workbook. Now, tomorrow I will check it first thing in class. Anyone who doesn't have every blank filled will get 10 points deducted from his grade total. Is that clear?"

Exercise 5–3 consists of 27 fill-in-the-blank statements, such as, "The first state to enter the union after the original _____ colonies was _____ in _____ ." The workbook is published as a supplement to the history text that Mr. Davis' class uses. Students who complete the assignment (and the vast majority do) spend about an hour finding from the textbook what goes in the blanks. Chapter 5 of the history text contains each of the 27 completed statements nearly verbatim. Few students recognize value in doing this assignment other than to keep them in Mr. Davis' good graces and prevent them from losing points from their grades.

The concern of this section is how teachers, such as Ms. Ramsen, can deal with incidences in which students choose not to attempt *meaningful* homework assignments. It is debatable as to whether or not it is even desirable for students to complete assignments, such as the one Mr. Davis gave, for which there is no worthwhile rationale. There is no *naturally occurring* consequence for failing to complete meaningless assignments. With his point deduction scheme, Mr. Davis imposed a contrived punishment for students' failure to fill in all the blanks.

## Strategies

The goal of Mr. Benge's first unit in the English course he is just starting with an eighth grade class involves improving students' essay writing abilities. His first homework assignment requires students to choose a topic for a two-page essay dealing with something from their neighborhood and then construct an outline listing the subtopics for the introduction, the main body, and the ending. A number of students ask Mr. Benge questions regarding how to do the assignment "right." He brushes off their questions and tries to assure them that if they will only do it the best way they know how, it will help him help them learn how to do it "right." He tells them that he will collect the work the next day and make suggestions on it that will help them fix it up so that eventually they will be ready to start writing the complete two-page essay. He tries to assure them that, although he will collect and comment on the work, it will *not* be graded. "How many points is this worth?" asks one student. "zero," replies Mr. Benge.

Christine, who like most members of the class does not yet know Mr. Benge well enough to trust what he says, thinks to herself, "I've never made an outline before. I don't know how to do this and since he's not grading us on it, I won't do it." The next day, Christine and several others do not have topics and outlines ready. Others present their attempts to Mr. Benge, but (as he expected) few are anywhere near a finished product. Mr. Benge analyzes each outline he receives and returns it to its owner with helpful suggestions and encouraging comments. Students refine their outlines in class by taking Mr. Benge's suggestions and individually showing them to him. He either makes further suggestions for refinement or okays the work and directs them to begin writing the essay.

Christine feels left out of the activities as she did not give Mr. Benge the opportunity to help her. She asks Mr. Benge if she can turn in the work the next day. He replies, "If you bring in your first outline tomorrow, I'll do my best to get to it and make suggestions. But, I may not have time. Do not write your essay until after I've approved your outline." At no time does Mr. Benge either ask Christine or others why they did not do the initial assignment, nor is he receptive to hearing their excuses. He only concerns himself with the business of getting the work done, not with why it was not done in the past.

The following day, Mr. Benge busies himself helping those who are on schedule with their assignments and does not find time to annotate the "late" ones in class. He takes those home and returns with them the next day. Until all those students who have kept up with the work have a satisfactory essay in hand, the procedures continue with students presenting homework to Mr. Benge who then makes suggestions and gives the next assignment. Mr. Benge administers a unit test that includes an item requiring an essay to be written. Christine feels her chances of doing well on the test are diminished because she was one day behind schedule throughout the unit and never did have the opportunity to have her final homework checked by Mr. Benge before taking the test. She vows to more diligently keep up with Mr. Benge's assignments in the future.

Ms. Simon is circulating among her first graders collecting handwriting homework that she had assigned the previous day. Passing Bruce's desk, she asks, "Bruce, may I have your writing homework?" Bruce: "I don't have it." Ms. Simon: "Oh! I'm sorry, Bruce. I really need it so I can look at it after school today. I know how we can solve the problem! I'll let you do it at one o'clock today. We're going to be baking pumpkin bread then, and you can use that time to do your writing homework." Bruce, who especially enjoys working on the class cooking projects, frowns, but Ms. Simon is already collecting the next student's homework.

## FAILING TO BRING MATERIALS

Ms. Watham directs her class to begin an in-class written assignment. Instead of beginning, Andrea tells her, "I don't have anything to write with. I forgot my pencil." Ms. Watham: "Here, you may borrow one of mine *this* time. Please don't make a habit of this." Andrea: "I won't. Thank you." Ms. Watham thinks to herself, "I'd better develop some strategies if this 'forgetting' becomes habitual."

Because failing to bring supplies and borrowing among students became a problem for Ms. Murphy's fourth grade class, the class established the following rules:

Borrowing supplies among students will not take place *during* class. A student who does not have needed school supplies may choose to either: (1) Purchase the needed items from the class store room, paying the marked price immediately; (2) Take the needed items from the store room and provide twice as many items to the store room supply the morning of the very next school day (e.g., if three sheets of paper are taken, six are provided the next day).

Students failing to replace twice what they took will be required to work off the price of the items during the free period the day after the items were taken. The work tasks will be determined by Ms. Murphy and will involve such jobs as cleaning out the classroom or straightening up the store room.

Mr. Emery requires his junior high male physical education classes to dress out in clean uniform shorts, t-shirts, socks, sneakers, and athletic supporters. Mark, one of his students, tells Mr. Emery before class while others are changing into their uniforms, "Coach, I brought my P.E. clothes home to wash and I forgot to bring them back today." Mr. Emery: "Well, you need today's workout and you may not do it in those street clothes. What are you missing?" Mark: "My shirt, shorts, socks, and jock." Mr. Emery: "You've got your tennis shoes?" Mark: "Yes." Mr. Emery: "Wait here, I think I can lend you some extra stuff, but you'll have to bring them back tomorrow cleaned." Mark: "Okay, Coach." Mr. Emery goes to his supply of P.E. clothes and purposely selects shorts that are baggy and an oversized shirt for Mark. Returning, he gives them to Mark. As he dresses, Mark looks at the ill-fitting outfit and thinks, "I hope I never forget my uniform again!"

## BEING UNDER THE INFLUENCE OF DEBILITATING DRUGS

### Teachers' Attitudes

Every school day in numerous urban, suburban, and rural school districts, tens of thousands of elementary, middle, junior high, and high school students attend classes under the debilitating influences of drugs (e.g., alcohol, marijuana, cocaine, legal prescription drugs, barbiturates, amphetamines, and heroin) (Shannon, 1986). Strangers to a community who are seeking a source for an easy buy of illegal drugs typically first try areas near high schools and junior high schools. Teachers respond to drug use by their students in a variety of ways:

1. Many teachers never become aware of their students' drug use although it is occurring at their schools and affecting the success of their learning activities. Such teachers remain naive because they do not "see" individual personalities in their classes. They visualize their classes as a mass of faceless students and think, for example, of their "third period European literature class" rather than "Clarence, Jean, Barbara, Mono, Sam, Oramya . . ." Typically, such teachers spend much of their time talking to their groups while staring at the back walls of their classroom. They do not look into any one student's eyes and do not distinguish between glassy-eyed stupors and bright-eyed alertness. Subtle and even dramatic personality changes go undetected. Students who are depressive in the morning and manic in the afternoon appear the same all day to these teachers.

2. Some teachers, who believe they have never before been around drug users, are so frightened by the prospects of drugs in their classrooms that they do not allow themselves to accept the possibility. "Deny what you don't like and you won't have to deal with it,"

## Table 9.1 Reference of Common Debilitating Drugs*

| Drugs | Slang Name | Medical Trade Name | Medical Uses | Drug Form |
|---|---|---|---|---|
| *Stimulants* | | | | |
| Cocaine | Big C, coke, blow white powder, gold dust, nose candy | | Local Anesthetic | Powder (white) Liquid |
| Crack | crack | | | Compressed powder (rocklike) |
| Amphetamines | "A", bennies, uppers, jellybeans, pep pills | Biphetamine, Delsoxyn, Dexedrine, Methamphetamine | Hyperkinesis | Tablets (var. color), Liquid |
| Phenmetrazine | | Preludin | Narcolepsy | Tablet, Liquid |
| Methylphenidate | | Ritalin | Weight Control | Tablet, Liquid |
| *Depressants* | | | | |
| Chloral Hydrate | Joy juice, mickey finn, knockout | Noctec, Somnos | Hypnotic | Tablet |
| Barbiturates | Barbs, black beauties, blue angels, pink ladies, sleepers, yellow jackets | Amobarbital, Phenobarbital, Butisol, Phenoxbarbital, Socobarbital | Anesthetic | Tablet, Liquid |
| Benzodiazepines | | Ativan, Valium | Anti-anxiety, Anti-convulsant Sedative, Hypnotic | Tablet, Liquid |
| Methaqualone | | Optimal, Parest Quaalude, Somnafac | Sedative, Hypnotic | Tablet, Liquid |
| *Narcotics* | | | | |
| Codeine | School boy | Methymorphine, Robitussin A,C | Analgesic | Tablet, Liquid |
| Heroin | "H", brown sugar, horse, joy powder, smack, white stuff | Diacetylmorphine | | Powder (white, gray, brown) |
| Hydromorphone | | Dilaudud Dilocol | Analgesic | Tablet, Liquid |
| Methadone | Dolly | Dolophine, Methadose, Methadone Hydrochloride | Analgesic | Tablet, Liquid |

| How Taken | Duration of Effect | Effects Sought | Signs and Symptoms of Use | Effects of Withdrawal |
|---|---|---|---|---|
| Injected, Ingested, Inhaled | 2–4 hours | Euphoria, alertness, activeness, prevent withdrawal discomfort | Individuals may have increased pulse and blood pressure, loss of appetite, insomnia, or become easily excitable. | Individual may become irritable, depressed, disoriented, apathetic, may tend to sleep for long periods of time. |
| Inhaled | 5–30 min/ chip | | Overdose symptoms: Individual may exhibit an increase in body temperature, hallucinations. | |
| Injected, Ingested | 2–4 hours | | | |
| Injected, Ingested | 2–4 hours | | | |
| Ingested, Injected | 2–4 hours | | | |
| Ingested | 5–8 hours | Euphoria, anxiety reduction | Individual may appear drunk without the alcohol smell. | Individual may exhibit anxiety, or insomnia. Individual may become delirious or convulsive. Possible death may result. |
| Ingested, Injected | 1–16 hours | | Overdose Symptoms: Individual may have cold, clammy skin, rapid and weak pulse, shallow respiration, and dilated pupils. Coma and possible death may result. | |
| Ingested, Injected | 4–8 hours | | | |
| Ingested | 4–8 hours | | | |
| Injected, Ingested | 3–6 hours | Euphoria, prevent withdrawal discomfort. | Individual may become drowsy, nauseated, and have constricted pupils. | Individual may exhibit yawning, runny nose, watery eyes, loss of appetite, irritability, chills, sweating, cramps, and nausea. |
| Injected, Inhaled | 3–6 hours | | Overdose Symptoms: Individual may have shallow respiration, clammy skin, and convulsions. Coma and possible death may result. | |
| Ingested, Injected | 3–5 hours | | | |
| Ingested, Injected | 3–5 hours | | | |

## Table 9.1 (*Continued*)

| Drugs | Slang Name | Medical Trade Name | Medical Uses | Drug Form |
|---|---|---|---|---|
| Morphine | "M", morph, dreamer, first line, white stuff | Morphine | Analgesic, Antitussive | Powder, Tablet, Liquid |
| Opium | Brown stuff, hop "O", tar | Paregoric, Parepectolin | Analgesic | Tablet, Liquid Plant resin |
| *Hallucinogens* | | | | |
| LSD | Acid, barrels, blue heaven, cubes, white lightning | | None | Tablet, Liquid |
| Mescaline, Peyote | Buttons, cactus buttons, mesc | | None | Tablet, Plant particles |
| Phencyclidine, Phencyclidine Analogs | PCP, angel dust, aurora borealis, dust, rocket fuel | Phencyclidine | Animal anesthetic | Tablet, Liquid, Powder |
| *Cannabis* | | | | |
| Hashish, Hashish oil | Hash, Black Russian Lebanese | | None | Solid resin (brown/black) |
| Marijuana | "J", Acapulco gold, Aunt Mary, grass, Columbian, hemp, Mary Jane, loco weed, pot, reefer | | None | Plant particles |

* This reference table is an incomplete reference. There are numerous drugs not listed that can be debilitating. Information given in "Signs and Symptoms" is generalized; individuals may react differently due to dosage and drug tolerance. (This table was compiled by Ruth Struyk.)

| How Taken | Duration of Effect | Effects Sought | Signs and Symptoms of Use | Effects of Withdrawal |
|---|---|---|---|---|
| Ingested, Injected, Inhaled | 3–6 hours | | | |
| Ingested, Inhaled | 3–6 hours | | | |
| Ingested | 8–12 hours | Insight, euphoria, distortion of senses. | Individual may exhibit hallucinations, and altered perception of time and distance. | |
| Ingested | 8–12 hours | | Overdose Symptoms: Individual may have longer, more intense experiences, and exhibit signs of psychosis. Possible death may result. | |
| Inhaled, Ingested, Injected | varies | | | |
| Inhaled, Ingested | 2–4 hours | Euphoria, diminished inhibitions, and perceptions. | Individual may have increased appetite, become disoriented, or paranoic. Possible psychosis may result. | |
| Inhaled, Ingested | 2–4 hours | | | |

is the message they subconsciously believe. These teachers avoid drug awareness seminars and depend on their experiences sitting in motion picture theaters watching dramatizations of heroin addicts in the acute stages of withdrawal as indicative of how drug users act. They are not familiar with the information provided by Table 9.1.

3. Some teachers welcome the mellow, nondisruptive behaviors displayed by many students when under the influence of at least some drugs (e.g., marijuana and barbiturates). "I wish he didn't use drugs at all, but I'd rather have him doped up than misbehaving," one teacher admitted. She continues, "He can sleep it off in my class. That way, he's not disturbing those that want to learn. I can't control their habits, so why try?" Similarly, there are teachers who encourage guardians to obtain medication for their "hyperactive" children.

4. There are teachers who react to student drug use by initiating a personal crusade against this "evil." Moralizing on the reasons why drugs should be avoided is usually ineffectual. Teachers who preach to students about the evils of drug use are often dealing with their own feelings of inadequacy. They may not be doing anything to effectively stem drug usage, but they can tell themselves, "I'm trying to do something about the problem."

5. Some teachers do not moralize about drug usage, but they do attempt to help students become more knowledgeable regarding the effects of drugs. These teachers alter curricula so that specific units about drugs are taught and so that problems involving drugs are used to intrinsically motivate students to engage in learning activities in science, mathematics, social studies, physical education, language arts, music, and other academic areas. The section, "Problem-Solving Learning Activities," from Chapter 6 treats of this type of learning activity. These teachers believe that it is better for students to choose whether or not to use drugs from an enlightened posture than to have to make that choice from a position of ignorance.

6. There are teachers who realize that they cannot be "all things" to their students and concentrate on helping students attain only those goals for which they are responsible. But, they also realize that students cannot be completely engaged in learning activities and, thus, efficiently achieve those goals while under the influence of mind-altering substances (Santrock, 1984). Such teachers believe that while they may not be able to control drug use outside their own classrooms, they can teach students to choose not to be under the influence of such substances when under their supervision.

## Strategies

The teachers appearing in the next four scenarios use the last of the afore-mentioned approaches to student drug use.

Royal, Paul, and Jake return from their lunch break to their sixth grade classroom grinning and glancing at one another. Ms. Jackson, their teacher, observes them carefully and finds their behavior, while not disruptive, strange for them. Ms. Jackson ignores the three boys for the first 10 minutes while she conducts a large group activity. As the class divides into smaller work groups and begins a second learning activity, Ms. Jackson individually engages each of the three in a conversation. She notices that Paul and Jake are less coherent than usual and that all three respond slower to questions than they normally do. Their eyes seem dilated more than one would expect in the daytime and she detects a sweet, musky odor when near Royal. She believes the three smoked marijuana during the lunch break. She thinks to herself, "I'm pretty sure this is the first time they've shown up in class stoned. I need to make sure it's the last. And I have to prevent others from modeling what they've done. They first need to understand that this won't be tolerated in our classroom. I should get them out of here while I think of what to do, but they should also be separated. I don't want them enjoying each other's company right now . . . ."

Ms. Jackson goes over to Royal, takes him by the hand, walks him out of the room, and without anger says, "You're in no condition right now to learn. There is no sense in you remaining here for this lesson." Royal: "But I didn't do anything!" Ms. Jackson: "I know you didn't. You're just not thinking as well as you usually do, and I think it's because you've been smoking marijuana or something else that messes up your mind. You wait for me in the time-out room until I have time to come and get you." Royal enters the time-out room adjoining the classroom. Ms. Jackson thinks, "Now, for the other two. I don't want them together. They should be alone to think. Where can I put Paul? – Let's see. – The library! – No, Ms. Green wouldn't understand. She'd likely do something stupid. I know, I'll send a note to Mrs. Lobianco in the office and ask if she can find a couple of inconspicuous places for both him and Jake to wait separately. She'll understand." Ms. Jackson writes the following note and seals it in an envelope addressed to Ms. Lobianco, the principal's receptionist and secretary:

Mrs. Lobianco:
I need to send Jake Abramson and Paul Guidry out of my room until 2:20 when I can retrieve them. Can you immediately locate two inconspicuous, quiet places (one for each as I don't want them together or anyone talking to them now)? My time-out room is occupied and I don't want either in the library.

Please return this note by way of Tyrone indicating whether or not you can work this out. If you can, I'll send Paul first and then Jake five minutes later. If either doesn't make it, send an aide to my room to let me know.

Thanks for your help. I apologize for this unforeseen trouble.

-Wilma Jackson

Ms. Jackson directs Tyrone to take the note. In 2 minutes, he returns with a reply from Ms. Lobianco, "It's all worked out; glad to help." Ms. Jackson directs Paul and then Jake to the office in a manner similar to the way she handled Royal. She thinks, "Now, what do I do? I'd like to turn the whole matter over to their parents. Jake's parents would handle it most effectively. But Royal's parents would just beat him. I don't want that. I don't really know Paul's parents. Actually, I wouldn't be too surprised if Paul's momma and daddy didn't share their dope with him. They seem so emotionally immature. I could just give them a stiff warning and tell them to make this the last time, but this is too serious. I'll call Jake's and Paul's houses tonight. But the Van Harpers will just mishandle it and not help Royal at all. I'm going to refer him to the guidance office; Hodge will handle it right. . . ."

After school, Ms. Jackson enters the time-out room and tells Royal, "I never want you to come into our class after smoking marijuana." Royal: "I didn't smoke anything!" Ms. Jackson: "I'm surprised, because you show the signs of having smoked something." Royal: "Well, I didn't!" Ms. Jackson: "I really don't care what you've already done or not done. I just want to make sure that you won't ever take anything like marijuana before coming to class in the future. Do you understand?" Royal: "Yes, but I didn't!" Ms. Jackson: "What is it that I'm trying to tell you?" Royal: "Not ever to show up in our class stoned." Ms. Jackson: "Very well, you understand. Now to help you from ever letting this happen, I am going to ask Mr. Hodge if he will assist you. If he agrees, he'll be calling you into his office to speak with you either tomorrow or the next day. Do you have anything you'd like to say?" Royal: "What about Paul and Jake, don't they have to do nothin'?" Ms. Jackson: "We're not concerned with Paul and Jake right now, only with you. Do you have anything else to say?" Royal: "No, nothing." Ms. Jackson: "Okay, now hurry along so you won't miss your bus. Have a pleasant night; I'll see you tomorrow."

Ms. Jackson brings Paul to the time-out room and engages him in a conversation. Ms. Jackson: "Paul, I never want you to come to class after smoking marijuana." Paul: "Who said I smoked it? Was it Royal? He smoked a lot more than me! Why are you puttin' it on me?" Ms. Jackson: "Be cool, Paul. I don't want to talk about Royal. It is you I'm asking to never use any kind of dope before or during school. I can't teach you when your mind's messed up. Tonight, I'm going to call your parents to see if I can get them to help you prevent this from happening again. I don't expect it to happen again, but if it does, I'm not going to call your parents again, I'm going to send you to Ms. Bannon, the principal. Do you know what that means?" Paul shrugs his shoulders. Ms. Jackson: "What do you suppose Ms. Bannon will do if I send you to her office?" Paul shrugs again. Ms. Jackson: "I don't know what that means." Paul: "I don't know what she'll do." Ms. Jackson: "Let's brainstorm the possibilities. You go first." Paul, grinning shyly: "She could just let it go." Ms. Jackson, not grinning at all: "That's one possibility. Here's another. She could expel you. Now it's your turn." Paul: "She could call the police." Ms. Jackson: "That's a very real possibility. Or she could call the juvenile authorities. I think we understand one another. That's good. Now, I know you've got somewhere to go, so be on your way. But first, how about a nice firm handshake? Take care; I'll see you tomorrow."

Jake takes his turn speaking with Ms. Jackson in the time-out room. Ms. Jackson: "Jake, I think you smoked marijuana or something that messed up your mind at lunch break today." Jake: "Yes." Ms. Jackson: "Thank you for being up front with me. I expect you never to come into our class in that condition again." Jake: "Okay." Ms. Jackson: "Now, I have a favor to ask of you." Ms. Jackson, watching to see if he appears to understand: "I want you to relate the whole incident to either your mother or your father after you get home. Have one of them call me to discuss it at this number and time." She writes down her phone number and a time interval and hands it to Jake. Ms. Jackson: "That's between seven and ten o'clock tonight. If I haven't heard from one of them by 10, I'll call your house.— Okay?" Jake: "All right." Ms. Jackson: "You take care; I'll see you tomorrow."

For the first 2 months that Joel has been in Ms. Bazinski's second grade class, he has virtually always appeared alert and active. At times, Ms. Bazinski finds Joel's behavior to be exhausting, as he displays a high energy level. But she always manages to help him direct that energy into constructive activities. Ms. Bazinski makes lesson plans so that when she wants Joel in a quiet, sedentary learning activity, she precedes it with a vigorous psychomotor activity.

One morning, Joel is uncharacteristically listless. He seems to want to just sit and stare. His eyes do not seem bright and mischievous as they normally do to Ms. Bazinski. She asks him, "Are you feeling poorly?" Joel: "No." Ms. Bazinski: "Are you tired?" Joel: "No." To Ms. Bazinski's amazement, Joel's listlessness continues through the next school day and she phones his mother, Ms. Logan. Ms. Bazinski: "Hi, Ms. Logan. This is Susan Bazinski, Joel's teacher at school. How are you tonight?" Ms. Logan: "Just fine. Is anything the matter?" Ms. Bazinski: "I'm not sure; that's what I've called to find out. Did I catch you at an inconvenient time?" Ms. Logan: "Oh, no. Things are quiet around here for a change. Is Joel giving you some kind of trouble? Is he failing?" Ms. Bazinski: "No, Joel is not giving me trouble and he's not failing." Ms. Logan: "Then what's the matter?" Ms. Bazinski: "Joel has always been so energetic in class, always eager to participate. But yesterday and today, he acted so tired and out of it." Ms. Logan: "Really!" Ms. Bazinski: "Yes, it is worrying me and I wonder if you have any explanations." Ms. Logan: "He shouldn't be tired. He used to hardly ever sleep through the night, but since he started his medication, he's gotten 10 good hours a night. Plus, he naps in the afternoon. So he shouldn't be tired." Ms. Bazinski: "What *medication,* Ms. Logan?" Ms. Logan: "Oh, the doctor prescribed something to settle him down." Ms. Bazinski: "Why? Is he sick?" Ms. Logan: "No, he's just hard to handle—always wiggling, won't sit still. He'd drive me up a wall and when the school bus driver complained that she couldn't handle him, it was just dangerous." Ms. Bazinski: "Who is the doctor?" Ms. Logan: "Dr. Herrold. He said Joel is hyperactive." Ms. Bazinski: "What is the medication?" Ms. Logan: "Dr. Herrold says it's a tranquilizer. Joel takes it twice a day. Life sure has been easier around here since he's been on it. It really works." Ms. Bazinski: "I guess that explains Joel's peculiar behavior at school." Ms. Logan: "What do you mean 'peculiar'?" Ms. Bazinski: "I mean it's just not like him to sit and stare and not participate the way he should." Ms. Logan: "But how can he learn if he won't sit down and be quiet?" Ms. Bazinski: "Ms. Logan, Joel can learn much better when he's active and alert than he can in a stupor. I would like for you to call Dr. Herrold tomorrow, and discuss this with him. I'd like to speak with him myself, after you've had a chance to explain the problem to him." Ms. Logan: "Maybe he can change his prescription." Ms. Bazinski: "Maybe so. I know I'd like to have the real Joel back in my classroom." Ms. Logan: "Okay, I'll call the doctor tomorrow." Ms. Bazinski: "Thank you very much. I'll call you at this time tomorrow night and you can let me know about your discussion with Dr. Herrold and what *you* decided." Ms. Logan: "All right." Ms. Bazinski: "You have been so helpful. I look forward to speaking with you tomorrow. Have a pleasant night and tell Joel 'good night' for me." Ms. Logan: "Oh, he's already asleep. Good-bye."

Jim comes into Mr. Terrell's fourth-period business law class glassy-eyed and moving in a peculiar mechanical fashion. Mr. Terrell watches him sit at his desk with his head seeming to bob around his shoulders like a doll with a spring neck. Jim seems to be making an effort to appear "straight," but Mr. Terrell is not deceived. Mr. Terrell decides not to deal with the situation at present. After class, he writes out an anecdotal account describing Jim's behavior in class that day. He sends copies to the principal and a trusted school counselor with notes requesting advice as to how he should handle the matter.

Through 10 years of schooling, Ray was never instructed by a teacher who utilized learning activities designed around problems that he had a felt need to solve. Not being intrinsically motivated to participate, Ray learned in ninth grade that by coming to class high on drugs, time seemed to pass more quickly and the boredom was not as insufferable. The drugs also seemed to relieve the anxiety he felt over his concern for peer approval.

Early in the beginning of Ray's eleventh school year, Ms. Koo-Kim, Ray's literature teacher, becomes aware that he is habitually stoned in her class. She thinks to herself: "I will not tolerate Ray or any other student wasting time in my class by being strung out. I'll definitely do something to either teach him to show up straight or not at all. But how? What strategy should I try? Maybe I should give him one warning and then let the office handle him if he shows up out of it again. But unless they catch him with the stuff on him, what can they do? There's no school rule against being high, just for possession and trafficking. I'll first see if I can entice him into wanting to participate in class. Maybe intrinsic motivation isn't just a textbook dream. First of all, I need to find out more about Ray. . . ."

After some observations, Ms. Koo-Kim thinks that Ray might have some interest in being an entertainer. She decides to give him the role of Macbeth in an upcoming class play during a unit on Shakespeare. She hopes he will discover that he cannot learn to perform to the satisfaction of his classmates when he is high. She figures that the responsibility of having them depend on him will either make or break him in the literature class.

Ms. Koo-Kim implements her plan and Ray begins to realize that he is unable to remember the lines he studies the night before when he is under the influence of drugs in class. Classmates' performances are affected by how well Ray does. Several times, Ray and other students suggest that he be replaced for the production. Ms. Koo-Kim persists in her expressions of confidence in Ray's will to succeed. Ray resolves to control his drug usage at least so that it does not interfere with his ability to be engaged during the unit on Shakespeare. Ms. Koo-Kim hopes that this is the beginning of the end of Ray attending her class while under the influence of drugs.

## BEING ABSENT OR TARDY

### School-Wide Policies for Extrinsically Motivating Student Attendance

Numerous school systems and individual schools, especially high schools, have policies such as the following one:

A student who is absent for an entire school day or from an entire class during a school day may not be admitted back into any of the classes that he or she missed before bringing a note, signed by a guardian, explaining the reason for the absence. The note will be evaluated by the school attendance official to classify the absence as either "excused" or "unexcused." The official will provide the student with an "admit slip" which teachers are required to see prior to allowing the student to return to individual classes.

A student who either arrives at school after the beginning of homeroom period or is late for any class must explain the reason for the tardiness to the attendance officer who will provide the student with an admit slip and categorize the tardiness either as "excused" or "unexcused." Teachers shall not admit tardy students into their classes without admit slips.

A student who accumulates three unexcused absences for a class during one grade reporting period or a student who accumulates a combined total of five unexcused absences and incidences of tardiness for a class period during one grade reporting period shall receive a failing grade for that class for that grade reporting period.

A student will be allowed to make up work missed during an excused absence and excused tardiness. Students may not be allowed to make up work missed during any unexcused absence or unexcused tardiness.

A student will be suspended from attending school for a week each time he or she accumulates a total of five unexcused absences for entire school days.

## Teachers' Policies for Extrinsically Motivating Student Attendance

Sometimes individual teachers, especially secondary school teachers, have rules for their classes similar to the following one:

Each student's course grade will be based on attendance, completion of assignments, scores on weekly tests, score on the final examination, and conduct in class. During the 45-day grading period, students have the opportunity to earn up to 500 points distributed as follows:

1. *Attendance (90 points):* For each complete class attended, the student will receive 2 points. A student who is tardy receives 1 point for that day. No points are received on days a student is absent.
2. *Completion of Assignments (90 points):* For each day a student satisfactorily turns in assigned homework on time and completes all in-class work, that student is credited with 2 points. Only 1 point is given on days in which assignments are either turned in late or unsatisfactorily done. No points are given on days that assignments are not turned in at all.
3. *Scores on Weekly Tests (160 points):* Eight 20-point weekly tests will be given.
4. *Final Exam Score (100 points):* The final exam will be an opportunity for each student to earn up to 100 points.
5. *In-Class Conduct (60 points):* Each student will begin the grade reporting period with 60 points. A student who is disruptive in a class or violates a classroom regulation will have points subtracted from that total in proportion to the seriousness of each offense.

A student's report grade will be determined by the number of points obtained during the grading period as follows: A for 468 to 500 points, B for 428 to 467 points, C for 388 to 427 points, D for 348 to 387 points, and F for 0 to 347 points.

## Irrationality of Some Popular Attendance Policies

Schools and teachers with policies similar to the two aforementioned examples attempt to extrinsically motivate students to attend classes with a system of rewards (or punishments, depending on how the reinforcements are viewed) that largely depend on students' desires to obtain high grades on reports. Such systems are inherently irrational for at least four reasons:

1. The purpose of grades is to communicate teachers' summative evaluations of students' achievement of learning goals. If in-class learning activities are relevant to student attainment of goals and grades are assigned based on students' achievement of those goals, then there is no need to *artificially* tie grades to class attendance. Students who are absent from classes in which *worthwhile* learning activities take place are far less likely to receive high grades than students who engage in those worthwhile learning activities. It is only when what goes on in class does not help students achieve goals that making grades directly contingent on attendance even remotely makes sense. In such unfortunate cases, the rationale is: "We want students to attend classes. Since what goes on in classes doesn't really help them achieve and, thus, does not naturally help their grades, we'll fabricate a relation between attendance and grades."
2. Many students, especially those with a history of obtaining low grades, are simply not motivated by the desire for high grades or the fear of low grades.
3. Not allowing a student to make up work missed for unexcused absences or tardiness is an admission that school work is unimportant. If work missed by an absent student is critical to that student's goal attainment, then not allowing her or him to do that work is leaving that student with a learning gap. How is a teacher supposed to deal with that student for the remainder of the school year when the student lacks some knowledge, skill, ability, or attitude that is a prerequisite for subsequent learning?
4. Responding to habitual absenteeism with suspensions seems counterproductive. Is the principle of satiation being applied?

## Strategies

Rather than depend on schemes for artificially tying grades to attendance, you, as a teacher, can make sure that students discover the natural connection among attendance, achievement, and grades. Here are three examples of teachers dealing with students' absenteeism:

As part of a language arts exercise, Mr. Kacala's third grade students compose letters to the mayor of their city suggesting ideas for reducing crime. The letters are written in class on a day when April is not in attendance. The next day when April returns, Mr. Kacala has the letters for the mayor displayed on the walls and directs each student to select a letter to talk to the class about, explaining what he or she likes and dislikes about the letter. Mr. Kacala stipulates that students may talk about a letter only if its author agrees to talk about the letter of that student in return. As the students go about reading the letters hanging on the walls and deciding who will critique whose letter, April says, "I want to talk about Steve's letter!" Steve: "Okay, then I get to do yours." April: "I don't have one because I wasn't here yesterday." Steve: "Let's ask Mr. Kacala what to do." Hearing about their problem, Mr. Kacala replies, "Gee! I'm sorry but if April does not have a letter, then she won't be able to talk about another's today." April: "But it wasn't my fault; I was sick yesterday!" Mr. Kacala: "I'm really sorry that you were sick yesterday. That's terrible and it kept you from writing a letter." April: "But I wanna—" Mr. Kacala: "I know you do. I'll tell you what. Just listen to the others talk about the letters today and after you get home today, you write your letter. Bring it tomorrow. Gretchen isn't here today. If she agrees, you can talk about each other's letters tomorrow or on whatever day she's back in school." April: "But I want to do Steve's today!" Mr. Kacala has already moved toward another group of students and is conversing with them.

Due to a dental appointment, Singh misses Mr. Shapiro's health science class one Tuesday. The next day, Singh listens to Mr. Shapiro's lecture befuddled and unable to follow the trend of thought. Several times within his lecture, Mr. Shapiro prefaces statements with, "As we discussed yesterday. . . ." Not having "discussed" anything with the class yesterday, Singh feels frustrated not being able to follow the lecture.

Afterwards, Singh approaches Mr. Shapiro with, "Man! I'm absent one day and now I'm two days behind! I couldn't follow a thing you said today just because I had an excused absence. You know I had to go to the dentist yesterday." Mr. Shapiro: "Yes, I was just thinking it was unfortunate that you couldn't schedule that appointment at another time. Anyway, after class, find someone who is willing to let you copy yesterday's notes. After you've gone over the notes, check with me in here at 7:45 tomorrow morning. I'll answer any questions I can before homeroom period begins. I'll also lend you some reading matter that'll help you catch up." Singh: "Thank you."

Willie approaches Ms. Grimes, his college botany teacher, and says, "Ms. Grimes, will we have a test on Tuesday of next week?" Ms. Grimes: "I'm not sure yet. It depends on how much progress we make before then. If the test isn't Tuesday, it'll be on Thursday of that week." Willie: "It's because I have to be out of town on that Tuesday and I don't want to miss a test. If we have one, will I be allowed to make it up? I really hate to miss, but I can't help it because —" Ms. Grimes (interrupting): "Why you'll be absent is irrelevant. Let's concern ourselves with what we should do about it." Willie: "Okay." Ms. Grimes: "Actually, I'd much rather you miss a test than a regular class meeting. I can easily administer an equivalent form of the test to you at another time. We can schedule a make-up test at your convenience." Willie: "And you won't take off because it's a make-up?" Ms. Grimes: "Why would I do that?" Willie: "That's what other teach—hey, that's great!" Ms. Grimes: "But, if we have a regular class on that Tuesday, that does present us with a problem. Who do you know in class that you can trust to help us and who you can easily get in touch with?" Willie: "Lamona or Edgar. Either one will help." Ms. Grimes: "Okay, get one of them to bring some cassettes and a recorder to class that Tuesday. I'll record the session for you and they can get the tapes to you. As soon as you return to town, listen to the tapes, get their notes, find out the assignment, and discuss the session with Lamona or Edgar. After you've done that, you can give me a call and we'll either talk about it on the phone or make an appointment to clear up any further questions you might have." Willie: "Hey lady, that's all right. Thank you. I'll do it. Really, I wouldn't miss your class if it wasn't for —" Ms. Grimes (interrupting): "Good-bye, Willie."

## CHEATING ON TESTS

### Nine Incidents

Angee gets up from her desk, walks over to the classroom pencil sharpener, and returns to her desk to complete the multiple-choice science test she and the rest of her sixth grade classmates are taking. During her walk, Angee looked on several other students' papers to find out how they responded to certain items that she couldn't answer.

A calculus teacher, Mr. Kruhl, scores test papers by writing down the number of points off by each item a student doesn't correctly answer. Mr. Kruhl does not mark anything by correctly answered items; he simply subtracts the number of points for incorrect items from the maximum possible score of 100. Jack, one of Mr. Kruhl's students, realizes this after his first calculus test is returned. When Jack is about to begin taking the second calculus test, he thinks, "I'll never have time to complete this 12-page monster in the 90 minutes Kruhl's allowing us. I'll just rip out pages 6 and 9 and discard them. He'll probably just pass over them and not realize they're missing. If he does catch it, I'll just say they were never there." Several days later, Mr. Kruhl returns Jack's paper with a score derived by subtracting the number of points off for incorrect items from 100. Jack's score is the same as it would have been if Jack had correctly responded to all of the items on pages 6 and 9.

June did not study for the history exam that Ms. Tolbert is giving today. Instead, June memorized the answers to an old unit test that Ms. Tolbert had administered to one of June's friends in a previously held class. June is overjoyed when Ms. Tolbert hands her a test identical to the one her friend shared.

Twelfth graders Kraemer, Tom, and Arthur engage Ms. Hubert in a lively conversation before school as their co-conspirator, Mary Ellen, steals four copies of the final physics exam scheduled for that afternoon off of Ms. Hubert's desk. During the morning study hall, the four students jointly figure out the answers and each fills out a copy of the test. They make sure that there are some minor discrepancies among their papers. When Ms. Hubert administers the test, the four carefully substitute their completed copies for the ones distributed by Ms. Hubert.

Sonia, an eighth grade student, runs a popular service for her school-mates at Abraham Lincoln High School. Sonia searches trash containers for used duplicating carbons and masters that have been discarded in the faculty lounge or school office. From her growing "test file," she provides test information to her many "friends." Sonia feels very popular with her peers.

"May I please be excused to go to the restroom?" Mickey asks Mr. Green during a fourth grade spelling test. Mr. Green: "Yes, but hurry so you will have plenty of time to finish your test." Mickey: "I will. Thank you very much." In the restroom, Mickey extracts the spelling list that earlier in the day he had hidden under a toilet. He quickly checks the spelling of the four words from the test that he does not know.

As Mr. Duetchman supervises a large group of high school students taking a two-day achievement test battery, he finds it curious that Donna frequently brings her elbows together and stares down the neckline of her dress. Not knowing what to do, he dismisses her behavior as a reflection of adolescent self-consciousness. Actually, Donna has a "cheat sheet" attached to the inside of her bra.

Ms. Bolden instructs her first graders to keep their test papers covered and not to let classmates see their answers while taking a math test. Ashley and Monica are sitting at the same table taking the test when Monica turns to Ashley and, pointing to one of her test items, says, "I forgot what this one is." Ashley: "Ms. Bolden said you weren't supposed to show me your paper! Cover it up." Monica: "Sorry! But I need some help on this one." Ashley: "Okay, don't show me your paper. Just read it to me." Monica: "What's this called?" Monica draws a rectangle in the air with her finger. Ashley: "Let me see what I just put for that. But don't look on my paper

**Illustration 9.3. Primary Grade Children, Like Ashley and Monica, Do Not Have an Adult's Concept of Cheating**

while I look. It's not allowed.'' Ashley turns back to Monica, still carefully covering her paper, and says, ''It's a rectangle.''

Freda takes a lengthy psychology test and leaves several short-answer, written-response items blank. Her teacher, Mr. Zabriski, scores the test and returns them to the class the following day. The items Freda left blank are marked with zeroes, but she quickly fills in the answers and approaches Mr. Zabriski, ''Mr. Zabriski, don't I get any credit for these? I thought they were at least partially correct!''

## Strategies

By violating rules under which a test is administered in order to correctly answer items which they otherwise could not answer, students contaminate the validity of that test. In other words, aside from being an unethical, distasteful practice, cheating leads to inaccurate and misleading test results. Students would have no inclination to cheat on a test if they believed that *accurate* information about their achievement in the hands of their teachers is more beneficial to them than is misinformation that deceives their teachers. Once again, three vital principles become apparent:

1. The self-worth students perceive and the respect, love, and esteem others (including teachers) feel for them should never be dependent upon their achievements.
2. Formative evaluations of students' achievements should be emphasized to a far greater degree than should summative evaluations.
3. Grades should only be used to communicate summative evaluations; they should not be used as a reward for achievements.

Given the unfortunate fact that there is an almost universal violation of these principles, you are virtually assured of encountering students with inclinations for cheating on tests. But even with these students, cheating is unlikely when:

1. *You set a businesslike tone and display an attitude that communicates that students are expected not to cheat.*
2. *Test administrations are closely supervised.* (Please note, however, that, as indicated by the example involving first graders Monica and Ashley in Ms. Bolden's class, the concept of cheating is not well-developed in young children (e.g., under the age of nine). Primary school children do not differentiate between obtaining a correct response with unauthorized aid and obtaining it without unauthorized aid (Pulaski, 1980). Teachers should observe whether or not young children respond on their own or with unauthorized aid. Steps should be taken so that such aid is not attainable. However, warning young students not to cheat or punishing them for behaviors that adults consider to be cheating is, for them, a frustrating experience that only teaches them they are not trusted. Even with older students, warnings not to cheat are futile and should be avoided. However, students should not be given reasonable opportunities to cheat.)
3. *The same form of a test is not used repeatedly.*
4. *You account for each copy of a test that is duplicated (copies can be numbered) and materials, such as duplicating masters, are secured.*
5. *You mark test papers so that points are added for correct responses rather than subtracting points for incorrect ones.*
6. *You annotate, as well as score, test papers.* (Not only does this practice provide helpful feedback to students, but it also helps you remember why you scored items as you did. Students are less likely to manipulate answers after the tests are returned if you have already commented on their answers.)

7. *Students are directed to check on whether or not their test copies contain all pages and are properly collated prior to beginning.*
8. *Students are not tested on their recall of material that seems unnecessary to memorize.* (When obtaining a grade on a test is the *sole* perceived purpose students have for memorizing what they know will be forgotten after the test, using crib notes seems like a sensible thing to do.)

Because a student cheats on a test is not a reason for recording a low score. Cheating does not reflect learning goal attainment (except in the rare case in which the learning goal is for the student to be honest). Thus, if a teacher knows that a student has cheated on a test, then the test results are not valid and *no score* should be recorded as if the student never took the test at all. A student's understanding of biology, for example, should not be judged by whether or not that student cooperated with the test-taking procedures. Judgments of how well learning goals are achieved should be withheld until after the student no longer displays the dishonest behavior and a valid measurement of achievement can be obtained (Cangelosi, 1982).

> While scoring a unit test he had administered to his tenth grade first-aid class, Mr. Broussard notices some inconsistencies in Joe's test responses. Joe's answers to a couple of the more difficult items on the test are correct, while he missed a number of items that measured simple rudimentary knowledge. Mr. Broussard asks himself, "How could he get these correct without knowing this?" Later, while scoring Remy's paper, Mr. Broussard notices that Remy answers the same difficult items using words very similar to those in Joe's responses. Mr. Broussard then compares their two sets of responses and notices some peculiar similarities. On the multiple-choice portions of the test, Joe's choices nearly always agree with Remy's. He finds it curious that the two would consistently choose the same distractors or foils for multiple-choice items that they both missed.
>
> Convinced that Joe copied from Remy's paper, Mr. Broussard begins planning how to deal with the situation. He thinks, "I should confront them both with this. Scare the hell out of them! But if I'm wrong, I'll only teach them they're not trusted. That could be damaging. They just might cheat from now on because they figured there'd be no trust to lose. But I really can't put any stock in Joe's test results and I need to know what he got out of this unit. I need an accurate score on him. Also, I don't want Joe to get away with this. I don't think he's cheated before. I should block any positive reinforcement so this doesn't become a pattern. I know! I'll 'lose' his test paper and schedule a retest for him with an equivalent form."
>
> The next day, Mr. Broussard distributes the scored and annotated test papers. Joe from his desk: "Mr. Broussard, you didn't give my test back." Mr. Broussard: "I didn't? Please come up here." Joe arrives and Mr. Broussard says softly, "You didn't get your paper back. What do you think

happened?" Joe: "I don't know. I took the test." Mr. Broussard: "Yes, I know. I remember going over it." Mr. Broussard pulls out his grade book and says, "Here, Joe, let's see if I recorded a score for you. No, there's no score here. Look." Joe sees the empty square. Mr. Broussard: "We'll just schedule a retest. How about tomorrow? I'll give you a test tomorrow." Joe: "That's not fair for me to have to take another test." Mr. Broussard: "Yes, I know. Now, let's see when we can schedule it. . . ."

Mr. Stoddard validates each sociology test that he administers to his classes before allowing the test results to influence evaluations he makes regarding students' achievement levels. From analysis of one set of test results and from his observations of some curious student behaviors during the administration of that test, Mr. Stoddard suspects that student cheating contaminated the accuracy of the test results. At the next class meeting, Mr. Stoddard announces, "The results I received from the test are invalid. There are some major discrepancies among the scores. Statistical analyses indicate the test was too unreliable to accurately indicate your levels of achievement. Therefore, I discarded the results and we will take a refined version of the test under more controlled conditions on Wednesday."

Ms. Maggio administers a problem-solving test to her fourth graders in which they are directed to work out in their heads a sequence of tasks that are presented on pages 39 and 40 of one of their textbooks. She instructs them to look at only those two pages in their books while working out the solutions and expressing answers on a sheet of paper. Ms. Maggio notices one student, Nettie, keeping an eye on her during the test. Nettie seems to manipulate her book suddenly whenever Ms. Maggio comes near or looks at her. Ms. Maggio suspects that Nettie has surreptitiously turned to the back of the book in which answers to the problems are given.

After the test, Ms. Maggio examines Nettie's answer sheet. Most of the responses are correct. She then engages Nettie in a private conference and presents one of the problems that Nettie answered on the test and asks her to solve it. Nettie is unable to come up with a solution this time. Nettie fails twice more to reproduce answers which she had written on the test earlier in the day. Ms. Maggio: "Nettie, I do not understand why you cannot figure out these answers now if you solved the problems during the test." Nettie: "I don't know." Ms. Maggio: "I will not check off that you can do these types of problems until you demonstrate to me that you can."

## Self-Assessment for Chapter 9

I. Which of the six approaches for teachers to respond to students' abuse of drugs listed on pages 245–250 do you most closely associate with your own philosophy? Explain in a paragraph why you prefer this approach.

II. Observe the students in someone else's class. Search for indicators of student daydreaming and mind-wandering. Describe what you observed in those students' behaviors that led you to believe that they had quietly become disengaged from the learning activity.

III. For each of the following examples presented in this chapter, write one or two paragraphs giving your view of the advantages and disadvantages of the way the teacher handled the off-task behavior; suggest how the approach could have been improved: (A) Ms. Searcy, page 234; (B) Mr. Cavallaro, page 235; (C) Mr. Legget, page 235; (D) Mr. Burns-Whittle, page 238; (E) Mr. Benge, page 243; (F) Ms. Murphy, page 244; (G) Ms. Jackson, page 251; (H) Mr. Broussard, page 263.

*Reviewing Your Self-Assessment* _____

Exchange copies of what you wrote in response to parts I, II, and III with others for copies of their responses. After reading one another's papers, discuss the differences and similarities among your answers.

## Supplemental Readings

Cain, H. D. (1980). *Flint's emergency treatment and management* (6th ed.). Philadelphia, PA: Saunders.

Cangelosi, J. S. (1982). *Measurement and evaluation: An inductive approach for teachers* (pp. 236–238). Dubuque, IA: Brown.

Carducci, D. J., & Carducci, J. B. (1984). *The caring classroom* (pp. 19–40). Palo Alto, CA: Bull Publishing.

Greenwood, G. E., Good, T. L., & Siegel, B. L. (1971). *Problem situations in teaching* (pp. 32–43, 67–72, 85–98). New York: Harper & Row.

Karlin, M. S., & Berger, R. (1972). *Discipline and the disruptive child: A practical guide for elementary teachers* (pp. 181–196). West Nyack, NY: Parker.

Maifair, L. L. (1986, October). Helping kids resist drugs. *Instructor, XCVI*, No. 3, 72–74.

O'Brien, R., & Cohen, S. (Eds.). (1984). *The encyclopedia of drug abuse* (pp. 316–320, 393–398). New York: Facts on File.

Santrock, J. W. (1984). *Adolescence: An introduction* (2nd ed.), (pp. 605–649). Dubuque, IA: Brown.

Seeman, H. (1984). A major source of discipline problems. *Educational Horizons, 62,* 128–131.

Shannon, J. (1986). In the classroom stoned. *Phi Delta Kappan, 68,* 60–62.

Tillman, M. (1982). *Trouble-shooting classroom problems.* Glenview, IL: Scott, Foresman.

# 10

# Dealing with Disruptive Behaviors

Chapter 10 is designed to provide you with some ideas for developing your own techniques for effectively handling both isolated incidents and patterns of disruptive behaviors. In particular the following types of disruptive behaviors are addressed: (1) disruptive talking; (2) interrupting; (3) clowning; (4) being generally discourteous; (5) failing to clean up; (6) vandalizing; (7) perpetrating violence against students; (8) perpetrating violence against teachers.

## DISRUPTIVE BEHAVIORS

Students reject opportunities to learn by displaying nondisruptive off-task behaviors; they suffer the consequences of their own choices. But students who behave disruptively also tread on the rights of other students to learn. You, as their teacher, can hardly ignore disruptive student behaviors. Some 29 scenarios of teachers dealing with disruptive student behaviors are provided in this chapter. You are urged to extract principles from these examples that will help you design strategies that will work for you and your students. Reflect on the pros and cons of how the teachers handled disruptions in these examples; please don't simply copy their methods.

## DISRUPTIVE TALKING

Ms. Bravo usually plans each school day so that her fourth grade students alternate learning activities in which they need to be rather quiet with learning activities in which talking with one another is not disruptive. Her students typically look forward to the learning activities that have hardly any restrictions on talking. One day during a quiet session in which the class is supposed to be individually working on some problems, sporadic conversations erupt among the students. Ms. Bravo finds the noise disturbing to those working on the problems. Realizing that students are anticipating playing "Who am I?" (the next learning activity scheduled to begin in 30 minutes) she blinks the classroom lights to get their attention and announces, "There is much too much talk for us to think on our own. I am starting my stopwatch now." She pushes a button on the chronograph on her wrist and continues, "I will keep my stopwatch running as long as there is noise in here. When the noise stops, my watch will stop. When the noise starts again, my watch will also. We will begin playing 'Who am I?' only after 30 more minutes of silence for working out these problems." In 5 minutes, the class is quiet and working and Ms. Bravo stops her watch. Eight minutes later, talking disrupts the work and Ms. Bravo accumulates another 6 minutes on the stopwatch waiting for silence. The required total of 30 minutes of silence is finally obtained with only one more interruption; this last one took only 3 minutes. She directs the class to begin playing "Who am I?" 14 minutes after the game was scheduled to start. However, the starting time for the silent learning activity scheduled right after "Who am I?" is not delayed. A number of students complain that the game was too short and they did not have enough time to finish.

There are 30 minutes remaining in Ms. Allen's fourth period Latin II class when she directs the students to begin work on a translation exercise from their textbooks. A number of students carry on conversations that are disturbing to others. Ms. Allen motions for silence, but talking continues to spring up around the classroom. Ms. Allen calls a halt to the translations saying, "Okay, class, please let me have your attention. I think each of us needs silence to properly translate these sentences. I'm sorry, but I see this isn't working. Let's hold off on these translations until you can get away by yourselves, either at home or during your free period. Just have them ready for class tomorrow. Right now, put your books away and we'll work together on our conversational Latin. Okay, here's what we'll do. . . ."

Mr. Haimowitz is explaining Ohm's Law to his physics class when he becomes annoyed by a conversation between two students, Walt and Henry. Without missing a word in his explanation, he moves between the students and continues speaking to the class. The two boys stop talking and appear to pay attention as long as Mr. Haimowitz is between them. Five minutes later, with Mr. Haimowitz lecturing from another area of the room, Walt and Henry are conversing again. This time, Mr. Haimowitz goes over to them, continuing with his lecture, picks up Henry's papers from the top of his desk, and motions Henry to follow him to another part of the room where there is a vacant desk. Mr. Haimowitz places Henry's papers on the desk top and Henry takes a seat. At no time during the incident did Mr. Haimowitz speak directly to either Henry or Walt, nor did he miss a word in his explanation of Ohm's Law.

Mr. Eglin is lecturing to a political science class when several students' conversations develop in the crowded lecture hall. Mr. Eglin lowers his voice below the level of the combined students' voices. Other students, who are now straining to hear Mr. Eglin's inaudible words, turn to those near them who are talking and tell them to be quiet. As the conversations cease, Mr. Eglin raises his voice so that he can again be heard.

Leora and Nan, two sixth graders, consider themselves "best friends." At school they are almost constant companions. Ms. Helmick, their teacher, believes their relationship is healthy and she doesn't want to discourage it. However, they have developed a pattern of talking, note passing, giggling, and looking at one another during quiet learning activities. Ms. Helmick has dealt with incidences of their disruptive talking individually as she would for isolated off-task behaviors. She now decides that their pattern of disruptive talking must somehow be modified. Careful thought leads Ms. Helmick to formulate the following alternative three plans:

1. Ms. Helmick will confront the two with the problem they have been creating. She will indicate that each time she recognizes that they are talking at an inappropriate time, she will signal them to leave the area where the learning activity is going on and to continue their conversation in the time-out room. They are to remain there until the learning activity that they disturbed is over.
2. Ms. Halmick will frequently schedule "free talk" sessions after quiet learning activities. Participation in the free talk sessions, in which students can socialize within certain guidelines, will be contingent on all students having quietly engaged in the previous quiet learning activity. Time wasted during the quiet activity due to disruptive talking is made up from time scheduled for the free talk session.
3. Each time Leora and Nan's talking disrupted a learning activity, Ms. Halmick will use the timer she wears on her wrist to keep account of the amount of time wasted. Leora and Nan would then be required to make up the lost time after school that day. Leora's and Nan's guardians will be made aware of this plan, so they can cooperate in having the two students get home on days they miss their buses.

Ms. Helmick is not yet sure which of the three plans she will try first. She has confidence in the first plan because she doesn't believe that Leora and Nan want to be excluded from class activities. In fact, incidents during class activities often stimulate their in-class talking. Furthermore, the principle of satiation may take effect and the girls could become "talked out." In the time-out room they would be deprived of much of the stimulations (e.g., seeing other students) for their conversations. Ms. Helmick thinks the second plan would bring peer pressure on Leora and Nan to control their disruptive talking. The third plan utilizes the power of negative reinforcement because they would control when Ms. Helmick stops her timer.

## INTERRUPTING

During a fifth grade math lesson, Mr. Caldwell asks Lorene, "What number multiplied by 7 is 42?" Lorene: "Uhh, let's see. I think—" Sandy interrupts, "Six because 42 divided by 7 is 6!" Lorene appears relieved because she has been taken off the hook. Sandy smiles. Mr. Caldwell is frustrated because his planned questioning strategy in which Lorene was to reason deductively has been disrupted. Sandy's interruption deprived Lorene of a learning experience. Mr. Caldwell, appearing quite disgusted, turns to Sandy, "Why did you interrupt?" Sandy: "I was just helping her out."

But Sandy did not help Lorene out at all. Unfortunately, students are often conditioned into believing that all teachers want from them are *the right answers*. They don't think processes and thinking skills are of concern to teachers. Furthermore, these students have learned to believe that they are constantly being tested. Thus, by popping up with the right answer, Sandy felt she could seize an opportunity to show off her knowledge and she could either gain Lorene's favor for "helping" her or outdo Lorene in a competition of "who knows the answer." Teachers in Ms. Caldwell's situation are in a dilemma. On one hand, they do not want to discourage the interrupting students' enthusiasm for the lesson, but they need to discourage such disruptions. Of course, teachers who implement the suggestions for conducting questioning and discussion sessions from pages 157–158 are not as likely to be faced with this dilemma.

Ms. Brittain has established the following procedure for her fourth graders to use during large group discussions. During a discussion session only the one person who has the floor may speak. A student may obtain the floor by raising his or her hand and being recognized by the student who at the time has the floor. A student who has the floor must relinquish it within one minute after another raises a hand. Ms. Brittain will intervene at any time in the process in order to assure each student a fair opportunity to speak and to keep the discussion focused on the agreed upon topic.

While discussing the differences between living in a large city and in a small town, Crystal has the floor and is explaining why she thinks it is easier to travel in a small town. Without raising his hand, Oral interrupts with, "Yeah, but in a big city you can take a subway and—" Crystal (interrupting): "I have the floor! I didn't call on you!" Oral: "But,—" Ms. Brittain (interrupting): "Oral, the procedure is to raise your hand and wait to be recognized before speaking. Now, I want to hear what Crystal was saying about traveling in a small town." The discussion continues as Ms. Brittain carefully monitors the session, watching to see if the less bold students are encouraged to speak.

Mr. Rutknecht is explaining how to bisect an angle with a straight-edge and compass when Debbie, one of his 34 students, interrupts with, "What size radius do you need for the first arc?" Mr. Rutknecht appreciates that Debbie has asked a question that is relevant to the topic. He wants to encourage her interest and that type of question. However, he doesn't want to positively reinforce interruptions. He responds to Debbie's out-of-turn question with only a frown and continues his explanation, watching for Debbie and other students to raise their hands. Momentarily, Lynn raises her hand and Mr. Rutknecht immediately recognizes her. Lynn asks a question and raises a point on which Mr. Rutknecht elaborates. Five students, including Debbie, raise their hands and two speak out without being recognized. Mr. Rutknecht cuts off the interrupting students and calls on those with hands raised. At one point, he thanks a student for her patience in waiting to be recognized.

"People moved west because . . . ," Maureen is saying to Mr. Peck's class when another student, Hugh, interrupts with, "They never would have moved if. . . ." Mr. Peck has had to deal with Hugh's interruptions in the past; he resolves to do something about the pattern. That night Mr. Peck thinks: "I will use the principle of extinction to help Hugh break this habit of interrupting speakers during class. I first need to identify the payoff he realizes from interrupting. What's the positive reinforcement? I really believe he likes being noticed. He wants the rest of the class and me to know what he knows. He thinks others are upstaging him by talking. It is a competitive thing. If it's attention he wants, I'll make sure he gets it when he's patiently waiting for his turn to talk; I'll keep him from getting attention when he interrupts. Each time he interrupts, I'll cut him off immediately by repeating the last words of whomever he interrupted. I won't even look at him. If he interrupts Sue, for example, I'll interrupt him and say 'Excuse me, Sue, you were saying you thought that . . .' and I'll let Sue go on. When Hugh remains quiet, I'll ask him for a comment or an opinion. That should positively reinforce a desirable alternative behavior. Now, I'd better work up a little tally sheet to help me measure how much progress Hugh makes while he's on this plan."

## CLOWNING

Mr. Holt's sixth grade class is engaged in a large group learning activity on nutrition when Vickie responds to one of Mr. Holt's questions with, "I'm not going to eat just anything. I'm careful about what I stick in my body." Woodrow stands up and yells out, "Here's something you can stick in your body!" Woodrow momentarily grabs his crotch. Laughter erupts around the room. Because Mr. Holt has thought about handling this type of situation prior to this time and follows the Teacher Process Model, he is able to process the following thoughts in his mind without a moment's delay: "Woodrow has never pulled this stunt before. He's only looking for attention. It's too bad they laughed at him. That's positive reinforcement and this could be the beginning of a pattern. I need to prevent this from happening again. But how? I have numerous options. I could just laugh along and not make a big deal of it. But no, I cannot display approval. I might just ignore it and try not to focus any more attention on him. But, damn it, they've already laughed at him! It's too late to ignore it. I could jerk him out of his desk and give him a good tongue-lashing, but that would just call more attention to him. That's what he wants. Of course, he's left himself very vulnerable for a comeback. It would be easy for me to turn this around and embarrass him with his own words. That maybe could serve as a punishment. But that would also be destructive; I'd never do that. It's never helpful to have a child lose face in front of peers. That could easily turn into a competitive thing between us; I can't afford that. I'm only glad no one in the class had a comeback for him. I must make sure I don't label him in any way. If I called him 'dirty' or 'rude,' he might learn to live up to that expectation. I could pretend that I did not understand the sexual connotation of his comment and respond as if he were really talking about nutrition. But that would be obvious dishonesty. No, I've got to handle this one head on."

Because Mr. Holt's mind was busy with the aforementioned thoughts in the moments immediately following the outburst of laughter, he was able to maintain a serious expression throughout. The class quickly realizes that Mr. Holt did not find Woodrow's clowning humorous. He turns to Woodrow and says, "I know you are trying to make us laugh. But I do not like to hear that kind of joke. You and I will talk about this for a few minutes after the class leaves for lunch today." Turning to Vickie, Mr. Holt says, "Excuse the interruption, Vickie. You were telling us that you choose your food carefully. Please continue."

It is the first week of the school year in Ms. Giminski's kindergarten class. Ms. Giminski has just started each student working individually in a language arts work assignment. Brian jumps up and begins dancing and gyrating in front of the others saying, "Watch me! Watch me!" Two students stop their work and giggle, but most just ignore him. Ms. Giminski thinks, "I hope this isn't a pattern for Brian. I'll bet this is what he does for attention at home." She picks up Brian's paper, takes him by the hand, and walks him over to an area of the room that is out of the view of the other students. She softly tells Brian, "Please sit here and finish your paper. Bring it to me only after all of these spaces are colored in. . . .

**Illustration 10.1. Mr. Holt's Response to Woodrow's Clowning Is Systematic, Thoughtful, and Decisive**

What are you going to do?" Brian: "Color all this and bring it to you." Ms. Giminski: "That will be fine!"

Over the next several days, Ms. Giminski watches for signs of Brian wanting to show off. She makes an effort to see that he gets attention at times when he is not trying to show off.

Holly's frequent out-loud quips, gestures, and facial contortions evoke laughter among her peers in Mr. Smith's tenth grade English class. Mr. Smith finds that occasional clowning is humorous and a healthy diversion from work. However, Holly's clowning has become so frequent that it is impeding class progress. Mr. Smith is beginning to fear what Holly will come up with and, consequently, phrases his words with care in order to avoid having Holly turn a serious comment into a joke. He decides to help her control her in-class clowning and thinks to himself, "I'm not going to continue to stand for Holly's habitual clowning. She's modifying my behavior so that I'm not as relaxed in class as I used to be. I'm afraid to smile for fear she'll think it's her cue to be on stage. . . . If I asked her why she was clowning or if I turned her jokes back on her, it'd embarrass her and she'd more likely try to regain face with the class by trying even harder to be funny. No, I never want for her to be embarrassed. That would make matters worse. She does it to gain favor and to relieve her boredom. . . . I know! I'll call her in for a private conference and be perfectly frank with her. I'll tell her how her clowning is making it difficult for me to do my job. I'll ask for her cooperation. If she agrees to try, I'll agree to help her succeed. We'll set up a secret code between us so that I can signal her when she is being dirsuptive and should stop whatever she's doing at the moment. The rest of the class will never know. She can also have a signal worked out for me when she feels the urge to clown; I'll help her pick an appropriate time and set her stage. We'll establish a real cooperative relationship. Now, I'd better come up with some alternative plans in case she doesn't go for this one. I hope she goes for the original idea because I don't want to have to sacrifice her welfare for the good of the class."

## BEING GENERALLY DISCOURTEOUS

Learning activities are generally more effective when they are conducted in an atmosphere of cooperation and mutual respect among participants. It is usually disruptive for a student to treat other students or a teacher in a disrespectful or thoughtless manner. Although the accepted rules of decorum and courtesy vary among the subcultures represented within the composition of many school populations, a teacher is responsible for establishing an environment in which students are unlikely to feel insulted, uncomfortable, or inconvenienced as a consequence of the rudeness of others.

Mr. Lowder assigns Mitch and Ward to be on the same basketball team during one physical education session. Mitch complains aloud in front of the class, "I don't want that queer, Ward, on my team. I'd rather not play." The following thoughts run through Mr. Lowder's mind: "Mitch is so competitive. I should just tell him, 'Fine! Than you don't play.' He could just sit on the sidelines. Maybe I could play in his place and show Ward that I'd like to be on his team. But I don't want to give the class the impression that their participation isn't critical. I'd like to do something to protect Ward's feelings. I know he's already allowed them to be damaged and I may make things worse by making a big deal out of this incident. I'll let it slide for now; if it recurs, I'll intervene. Maybe I should let Mitch know that I don't approve of such behavior. I'll use Glasser's approach in a conference with Mitch."

Several of Ms. Belcher's second graders begin jockeying and shoving to obtain a place near the front of the line that they are forming in preparation for going to the auditorium for a puppet show. "Hey, I'm first; get away!"

Jack yells as Ellis pushes his way to the front. Ms. Belcher observes the scene for a minute as the more aggressive students manage to be near the front of the line and crowd toward the exit. In a very calm voice, Ms. Belcher announces, "Okay, keep your places in line. We're going to stretch our legs a bit and take a walk around the room before leaving." Noticing that Cheri is last in the line, Ms. Belcher continues, "Cheri, you lead the line around the back wall, over along the side wall, past the front, and then lead the line out of the door. I'll get in behind Ellis and shut the door as I leave." Surprised by the strange route they take exiting the room, the students turn silently and follow Cheri to the auditorium. Cheri beams as Ellis and Jack roll their eyes in disgust.

Susan, a seventh grader, is working on a problem-solving assignment when she exclaims in a rather curt voice to Ms. Comeaux, her teacher, "I can't do this ass-hole crap! It's so stupid!" Ms. Comeaux: "I can tell you're frustrated. The problems are difficult. When you are ready for me to help you with them, tell me in a courteous way using only words that are acceptable to me."

Mr. Turner's social studies students are engaged in small group discussions when he overhears Kendall tell Russ, "You wouldn't think that if you weren't such an ugly slob!" Mr. Turner: "Kendall, I get so angry when you speak rudely that I cannot understand what you're trying to say." Mr. Turner hopes that he has reminded the group that impolite, thoughtless talk is unacceptable during his learning activities. He wants to avoid an inane, nonproductive exchange on why Kendall spoke rudely. He does not think that it would be wise to appear as if he were trying to protect Russ, so he doesn't say anything like, "Russ is not an ugly slob! I like him very much." He believes that would display a lack of confidence in Russ being able to deal with his own feelings. The focus is on terminating the rude behavior and getting on with the business at hand.

## FAILING TO CLEAN UP

A classroom in disarray, a littered playing field, inaccessible equipment, unattractive surroundings, damaged supplies, and an unprepared activity area interfere with the effectiveness of learning activities. Thus, by failing to clean up after themselves, students can be disruptive.

Ms. Johnson frequently schedules her third graders' school days so that learning activities that require students to pick up materials afterwards are followed by activities that students genuinely enjoy. Initiation of an antici- pated enjoyable activity is always contingent on the classroom being in acceptable order as specified by Ms. Johnson.

Ms. Lambert usually gives her tenth grade biology students some time to begin their homework assignment in class. However, she never informs them of the assignment until the lab area meets her standards for cleanliness and order.

Each student in Mr. Ditty's art class has her or his own container for keeping supplies. Mr. Ditty directs his students to clean their materials and put them away for the next day. Juan and Candy leave some of their brushes, paints, cloth, and paper. Mr. Ditty notices this before they leave, but says nothing. He cleans up after them, placing their equipment in the general art supply closet. The next day, Juan complains, "Where's my thin brush? And I'm out of paper; I had plenty yesterday!" Candy: "I can't find my green paint." Mr. Ditty: "Oh, that must have been your stuff I cleaned up yesterday. I'm sorry, but I mixed them up with the general supplies. You need to purchase more."

## VANDALIZING

Vandalism, like general discourtesy and an unkempt classroom, can be extremely disruptive to a learning environment. School-level vandalism (e.g., breaking windows or arson) should be handled by school-level, system-level, and law-enforcement authorities. It is wise for you, as a teacher, to avoid playing the role of detective with your own students. Antagonism between teacher and students is a likely consequence. Repeat vandalism may be encouraged by students' desire to continue the "cops and robbers" game that a teacher has initiated. Besides reporting vandalism to authorities and cooperating with their investigations, you may try to prevent acts of vandalism from being positively reinforced.

Ms. Romano enters her equipment room to prepare for the day's physical education classes when she discovers the soccer balls she plans to use deflated and flattened. The nets of the six portable soccer goals are cut and unusable. In horror she thinks, "Who would have done this? This screws up my whole day! The girls will be on the field in 6 minutes and we are scheduled to play soccer first period. If I ever catch the little—!" Ms. Romano composes herself and begins thinking, "Barbara, Evelyn, Tamaria, and some of the others have been complaining about having to play soccer during first period. They said it was too hot and it made their hair a mess for the whole day. I wonder if it's one of them. Well, I don't know that. I could hardly find out if I tried. But I do know that a lot of the girls would love to use this as an excuse to avoid going out and working up a sweat."

Ms. Romano walks over to the locker room where her students are changing. She announces, "Let's go, ladies! We meet on the soccer field at exactly 9:20." "Do we have to? It'll be too hot today, Ms. Romano!" complains one student. Ms. Romano makes no response and heads for the field. Outside, she tells the class, "We will not be able to play soccer today because the equipment has been damaged." Barbara: "Then why are we dressed out on the soccer field?" Ms. Romano: "Because it is critical that we do an aerobic type activity today and the soccer field is as good a place as any to get your hearts and lungs working. Just because we can't play soccer, doesn't mean we can't get the same benefits that a vigorous soccer game affords us." Some students begin to moan and complain to one another. Ms. Romano puts them through an especially fatiguing routine of calisthenics. After the session, the students are dragging themselves and perspiring with tousled hair as they enter the showers. Ms. Romano reports the vandalism to her immediate supervisor who makes arrangements to repair the damages and prepares a report for the principal.

## PERPETRATING VIOLENCE AGAINST STUDENTS

Generally speaking, if a student strikes a teacher or other adult school personnel, that student is in serious trouble with school authorities and possibly with law enforcement authorities. Expulsion or suspension from the school is a likely consequence. Although society, including parents and school personnel, tends to view an unarmed assault of one student on another as not terribly serious, students have as much right as do their teachers to feel safe and secure from violence while under the supervision of school personnel.

Ms. Duke found it odd that Frank, Maunsell, Mickey, and a few other of her fifth grade boys chose to spend their time before school and during their recess break in the classroom with her. "Why don't you men go out and get some fresh air while you still have the chance?" she asks. They shrug sheepishly and remain with her. She finds Mickey's absentee pattern curious. He seems perfectly healthy on Monday, Wednesday, and Friday of each week, while being excused for "illness" on Tuesday and Thursday. Other puzzling occurrences involving the boys (e.g., their homework papers are wet and crumpled all on the same day with no apparent explanation) cause Ms. Duke to wonder what is going on. These boys choose to spend virtually all their time at school in her company, yet Ms. Duke has the distinct impression that they are uncomfortable around her and prefer being elsewhere. The students offer no explanation.

Ms. Duke begins making observations. Instead of staying in her room just before school begins in the mornings, she walks the grounds where most of her students are at that time. She notices that Bobby, Ronald, Stan, and Winslow nearly always hang around together and that her "followers," Frank, Maunsell, and Mickey, appear particularly uneasy as Bobby and his companions greet her with, "Good morning, Mrs. Duke!" Soon, Ms. Duke surmises that Ronald, Stan, and Winslow are terrorizing fellow students to the point that Frank's, Mickey's, and Maunsell's opportunities to learn are being hindered. The following thoughts run through Ms. Duke's mind: "I can't stand bullying! What do those creeps think they get out of terrorizing others? They must really be miserable with themselves to act so miserably toward their classmates! I can't conduct effective learning activities in an environment filled with fear. What should I do? If I confront that gang with what I suspect, they'll think Maunsell and the rest of the victims tattled on them and they'll just make life more miserable for them. We need more adults to supervise the school grounds, the bus stop, the buses, the halls! Good grief! Do we need a police state? I'll try one tactic and if it doesn't work, I'll find a way to sit on those bullies so they become the ones imprisoned by having to hang around me all day. But first I'll pair Maunsell and Bobby together in a joint project where they have to meet me before school. That'll begin breaking up the gang and maybe the two will start cooperating. If that seems to show some progress, I'll work some of the other bullies into cooperating roles with the victims. Oh! Listen to me! I'm labeling them. I'd better watch my language and not even think such characterizations as 'bullies' and 'victims.' . . . I don't know if this plan will work at all. Why should I force them together? Maybe I should, instead, call a class meeting and discuss the problem openly with the group and have them initiate a proposal. . . . Then they'd probably come up with a vigilante plan with Bobby and his gang as the main 'hit squad.' That's an idea! Put them in charge of making the school grounds safe. . . . Forget it. I'll stick with the plan of splitting the gang and motivating some cooperation between the antagonists. . . . Okay, I need to work out the details. . . .

Ms. Duke's plan has a chance of working because she focused on her task of making the learning environment conducive to on-task behavior. She was not overly concerned with punishing those that perpetrated the terror or teaching them some lifelong moral lesson. She concentrated on stopping the disruptive behaviors and preventing recurrences. She controlled her anger. She abhorred Bobby's, Ronald's, Stan's, and Winslow's antisocial behaviors and determined not to tolerate such activities. But she also recognized that they need a more constructive way of dealing with their own insecurities, a way that doesn't step on the rights of others. This realization made it possible for her to calmly think through a plan for dealing with the situation.

Here are two more examples of teachers dealing with student violence:

Ms. Saunders, a librarian at Bishop Vincent High School, is supervising activities in the library when Stanley, an eleventh grade student, bursts into the room and confronts Ronny, another student who is seated at a table. Stanley: "You little piece of shit! You owe me!" Ronny pulls a small knife from his pants, gets up, and faces Stanley. Displaying the knife, he says, "Get away from me, or I'll cut your goddamn throat out!" Stanley: "You wouldn't. . . ." Ms. Saunders has made her way to the two and yells, "Enough!" Convinced the two see her, she steps between them with her back to Stanley and facing Ronny. She attempts to present a stern, but nonthreatening posture to Ronny. She does not want to raise either student's level of anxiety. "Stanley," she firmly says, "I want you to turn around and walk out of the door right now. You can wait for us in the hall." Some of the other students in the library are gathering around as others back away from the scene. Stanley: "I don't have to. . . ." Ms. Saunders (still with her back to Stanley): "Be cool, Stanley. You're right. You don't have to, but be cool and do it anyway." Ronny: "Yeah, why don't. . . ." Ms. Saunders (interrupting): "Ronny, shut up! And the rest of you in here get back to what you were doing. This whole incident is over. Hurry up! You've got work to do." Surprised, Stanley leaves and other students hesitatingly move back to their places and in wonderment leave Ronny and Ms. Saunders standing face-to-face with the knife between them. Calmly and softly, Ms. Saunders tells Ronny, "It's okay, now there's no longer a need for that knife to be out. So put it back in your pocket. I'll have to report this incident to Mr. Civello. I'm sure he'll be calling you to his office. If I were you, I'd get rid of that knife before he calls you. You can dispose of it yourself after you're through working here or, if you like, I'll get rid of it for you now. If you give it to me, no one will ever see it again."

Ronny lowers the knife and puts it back in his pants. Ms. Saunders walks back to her desk where she calls Mr. Civello's office to report the situation. Ronny returns to where he was seated before, but then immediately gets up, goes over to Ms. Saunders, and asks, "If you get rid of this for me, will it go easier on me?" Ms. Saunders: "It might." Ronny: "Here." He hands her the knife. With Ronny still standing there, Ms. Saunders completes her report over the phone. The dean of students, Mr. Civello, handles the matter, taking disciplinary action against both students.

Ms. Silverstein's fourth graders are working individually at their places on an assignment as she helps Zachary at his desk. Suddenly she hears Beth scream, "Stop it!" She turns to see Roxanna on the floor crying, "Ow!, Oh, ow!" Roxanna has fresh scratch marks extending from one cheek down to the side of her neck. Beth is standing over her. "She clawed me!" screams Roxanna as she continues to cry. Ms. Silverstein is uncertain as to what happened, but rather than investigate the cause, she decides to deal with Roxanna's immediate need. She bends over Roxanna, cradles her head with her arm, and says, "You are hurt. I'm sorry."

Ms. Silverstein softly strokes Roxanna's hair and says, "I can see why you're crying." Roxanna: "She clawed me! I hate. . . ." Ms. Silverstein (interrupting): "Don't talk now, we have to clean those scratches." Beth: "Well, she poked me firs—" Ms. Silverstein (interrupting and not even looking at Beth): "Enough talk. I don't want to hear anything until we've taken care of Roxanna's scratches. Zachary, please go get two tissues from my desk. Wet one at the sink and leave one dry and bring them both to me. Nadine, bring me the first-aid kit, please. The rest of you get back to work."

As Ms. Silverstein helps Roxanna to her feet and walks her to the back of the room, she thinks to herself, "I've bought some time to figure out how to handle this and prevent it from happening again. This'll also give those two time to cool off. I can deal with them more effectively when they're over their anger." She thanks Nadine and Zachary for their help and administers to Roxanna's scratches. Ms. Silverstein thinks: "I'll talk to both of them together and get them to examine their own actions. But when? This has to be handled before they leave school today. It's going to be inconvenient, but I must meet them after school. It'll be hard on me today, but a lot easier in the long run. If this becomes a pattern with Beth, I'll have hell to pay for the rest of the year. The inconvenience today will be a good investment for the future."

Nine minutes after everyone is back on-task, Ms. Silverstein beckons Beth and Roxanna to her desk. Ms. Silverstein: "Roxanna, what are you planning to do after the final bell today?" Roxanna: "I have a Brownie meeting. Mrs. Sheirer is picking us up." Ms. Silverstein: "Where is the meeting?" Roxanna: "At Ellie's house." Ms. Silverstein: "When will it be over?" Roxanna: "I don't know." Ms. Silverstein: "Is Ellie's house far from here?" Roxanna: "It's just over the other side of the hill." Ms. Silverstein: "Could you show me how to get there?" Roxanna: "Yes." Ms. Silverstein: "Thank you. Beth, what do you do after school today?" Beth: "I catch bus 57." Ms. Silverstein: "Do you go straight home from the bus?" Beth: "Yes." Ms. Silverstein: "Who will be there when you arrive?" Beth: "My dad." Ms. Silverstein: "Thank you." Beth: "Ms. Silverstein, Roxanna poked . . ." Ms. Silverstein (interrupting): "Not now. We'll talk about it after school. You will miss your bus today, Beth. So I will call your dad and make arrangements for you to get home. Roxanna, I'll meet Ms. Sheirer and explain to her that you'll be late for Brownies. Both of you are to stay right here after the last bell so we can talk about how to prevent today's incident from ever happening again. I'll make arrangements for you to get to where you need to be after our talk. Now, go back to your places and get on with your work."

After the last bell, Roxanna and Beth wait alone in the classroom as Ms. Silverstein informs Ms. Sheirer that Roxanna will be late and that she'll drive her to Ellie's house herself. Ms. Silverstein then phones Beth's father.

Arriving back in the classroom, Ms. Silverstein says, "Beth, your father will pick you up in 30 minutes. We have until then to talk about what happened today." Roxanna: "I didn't do nothin' to her!" Beth (interrupting): "I guess jabbin' me through my ribs is nothing!" Roxanna: "I was just playing. You didn't have to try to kill me with your claws!" Beth (holding up her hands in a claw-like manner): "You ain't seen nothin' yet!" Ms. Silverstein: "Would you like to know what I think, Beth?" Beth (returning to a normal, nonthreatening posture): "What?" Ms. Silverstein: "Please answer me with a more pleasant tone." Beth: "Yes, ma'am." Ms. Silverstein: "Roxanna, are you ready to hear what I think?" Roxanna: "Yes, ma'am." Ms. Silverstein: "I think that Roxanna poked Beth as she passed her desk. And Roxanna did it just to be friendly, sort of like saying, 'Hello, Beth. Look at me. I'm here.' Is that right, Roxanna?" Roxanna: "Yes." Beth: "But. . . ." Ms. Silverstein (interrupting): "Shh! But Roxanna poked Beth too hard and it disturbed her while she was working. Is that right, Beth?" Beth: "Yes, ma'am." Ms. Silverstein: "And Beth got so annoyed that without thinking, she struck out at Roxanna and hurt her. If Beth had thought first, she would never have scratched Roxanna. . . . Now, I don't care who *was* right and who *was* wrong. I only care that none of my students hurts one another again. If Beth hadn't lost control of her temper, but just ignored Roxanna's poke, everything would be okay now. And if Roxanna hadn't bothered Beth while she was working, this wouldn't have happened. Am I correct?" Beth and Roxanna both nod in agreement. Ms. Silverstein: "Beth, will this ever happen again?" Beth: "Not if she doesn't. . . ." Ms. Silverstein (interrupting): "Beth, either one of you is capable of keeping this from happening again. No matter what anyone else does, are you going to let this happen again?" Beth: "No, *I* won't." Roxanna: "Me neither." Ms. Silverstein: "Wonderful! We'll wait here until it's time for Beth's Dad to be out front and then I'll take Roxanna to her Brownie meeting."

## PERPETRATING VIOLENCE AGAINST TEACHERS

### Causes

A student may choose to physically abuse a teacher for one of the following four reasons:

1. *The student feels backed into a corner and that striking out at the teacher is the only way to maintain "face" with peers.* Here is an example:

Ms. Mildred is lecturing to one of her eighth grade classes when she becomes annoyed by the off-task conversation that Jim and Jan are carrying on from their places in the room. Ms. Mildred stops her lecture and scolds, "Can't you two be quiet? You're forever chattering. Jim, if you'd listen in class instead of mooning over Jan all the time, you wouldn't be flunking!" Jim is overwhelmed with embarrassment. He, in fact, is very fond of Jan and feels that Ms. Mildred has challenged his status with Jan and his other peers. He tries to save face by verbally striking out. "I never mooned anybody!" Jim curtly barks at Ms. Mildred. Ms. Mildred gets embarrassed herself and yells, "What? That's not what I meant! You come right here, young man, and apologize to me!" Jim slowly shuffles his way up to Ms. Mildred with a grin on his face, shifting his eyes to see who is watching him. Ms. Mildred: "Wipe that stupid grin off your face! There's nothing funny about your impudence!" Jim looks down, trying not to laugh, but he is overcome by his concern for what his classmates are thinking and covers his fear and anger with laughter. "You wipe that smile off and apologize," says Ms. Mildred standing face-to-face with Jim. Jim wipes his mouth with his hand and says, "There, I wiped it off." But he bursts out laughing as he hears others in the room giggling. Furious that Jim is making her look bad in front of the class, Ms. Mildred tries to gain the upper hand with a show of authority. Ms. Mildred: "You know I can make you sorry you ever set foot in this school! You either say 'I'm sorry' to me right now or you'll find out just how tough I can be!" Jim believes that this confrontation has gone too far for him to back down without losing the respect of his classmates. Panicking and seeing no other way out of the situation, he suddenly appears very serious. Gritting his teeth, he says in a low voice, "Go play with yourself, you old bitch!" Jim shoves Ms. Mildred using both hands on her shoulders. She tumbles over backwards as he runs out of the room.

Within a week, Jim is expelled from the school and enrolled in an alternative school for students who have committed "first class" offenses according to school board policy.

2. *The teacher is in a position of being an accessible target for the student at a moment when the student is reacting angrily.* Three examples follow:

Mr. Diel is returning to his classroom where several tenth graders are located waiting for the beginning of the next period. Suddenly, he observes Kraemer leap at Danny and yell, "What did you call me? . . . Hey boy, don't ever say that to me again! Understand?" Danny is about to respond when Mr. Diel arrives from behind and touches Kraemer on the right shoulder and says, "Easy Kraemer. . . ." Kraemer wheels around and swings his right arm so that his elbow catches Mr. Diel in the mouth. A tooth is broken and blood spurts from Mr. Diel's lip.

Finis is a twelve-year-old student participating in an intramural basketball game refereed by Mr. Leblanc, a physical education teacher. The game is closely contested when Mr. Leblanc calls a personal foul on Finis. "You, number three–two," Mr. Leblanc yells coming face-to-face with

Finis in the tradition of basketball officials. Finis believes that he is not guilty of the foul; he thinks he was fouled instead. "Get your hand up, thirty-two!" Mr. Leblanc yells in Finis' face. Finis: "I didn't do. . . ." Mr. Leblanc (interrupting): "Technical foul!" Finis, feeling frustrated and helpless, lashes out at the nearest accessible target by striking Mr. Leblanc on the nose with his fist.

Ms. Blouin teaches a class of 11 students who are classified as emotionally handicapped. Two of her students, Suzanne and Paul, habitually express their feelings by physically striking out at Ms. Blouin. Ms. Blouin has been kicked, bitten, pushed, scratched, and slapped by these two students. To help her deal with the situation, avoid being victimized by them, and prepare for similar situations in the future, Ms. Blouin completes a course in self-defense techniques especially designed for teachers. Ms. Blouin is now able to protect herself from such abuse without a high risk of injury to Suzanne, Paul, or any other student who might attack her or attack another student. The self-defense techniques she uses immobilize students without harming them.

3. *The student attempts to either experience control over authorities, win favor with peers, seek revenge on an authority, or relieve boredom by carrying out a prank that endangers the well-being of a teacher.* Here is an example:

Ms. Heidingsfelder, a compensatory education teacher at Blackhawk High School, is driving home after work when she is startled by the sound of an explosion from under her car. A tire blows out, she loses control of the vehicle, crosses a lane with oncoming traffic, and comes to a stop in a ditch on the side of the road. Fortunately, she is uninjured and the car suffers only the damaged tire which she replaces.

Ms. Heidingsfelder does not suspect that her "accident" is anything more than that until the following school day. Several students in her third period class question her: "Ms. H, are you okay?" "Did you drive your bug to school today?" "Did anything happen to you after school yesterday?" Thinking quickly, she concludes that she had been the victim of a booby trap. Believing she can hardly find the responsible criminals among the students, she decides not to give them the satisfaction of knowing that the prank worked. She replies, "I'm fine; it's awfully nice of you to ask. Why do you ask if anything out of the ordinary happened after school yesterday?"

4. *The student feels obliged to defend herself or himself against a perceived danger that the teacher poses.* Here's an example:

Mr. Moe, an assistant principal at Greenfield Creek Junior High, is six-feet-five and weighs nearly 300 pounds. He finds that his reputation as a strict disciplinarian who'll "knock your head off rather than look at you" helps him with his primary responsibility of maintaining order in the school. One day, Mr. Moe surprises Rudolph, a ninth grader, smoking marijuana in the boys' restroom. Panicked at the sight of the towering figure of the man with the infamous reputation, Rudolph spots a large wrench, inadvertently left on the floor by a custodian. He grabs it and throws it at Mr. Moe's head.

## Strategies

You can reduce your chances of being a victim of student violence by adhering to the following principles:

1. You are not intimidated by the fear or threat of violence.
2. You do not pose a threat to students. This includes not perpetrating violence on them (e.g., by using corporal punishment or by roughly handling them) nor competing with them for esteem from others (especially their peers). You never try to show up a student.
3. You use physical force with students *only* in drastic situations in which it is the only reasonable means for restraining them from harming themselves or another. Physical force is never used to punish or hurt, only to restrain in certain unusual situations.
4. You are sensitive to potentially volatile situations and do not make yourself available as a target when students are likely to unthinkingly react aggressively.
5. You avoid making ultimatums in which the consequence of students' noncompliance is the most severe sanction you can levy. (If you commit yourself to administering the severest penalty available to you, then students have nothing left to lose by displaying even less desirable behaviors than those that initially led to the unpleasant situation.)
6. You simply should never tolerate violent behavior in your presence. You have every right to use the full power of the legal system to prevent violence or the threat of violence from hindering you from effectively meeting your professional responsibilities.

## Self-Assessment for Chapter 10

I. Observe the students in someone else's class. Identify three incidents of disruptive student behaviors. For each, write two paragraphs *describing* the dirsuptive behavior and what the teacher did to deal with it. Make sure that you only describe what happened. For this exercise, do not write about your value judgments regarding the teacher's method of handling the disruption.

**II.** For each of the following examples presented in this chapter, write one or two paragraphs giving your view of the advantages and disadvantages of the way the teacher handled the disruptive behavior; suggest how the approach could have been improved: (A) Ms. Bravo, page 266; (B) Ms. Allen, page 267; (C) Mr. Haimowitz, page 267; (D) Ms. Helmick, page 268; (E) Ms. Brittain, page 269; (F) Mr. Peck, page 270; (G) Mr. Holt, page 270; (H) Mr. Smith, page 272; (I) Ms. Belcher, page 273; (J) Mr. Ditty, page 275; (K) Mr. Duke, page 276; (L) Ms. Saunders, page 277; (M) Ms. Silverstein, page 278; (N) Ms. Mildred, page 280; (O) Ms. Heidingsfelder, page 282.

*Reviewing Your Self-Assessment* ———————————————————

Exchange copies of what you wrote in response to parts I and II with others for copies of their responses. After reading one another's papers, discuss the differences and similarities among your answers.

## Supplemental Readings

Greenwood, G. E., Good, T. L., & Siegel, B. L. (1971). *Problem situations in teaching* (pp. 44–51, 117–122). New York: Harper & Row.

Karlin, M. S., & Berger, R. (1972). *Discipline and the disruptive child: A practical guide for elementary teachers* (pp. 102–130). West Nyack, NY: Parker.

Kerr, M. M., & Nelson, C. M. (1983). *Strategies for managing behavior problems in the classroom* (pp. 201–249). Columbus, OH: Merrill.

Mendler, A. N., & Curwin, R. L. (1983). *Taking charge in the classroom: A practical guide to effective discipline* (pp. 141–182). Reston, VA: Reston Publishing.

Swick, K. J. (1985). *Disruptive student behavior in the classroom* (2nd ed.). Washington, DC: National Education Association.

Wilde, J. & Sommers, P. (1978). Teaching disruptive adolescents: A game worth winning. *Phi Delta Kappan, 59,* 342–343.

# part four

# Why Do Proven Methods Sometimes Fail?

# How Do You Make Proven Methods Work for You?

# Incorporating New Ideas Into Your Teaching Style

Chapter 11 is intended to remind you of the following as you select ideas and methods gained from this book and choose to apply them to your own teaching situation:

1. Some methods for gaining students' cooperation may not work as effectively as you'd like until you've had some experience using them and thereby refined your skills with those methods. For example:

    A. One section of Chapter 4 suggests that you will establish more productive communication patterns with your students by using descriptive instead of judgmental language. However, most people are not in the habit of considering their words carefully enough to consistently express themselves descriptively. Consequently, you may find that it takes consistent effort practicing descriptive language with your students before descriptive phrases flow from your tongue, and you begin to reap the benefits from this technique.

    B. A section of Chapter 6 urges the use of problem-solving learning activities (e.g., Ms. Olson's math lesson beginning on page 135 and Ms. Piscatelli's history lesson beginning on page 136) to intrinsically motivate students to achieve learning objectives. However, until a teacher has observed students for a while and is thoroughly familiar with the subject matter of a particular learning unit, it may be extremely difficult for that teacher to identify interesting problems on which to focus. Familiarity with both students and subject matter should increase with teaching experience. If you are not used to conducting problem-solving learning activities, but are convinced of the advantages of doing so, then you are advised to begin on a small scale only with learning units that readily lend themselves to that approach. In time you will build both your repertoire of learning units that utilize the problem-solving approach and your abilities to design such units.

C. Throughout this text, and especially in Chapter 7, you have been encouraged to respond to your students' off-task behaviors via the Teaching Process Model, just as you should for the teaching of academic learning units. In the episode beginning on page 186, Ms. Reid effectively handled a rather nasty situation because she consciously organized her thoughts around the Teaching Process Model. You may have to face a number of discipline problems before you have utilized the Teaching Process Model enough times to make it consistently and efficiently work in your favor.

D. As indicated by a section of Chapter 8, the principle of extinction can be a powerful weapon in your arsenal against off-task behavior patterns. However, unless you can identify the positive reinforcers that lead a student to be habitually off-task, then you can hardly take advantage of extinction. As an observant, thinking teacher you will, with experience, develop your abilities to identify what positively reinforces your students' habits.

2. Because of differences between you and other teachers and between your circumstances and theirs, what works for other teachers may not work for you. However, your knowledge of what other teachers do to teach their students to be on-task is a major source of ideas for originating your own systematic approach. For example:

A. Ms. Phegley's activities that are described in the scenario beginning on page 59 exemplify the sort of things teachers can do during the first week of a school term to establish a learning environment that encourages students to cooperate. There are probably legitimate reasons why you should not try to copy just what Ms. Phegley did when you begin your next new term as a teacher. Unlike Ms. Phegley, you may not feel comfortable putting your hands on your head as a cue for your students to listen to your directions and do nothing else. Maybe your students are too old for that sort of thing. But surely, you can learn from Ms. Phegley's methods by thinking of ways that you can, nonverbally, but comfortably, establish cues for your students to follow your directions during the first week of a school term.

**B.** Mr. Cooper uses a democratic process in determining a classroom procedure in the example beginning on page 125. Perhaps a democratic process is too inefficient for you to use in establishing your own procedures or rules of conduct. However, your knowledge of what Mr. Cooper did can help you clearly distinguish for your students those times when they are to focus on management matters from those when the class is concerned with achieving some academic learning objective from the curriculum.

**C.** In the example beginning on page 235, Mr. Legget took some rather extraordinary steps to deal with the problem of student mind-wandering and daydreaming in his class. Most teachers would not choose to try Mr. Legget's elaborate scheme. However, Mr. Legget's method illustrates some important ideas that can be utilized to improve other more conventional approaches.

It is inadvisable for you to try to revolutionize your teaching style all at once; ideas and methods new to you should be tried cautiously and conservatively. But they should be tried if they have a documented record of success. Those suggested by this book do have such a success record for gaining students' cooperation. For some that you try you can expect immediate success; others must be practiced for a while before the benefits can be enjoyed. Please reread the first two paragraphs of the section near the beginning of Chapter 1 entitled "The Difference Between a Miserable and a Pleasant Teaching Experience."

May you have a satisfying teaching career.

# References

Abernathy, S., Manera, E., & Wright, R. (1985). What stresses student teachers most? *The Clearing House, 58,* 361–362.

Anderson, L. W. (1976). An empirical investigation of individual differences in time to learn. *Journal of Educational Psychology, 68,* 226–233.

Arnold, D., Atwood, R., & Rogers, V. (1974). Question and response levels and lapse time intervals. *Journal of Experimental Education, 43,* 11–15.

Ashlock, R. B. (1976). *Error patterns in computation: A semi-programmed approach* (2nd ed.). Columbus, OH: Merrill.

Azrin, N. H., Hake, D. G., Holz, W. C., & Hutchinson, R. R. (1965). Motivational aspects of escape from punishment. *Journal of Experimental Analysis of Behavior, 8,* 31–44.

Azrin, N. H., Hake, D. G., & Hutchinson, R. R. (1965). Elicitation of aggression by a physical blow. *Journal of Experimental Analysis of Behavior, 8,* 55–57.

Azrin, H. N., Hutchinson, R. R., & Sallery, R. D. (1964). Pain-aggression toward inanimate objects. *Journal of Experimental Analysis of Behavior, 7,* 223–228.

Bandura, A. (1965). Behavior modification through modeling procedures. In L. Krasner & L. P. Ullman (Eds.), *Research in behavior modification* (pp. 310–340). New York: Holt, Rinehart and Winston.

Bell, L. C., & Stefanich, G. P. (1984). Building effective discipline using the cascade model. *The Clearing House, 58,* 134–137.

Berg, F. (1986). *Listening for the hard of hearing students.* San Diego, CA: College Hill Press.

Bongiovanni, A. F. (1979). An analysis of research on punishment and its relation to the use of corporal punishment in the schools. In I. A. Hyman & J. Wise (Eds.), *Corporal punishment in American education* (pp. 351–372). Philadelphia: Temple University Press.

Borg, W. R. (1980). Time and school learning. In C. Denham & A. Lieberman (Eds.), *Time to Learn.* Washington, DC: National Institute of Education.

Bowman, R. (1983). Effective classroom management: A primer for practicing professionals. *The Clearing House, 57,* 116–118.

Boynton, P., Di Geronimo, J., & Gustafson, G. (1985). A basic survival guide for new teachers. *The Clearing House, 59,* 101–103.

Brophy, J. E., & Putnam, J. G. (1979). Classroom management in the elementary school. In D. L. Duke (Ed.), *Classroom management: The seventy-eighth yearbook of the National Society for the study of education* (pp. 182–216). Chicago: The University of Chicago Press.

Brown, D. (1971). *Changing student behavior: A new approach to discipline.* Dubuque, IA: Brown.

Cain, H. D. (1980). *Flint's emergency treatment and management* (6th ed.). Philadelphia: Saunders.

Cangelosi, J. S. (1980). *Project G.R.E.A.T. needs assessment report.* Tallahassee, FL: Florida Department of Education.

Cangelosi, J. S. (1982). *Measurement and evaluation: An inductive approach for teachers.* Dubuque, IA: Brown.

Cangelosi, J. S. (1986). *Cooperation in the classroom: Students and teachers together.* Washington, DC: National Education Association.

Canter, L. (1978). Be an assertive teacher. *Instructor, 88,* 60.

Canter, L., & Canter, M. (1976). *Assertive discipline: A take-charge approach for today's educator.* Seal Beach, CA: Canter and Associates.

Carducci, D. J., & Carducci, J. B. (1984). *The caring classroom.* Palo Alto, CA: Bull Publishing.

Charles, C. M. (1983). *Elementary classroom management.* White Plains, NY: Longman.

Charles, C. M. (1985). *Building classroom discipline: From models to practice* (2nd ed.). White Plains, NY: Longman.

Clark, L. H., & Starr, I. S. (1981). *Secondary and middle school teaching methods* (4th ed.). New York: Macmillan.

Corno, L., & Snow, R. E. (1986). Adapting teaching to individual differences among learners. In M. C. Wittrock (Ed.), *Handbook of research on teaching* (3rd ed.). (pp. 605–629). New York: Macmillan.

Cunningham, A. R. (1983). The deportment chart: A student management tool that could help a classroom teacher. *The Clearing House, 56,* 421–422.

Delgado, J. M. R. (1963). Cerebral heterostimulation in a monkey colony. *Science, 141,* 161–163.

Denham, C., & Lieberman, A. (Eds.). (1980). *Time to learn.* Washington, DC: U.S. Department of Education and the National Institute of Education.

Dewey, J. (1933). *How we think* (rev. ed.). Boston: Heath.

Doyle, W. (1986). Classroom organization and management. In M. C. Wittrock (Ed.), *Handbook of research on teaching* (3rd ed.) (pp. 392–431). New York: Macmillan.

Dreikurs, R. (1968). *Psychology in the classroom* (2nd ed.). New York: Harper & Row.

Dreikurs, R., Grunwald, B., & Pepper, F. (1982). *Maintaining sanity in the classroom* (2nd ed.). New York: Harper & Row.

Duke, D. L., & Jones, V. F. (1984). Two decades of discipline—Assessing the development of an educational specialization. *Journal of Research and Development in Education, 17*, 25–35.

Dunlap, K. (1919). Are there instincts? *Journal of Abnormal Psychology, 14*, 307–311.

Emmer, E. T., Evertson, C. M., & Anderson, L. M. (1980). Effective classroom management at the beginning of the school year. *Elementary School Journal, 80*, 219–231.

Emmer, E. T., Evertson, C. M., Sanford, J. P., Clements, B. S., & Worsham, M. E. (1984). *Classroom Management for Secondary Teachers.* Englewood Cliffs, NJ: Prentice-Hall.

Evertson, C. M., & Emmer, E. T. (1982). Effective management at the beginning of the school year for junior high classes. *Journal of Educational Psychology, 82*, 329–350.

Evertson, C. M., Emmer, E. T., Clements, B. S., Sanford, J. P., & Worsham, M. E. (1984). *Classroom Management for Elementary Teachers.* Englewood Cliffs, NJ: Prentice-Hall.

Fisher, C. W., Berliner, D. C., Filby, N. N., Marliave, R., Cahen, L. S., & Dishaw, M. M. (1980). Teaching behaviors, academic learning time, and student achievement: An overview. In C. Denham & A. Lieberman (Eds.), *Time to learn* (pp. 7–32). Washington, DC: National Institute of Education.

Gallup, A. M. (1986). The 18th Annual Gallup Poll of the public's attitudes toward the public schools. *Phi Delta Kappan, 68*, 43–59.

Ginott, H. G. (1965). *Parent and child.* New York: Avon Books.

Ginott, H. G. (1972). *Teacher and child.* New York: Avon Books.

Glasser, W. (1965). *Schools without failure.* New York: Harper & Row.

Glasser, W. (1977). Ten steps to good discipline. *Today's Education, 66*, 60–63.

Glasser, W. (1978). Disorders in our schools: Causes and remedies. *Phi Delta Kappan, 59*, 331–333.

Glasser, W. (1986). *Control theory in the classroom.* New York: Harper & Row.

Glickman, C., & Wolfgang, C. (1979). Dealing with student misbehavior: An eclectic review. *Journal of Teacher Education, 30*, 7–13.

Gold, S. R., & Cundiff, G. (1980). Decreasing the frequency of daydreaming. *Journal of Clinical Psychology, 36*, 116–121.

Goodlad, J. I. (1984). *A place called school: Prospects for the future.* New York: McGraw-Hill.

Gordon, T. (1974). *T.E.T.: Teacher effectiveness training.* New York: Peter H. Wyden.

Greenwood, G. E., Good, T. L., & Siegel, B. L. (1971). *Problem situations in teaching.* New York: Harper & Row.

Harris, T. A. (1969). *I'm OK–you're OK: A practical guide to transactional analysis.* New York: Harper & Row.

Homme, L. (1973). *How to use contingency contracting in the classroom.* Champaign, IL: Research Press.

Hyman, I. A. (1978). A social science review of evidence cited in litigation on corporal punishment in the schools. *Journal of Child Psychology, 30,* 195–199.

Hyman, I. A., & Wise, J. H. (Eds.). (1979). *Corporal punishment in American education.* Philadelphia: Temple University Press.

Johnson, D. R. (1982). *Every minute counts: Making your math class work.* Palo Alto, CA: Seymour.

Johnson, D. R. (1986). *Making minutes count even more: A sequel to every minute counts.* Palo Alto, CA: Seymour.

Jones, F. (1979). The gentle art of classroom discipline. *National Elementary Principal, 58,* 26–32.

Jones, V. F., & Jones, L. S. (1986). *Comprehensive classroom management: Creating positive learning environments* (2nd ed.). Boston: Allyn & Bacon.

Joyce, B., & Weil, M. (1980). *Models of teaching* (2nd ed.). Englewood Cliffs, NJ: Prentice-Hall.

Karlin, M. S., & Berger, R. (1972). *Discipline and the disruptive child: A practical guide for elementary teachers.* West Nyack, NY: Parker.

Kerr, M. M., & Nelson, C. M. (1983). *Strategies for managing behavior problems in the classroom.* Columbus, OH: Merrill.

Klinger, E. (1978). Modes of normal conscious flow. In K. S. Pope & J. L. Singer (Eds.), *The stream of consciousness.* New York: Plenum.

Kohut, S., & Range, D. G. (1979). *Classroom discipline: Case studies and viewpoints.* Washington, DC: National Education Association.

Kounin, J. (1977). *Discipline and group management in classrooms.* New York: Holt, Rinehart and Winston.

Kounin, J., & Sherman, L. (1979). School environments as behavior settings. *Theory Into Practice, 18,* 145–151.

Krumboltz, J. D., & Krumboltz, H. B. (1972). *Changing children's behavior.* Englewood Cliffs, NJ: Prentice-Hall.

Lasley, T. J. (1985). Fostering nonaggression in the classroom: An anthropological perspective. *Theory Into Practice, 24,* 247–255.

Latham, G. I. (1984). *Time-on-task and other variables affecting the quality of education of handicapped students.* Logan: Utah State University.

Lessinger, L. (1970). *Every kid a winner: Accountability in education.* New York: Simon & Schuster.

Loo, C. M. (1977). *The differential effects of spatial density on low and high scorers on behavior problem indices.* A paper presented at the annual meeting of the Western Psychological Association, Seattle, WA.

Lyerly, K. Z. (1982). *Daydreaming and its implications to reading instruction among gifted children.* Unpublished master's thesis, the University of North Florida, Jacksonville.

Maifair, L. L. (1986, October). Helping kids resist drugs. *Instructor, XCVI,* No. 3, 72–74.

Martin, G., & Pear, J (1983). *Behavior modification: What it is and how to do it* (2nd ed.). Englewood Cliffs, NJ: Prentice-Hall.

Maslow, A. (1962). *Toward a psychology of being.* New York: Van Nostrand.

McDaniel, T. R. (1986). A primer on classroom discipline: Principles old and new. *Phi Delta Kappan, 68,* 63–67.

McGarity, J. R., & Butts, D. P. (1984). The relationship among teacher classroom management behavior, student engagement, and student achievement of middle and high school science students of varying aptitude. *Journal of Research in Science Teaching, 21,* 55–61.

McLemore, W. P. (1981). The ABC's of classroom discipline. *The Clearing House, 52,* 205–206.

Mendler, A. N., & Curwin, R. L. (1983). *Taking charge in the classroom: A practical guide to effective discipline.* Reston, VA: Reston Publishing.

Morales, C. A. (1978). Discipline: Applicable techniques for student teachers. *Education, 101,* 122–124.

National Commission on Excellence in Education. (1983). *A nation at risk: The imperative of educational reform.* Washington, DC: U.S. Government Printing Office.

National Education Association. (1972). *Report of the task force on corporal punishment.* Washington, DC: National Education Association.

O'Brien, R., & Cohen, S. (Eds.). (1984). *The encyclopedia of drug abuse.* New York: Facts on File.

Paley, V. G. (1986). On listening to what children say. *Harvard Educational Review, 56,* 122–131.

Parker, W. C., & Gehrke, N. J. (1986). Learning activities and teacher decisionmaking: Some grounded hypotheses. *American Educational Research Journal, 23,* 227–442.

Petreshene, S. (1986, September). Management made easy. *Instructor, XCVI,* No. 2, 70–74.

Petreshene, S. (1986, October). What can you do in 10 minutes? Transition activities that make kids think! *Instructor, XCVI,* No. 3, 68–70.

Pratt, D. (1980). *Curriculum design and development.* New York: Harcourt Brace Jovanovich.

Presbie, R. J., & Brown, P. L. (1985). *Behavior modification* (2nd ed.). Washington, DC: National Education Association.

Pulaski, M. A. S. (1980). *Understanding Piaget: An introduction to children's cognitive development* (2nd ed.). New York: Harper & Row.

Reardon, F. J., & Reynolds, R. N. (1979). A survey of attitudes toward corporal punishment in Pennsylvania schools. In I. A. Hyman & J. H. Wise (Eds.), *Corporal punishment in American education.* Philadelphia: Temple University Press.

Rich, J. M. (1984). Discipline, rules, and punishment. *Contemporary Education, 55*, 110–112.

Robert, S. C. (Ed.). (1970). *Robert's rules of order* (rev. ed.). Glenview, IL: Scott Foresman.

Rogers, C. R. (1969). *Freedom to learn.* Columbus, OH: Merrill.

Rogus, J. F. (1985). Promoting self-discipline: A comprehensive approach. *Theory Into Practice, 24*, 271–276.

Rose, T. L. (1984). Current uses of corporal punishment in American public schools. *Journal of Educational Psychology, 76*, 427–441.

Rosenshine, B., & Stevens, R. (1986). Teaching functions. In M. C. Wittrock (Ed.), *Handbook of research on teaching* (3rd ed.) (pp. 376–391). New York: Macmillan.

Rosenthal, R., & Jacobson, L. (1968). *Pygmalion in the classroom: Teacher expectations and pupils' intellectual development.* New York: Holt, Rinehart and Winston.

Rust, J. O., & Kinnard, K. Q. (1983). Personality characteristics of the users of corporal punishment in the schools. *Journal of School Psychology, 21*, 91–105.

Salter, A. (1949). *Conditioned reflex therapy.* New York: Farrar, Straus & Giroux.

Santrock, J. W. (1984). *Adolescence: An introduction* (2nd ed.). Dubuque, IA: Brown.

Seeman, H. (1984). A major source of discipline problems. *Educational Horizons, 62*, 128–131.

Shannon, J. (1986). In the classroom stoned. *Phi Delta Kappan, 68*, 60–62.

Skinner, B. F. (1953). *Science and human behavior.* New York: Macmillan.

Skinner, B. F. (1954). The science of learning and the art of teaching. *Harvard Educational Review, 24*, 86–97.

Strike, K., & Soltis, J. (1986). Who broke the fish tank? And other ethical dilemmas. *Instructor, 95*, 36–39.

Strom, R. D. (1969). *Psychology for the classroom.* Englewood Cliffs, NJ: Prentice-Hall.

Sulzer-Azaroff, B., & Mayer, G. R. (1977). *Applying behavior analysis procedures with children and youth.* New York: Holt, Rinehart and Winston.

Swick, K. J. (1985). *Disruptive student behavior in the classroom* (2nd ed.). Washington, DC: National Education Association.

Swick, K. J. (1985). *Parents and teachers as discipline shapers.* Washington, DC: National Education Association.

Tillman, M. (1982). *Trouble-shooting classroom problems.* Glenview, IL: Scott, Foresman.

Tobbin, K. (1986). Effects of teacher wait time on discourse in mathematics and language arts classes. *American Educational Research Journal, 23*, 191–200.

Ulrich, R. E., & Azrin, N. H. (1962). Reflexive fighting in response to aversive stimulation. *Journal of Experimental Analysis of Behavior, 5,* 511–520.

Van Dyke, H. T. (1984). Corporal punishment in our schools. *The Clearing House, 57,* 296–300.

Van Horn, K. L. (1982, April). *The Utah pupil/teacher self-concept program: Teacher strategies that invite improvement of pupil and teacher self-concept.* Paper presented at the annual meeting of the American Educational Research Association, New York.

Walker, J. E., & Shea, T. M. (1984). *Behavior management: A practical approach for educators* (3rd ed.). St. Louis: Times Mirror/Mosby.

Watson, J. B. (1914). *Behavior: An introduction to comparative psychology.* New York: Holt, Rinehart and Winston.

Webster, N. (1979). *Webster's deluxe unabridged dictionary* (2nd ed.). New York: Simon & Schuster.

Welsh, R. S. (1985). Spanking: A grand old American tradition? *Children Today, 14,* 25–29.

Wilcox, R. T. (1983). Discipline made gentle. *The Clearing House, 57,* 30–35.

Wilde, J., & Sommers, P. (1978). Teaching disruptive adolescents: A game worth winning. *Phi Delta Kappan, 59,* 342–343.

Wittrock, M. C. (1986). Students' thought processes. In M. C. Wittrock (Ed.), *Handbook of Research on Teaching* (3rd ed.) (pp. 297–314). New York: Macmillan.

Wolf, M. M., Hanley, E. L., King, L. A., Lachowicz, J., & Giles, D. K. (1970). The timer game: A variable interval contingency for the management of out-of-seat behavior. *Exceptional Children, 37,* 113–117.

Wolfgang, C. H., & Glickman, C. D. (1986). *Solving discipline problems: Strategies for classroom teachers* (2nd ed.). Boston: Allyn & Bacon.

Wolpe, J., & Lazarus, A. A. (1966). *Behavior therapy techniques: A guide to the treatment of neuroses.* Oxford, England: Pergamon.

Wood, F. H. (1982). The influence of public opinion and social custom on the use of corporal punishment in the schools. In F. H. Wood & K. C. Lakin (Eds.), *Punishment and aversive stimulation in special education: Legal, theoretical and practical issues in their use with emotionally disturbed children and youth* (pp. 29–39). Reston, VA: Council for Exceptional Children.

Woolridge, P., & Richman, C. L. (1985). Teachers' choice of punishment as a function of a student's gender, age, race, and IQ level. *Journal of School Psychology, 23,* 19–29.

Zumwalt, K. K. (Ed.). (1986). *Improving teaching: 1986 ASCD yearbook.* Alexandria, VA: Association for Supervision and Curriculum Development.

# Index

It was getting dark as they picked up speed across the open water. The black clouds were beginning to spit rain. As they got closer to the island, Purse could see the Trieu Bleu. The shiny, white yacht glowing in the greenish light—the boat, he couldn't help remembering, where he and Trieu had made love just the week before—was anchored maybe a hundred yards or so off the beach. Mike veered off to the left to the other end of the small island. He kept looking up at the clouds. Purse had on a little jacket, but none of them had rain coats, or life preservers.

The misting rain let up for the moment, and Mike dropped them off at a fishing pier around the curve of the island, about a quarter mile from the yacht. Aboy paid him $20 and reminded him that he was to be back in two hours.

Mike turned his little boat back toward the mainland, and Purse and Aboy started strolling up the wide, sandy beach toward the yacht, the roar of the surf and the wind making it hard to hear themselves think, much less talk. They paused now and then to pick up shells. Purse got so interested in the shells and sand dollars that he almost forgot why they were on the island.

As they got closer to the boat, Aboy nodded toward the dunes about a hundred yards from the surf. They headed that way, using the dunes to hide their approach, and continued through the soft sand toward the Trieu Bleu. Once they got even with it, they peered through the sea grass growing atop the dunes and tried to make out what was going on aboard the yacht. It was almost dark, but they could see four men on the deck, drinks in hand, occasionally gesturing toward the dark clouds. Purse couldn't make out who they were, and neither could Aboy, even through his camera viewfinder.

A huge peal of thunder and a spectacular slash of lightning over the Gulf sent the men hurrying inside. Rain began to fall even harder. It was cold.

"So what do we do?" Purse shouted to Aboy.

Aboy looked toward the mainland, looked back toward the yacht. "It's dark," he yelled. "Let's do what we came to do. For Red's sake."

He pulled his soggy straw hat down on his head and cinched up the string under his chin. They scrambled over the dunes and headed toward the beach, like D-Day marines in reverse. They slowed down—actually Purse fell down—when they hit the cold water, angling toward the yacht, their eyes peeled for a searchlight, for anyone looking their way through the windows. The rain and the dark made them almost invisible—at least they hoped it did—except when lightning lit up the sky. Purse was scared and cold, but Aboy seemed to have no fear. He plowed through the water like a seagoing Clydesdale, camera held above his head. Purse followed.

It only took them about 10 minutes, but every time Purse got a mouthful of cold salt water, he thought about turning back. They never had to resort to swimming, but once they got to the boat, the water was chest-deep, and the waves nearly knocked them off their feet. They hadn't thought about—at least Purse hadn't —how they would pull themselves onto the deck. Fortunately, the small ladder at the stern that snorkelers used made it fairly easy for them.

Purse clambered up first, looked to his left, to his right and then nodded for Aboy to follow. Purse was shivering from the cold, and the rain was coming down harder. They saw no one, although Purse could tell through the closed blinds that the lights were on in the salon.

The big picture window was closed against the wind and rain, but the side windows, under an awning, were open, probably for the fresh air. They could see into the salon, where four men were having drinks and talking easily, although it was hard to hear what they were talking about. Sitting in an overstuffed easy chair near the dogs-in-the-bordello picture was weaselly Nabob Slidell, the light glinting off a new pair of glasses. On the long, white couch was Calvin Locke, legs crossed in a casual way, one arm draped over the back of the couch. A middle-aged Asian man Purse didn't recognize, although he guessed it was Trieu's husband, also sat on the couch. In a chair near Nabob, looking sort of ridiculous in a bright Hawaiian shirt and seersucker slacks and sipping some sort of pink drink in a tall glass was that gray-haired symbol of Lutheran probity and legal rectitude, Judge Luther Sanders himself. Purse noticed a little paper umbrella on an end table beside his chair.

"The fix is in," Aboy muttered, trying to maneuver his camera so that one shot would capture the whole room.

"Wait for a lightning flash," Purse whispered. "That way they won't notice."

They waited, and suddenly music started up, country and western music, Garth Brooks singing "Friends in Low Places." They noticed everyone in the room turn eyes right, where Trieu came slithering out of the bedroom. She wore the same white outfit she was wearing that first night he and Aboy had seen her, that night at the Wagon Wheel. With the judge in her sights, playing peekaboo with her long, liquid ebony hair, she made her way across the room, dipping and swaying like a cobra. To Purse, she didn't look 35. He wondered if Aboy was right about that.

She came to a stop directly before the judge's chair, and as she swayed and turned, her legs spread wide, she teased her blouse out of her pants and began to slowly remove it, off one lovely brown shoulder, then the other. Once she had it all the way off, she began slowly sliding the armadillo-buckled belt through the pant loops while Garth Brooks kept time to her slow strip. She doubled the belt and popped it like a whip, inches away from the judge's nose.

Gracefully, she managed to get the pants off over her white doeskin boots and with nothing on but the boots and a lacy pair of red panties, the same ones, Purse was thinking, he had seen in Dallas underneath the waterfall sign. She leaned over the judge, her pert breasts brushing his face. As Garth wailed about going on down to the Oasis, she balanced herself like an Olympic gymnast on the arm rests of the judge's chair and flipped into a hand stand, red-nailed toes pointed toward the ceiling. She held the arrow-straight pose for a few seconds, her hair pooling into the judge's seersuckered lap, before smoothly doing a tuck and roll into that same lap.

The judge looked hypnotized, and when Purse glanced at Aboy he seemed to be in the same state of mind. His big red face glued to the glass, camera down at his side, he looked like he wanted to ooze through the window. Lightning flashed and then thunder, but Aboy didn't seem to notice.

"Take a picture," Purse hissed. Aboy managed to squeeze off several.

What Purse felt as he stood there and watched was rage and hurt and deep, deep anger—anger at Trieu but mainly anger at himself for having been so stupid. He groaned, and without thinking what he was doing, he banged his fists against the wall beside the window. Twice, maybe three times.

That stopped the strip tease. Trieu hopped off the chair and reached for her pants.

"What was that?" Purse heard Nabob ask.

The banging snapped Aboy out of his trance too. Both their heads swiveled toward the dark, choppy water below them, looking for a way to escape the boat. Go over the edge right where they were standing and make a swim for it? Race around to the other side?

Purse heard the engine begin to rumble and suddenly they were moving, away from the island. He sensed a person near the bow.

"Hold it!" a deep voice commanded.

Coming toward them was Ngo, the unsmiling brute who had served dinner when he and Trieu were aboard the yacht. He was so tall his shaved head nearly grazed the canvas awning. Purse started to call out to him, tell him who he was, but then lightning flashed and he saw the pistol.

Panicked, Purse ran the other way, sliding as he turned the corner and almost going overboard. Aboy, maybe not seeing the gun, lumbered toward Ngo, plowing into him headfirst. Purse raced past Nabob and friends, who had come out on deck to see what was going on. He came around behind Ngo and Aboy, both sprawled on the deck, both scuffling for the gun. Aboy got to his knees and then to his feet, but Ngo sliced his legs out from under him with a karate scissor kick and then kicked him under the railing and into the water.

Purse vaulted over the railing into the cold water right behind where Aboy had gone in. Like a big pastel-blue whale, Aboy surfaced beside Purse, snorting and spitting water. They started swimming toward the island as the yacht picked up speed away from the island. With his clothes and boots weighing him down, he wasn't sure he could make it. He glanced back at Aboy. He was drawing in air in harsh, jagged gasps but swimming. He caught a glimpse of Ngo on the back of the deck, his bald head gleaming. He was peering into the dark, choppy water, his legs spread for balance, both hands aiming the pistol. Purse turned and kept swimming. Seconds later, he heard what sounded like the flat slap of a pistol shot, and then another. He kept swimming.

All was quiet except for the waves and the slowly fading rumble of the yacht's engine. Swimming slowly through the cold water as it rolled toward the beach, he had gone another 50 yards or so before he realized Aboy was not with him. He stopped and shouted, nearly choking on salt water when he opened his mouth. The Trieu Bleu was pulling steadily away, but he saw no sign of Aboy. He shouted over and over, treading water. His boots pulling him under, he kept treading until he was so cold and wet and tired he was afraid he wouldn't make it in. Finally, he let the tide wash him onto the beach. He stood up. The surf knocked him down. He stood up again.

The boat was no longer in sight. Neither was Aboy. He ran up and down the beach, like an abandoned puppy, looking out to sea for his friend. Rain began to fall, and still he stood there, staring into the water, the waves pulling at his feet. Knowing Aboy, he thought he might be playing a trick. Maybe he had floated down the beach a ways, was going to come walking up any minute. Maybe he would made his way back onto the boat. Maybe Ngo had shot him.

For maybe an hour, he stood there in the surf, peering out at the waves. He was shaking so hard, he could barely stand. Maybe Mike will show up, he told himself, but he knew he wouldn't.

Finally he turned and stumbled out of the water and across the sand to the dunes. The rain gradually stopped, but he was so cold he couldn't stop trembling. He tried to burrow into the tall grass and soft, wet sand, trying to protect himself against the wind. It was no use. Every half hour or so through the long night, he stood up and looked out to sea. More than anything he ever wanted in his life, he wanted to see Aboy.

The rain let up, and he lay on his back in the sand. The pure black sky above him was pricked with a billion stars.

## ★ ★  TWENTY-TWO  ★ ★

On a Saturday morning in April, on what promised to be the first really warm weekend of the year, he made the 80-mile drive from Alpine down to the ghost town of Terlingua, in the Big Bend. He stopped in at Swofford's General Store and borrowed a raft from Roy Swofford, an old miner he had met when he first got to Alpine. A short, seam-faced man who had lived in Terlingua for 60 years or so, Roy was still waiting for another copper strike. Purse told him he would need a ride back out of Santa Elena Canyon the next afternoon.

"Nothing better to do," the old man said, taking a draw on a hand-rolled cigarette as he sat on the wooden bench under the store's covered porch. "I'll come get you. You take care."

The morning was clear and cool, the air tangy with the smell of salt cedar. The water level in the Rio Grande was high from snowmelt upriver in New Mexico, and the occasional rapids, their bubble-hiss urgency propelling him into long, slow stretches of gently flowing river, made for a wonderful day.

He made it to his usual camping place about sundown, setting up his pup tent in a meadow underneath a high, craggy cliff on the Mexican side of the river. He hacked a dead mesquite limb into firewood, got a fire going and hauled up his ice chest. Lifting out a t-bone steak, he rubbed it with butter, cracked pepper and salt and then, when the fire blazed, laid the meat directly in the flames to sear it quickly. He buried a potato to bake in the glowing ashes. Except for the soughing sound of doves settling in for the evening in a nearby stand of cottonwoods and the gurgle and brush of the river as it flowed south, it was quiet. His cooking sounds echoed off the canyon walls.

After the steak and a couple of beers, he sat on a log-sized piece of smooth driftwood for a while, his bare feet in the cool sand, and let his mind drift like the river. The aloneness was good, as usual.

Along about 10, he spread out his sleeping bag. He decided it was warm enough to sleep outside the tent. Lying on his back and looking up at the sky, watching for the quick occasional smudge of a falling star, he saw Cassiopea, Arcturus, Vega. He saw the bright Orion and the Twins. His Mama had taught him how to read the sky when he was a little boy, and the three of them lay out in the back yard on a blanket on summer nights, waiting for the house to cool down before they went to bed.

His mind, as usual, drifted back to Santa Lucia. It had been six months and still he had nightmares now and then about what happened.

That night. That long, long night. He remembered drifting off to sleep for a few minutes, waking up stiff and sore from the cold. He remembered standing in the wind atop the dune maybe a dozen times and staring out at the constantly roaring surf.

The next morning. He remembered walking along the beach all the way around the island. It took about two hours. No sign of Aboy.

About noon he stowed away on an excursion boat that had brought some Minnesota elderhostel people out to the island to collect shells. Back on the mainland, he caught a ride in the back of a pickup with two men delivering fresh shrimp to a restaurant on the outskirts of Minerva. The Crusher was just where he had left it in the parking lot of El Corral. He tried to brush as much sand off himself as he could before he climbed behind the wheel and headed north. Twice he nodded off and veered onto the gravel shoulder, and twice he pulled into a roadside park for a nap.

All the way home he was trying to decide what to do. He knew he had to tell somebody what had happened, but he didn't know who. What he was hoping was that, for whatever reason, Aboy had made it back to Austin without telling him, or at least had called in from Minerva.

When he got home, he called Joe Frank. "Something bad's happened," he said.

"You're telling me," he said. "Get on down here to the campaign."

Probably he was talking about Trieu's husband and the other stuff Aboy had managed to find out. Not about what had happened to Aboy himself.

He threw his wet, filthy clothes out the front door, took a quick shower and changed into a clean pair of jeans. Downtown, the campaign headquarters was crowded as usual. He found Joe Frank in his back office, by himself. He walked in and tried to stare into his eyes, tried to gauge what he knew.

"Did Aboy get ahold of you?" Joe Frank asked.

"When?"

"Yesterday afternoon. From down at Minerva."

He didn't answer. He looked down at his feet and tried to hold back the insistent tears. "Aboy's dead," he finally managed to say.

Aboy's body washed up on the island two days later. He still had his straw hat around his neck. By then Purse had told his story countless times—to Joe Frank, to Red, to the Texas Rangers. Over and over to the Rangers. They wanted to throw him in jail for not going to the Minerva authorities immediately. One of them kept calling him Wily Chappaquidick.

The official cause of death was accidental drowning. No gunshot wounds were found. Calvin Locke admitted to being on the Trieu Bleu that night. Proudly. Ly Tong Nguyen was a "dear friend and close business associate," he said. They were relaxing on the boat and talking about import/export plans in the Sisco administration's Department of Commerce. Ly, he said, would be a trusted adviser to the new senator.

Aboy's death was "regrettable," Locke said in a written statement. He and Senator-elect Sisco were sorry it happened, even if "Mr. Suskin was known to play fast and loose with political ethics."

Judge Sanders denied being on the boat. He had spent a quiet evening at home with his family on the night in question, he said, watching Andy Griffith and Barney on TV. His wife backed him up. It was an episode that featured Floyd the barber, she recalled.

Aboy's camera, and whatever was on it, wasn't found, not right then, anyway.

Although the papers had a field day speculating about what Aboy was doing on the coast, whether he was stalking Locke or looking for dirt on Nabob or whatever, they didn't seem particularly interested in investigating the Sisco-Nguyen connection. After some obituaries about Aboy's colorful life and career, the story pretty much died.

Three days after Aboy's body was discovered, Judge Sanders on a Friday afternoon issued his ruling on the election. Even though he found evidence of fraud in several precincts around the state, he did not consider it feasible to call for a new election. The state needed continuity, he wrote. The election result would stand.

Red announced that she would keep fighting in the courts, but everybody knew it was all over. By the time it got all sorted out, Jimmy Dale would be as well rooted in Washington as a springtime jimson weed.

Purse left town that very night. He packed everything he thought he would need into the Crusher, tossed Willis Seymour the keys to the trailer and told him to send the fifty-dollar security deposit to his Mama. His plan was to drive west, just as far as he could go, or as far as the Crusher held out, before he stopped. Maybe he would drive all the way to the West Coast, maybe to San Diego.

The Crusher gave up the ghost before Purse did. They made it about 400 miles before the old Land Cruiser blew a head gasket on IH-10, 25 miles east of Van Horn. He bequeathed it to the tow truck driver/mechanic as payment for hauling it into town. The next day he found a yellow and white '62 Ford pickup in great shape for its age, and made his way down to Alpine. He moved into a little one-bedroom stucco house he could afford to rent and, right after the first of the year, signed on for substitute teaching in a local elementary school.

He was rafting the river on the January day Jimmy Dale Sisco took the oath of office in D.C. Sisco had a ceremonial swearing-in back in Austin, while sitting atop a golden palomino. Purse saw the story the next day in the *Alpine Avalanche*.

*"I'm nobody, who are you? Are you nobody too?"*

He thought of those lines floating down the river on that April morning. He thought about how he had quoted them to Trieu, or whatever her name was, that delirious night at her place, the night that opened up his Pandora's package of miseries. After his 15 minutes of fame with Red had come to an end, he liked being nobody. His folks had been satisfied with their lot in life; he would be too. Like his mamma and daddy. Like Uncle Amos. Uncle Clyde. Their biggest moments in life had been their occasional weekend noodling on the Brazos. Not hobnobbing with a U.S. senator. Or almost senator.

After making pretty much of a mess of every ambition he had tried to have, whether personal or professional, he liked being responsible only for himself. He liked not having to carry somebody's purse.

He lay back on the raft and let the river take him on down, toward the high walls of Santa Elena Canyon. Staring up at the sky, the green water gently lapping at the raft, he thought again about Aboy. He wondered what his friend thought about in those final minutes of his life. Did he panic as the waves pulled him under? Did he trust in his God, his all-powerful Pappy, to save him? Or did he just have faith that whatever happened, it would all be okay?

"Trust and obey," he used to sing, "for there's no other way." Maybe he was right, but Purse realized that as long as he lived he would never know for sure. He would never know.

High in the clear blue sky above the river, a hawk coasted on the wind currents, its wings barely flapping. Purse closed his eyes. For a little while, he thought about giving in to the flow. He would just float on down the Rio Grande a thousand miles, until it emptied into the Gulf. He would trust and obey the big river, nothing else. It was a calming thought, the state of being nobody, of being an insignificant speck on the stream of life.

But then he remembered the dams and the lakes and the irrigation locks. He would have to clamber ashore and do some heavy portage, over and over, before the river emptied him into the sea. From the cliffs on the Mexican side, he heard the faint tinkle of a goat bell, and he raised up on his elbows and looked around. High above the river, he saw a young Mexican boy standing among his flock in the spring grass. He saluted. The youngster took off his straw hat and waved it above his head.

Seeing him reminded Purse of Luis and Olga and Anna Maria and all their little fourth-grade classmates who would be trudging into his Alpine classroom on Monday. He thought about the little Ninja Turtle backpacks on their skinny little shoulders, their black eyes shining. Sometime during the day, maybe while they rested after lunch, they would do poetry. Maybe they would dive into Emily Dickinson. Or Pablo Neruda.

# ★ ★ EPILOGUE ★ ★

The story wasn't over, of course. Are stories ever over?

The man on the palomino, Jimmy Dale Sisco himself, served only two years as U.S. Senator before the roof fell in, just as Aboy and Bill Young and Mary Ann Wright and so many others had predicted. Two years were more than enough for the people who had voted for him.

He was forced out of office after he and Calvin Locke and their bosom buddy Ly Nguyen got embroiled in what the press loved calling Shrimpscam. It was a nefarious scheme that bilked several thousand hardworking Vietnamese fishermen and their families living on the Gulf Coast out of their hard-earned savings.

Months after Aboy's death, a Santa Lucia shell collector was strolling along the beach one morning after a winter storm. She reached down to pick up a shell and found Aboy's camera, partially buried in the sand. Photos from that camera, a half dozen or so, helped send Jimmy Dale and friends up the river. The governor appointed a retired judge to serve out his term.

Nabob Slidell went to jail for a couple of years and found he had a friend in Jesus there. His path in life turned out to be the reverse of his old comrade-in-arms, Purse's friend Aboy. Nabob started a prison ministry he called "The Key." It was a big success, and years later Nabob had stayed true to his calling.

Purse saw him on TV once. He was wearing a black suit over a white T-shirt. When the suit jacket opened up, you could see a picture across his by-then ample chest, a picture of Jesus on water skis. The caption read, "HE'S UP!"

Alma Barbero—Purse could never help himself; she would always be Trieu Au Nguyen to him—turned state's evidence against her husband and never served a day in prison, despite her deep involvement in Shrimpscam. Purse heard that she lived in Los Angeles for a few years, divorced her husband while he was behind bars, and then moved to Hong Kong, where she was allegedly involved in real estate.

Rose Marie Ryder stayed in the public eye during Jimmy Dale's ill-fated term in Washington and during his trial. In fact, she never stopped running for the Senate, running flat out. When the special election came about, she was ready. ("DON'T BE BLUE/VOTE RED!") She ran again and easily defeated a governor with his eye on Washington, but who couldn't shed the taint of the brief and disastrous Sisco administration.

It was almost as if the voters were doing penance for the mistake they had made six years earlier. Mary Ann Wright, "Cyclone Mary, Child of Destiny," lived long enough to fly to Washington as a guest of honor at the inauguration of U.S. Sen. Rose Marie Ryder.

Red was a good senator, not spectacular but honest and steady and fair. She did the best she could to make sure that the jam jar was down on the lower shelf, for the people (although she never got around to pushing the booty-wearing cockfight bill that Aboy had championed.)

When her term was up, she could have been re-elected, but she decided not to seek another term. Purse always believed she was tired. She got herself appointed as ambassador to a Caribbean island nation. After a couple of years, she came back to the States, served on boards, lobbied a bit and made a bunch of money.

Axel Grenon was her official escort and steady pal during the first couple of years in Washington. You would see his picture on the society pages, escorting the senator as they showed up at parties and openings and so forth. After a little while he got bored. He went back to France, where he made several famous movies. The best known was the award-winning "*Gobe Tout*," an absurdist look at American politics starring the comedian Jerry Lewis as a U.S. president. It was big at Sundance.

After Red left Washington, she divided her time between Austin and New York City. Friends report she was happy.

So was Raenell Sitton. She moved back to Texarkana after the first campaign and used what she had learned around the Capitol to run for the state legislature. She was elected six times. During her fourth term, she married a banker named Sid Freeze from Arkadelphia, Arkansas; Sid and Raenell had three children. She opened Rosebud, a steak restaurant in Texarkana, on the Texas side of the line. On the menu is "The Aboy," a 72-ounce sirloin. Anyone able to eat it all at one sitting doesn't have to pay.

Jo Lynne James was happy. She married E. B. Schmedley not long after she left Purse standing on his mama's porch. She and E.B. were married a little over five years, living in a brand-new pre-fab house outside Elm Mott, until the hot summer night E.B's '57 modified Buick Century spun out on slick asphalt at the Heart-O-Texas Speedway and was hit broadside by a souped-up '56 Ford Victoria driven by the grandson of Purse's old highway-trash buddy, Rufus Cuttrell. Jo Lynne was left a widow before she was 30, with two young sons to take care of. She and Trudi Bulin remained partners at Hair Apparent, until she married again, retired from the beauty business and moved to South Texas.

Her erstwhile beau, Roy Towsen, was waiting in the wings when E.B. ascended to that great oval in the sky. Fortunately, she stuck to her promise never to ride with Roy again.

Roy survived his heartbreak. He still drives a bobtail truck for All Thumbs, a company that leases juke boxes and electronic video games. He spends his Saturday nights in the pit crew at the Heart-O-Texas Speedway. He's a lug-nut maniac, known for miles around.

Twin brother Ray is doing well. He owns Bide-a-While, a chain of funeral parlors that was among the first in the nation to feature drive-up viewing of the deceased, complete with funeral music you can tune in on your car radio. Ray, who also preaches on the side, is married to Rae-Harvey Pierce.

Ray-Harvey's old flame, Jo Lynne's little big brother Weevil, got religion, at least for a while. Ray Towsen's way with God's Word softened his hard, hard heart.

It didn't last. Once Ray's church, Praiseland Community Church of God in Christ Sanctified, started growing, and the Sunday collection plates started overflowing, the old Weevil reverted to his pre-Born Again ways. As one of the regular ushers who passed the collection plate every Sunday, he started skimming the take. Ray caught on and called the authorities. When two of Elm Mott's Finest arrived at the church on a Sunday morning to arrest him, Weevil ran out the back door, jumped into his cherry-red Plymouth Fury and took off, tires squealing, oversized engine gurgling and growling. He missed a curve on the Old Wilson Road, plowed into those banties his sister and Purse had gone to see years earlier and ended up back in prison as an habitual criminal.

As for the Purse Bearer himself, he stayed away from any official role in Red's campaign. Even though she had Sue Bee call him, and even though he was tempted, he finally said no thanks. He remained a supporter from afar. He was afraid he was Red's bad-luck charm.

Besides, he had a life of his own by then. He knocked around Alpine for a couple of years, rafting the Rio Grande whenever he had the time. He even went back to school and got himself a teaching certificate at Sul Ross State University. For going on 20 years now, that's what he's been doing, teaching junior high English in San Diego—San Diego, Texas, that is—where most of his students are just learning the language. Most days, he tells people, he feels like he is too.

After all these years, he still thinks about his friend. He thinks about him often. Aboy is buried in a little country cemetery in East Texas, not far from Crockett, in the same plot as his daddy, the Memory Man. Maybe once a year, Purse makes the long drive. He will sit on a little stone bench beneath a live oak tree, open a package of Mrs. Baird's powdered donuts and a quart carton of milk and tell his friend the latest good jokes he's heard, the dirtier the better. He can hear that rumbling laugh.

He knew Aboy didn't want to die when he did, he was having too much fun. But if anyone was ever prepared to die, Aboy was. He was truly a man of faith, Purse always believed. He trusted, even if he didn't always obey. He trusted that it would turn out all right, no matter what happened.

The two friends have a lot to talk about whenever Purse pays a visit. He tells Aboy about the family, tells him about Raenell. He tells him about his ten years in politics—five terms on the San Diego City Council. "I'm a politician," he reminds Aboy, "and it's primarily because of you."

Occasionally he'll recall how all through Red's campaign, whenever he made a mistake or Red got upset with him, Aboy would tell him not to get down on himself, not to slink away from life. Aboy knew him well enough to know he had a tendency in that direction. He knew Purse's mama, knew that's what she did. It took Purse a while to learn that lesson, years in fact.

Purse wouldn't tell just anybody, but he still seeks out Aboy's political advice, and since Aboy was the one who enticed him back into politics, he listens hard to what his old friend has to say. Driving back home from the quiet, peaceful graveyard—the radio off, the car windows down, not much on the road but the occasional dead armadillo—answers usually come.

One other thing: He married a lovely, young widow with two handsome boys. They're nearly grown now. Both of them like fast cars.

# ★ ★ ACKNOWLEDGMENTS ★ ★

Wily T. Foxx came to life many years ago on a long drive from Austin to the little West Texas town of Lorenzo to interview a newly elected state representative for the *Texas Observer*. As editor of the *Observer*, I hoped that a fictional Foxx would allow me to convey some of the wondrous absurdities I encountered daily around the Texas Capitol (absurdities similar to what my predecessor, the late Molly Ivins, was able to capture in her own inimitable way). It was a long time ago, but my *Observer* buddies, Geoff Rips and Frances Burton, helped me to bring young Wily to life, even if they didn't realize it at the time.

So did my friend John Donisi, who had a few real-life purse-bearing duties of his own when we both worked for Texas Governor Ann Richards a decade beyond my *Observer* years. I'm grateful to John and to Mary Beth Rogers, Deece Eckstein, Bill Cryer, Rafe Bemporaud, Margaret Justus, Chuck McDonald, Dorothy Browne, Suzanne Coleman and so many other Richards staffers who shared with me the experience of a lifetime. I'm grateful to Ann, as well. (By the way, any resemblance between Rose Marie Ryder and a certain Texas governor is purely coincidental.)

I'm grateful also to my old friend and fellow writer Tom Dodge, the sage of Midlothian, who read the manuscript and offered helpful suggestions, and also to my brother, Ken, who—his wife Susan reported—laughed out loud at all the right places.

Finally, I'm grateful to my fellow Texans. I left *The Washington Post* a few years ago to come back home—home to Texas. The Lone Star State, like family, can be infuriating at times, and yet it is my place, for good or ill. I hope *The Purse Bearer* captures something of my affection for and my fascination with Texas, our Texas.

Joe Holley
Houston, Texas

# ★ ★  ABOUT THE AUTHOR  ★ ★

Joe Holley is currently the politics editor and "Native Texan" columnist for the *Houston Chronicle*. A native Texan himself, he has been an editorial writer and opinion pages editor for the *San Antonio Express-News*, a staff writer for *The Washington Post* and a regular contributor to *Texas Monthly* and *Columbia Journalism Review*. He has been a Duke Media Fellow and a Eugene C. Pulliam Editorial Fellow, and has received numerous journalism awards. Holley followed Texas legends like Molly Ivins and Jim Hightower as the editor of *The Texas Observer* — and he spent time in the political trenches working for Texas Governor Ann Richards. Holley knows Texas politics inside and out.

Holley is the author of two books, *My Mother's Keeper* (1997), which received the Carr P. Collins Award for Nonfiction from the Texas Institute of Letters to the year's best work of nonfiction, and *Slingin' Sam: The Life and Times of the Greatest Quarterback Ever to Play the Game* (2012), a biography of Texas football hero Sammy Baugh.

**W**ings Press was founded in 1975 by Joanie Whitebird and Joseph F. Lomax, both deceased, as "an informal association of artists and cultural mythologists dedicated to the preservation of the literature of the nation of Texas." Publisher, editor and designer since 1995, Bryce Milligan is honored to carry on and expand that mission to include the finest in American writing—meaning all of the Americas, without commercial considerations clouding the decision to publish or not to publish.

Wings Press intends to produce multi-cultural books, chapbooks, ebooks, recordings and broadsides that enlighten the human spirit and enliven the mind. Everyone ever associated with Wings has been or is a writer, and we know well that writing is a transformational art form capable of changing the world, primarily by allowing us to glimpse something of each other's souls. We believe that good writing is innovative, insightful, and interesting. But most of all it is honest.

Likewise, Wings Press is committed to treating the planet itself as a partner. Thus the press uses as much recycled material as possible, from the paper on which the books are printed to the boxes in which they are shipped.

As Robert Dana wrote in *Against the Grain*, "Small press publishing is personal publishing. In essence, it's a matter of personal vision, personal taste and courage, and personal friendships." Welcome to our world.

WINGS PRESS

Colophon

This first edition of *The Purse Bearer*, by Joe
Holley, has been printed on 70 pound Edwards
Brothers plain text paper containing a percent-
age of recycled fiber. Titles have been set in
Birch type, the text in Adobe Caslon type. All
Wings Press books are designed and pro-
duced by Bryce Milligan.

On-line catalogue and ordering:
www.wingspress.com

Wings Press titles are distributed
to the trade by the
Independent Publishers Group
www.ipgbook.com
and in Europe by
www.gazellebookservices.co.uk

*Also available as an ebook.*